VERTICAL

MuseumsEtc

STREET LIFE IN LONDON

CONTEXT AND COMMENTARY

STREET LIFE IN LONDON

Context and Commentary

Emily Kathryn Morgan

MUSEUMSETC | EDINBURGH & BOSTON

FOREWORD

Michael Pritchard
Director-General
The Royal Photographic Society

THE GROWTH OF interest in street photography over recent years has lent a new relevance to John Thomson's work as a photographer and a proper reappraisal of his pioneering work encapsulated within *Street Life in London* (1877-78) is overdue.

Thomson's early work as a photographer in Asia, particularly China, went beyond simply travel photography. He brought his own intellect to bear on what he was photographing, frequently adding context and an informed written narrative to his images. His considerable inter-personal skills helped him to develop relationships that gave access to people and remote areas. Inevitably, Thomson brought his own values and cultural background to his work but he also imparted a respect for those he was photographing and writing about and, on occasion, he was quick to point out where Europeans could learn from their Asian counterparts.

The techniques and experience that Thomson developed in Asia he brought to bear closer to home in London. With his close collaborator, Adolphe Smith, Thomson's photographs of the "true types of the London Poor" showing the "harder phases of life" and their joint texts were both documentary in style and an ethnographic study of a section of Victorian society that was of growing interest, much as Thomson's earlier work in Asia had been. His outdoor studies were ground-breaking, despite the considerable technical obstacles, and have a realism that transcends their obvious posing. Had the project been started only a few years later a more discreet, snapshot style, of photography would have been possible, although it is unlikely that the photography would have been any more powerful.

Thomson's *Street Life* can be seen as the precursor to the more candid street photography of Paul Martin and the early social documentary work of Jacob Riis, and was important in establishing a model for twentieth century ethno-photography and anthropological work. This reappraisal is timely.

Dr Michael Pritchard
Director-General
The Royal Photographic Society

CONTENTS

INTRODUCTION

THIS BOOK EXAMINES the 1877-78 publication *Street Life in London*, by journalist Adolphe Smith and photographer John Thomson. *Street Life in London* aimed to reveal to readers, through novel use of photographic illustrations combined with essays, the conditions of a life of poverty in London. Now regarded as a pioneering photo-text and a foundational work of socially-conscious photography, *Street Life in London* did not achieve commercial success in its own time. This book aims to demonstrate how *Street Life in London* was subject to and shaped by a variety of interests and forces; to understand why it failed; and to place it within the overarching contexts of Victorian social exploration and street typology.

The first chapter of this book lays the historical and theoretical groundwork for what comes after. It introduces *Street Life in London* in some depth and demonstrates, through close reading of a single image and accompanying text, how word and image in the publication sometimes function in union, and sometimes at cross-purposes. This chapter also offers a history of the reception of *Street Life in London* from the mid-twentieth century to the present day.

The second and third chapters examine the biographies and *oeuvres* of, respectively, John Thomson and Adolphe Smith. Each author had had, prior to engaging with the project, a series of remarkable, formative life experiences paralleled by few others in polite Victorian society. Each found himself indelibly marked by his familiarity with the world beyond the British Isles, and so each brought a variety of motivations to the creation of the publication. Both men wrote extensively and well, before and after *Street Life in London*, and both revealed something of themselves in their other productions. Hence each chapter examines not only the life but also the other productions of its subject, to help illuminate what the two men hoped to accomplish with their innovative project.

The fourth chapter examines the literary and pictorial context into which *Street Life in London* emerged. It identifies literary themes common in works of urban spectatorship, and provides an overview of the literature of street and slum exploration up to 1877. The chapter concentrates in particular on Henry Mayhew's *London Labour and the London Poor* and the various works of urban explorer James Greenwood, two predecessors whom Smith and Thomson acknowledged outright in the Preface to *Street Life in London*. Thereafter it moves into an examination of pictorial models for *Street Life in London*, looking at the concept of the "type" and at Victorian street photography prior to 1877.

The fifth chapter looks at *Street Life in London* as a physical object, and examines the role of the publisher in determining its various formats. Physical copies of *Street Life in London* serve as a primary source of evidence for the marketing and distribution of the publication, and afford insight into the publisher's aspirations for the work. The chapter also discusses how the project was received, and demonstrates that although mostly well-regarded by critics, *Street Life in London* did not sell. The chapter then considers the timeline on which Smith and Thomson made the publication, the methods they employed, the locations where they worked, and the audience they hoped to reach.

The sixth and seventh chapters incorporate the findings of the previous five into close readings of images and texts throughout *Street Life in London*. The publication was never a monolithic production, but always the result of a variety of competing interests and vantage points: the two authors', the publisher's, the public's. Likewise, as a serial, *Street Life in London* evolved over the course of its year-long publication. Chapters Six and Seven track this evolution. Chapter Six examines the authors' original aims for the publication as stated in their Preface, in particular their desire to combine photography and text to produce "true types of the London poor." The chapter considers the concept of "true type," and examines how the first two monthly issues of the publication set the stage for what was to follow. Chapter Seven looks at the publication specifically as a serial photo-text, tracking how the authors' ambitions changed during the course of publication. It pays particular attention to instances in which image and text work especially well together, and those in which image and text work at cross-purposes. Overall, these two chapters demonstrate that *Street Life in London* was a fundamentally multivocal production. The authors attempted to join their own, their informants', and their subjects' voices in harmony, but the publication slid frequently into cacophony instead. Victorian readers found this visual and textual noise ultimately unappealing, but it proves one of the publication's greatest sources of pleasure for readers today.

CHAPTER ONE

REVISITING AND RE-EXAMINING STREET LIFE IN LONDON

IN FEBRUARY 1877, publisher Sampson Low, Marston, Searle and Rivington began the release of *Street Life in London* as a monthly serial publication. Authors Adolphe Smith and John Thomson professed a philanthropic mission: to reveal to readers, through novel use of photographic illustrations combined with essays, the conditions of a life of poverty in London. The series ran through January 1878, each monthly installment including three photographs and three accompanying essays. Thomson, a photographer, made all the pictures and wrote or contributed to about one-third of the texts. Smith, a journalist, wrote the rest. At the end of 1877, the publication was also issued as a single-volume book.

Collections of prints profiling "street types," a kind of vernacular taxonomy of street labor, had been popular among Europeans for centuries. From the mid-nineteenth century a separate, textual literature of urban exploration and social reform had also burgeoned. But image and text had rarely been brought together, and the young medium of photography – invented less than four decades before – had never been pressed into service to represent the poor in the context of the streets on a large scale. With *Street Life in London*, Smith and Thomson proposed something radical: taking the camera into the streets to produce a series of "true types of the London Poor."[1] These "true types" would profile the poor in word and image, not categorizing and taxonomizing but rather individualizing and contextualizing, augmenting factual written accounts of the reality of poverty with the concrete immediacy of photography.

Critics, however, seemed not to understand, professing skepticism from the start. "We hardly see how such a periodical can possibly live a long time," one wrote before the first installment had even appeared. "[S]treet-types in London are not very numerous, or, at any rate, such as would interest are not, and therefore the task of pourtraying [*sic*] London street-folk must soon come to an end."[2] When issues of the periodical began to appear, some gave positive reports, more progressive critics admiring the serial's ambition and deeming it "important to the sanitarian, the citizen, and the philanthropist."[3] But after just two months' installments, others began to complain. "[O]ne photograph presents the back view of a hansom cab and cabman – now, the typical cabman is the picture wanted," wrote one. The photographs deviated too dramatically from what this critic expected of a "street type." The critic demanded to "see the faces of the street-folk, not the streets or alleys in which they stand."[4] For that writer and others, *Street Life in London* provided too much context, too much information about the streets themselves and too little about the colorful characters within them. By the fourth monthly issue of the serial, Thomson and Smith had begun to alter their representations of the streets in both image and text, hoping to match the audience's demands. After just one year, having failed to satisfy critics or attract buyers, the serial folded.

In the 1950s and 60s, as interest in photography grew, scholars rediscovered *Street Life in London.* The very excess of pictorial information, the very contextualization that stymied Victorian critics, thrilled later viewers. Early historians of photography dubbed Thomson "the first photojournalist," and deemed the publication a foundational work of documentary photography.[5] Some, in their excitement over the publication's images, disregarded the texts – and Thomson's coauthor, Adolphe Smith – almost entirely. Virtually all of these historians thought of *Street Life in London* primarily as a book, not as a serial. Although more recent scholarship has corrected these oversights to some degree, to date there has been no sustained examination of *Street Life in London* as it appeared in, and to, Victorian Britain, and no consideration of how its serial format might have affected its appearance and content.

This book revisits and re-examines *Street Life in London*. Far from being a self-contained and monolithic work, *Street Life in London* was contingent, multiply-committed, and conflicted, subject to and shaped by a variety of interests and forces. First, the work had two authors, each of whom brought his particular aspirations, experiences and agenda to the table. Prior to undertaking *Street Life in London*, Thomson had lived and photographed in Asia for ten years, and he brought to his street photographs a semi-anthropological detachment. At the same time, while in Asia he had begun to develop an innovative approach to street photography, and in *Street Life in London* he sought to continue innovating, to create naturalistic photographs of street laborers and to restore to the imagery of poverty some of the liveliness and multiplicity of the streets themselves. For his part, Smith's attitudes toward poverty and labor were shaped by his experiences during the Franco-Prussian War and the subsequent Paris Commune, where he had served as a medic. A lifelong socialist, he brought to *Street Life in London* a political agenda: to convince his readers of the injustice of social inequality and to demonstrate the pressing need for public programs and social services to alleviate the conditions of poverty. In some entries the authors' interests came together to produce a photo-text of remarkable power; in others they looked past each other or worked at cross-purposes, leading to dissonance between text and image.

Second, *Street Life in London* did not exist entirely in a class by itself. Many works of social reportage and studies of street poverty, both textual and pictorial, had appeared before it; indeed, the genre of urban spectatorship, even spectatorship specifically focused on London, was a venerable one in 1877. Although Smith and Thomson desired to combine photography and text in an innovative fashion, updating the literature of street typology and urban spectatorship, *Street Life in London* was in many ways indebted to its progenitors, a debt its authors acknowledged openly.

Finally, as a serialized work it unfolded over time, rather than appearing complete and *en bloc*. By the time it was published as a single-volume work, most of its contents had already been seen by the public. Public commentary and criticism of the earlier installments in the serial, and the publisher's concerns about poor sales, affected the appearance and content of later installments.

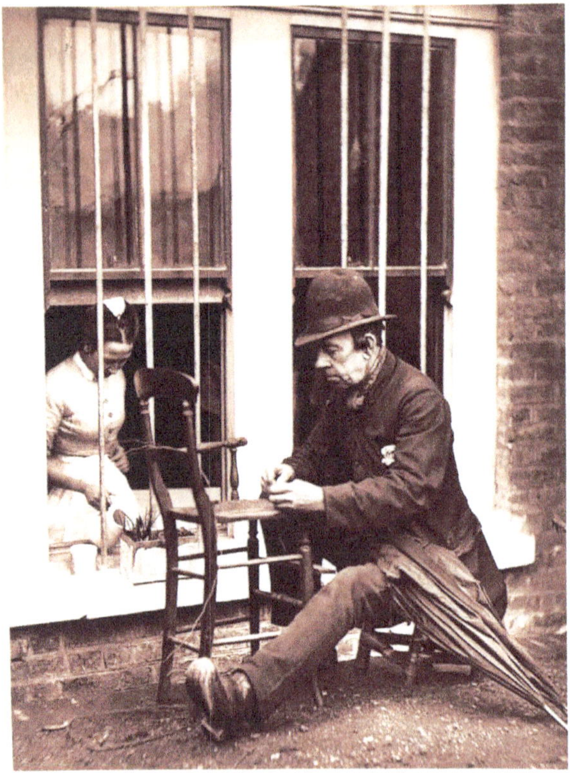

FIG 1.1: John Thomson, *"Caney" the Clown*, from Adolphe Smith and John Thomson, *Street Life in London* (London: Sampson Low, Marston, Searle and Rivington, 1877-78). Woodburytype. Private Collection.

"Caney" the Clown: an introductory case-study

This project illuminates the circumstances of *Street Life in London's* conception and execution, contextualizing it within a range of discourses and analyzing the relationship between text and image throughout. Like many books containing both image and text, the pictures and words in *Street Life in London* sometimes work in concert, sometimes at odds. Words may amplify the story the picture tells silently and contribute information not present in the image. But words may also serve to curtail the picture's function, to guide the reader to one of several possible meanings and thus to eliminate other potential meanings of the image.[6] In the combination of text and image there may be an abundance of information, or there may be a lack. Indeed, abundance and lack often coexist. *"Caney" the Clown*, an entry from the May, 1877 issue of *Street Life in London*, serves as an excellent starting point from which to demonstrate how the various phenomena that come together in the publication, including the two authors' sometimes-duelling agendas, can result in a kind of resonant disconnect between text and image.

In the center of the photograph (Figure 1.1), Thomson depicts a man seated on a low stool with legs of uneven length. He faces a low-backed chair, making repairs to its seat. He works outside, in an unpaved street without a sidewalk – an alley, perhaps – next to a brick building with a vertically barred window. Through the barred window we see a young woman watering a tiny garden potted in a reclaimed box. The two subjects' heads are just about a meter apart, inclined toward one another, but they do not share a space. The heavy bars on the windows separate them. These are not prison bars: their purpose is to exclude, not to contain. The man and woman are physically proximate but socially distant, alienated from one another.

Adolphe Smith's accompanying four-page essay, like many in the publication, discusses its subject at length and makes connections to overarching social concerns of the day. As he does throughout the publication, Smith packs a lot into this essay. Words amplify where the image cannot. But there is also much Smith fails to explain, leaving lacunae of meaning over which the reader/viewer ponders.

Smith begins with a biographical sketch of the principal subject, but his essay ultimately becomes an epic tale of the reversal of fortune. In the process, it also gives account of a panoply of Victorian labor forms and practices. The central figure here, as his name implies, repairs cane-bottomed chairs and was once a professional clown. He rose to a fair degree of fame through hard work and temperance: after running away from a boyhood career as a sailor, a profession replete with drunkenness, he came eventually to circus life, working his way up from day-laborer, to a position as human punching-bag for clowns, to full-fledged pantomime performer. But clowning was hard work and his exertions nearly killed him. A series of burst varicose veins ended this career, and medical costs bankrupted him. Propelled to success by his will, he was betrayed by his body. Taking pity on him, another pauper taught him to mend umbrellas and cane-work furniture, permitting him to "eke out a wretched existence at desultory and humble labour."[7] His hardships, combined with the medical necessity of curbing the enthusiasm that caused his medical problems in the first place, have imprinted themselves on his very physiognomy: "in him, as in others," Smith writes, "we find the indelible stamp denoting a hard life of struggle and adversity."[8]

Smith moves from this compelling story into a discussion of the chair-caning industry, allowing him to illuminate not only the work of "Caney" and other repairers but also that of the individuals and families engaged in making the goods in the first place. Centered in the countryside outside London, the industry occupied a liminal space between cottage production and mass manufacture: the chairs were made by entire families working out of their homes, but these families functioned like tiny factory units, forming assembly lines and turning out their products in large numbers. The speedy construction of the chairs led to equally speedy deterioration, so the industry of caned-chair-making quickly generated the offshoot profession of caned-chair-repairing. The repair of the chairs, too, was a marginally professionalized occupation, with some workers accepting regular but ill-paid employment in furniture dealerships and others, like Caney, opting for "wandering through the streets, cane in hand, soliciting from door to door, for a solitary [but better-paid] 'job.'"[9]

Smith moves from biography into labor context, using the individual story as entrée to overarching concerns. He deploys this formula often throughout *Street Life in London*. But here, as also throughout the publication, he refers very little to the image itself. He treats the photograph as illustration – an instance of the chair-caning clown caning a chair – not as a medium capable of communicating on its own. It is not a picture but a picture *of something*. The dynamics of the picture, its composition and structure, do not interest him; nor do the circumstances under which it was made. Smith writes around the image, rather than speaking directly to or about it.

As such, the reader learns much about things that interested Smith, but nothing at all about things he chose to ignore. He makes no mention, for example, of the woman in this picture, though her presence in the image cannot have been accidental. In 1877, one did not appear in photographs on a regular basis and street-photography was virtually unheard-of. The appearance of a photographer in the alley behind the house, accompanying the chair-repairer, can only have been an extraordinary event. This woman either asked Thomson to let her participate or he persuaded her to appear, perhaps because he wanted the image to seem more pleasing and aesthetically balanced, or because he wanted the household to seem a living thing rather than just a backdrop. Either way, her presence in the picture was calculated.

Hence Smith's failure to mention her makes her a more, not less, intriguing figure. Who is she? She wears the clothing of a servant, so this is probably not her own house but her employer's. Like Caney, she depends on the house for her livelihood, so in that way the two occupy similar social niches. But she has regular employment, while Caney makes his living piecemeal. She labors within the house, he without.

His labor is auxiliary to the needs of the household, hers central to it. To the people within the house, he is invisible; to the world outside, she is. Her presence broadens the image's topicality with regard to the variety of labor in London, but rather than take advantage of this iconographic richness Smith simply ignores her.

It is possible Smith never met the woman. He may not have been present when Thomson made the photograph, conducting his interview of Caney later and separately. The two authors operated independently of one another at least some of the time. Rather than imagine a story for her, Smith simply eliminated her from his narrative. Domestic labor was, anyway, too big a subject to address here, simultaneously too mundane and too complex to contain in a book about work. Everyone had a servant or two. Everyone knew how a household ran. No one wanted to read about such subjects.[10] This girl's appearance in the window marks the only time in *Street Life in London* in which domestic labor makes such an appearance. Smith disregards her and her work, and they disappear again.

Smith and Thomson understood, and designed their book in part to convey, the idea that a text-image combination can be greater than the sum of its parts. But the relationship between word and picture is complex, and throughout the book it shifts. Sometimes text and image work well together. Other times they go off in different directions or even work against one another. The dynamic of the two forms is fraught with fissures and cracks. As such, readers must fill in the gaps for themselves: one of the great frustrations of reading *Street Life in London*, and one of its great pleasures as well.

Methods and historiography

Roland Barthes illuminated in the 1960s how a photograph's textual surround may undercut the image's inherent "polysemy" through the functions of "anchorage" and "relay." An anchoring text selects out one particular meaning for the image from a range of possibilities and promotes it as the correct or sole meaning, suppressing others. In a relaying text, image and word work in a complementary fashion to convey a single idea or advance a narrative.[11] Barthes effectively conveyed the fundamental idea that a photograph and a text together may mean more, and certainly mean differently, than the two forms separately.

Many subsequent investigators have built on this understanding, some of them focusing on the way text and image, when put together in sequence as in a book, may be made to convey a truly complex set of meanings. Alan Trachtenberg's *Reading American Photographs* provides the best model for comprehending such sequenced works. Images, writes Trachtenberg:

> *...cannot be trapped readily within a simple explanation or interpretation. They have a life of their own which often resists the efforts of photographers and viewers (or readers) to hold them down as fixed meanings.*[12]

The photographer may enrobe his images in a textual surround, but deep or unintended meanings come through nonetheless. Mathew Brady's *Gallery of Illustrious Americans*, for instance, combined lithographs (from daguerreotypes) of famous Americans, including politicians from both North and South, with biographical sketches. Published just after a threat of secession by Southern states in 1849, the publication intends to laud these great Americans' personal triumphs and heroism but is, Trachtenberg demonstrates, driven at heart by a "fear of disunion descending into fratricide."[13] Photographers may even draw deliberately on the power of sequencing: documentary photographer Lewis Hine, for instance, understood the inadequacy of the photograph as a means of communication in and of itself, and used sequencing to engage the reader-viewer in:

> *the* process *of communication... inventing presentational forms through which social information might become the viewer's own concrete experience... [and awaken] the viewer's awareness of and imaginative empathy with the pictured others...*[14]

Following Trachtenberg, Carol Armstrong applies the idea of sequential reading specifically to early English photobooks in *Scenes in a Library: Reading the Photograph in the Book, 1843-1875.*[15] As with *Street Life in London*, the photographs in the books which Armstrong examines have repeatedly been plucked from their contexts and shown in museums in "modernist, ambiguity-celebrating" exhibitions, in which the photographs appear entirely divorced from their original textual surrounds:

> *The history of photograph collecting and of the art museum's colonization of the historic photograph is rife with removals from the photograph's printed context, be it cut from the album series or from the pages of a book.*[16]

Armstrong reinscribes the photographs in their series and performs throughout her study what she calls "an oscillation between close looking and equally close reading," examining works by William Henry Fox Talbot, Anna Atkins, Francis Frith, and others.[17] I follow Armstrong and Trachtenberg in reenacting, with *Street Life in London*, the simultaneous reading and viewing that it expected of its nineteenth-century audience.

Early scholarship on *Street Life in London* is synonymous with scholarship on John Thomson himself. As with many other photographers, scholarly treatment of Thomson's life and works expanded dramatically between the 1960s and the 1980s, part of the overall growth in the market for both historic and contemporary photography. In 1958 next to nothing was known about John Thomson or his work; by the late 1990s Thomson had received several solo exhibitions, was covered in most major survey books on photography, and had been the subject of multiple monographs.

The compelling qualities of Thomson's photography – his artful and natural compositions, his sensitive and empathetic depictions of his subjects, and his extraordinary technical command – assured him a place in the history of the medium. Early collectors of photography knew and prized Thomson's photographs. The industrialist Alden Scott Boyer, for one, included the 1877 single-volume edition of *Street Life in London* and several other Thomson books in the collection he donated to the George Eastman House in 1951.[18] Because the Eastman House was recognized at the time as one of the few places one might seriously study photography's history, Boyer's collection helped to shape the history of the medium as it evolved.

Through the Boyer donation Thomson's work came to the attention of Beaumont Newhall, curator at the Eastman House from 1948 and among the first scholars to pay attention to photography as a museum-worthy art. Newhall later included Thomson in *The History of Photography*, one of the earliest textbooks on the medium as an art form. Thomson makes his appearance in the fourth edition of Newhall's book, published in 1964, in a chapter titled "Documentary."[19] Newhall reproduces in the chapter only images from *Street Life in London*, mentioning Thomson's Asian work just briefly. The vision of Thomson as a socially-conscious photographer and of *Street Life in London* as a work of proto-documentary photography thus became codified in photography's official history.

Helmut Gernsheim, also a collector and one of the medium's earliest historians, acquired works by

Thomson in the 1940s.[20] By 1955 he had incorporated Thomson into his own textbook on the medium, *The History of Photography from the Earliest Use of the Camera Obscura in the Eleventh Century up to 1914*. Thomson and *Street Life in London* appear as the first entry in Gernsheim's chapter on "Documentary and Press Photography," where Gernsheim singles out one *Street Life* image, *The Crawlers*, as particularly "modern."[21] Gernsheim's understanding of Thomson's *oeuvre* subsequently broadened, and he cited Thomson's travel photography in later histories, but his vision of Thomson as a documentarian did not fundamentally change. "Thomson's purpose [in *Street Life in London*] was not to make pictures but to document the life of the poor," he asserted in *Creative Photography: Aesthetic Trends 1839-1960*.[22]

Intensely interested in photojournalism, these historians saw Thomson as a precedent for the compassionate documentarians of the early-to-mid twentieth century. This desire to place Thomson within a teleological history of the medium led some to focus on Thomson's street photography and to neglect his massive body of non-street work, including typological photographs, landscapes, and the many portraits he created both in Asia and as a "fashionable" photographer to wealthy and aristocratic Londoners. Almost always, these historians placed Thomson in chapters devoted to "documentary" or the use of photography for making "records."[23]

Many of these historians rightly recognized the aesthetic innovations of *Street Life in London*, but they attributed the values of twentieth-century documentary photographers to Thomson: an interest in social justice, a desire to reveal and thus perhaps to alleviate human suffering. One article even designates Thomson "the first photojournalist."[24] The problem with such an anachronistic formulation is not that Thomson did not possess these values, but that he could not have conceived them in precisely the same way a contemporary photographer might. Documentary, as a paradigm, did not exist.

Indeed, "documentary" is a remarkably imprecise term. As William Stott pointed out in 1973, the word "document," from which it derives, "has *two* meanings, only one of which is in the dictionary."[25] The dictionary defines a document as an objective record, but "documentary" has been used with remarkable frequency to refer to accounts – in image, word, film and other representational modes – which, while non-fictional, preserve a personal point of view, a personal experience.[26] A "documentary" photograph may be a dryly factual image of, say, a railroad bed. It may be a deeply moving image of a person dying slowly of disease, or of a body photographed at the very moment a bullet pierces it. The subjects may be unaware of the photographer, or posing self-consciously for the camera. The meanings of ostensibly documentary images may be, and have been, contested.[27] Overall, "documentary" as a term has suffered from overuse, to the extent that it has become almost meaningless. Applying it to *Street Life in London*, as early studies of the work tended to do, does not help us to understand how Smith and Thomson conceived their publication or how it functioned in its own time.

But understanding of Thomson's *oeuvre*, and of *Street Life in London* in its original context of Victorian England, did begin to deepen even as early as the 1950s. In 1957, Robert Doty published a brief article examining *Street Life in London*, drawing on the publication itself and on some critical reception of it. Doty recognized the publication's innovations as an early work of street photography, and he contextualized it within Thomson's overarching career though he knew little of Smith.[28] In 1969, when publisher Benjamin Blom reissued *Street Life* as a book, it became available to a wider audience. The unsigned "Publisher's Note" in the reprint also served as the first attempt to contextualize the work within Victorian London, noting its descent from the lineage of social investigation literature and in particular from Henry Mayhew's *London Labour and the London Poor.* Although it got some details wrong – the reprint misspells Thomson's name as "Thompson" throughout, and the note claims Adolphe Smith's "real name was Adolphe Smith Headingly," when in fact this was an alias he used on occasion – the Publisher's Note effectively located *Street Life in London* in the milieu of Victorian England and established the work's revolutionizing agenda.[29] It cited Smith's service at the International Trades Union Congresses and his "indefatigable concern for the worker and the quality of working class life," and discussed the "naturalness" of Thomson's photographs and the publication's use of the Woodburytype process for printing photographs. It also briefly outlined Thomson's other work, including his endeavors in Asia and his many years as a high-end portrait photographer.

From 1969, then, *Street Life in London* moved out of the realm of esoteric photographic knowledge and into the burgeoning body of widely accessible historic photography.[30] Understanding of the publication, and of Thomson's greater body of work, began to expand. Historians of Asian art and culture, among others, began to examine Thomson's work as evidence and as art.[31] And in 1978, Elliott Parker wrote of Thomson's position, beginning in the 1880s, as an instructor in photography to explorers under the aegis of London's Royal Geographic Society.[32]

By 1977 *Street Life in London* had become part of the photographic canon to the extent that critic and theorist Susan Sontag could write of it as one of the earliest examples of what she called "class tourism" photography. Sontag famously distrusted photography, and socially-committed or "documentary" photography made her particularly uncomfortable. "Photography has always been fascinated by social heights and lower depths," she wrote in *On Photography:*

> *Social misery has inspired the comfortably-off with the urge to take pictures, the gentlest of predations, in order to document a hidden reality... Gazing on other people's reality with curiosity, with detachment, with professionalism, the ubiquitous photographer operates as if that activity transcends class interests, as if its perspective is universal... Perhaps the earliest model of the sustained look downward are the thirty-six* [sic] *photographs in* Street Life in London *(1877-78) taken by the British traveler and photographer John Thomson.*[33]

Street Life in London thus became, for Sontag, a root from which the creeping growth of documentary photography issued forth. Because Thomson worked in both Asia and England, photographing both ethnic others and the English poor, *Street Life in London* exemplified for Sontag the nature of socially conscious photography as a form of internal colonialism.

John Tagg likewise offered a vision of the functions of photography with relation to – and in service of – the mechanisms of power in *The Burden of Representation*. In this collection of essays, Tagg examined "the ways in which photography has been historically implicated in the technology of power-knowledge," looking at photography as a form of evidence, a means of classification, a source of information and a method of oversight.[34] He identified an increasing impulse in the later nineteenth century to objectify the powerless and thus, under the aegis of humanism, to fix them within a system of power relations.[35] John Thomson's photographs for *Street Life in London*, he contended, were a manifestation of this impulse.

When they were published, studies like Sontag's and Tagg's complicated, in far-reaching ways, the relatively simplistic understanding of photography that had existed up to that point: as "truth;" as a technology equally capable of producing functional imagery and works of great art; as evidence. Both offered views of photography incredibly wide in scope and shockingly innovative. But this breadth came at the expense of the detail, the small view. Sontag and Tagg described how the act of representing someone might become a means of exerting power, but in the case of *Street Life in London* neither followed this process into the individual object.

This is the crux, and the weakness, of Structuralism: it offers a long view of the medium and its social functions, but at the expense of specificity, of detail, and of complexity. One goes looking for hegemony and finds it everywhere, but the brush is too broad. In the case of *Street Life in London* such an approach disregards the sometimes-extraordinary detail the book provides about the many individuals profiled within, and as such actually perpetuates the very hegemonic dynamic it aims to critique. Closer examination of the object permits individual voices to emerge – both those of the creators, and those of the subjects. In examining *Street Life* it is necessary to bear in mind the colonialist and hegemonic functions of photography described by Sontag, Tagg and others, but such approaches go only so far in illuminating how *Street Life* operated, how it might have expressed or even subverted such functions.

By the early 1980s other scholars had begun to pay just such close attention to *Street Life in London*. In 1983, Ialeen Gibson-Cowan pointed out in a symposium talk that there were deep disparities between the present-day perception of *Street Life in London* as a work of documentary photography and the perceptions of it on its publication in 1877.[36] She expanded on this talk in a 1985 article for *Creative Camera*, one of a series of articles she wrote on Thomson.[37] Prior historians assumed Thomson's work expressed his compassion for his subjects, but as Gibson-Cowan notes, this was not in keeping with how he saw himself, and how others saw him, in his own time. She proposes that Thomson's motivation for undertaking *Street Life in London* was more educational than sociological: he saw the project as "an opportunity to broaden the scope of photography's educational role," a cause in which he believed deeply.[38] She contradicted many previously-accepted notions about Thomson and, as such, contributed significantly to the establishment of the photographer as a complex, multi-dimensional figure grounded in a specific historical milieu.

Gibson-Cowan asks in her 1985 article on *Street Life* a number of salient questions. How was the serialized *Street Life in London* structured? What was the relationship and division of labor between Thomson and Smith? What were the two men attempting to accomplish? Gibson-Cowan determined, among other things, that Adolphe Smith was related by marriage to the publisher Blanchard Jerrold (Smith's father-in-law) and, through Jerrold, to the great urban explorer Henry Mayhew (Jerrold's brother-in-law).[39] She posited that much of the impetus for *Street Life in London* lay with Smith; that *Street Life in London* was not financially successful; and that ultimately one must regard the publication as an "abortive effort." The first scholar to examine *Street Life in London* as a serial, she identified a "lessening of... editorial direction" in later issues of the serial, as compared with the first two or three monthly installments.[40]

Gibson-Cowan's are the first studies to pay such close attention to *Street Life in London*, to regard it as a product of its own time, to examine it as a serial rather than as a single-volume publication, and to delineate the specifics of its execution. But her speculations also miss the mark. She claims that later issues of the serial are more disorganized and less thematically-unified than early issues, a claim I dispute. She agrees with the Victorian critic who called for clearer presentation of the workers' faces in the photographs, not recognizing that the critic's disapproval resulted from a desire for more traditionally typological, less-dynamic imagery and not, as she imagines, from a forward-leaning impulse to look poverty full in the face.[41] Additionally, Thomson probably did not cease signing his text contributions out of a desire to "distanc[e] himself from the venture," but rather because he regarded many of his texts as collaborations, having either co-written them with Smith or quoted heavily from a variety of informants.[42]

Finally, she posits that *Street Life in London* failed commercially in part due to its uncomfortable similarity to another body of photographs produced in the 1870s. Social reformer Thomas Barnardo, operator of a series of homes and ragged schools for orphans and street children, was accused of posing and costuming the children in order to make "before-and-after" pictures showing the beneficial effects of his institutions on their well-being. Barnardo's photographs were the subject of a series of hearings in 1877, and thus the case was receiving publicity at the same time that Smith and Thomson's publication was appearing. But in speculating about this connection, Gibson-Cowan overstates the public's inclination to draw parallels between the Barnardo pictures and *Street Life in London*. She also overlooks the fact that throughout 1877, even during the Barnardo hearings, copies of the monthly serialized *Street Life* continued to carry advertisements for Barnardo's homes inside their covers, an association the publishing company would surely have discontinued if it perceived the connection between the two to be deleterious to sales of *Street Life in London*.

A major monograph on the photographer, Stephen White's *John Thomson: A Window to the Orient* (published in the UK as *John Thomson: Life and Photographs*), appeared in 1985.[43] As a collector and gallery owner, White amassed the largest-ever collection of Thomson's work.[44] In his monograph, White aimed to expand understanding of Thomson's work beyond *Street Life*, writing of the latter only briefly in comparison with longer sections on Thomson's photography in Asia and Cyprus.[45] White's monograph, which was also the first attempt at a biographical treatment of Thomson, marks a shift in perception of the photographer: once seen as a maker of photojournalistic images who happened also to have traveled in Asia, Thomson became a great travel photographer, and *Street Life in London* effectively a book of travels within London.

Jeff Rosen's 1993 "Posed as Rogues: the Crisis of Photographic Realism in John Thomson's *Street Life in London*" revisits some of the questions raised by

Gibson-Cowan in her articles of the 1980s. He makes some sound assessments of the publication. Smith and Thomson, for instance, clearly did desire to make the poor seem more respectable, more "deserving" of public sympathy and support.[46] Rosen also gestures toward, but does not pursue, an idea I explore in greater depth, the notion that Smith and Thomson altered *Street Life in London* over time to satisfy critics and increase the publication's appeal to potential buyers.[47] And he points out the clear manipulations present in some *Street Life* images: one has been cropped, and two others have had their backgrounds entirely masked out.

Rosen agrees with Gibson-Cowan that *Street Life* pretty clearly failed in its ambitions. He attributes this failure specifically to "a broader crisis in the politics of photographic representation that emerged in England during this period."[48] He explores in greater depth Gibson-Cowan's proposal that the scandal over Thomas Barnardo's manipulated photographs of children from his homes put the Victorian public off the idea of socially-conscious photography. "The publishers of *Street Life in London* could not have escaped the Barnardo headlines without understanding how their enterprise could be tarnished with similar accusations," Rosen writes. But again, if that is the case then why did the dust jackets of monthly installments of the serialized *Street Life* continue to carry advertisements for Barnardo's Homes? Like Gibson-Cowan, he overstates this connection.

Throughout his article, Rosen also erroneously attributes the impetus for the publication to Thomson. He cites Thomson as the sole originator of the ideas expressed in the publication's Preface, for instance. He believes that the Preface's repeated references to the truthfulness and faithfulness of photography constituted a statement of ideology on Thomson's part, and that Thomson intended the photographs in his book to take the place of the "vast array of statistics and figures" that Mayhew and other social explorers had deployed.[49] He does not take into account Smith's influence on the publication or acknowledge the publishers' fair amount of influence as well. The publication, in Rosen's hands, becomes essentially the product of Thomson's artistic vision. At the end of the day he presents *Street Life in London* as an underdetermined production, attributing to the photographer too much intentionality and control.

Thomas Prasch addressed *Street Life in London* as part of his 1994 dissertation, "Fixed Positions: Working-Class Subjects and Photographic Hegemony in Victorian Britain."[50] Prasch examines a wide variety of photographic projects, including depictions of agrarian laborers in art photography, the photographic advertisements produced by Barnardo for his Homes, the prints-from-photographs in Henry Mayhew's 1851 *London Labour and the London Poor*, and *Street Life in London*. Prasch views such photography as a means by which the middle and upper classes in Victorian Britain maintained hegemony over the working classes. "Victorian photographs of workers," he writes, "are not produced by the workers themselves. They are the creation of middle-class photographers whose own aims in training their cameras on workers must be interrogated."[51]

But although Prasch examines *Street Life in London* carefully and closely, the broad scope of his study necessarily prevents concentration on the details of any single production, and his focus on photographic representation leads him to neglect the work's texts. Like most scholars before him, Prasch treats *Street Life* as a single-volume work and does not consider its evolution over the year of its publication. Also like others, Prasch neglects Adolphe Smith's contributions in favor of Thomson's, making Thomson the driving force behind the work. The oversight is particularly noticeable here because Smith, a confirmed socialist, desired to upend the very hegemonic relationships

Prasch examines in the study.

Richard Ovenden's *John Thomson (1837-1921) Photographer* appeared in 1997.[52] Ovenden's monograph treats Thomson's life in considerable detail, providing the weightiest and most comprehensive study of the photographer's life, travels, and imagery to date. Ovenden offers particularly sensitive analyses of Thomson's books, placing them within the overarching context of book production and marketing in Victorian Britain and considering them as physical objects. He traces the process of publication for several of Thomson's books and situates them within the context of photographically-illustrated publishing in the nineteenth century. He proposes that Thomson cared deeply about the print quality of photographs as they appeared in his publications, a concern that led Thomson to choose fine, if expensive, print processes and to supervise printing of many of his books quite closely.[53] It also affected his professional associations: only certain publishers – like Sampson Low and Co., with whom Thomson was affiliated for several years – were willing to take on such labor-intensive and costly ventures.

Ovenden discusses *Street Life in London* at length, both as a physical object and with regard to its contents. He emphasizes that the publication originally appeared as a serial, and he elucidates the format and benefits of the woodburytype process for reproducing photographs. Drawing on advertisements and announcements in publishing trade journals, Ovenden reveals Thomson's hectic, even frenzied engagement in multiple projects in 1875-77, making it clear that the photographer could hardly have given *Street Life in London* his sole attention for an extended period of time.[54] He also defends Thomson against accusations by other scholars that the photographs in *Street Life* were staged, pointing out correctly that Thomson could hardly have done otherwise in 1877, given the technologies and equipment available at the time. Finally, Ovenden acknowledges Adolphe Smith's contributions more clearly than any prior historian.[55]

James R. Ryan's 1997 *Picturing Empire: Photography and the Visualization of the British Empire* discusses *Street Life in London* as one aspect of its overall treatment of photography in the service of Victorian imperialism. Most of Ryan's book examines photographs made outside the British Isles, including those Thomson made in Asia. But in one chapter, titled "'Photographing the Natives,'" Ryan devotes several sections to classificatory and exploratory photographs made in England, including those of *Street*

Life in London, in an endeavor to demonstrate "how the domestic and the imperial were interlinked through practices of representation."[56]

Ryan relies largely on secondary research and on his own readings of *Street Life*, so he contributes little to understanding of the book's origins.[57] He does, however, contextualize the book within a greater literature on slum tourism in the 1860s and 70s, going beyond Mayhew to bring in James Greenwood's sensational exposés and the works of other social explorers. He demonstrates how Thomson, like these other writers:

> *reinforc[ed]... imaginative processes whereby the Far East was mapped on to the East End of London; both became areas of darkness, danger and the 'unknown,' to be explored and subjected to scrutiny.*[58]

In this, Ryan reveals that his interest in *Street Life* lies solely with Thomson's contributions, again virtually ignoring the contributions of Smith. Ryan thus misunderstands the project, because while it is true that Thomson did make comparisons between the peoples he encountered in Asia and those he photographed in London, Smith never made such associations. And even in Thomson's photographs, a viewer unaware of Thomson's Asian photography – as most Victorian readers probably were – would be hard-pressed to see direct, visual analogies between the street figures of London and those of Asia. If one examines *Street Life in London* in itself and in its entirety, not as a simple extension of Thomson's Asian *oeuvre* and not focusing solely on Thomson's contributions, the notion that the publication as a whole maps the Far East on to the East End evaporates.

In her 2002 article "*Street Life in London* and the Organization of Labour," Angela Vanhaelen examines, to the greatest extent of any author, the contributions of Adolphe Smith. She emphasizes that one must understand Smith's political views to understand the true goals of the publication. For instance, she notes his involvement with the Trades Union Congress, an organization that emphasized self-sufficiency and the benefits of collective societies and communitarian efforts among laborers. She finds such rhetoric employed in many of Smith's texts for *Street Life in London*. Vanhaelen also discusses what *Street Life in London* can contribute to the understanding of photography as a whole. Specifically, she writes, it offers a view of photography that is neither "inherently repressive [n]or inherently democratic."[59]

Vanhaelen takes a holistic approach to the publication, contending that it "defined, classified and organized [its subjects] in terms of their labour," and that it attempted to promote a view of the poor as "for the most part... hard-working, independent, and honest people who are linked by the bonds of family, neighbourhood, and friendship."[60] She identifies correspondences between disparate entries in the publication. For instance, she notes that one pair of photographs – "The Temperance Sweep" and "Dealer in Fancy-Ware" – was made in the same location; and she points out that subjects appearing in one entry sometimes act as informants, introducing Smith and Thomson to subjects appearing in other entries.[61] Because of such connections between entries, and thus between individuals represented in the publication, the London streets as Smith and Thomson represent them come to seem not like a cacophony, but like a community.

Most recently, scholarship has focused more on Thomson's Asian productions than on *Street Life in London.* This has to do in part with the survival of materials. Thomson himself regarded his work in Asia and Cyprus as his most important, and it was these negatives, not his work from *Street Life in London* or from his decades-long studio practice, for which he made careful archival arrangements. His negatives survive in the collection of the Wellcome Library, London. Most recently this material has appeared in the exhibition and publication *China through the Lens of John Thomson*, constituted from the Wellcome collection.[62] Such recent exposure reinforces the perception of Thomson as primarily a travel photographer. Clearly, perception of his work has shifted over the past several decades: from "the first photojournalist," he has become an intrepid journeyer and interpreter of cultures. This trend is in fact a kind of reversion: present-day perception of Thomson now closely resembles perception of the photographer in his own time, when he was regarded as primarily a travel photographer and ethnographer, with special expertise on China.

Adolphe Smith, for his part, has received little attention beyond the brief discussions of his life and work contained within studies like Vanhaelen's. Welcome mentions of his vast, tireless later exertions as an activist journalist, traveling and reporting on issues of sanitation and public health worldwide, appear here and there on occasion, but for the most part he has become virtually invisible.[63] His contributions to *Street Life in London* thus appear, from the vantage point of the current day, to have been his greatest achievements, when they were in fact just one early endeavor in his lengthy, prolific career.

Adolphe Smith was not the most radical of socialists, but he certainly was a socialist. His commitment to the vision of a classless society existed before and during, and persisted long after, production of *Street Life in London.* To see *Street Life in London* as simply and wholly a product of class dominance one must essentially ignore Smith, as many scholars have. This book will examine *Street Life in London* as a complex production, recognizing the class dynamics present in the publication but regarding it as more than a hegemonic exercise.

NOTES

1 The Authors [Adolphe Smith and John Thomson], "Preface," *Street Life in London* (London: Sampson Low, Marston, Searle & Rivington, 1877), n.p.

2 "Photography in and Out of the Studio: More Photographic Publications," *Photographic News*, 26 January 1877, 37.

3 "Annotations: London Street Life," *Lancet* 109, no. 2789 (10 February 1877), 213.

4 "Street Life in London," *Lloyd's Weekly London Newspaper*, 11 March 1877, 5.

5 "The First Photojournalist: John Thomson," *Creative Camera* 43 (1968), 23.

6 See Roland Barthes, "The Rhetoric of the Image," in *Image-Music-Text*, trans. Stephen Heath (New York: Hill and Wang, 1978), 38-41.

7 Adolphe Smith, "'Caney' the Clown," *Street Life in London* (London: Sampson Low, Marston, Searle and Rivington, 1877), 45.

8 Ibid.

9 Ibid., 46.

10 Leonore Davidoff has written trenchantly on the subject of domestic labor's invisibility, both in the Victorian era and to economists and historians looking backward at Victorian England from the perspective of the twentieth century. Davidoff's own studies, collected in her book *Worlds Between*, were among the first serious scholarly examinations of domestic labor. Leonore Davidoff, *Worlds Between: Historical Perspectives on Gender and Class* (New York: Routledge, 1995), see especially Introduction, 1-17.

11 Roland Barthes, "The Rhetoric of the Image," 38-41.

12 Alan Trachtenberg, "Preface," *Reading American Photographs: Images as History, Mathew Brady to Walker Evans* (New York: Hill and Wang, 1989), xv.

13 Trachtenberg, "Illustrious Americans," in *Reading American Photographs*, 52.

14 Trachtenberg, "Camera Work/Social Work," in *Reading American Photographs*, 203.

15 Carol Armstrong, *Scenes in a Library: Reading the Photograph in the Book, 1843-1875* (Cambridge, MA: MIT Press, 1998).

16 Armstrong, "Introduction," in *Scenes in a Library*, 2.

17 Ibid., 3.

18 "The Boyer Collection," *Image* (Rochester, NY) 2, no. 7 (October 1953), 1-8. The article gives broad information on Boyer and his collection.

19 The first three editions of Newhall's history are, in order by date: *Photography 1839-1937* (New York: The Museum of Modern Art, 1937); *Photography: A Short Critical History* (New York: The Museum of Modern Art, 1938); *The History of Photography from 1839 to the Present Day* (New York: The Museum of Modern Art, 1949). Thomson appears in the fourth edition, *The History of Photography from 1839 to the Present Day* (New York: The Museum of Modern Art / Rochester, NY: The George Eastman House, 1964), 137-39.

20 Helmut Gernsheim, *Incunabula of British Photographic Literature, 1839-1875* (London / Berkeley: Scolar Press, 1984), 9.

21 Helmut Gernsheim and Alison Gernsheim, *The History of Photography from the Earliest Use of the Camera Obscura in the Eleventh Century Up to*

1914 (London: Geoffrey Cumberledge / Oxford University, 1955), 340. Gernsheim himself puts the word "modern" in quotes.

22 Helmut Gernsheim, *Creative Photography: Aesthetic Trends 1839-1960* (New York: Bonanza Books, 1962), 154.

23 See also Aaron Scharf's 1976 *Pioneers of Photography*, in which a chapter called "The Indelible Record" opens with a spread of images from *Street Life in London*. Aaron Scharf, *Pioneers of Photography* (New York: Harry N. Abrams, 1976), 122-23.

24 "The First Photojournalist: John Thomson," 22.

25 William Stott, *Documentary Expression and Thirties America* (New York: Oxford University, 1973), 5.

26 Ibid., 6-7.

27 To give just one example, what does it mean for the truthfulness of an image if the photographer moves a cow skull from grass to cracked earth before photographing it, the better to convey the desperation of a drought? Just such a controversy arose over two photographs made by Arthur Rothstein, who was employed by the Farm Security Administration during the Depression. They revealed that the skull had been moved, causing an uproar over the legitimacy of claims that the situation in rural America was truly as dire as the FSA photographers were making it seem.

28 Robert Doty, "Street Life in London: A Review of an Early Use of Photography in Social Documentation," *Image* (Rochester, NY) 6, no. 10 (December 1957), 240-45.

29 "Publisher's Note," *Street Life in London* (New York/London: Benjamin Blom, 1969), n.p.

30 Helmut Gernsheim writes that he paid five guineas (five British Pounds and five shillings, or about $200 in US dollars of the time) in 1948 for his copy of *Street Life in London*. In 1977, one hundred years after its publication, a copy of *Street Life* sold at Sotheby's for £3850, a growth in value of roughly 9600%. Gernsheim, *Incunabula*, 9.

31 See John Warner, "John Thompson [sic]: Compassionate Photographer," *Arts of Asia* 6 (1976), 42-53, which includes a selection of fifteen images from the 1872-74 publication *Illustrations of China and its People*, accompanied by Thomson's own texts.

32 Elliott S. Parker, "John Thomson, 1837-1921: RGS Instructor in Photography," *Geographical Journal* (London) 144, no. 3 (November 1978), 463-71.

33 Susan Sontag, "Melancholy Objects," *On Photography* (New York: Picador/Farrar, Strauss and Giroux, 1977), 55-57. *Street Life in London* actually incorporates thirty-seven photographs, because one entry, "Clapham Common Industries," includes two pictures rather than the usual one.

34 John Tagg, "Evidence, Truth and Order: Photographic Records and the Growth of the State," in *The Burden of Representation: Essays on Photographies and Histories* (London: Macmillan, 1988), 65.

35 John Tagg, "A Means of Surveillance: The Photograph as Evidence in Law," in *The Burden of Representation*, 90-92. Tagg's more recent work continues to explore photography not as a medium but as a discourse and to articulate the relationship between representation and power. See e.g. *The Disciplinary Frame: Photographic Truths and the Capture of Meaning* (Minneapolis/London: University of Minnesota Press, 2009).

36 Margaret Harker, "Scottish Contributions to Photography: The Symposium (continued)," *The British Journal of Photography* (20 May 1983), 527. Harker gives account of Gibson-Cowan's talk on 526-27, though the talk itself is not reprinted.

37 Ialeen Gibson-Cowan, "Thomson's Street Life in Context," *Creative Camera* 251 (November 1985), 10-15; see also Ialeen Gibson-Cowan, "John Thomson on Cyprus," *Photographic Collector* 5, no. 3 (1986), 309-19; John Thomson, *Through Cyprus with the Camera in the Autumn of 1878*, 2 vols. (London: Sampson Low, Marston, Searle and Rivington, 1879); Rpt. 1 vol. (London: Trigraph, 1985), with an essay by Ialeen Gibson-Cowan, ix-xvii.

38 Ialeen Gibson-Cowan, "John Thomson's Street Life in Context," 10.

39 Ibid.

40 Ibid.

41 Ibid., 13.

42 Ibid., 14.

43 Stephen White, *John Thomson: A Window to the Orient* (published in the UK as *John Thomson: Life and Photographs*) (New York / London: Thames and Hudson, 1985).

44 White's collection now resides at the Tokyo-Fuji Art Museum, Tokyo. See Richard Ovenden, "Thomson, John (1837-1921)," *Oxford Dictionary of National Biography Online*, http://www.oxforddnb. com/view/article/38593 (accessed 4 January 2010).

45 This was, in part, due to the pressures of publication. Nonetheless, the intent of this publication, and of the exhibition it accompanied, was to publicize Thomson's travel photographs. See Robert Sobieszek,

"Preface," in Stephen White, *John Thomson*, 7-8.

46 Jeff Rosen, "Posed as Rogues: The Crisis of Photographic Realism in John Thomson's Street Life in London," *Image* (Rochester, NY) 36, nos. 3-4 (Fall/Winter 1993), 24.

47 Ibid., 29.

48 Ibid., 9.

49 Ibid., 17.

50 Thomas Prasch, "Fixed Positions: Working-Class Subjects and Photographic Hegemony in Victorian Britain" (PhD diss., Indiana University, Bloomington, 1994).

51 Ibid., 9.

52 Richard Ovenden, *John Thomson (1837-1921) Photographer* (Edinburgh: National Library of Scotland / Stationery Office, 1997).

53 See Ibid., especially Chapter Two, "Publication," 29-44.

54 Ibid., 34-38.

55 Ibid., 86.

56 James R. Ryan, *Picturing Empire: Photography and the Visualization of the British Empire* (Chicago: The University of Chicago Press, 1997), 174.

57 Ryan's study does demonstrate how, without documentation, two scholars may arrive at separate conclusions using the same evidence: in mentioning an abbreviated version of *Street Life in London* called *Street Incidents*, for instance, he notes that *Street Life* merited such an abridgement because it "would appear to have sold well," a conclusion opposite from Gibson-Cowan's assertion that *Street Incidents* represented the publisher's endeavor to rid itself of excess stock. Ibid.

58 Ibid., 180.

59 Angela Vanhaelen, "Street Life in London and the Organization of Labour," *History of Photography* 26, no. 3 (Autumn 2002), 198.

60 Ibid., 191.

61 Ibid., 199.

62 John Thomson et. al., *China Through the Lens of John Thomson 1868-1872* (Bangkok: River Books, 2010).

63 See e.g. Louise Carroll Wade, "The Problem with Classroom Use of Upton Sinclair's The Jungle," *American Studies* 32, no. 2 (Fall 1991), 79-101.

CHAPTER TWO

JOHN THOMSON: LIFE AND WRITINGS

JOHN THOMSON CAME to *Street Life in London* already a seasoned photographer and traveler, his life and attitudes shaped by the ten years he lived in Asia from 1862-72. His prior experiences influenced the choices he made and the opportunities he pursued after his permanent return to Britain. *Street Life in London* was, at least in part, the product of these experiences.

This chapter focuses on Thomson as an individual, giving a brief biographical sketch and examining his work and writings beyond *Street Life in London*. Details of Thomson's biography are relatively well-known, but revisiting them permits placement of *Street Life in London* within the context of not only his life and activities but his overarching interests and motivations. Understanding the latter proves critical to analysis of the publication. Thomson's writings also provide a steady source of information not only about his movements and activities, but also his attitudes and his outlook. In particular, Thomson published several books for which he both made the images and wrote the accompanying text, demonstrating his sophisticated understanding of the photo-text form. By the time he arrived at *Street Life in London* he clearly recognized the profound effect text could have on the meaning of an accompanying image and vice versa.

In publishing, Thomson catered to audiences interested in a variety of subjects: anthropology, travel, exploration, and the science of photography, among others. Though most of his writing was expository, not autobiographical, one finds in his diverse productions a singular voice and a consistent set of concerns. Thomson's writings and photographs reveal him to have been quintessentially Victorian in many ways: assured of British cultural superiority, confident in the value of science and technology, endlessly curious and almost indefatigable. But they reveal, too, the depth of his thinking about his surroundings, his willingness to change his opinions and to reevaluate his own deeply-held convictions. During the decade he spent in Asia he became more open-minded, more receptive, less prejudiced in a variety of ways. He would later bring those attitudes to bear in *Street Life in London.*

Thomson's life

Thomson was born in Edinburgh in June 1837 to William Thomson and Isabella Newlands Thomson.[1] His father owned a tobacco shop, and the family seems to have been solidly middle-class and well-connected in Scottish intellectual society.[2] After his early schooling Thomson apprenticed with an optician and maker of scientific instruments. From there he went to the Edinburgh School of Arts, where he excelled in his fine arts and chemistry courses. Sir David Brewster, Director of the School of Arts during the years Thomson attended, was an early enthusiast of photography, and students there may have received some exposure to it.[3] Certainly Thomson's knowledge of optical and scientific equipment through his apprenticeship, combined with his formal education in both chemistry and the fine arts, constituted ideal training for a photographer in these early days of the medium. There is no record of how he learned to photograph, but for a man with his background and connections – both personal and professional – the necessary information and equipment would not have been hard to acquire.

In late 1861 or early 1862, Thomson traveled to the British colony of Singapore to join his older brother William, already working there as a watchmaker. By June 1862 Thomson was advertising as a photographer. The Thomson brothers also worked together, making watches, optical devices, and other scientific instruments. Singapore was a point of interchange for Asian traders doing business with European and Middle Eastern contacts. The constant flow of traffic in and out of its ports and the frequent arrival of new residents virtually ensured that a portrait photographer like Thomson would have no shortage of customers.[4]

But when trade slumped, demand for photographs did as well. Thomson's brother William, an alcoholic, added to his burdens, rapidly accumulating business and personal debts. It fell to John to satisfy his brother's creditors, a concern that occupied him for many of the years he lived in Asia.[5] The practice of portrait photography, too, could be both exacting and stultifying. Constant need for speedy processing and printing of negatives made for never-ending busywork, and one's reputation and livelihood depended on the timely output of quality work that satisfied one's sitters. There was little real excitement or space for innovation in portrait-making. Thomson left no record indicating precisely why he decided to branch beyond portraiture and to begin the photographic travelogues that ultimately made his name, but it seems likely that business uncertainties and monetary woes, combined with his intense desire to explore cultures utterly unlike his own, contributed to his decision.

He made a number of journeys in the early years of his stay in Asia. The most impactful on his development as explorer-photographer came four years in, when he traveled to Siam and Cambodia in 1865-66.[6] The journey began auspiciously, as Thomson met and photographed Mongkut, King of Siam. From there he headed into the jungle of Cambodia, accompanied by a British diplomat, H G Kennedy. Thomson had heard and read about a spectacular ruined city called Angkor, located deep in the jungle, and had become intensely interested in photographing it. The two men departed from Bangkok in early 1866, traveling first by boat and then over land.[7] A veritable troop of porters accompanied them to transport their luggage, which included Thomson's cumbersome assortment of photographic chemicals and equipment. His ambition to become the first person to photograph these ruins nearly killed him: he contracted "jungle" (malarial) fever and suffered three days of delirium while Kennedy hovered nearby to care for him. After the fever broke, it took him nearly two weeks to recover enough to continue the journey.[8]

After more travails, the party reached Angkor and Thomson began surveying and photographing the ruins, concentrating in particular on one great temple, Angkor Wat. The photographs reveal its architectural magnificence and catalogue its relief sculptures. They show long, straight, colonnaded passages and walls decorated with roiling battle

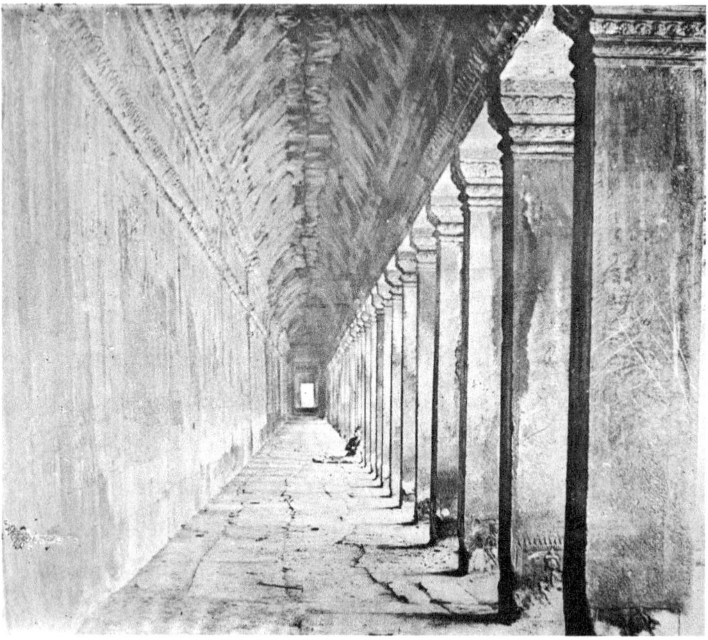

FIG 2.1: John Thomson, "Nakhon Thom, Cambodia," 1866, from *The Antiquities of Cambodia*, 1867. Digital positive from a wet-collodion negative. Courtesy of the Wellcome Library, London, record no. 19194i.

scenes and lush vegetal patterns (Figures 2.1, 2.2, 2.3). The pictures testify to the site's grandeur, and to the sense of romance in its decay and progressive reclamation by the jungle. Thomson was not the first to depict the site in images; the reports by French explorer Henri Mouhot that had piqued his interest in the first place contained illustrations from Mouhot's own sketches.[9] But photographs carried for Victorian audiences a testimonial quality that other illustration formats did not. In Thomson's images, the ruins would come alive for viewers.

The trip was Thomson's first great success as an explorer. He emerged from his brush with death with a terrific story to tell, a remarkable set of photographs, and a new-found authority as explorer of the world's remote places. It was with such authority that he returned to Singapore and then, shortly thereafter, sailed for Britain.[10] He would remain at home for just over a year, returning to Asia in 1867.[11]

His stay in Britain more than fulfilled his hopes for an enhanced reputation. On the strength of his images he was awarded a fellowship in the Ethnological Society of London in 1866. He presented a paper on Angkor Wat and the peoples of Cambodia to the Geographical and Ethnological Section of the British Association for the Advancement of Science

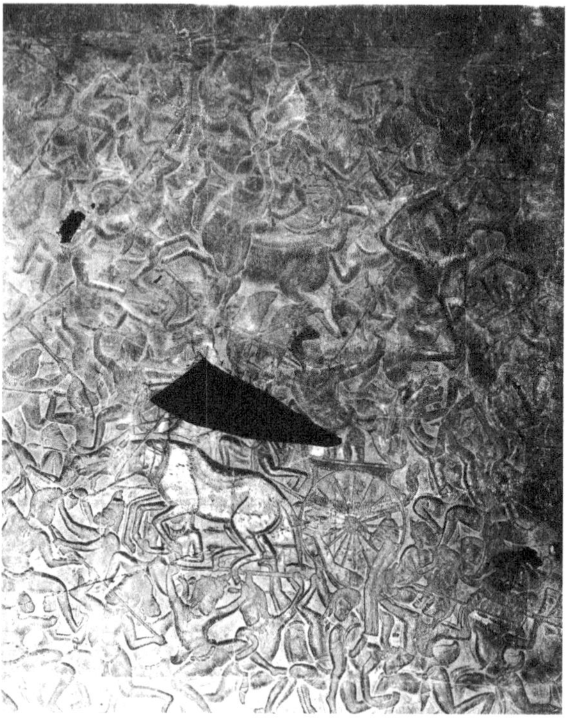

FIG 2.2: John Thomson, "Bas-Relief with Scenes from the Mahabharat, Nakhon Wat, Cambodia," 1866, from *The Antiquities of Cambodia*, 1867. Digital positive from a wet-collodion negative. Courtesy of the Wellcome Library, London, record no. 19130i.

in the autumn of the same year, and in November he won election to the Royal Geographical Society (RGS).[12] His photographs were exhibited in Edinburgh and published in the *Illustrated London News*. He also wrote articles for various photographic journals on technical subjects, including a series on how to photograph in tropical climates.[13] In 1867, Edinburgh publishers Edmonton and Douglas issued Thomson's *The Antiquities of Cambodia: A Series of Photographs Taken on the Spot*, a lavish production illustrated with actual albumen photographs. On top of this success, at one of his lectures at Edinburgh's Industrial Museum in 1867 he met a young woman named Isobel Petrie. By the time he returned to Asia they were engaged.[14]

Back in Asia, he moved his photography business from Singapore to Hong Kong. Hong Kong was, like Singapore, a trading hub and hence a center of intercultural interaction. It also had a larger community of Scots, making it a more inviting place for Thomson's young fiancée, Isobel, who joined him there. By 11 March 1868, Thomson's photographic studio was open, and in November he and Isobel were married.[15] In 1869 she gave birth to their first child, William, known as Willie. But Isobel's health suffered, as did the baby's, in the tropical climate of Hong Kong. Illnesses were rampant among Europeans in the

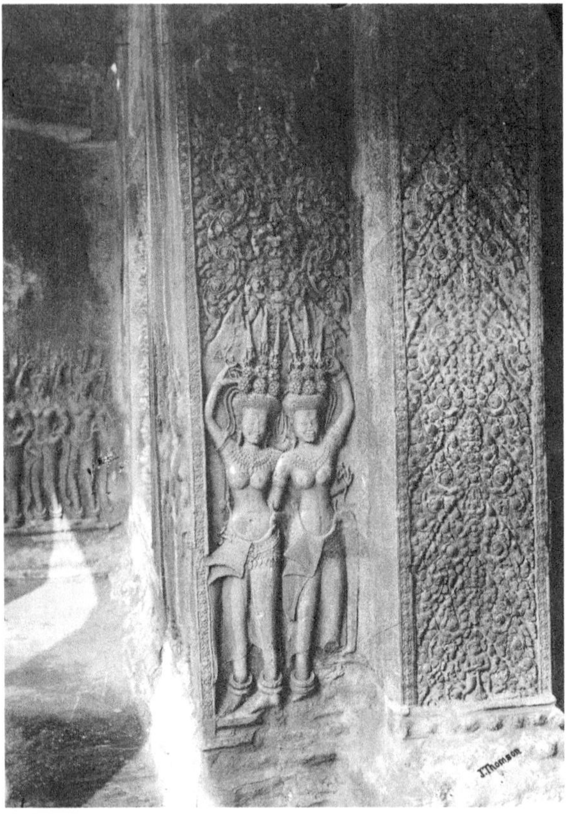

FIG 2.3: John Thomson, "Bas-Relief on a Pilaster, Nakhon Wat, Cambodia," 1866, from *The Antiquities of Cambodia*, 1867. Digital positive from a wet-collodion negative. Courtesy of the Wellcome Library, London, record no. 19152i.

colonies, and mortality rates were high. She justifiably feared for her own and her child's life. When she became pregnant again in 1870, she decided to leave John in Asia and return to Scotland with Willie.[16] When they departed on the months-long sea journey home, the boy was seven months old. A second baby, named John Newlands and called Newlands, was born after Isobel's return to Scotland. The couple had been married only a year and a half when she left Asia, and then faced a separation of more than two years. When John returned from Asia for the final time in late 1872, he arrived home to his wife, three-year-old Willie, and Newlands, the two-year-old son he had never met.

Thomson undertook his explorations and made his photographs not only for the thrill and enjoyment of it, but to satisfy an onerous set of financial burdens, supporting himself and his growing family while contending with his brother's creditors. His accumulation of negatives, which intensified during the two years he was separated from his wife, begins to read as an endeavor in economic prospecting. During that period, he traveled intensively inside China, moving into territories far outside those usually visited by Europeans. His sense of wonder at the beauty and strangeness of his surroundings comes through in his photographs and writings; but his desire for adventure was held in check by familial obligations. He began to forgo journeys, including one to Mongolia, as his longing for his family intensified.[17] Torn between a sense of adventure and one of obligation, Thomson became a family man.

On his return to Europe in 1872, Thomson spent little time reacquainting himself with his Scottish homeland, instead moving with his family to London. He immediately set about integrating himself into the various communities – photographic, geographic, ethnographic – with which he felt most closely allied by his own interests and experiences. He also pursued publishing endeavors, taking advantage of the widespread curiosity about all things Asian. Before the end of 1872, he had secured publication plans for two books of his Chinese images: *Foochow and the River Min*, a lavish book privately printed for a small group of subscribers; and the four-volume *Illustrations of China and Its People*.[18]

The latter work, which Thomson and many others in his lifetime regarded as his masterpiece, marks the beginning of his association with the publisher Sampson Low and Co., among the most important professional affiliations of his career. Between 1872 and 1878 Thomson worked on a number of projects for Low and Co., including *Street Life in London*. He also translated several texts from French into English for the company, including a travelogue of Spain and two editions of a popular practical handbook for photography.[19] Given that he probably worked on many of these projects, including *Street Life in London*, simultaneously, the period of his affiliation with Low and Co. must have been busy indeed.

After completing work on *Street Life* in 1877, Thomson encountered another opportunity to use his rare skills as field photographer and explorer. In the fall of 1878 he traveled to Cyprus, which had recently come under British administration after centuries of Turkish rule. British audiences were tremendously interested in the island, and Thomson shrewdly decided to take advantage of public curiosity. Within two months of the takeover in summer 1878 Thomson sailed for the island, landing in early September.[20] The photographs he made there, along with his characteristically informative and entertaining text, appeared in two volumes in early 1879. *Through Cyprus with the Camera in the Autumn of 1878* was a hit: praised by critics and fellow-photographers, it garnered Thomson yet more attention as explorer-with-a-camera.[21]

The journey to Cyprus was to be Thomson's last major expedition. Firmly ensconced as a member of the British community of explorers, and widely respected among photographers, Thomson concerned himself after 1879 with establishing a settled photography business in London. In the early 1880s he opened a portrait studio in London and began to accumulate a clientele composed of wealthy, socially-connected, and even aristocratic patrons. Thomson's field ability served him well in his portrait business, allowing him to visit clients at home rather than requiring their presence in his studio. Sitters clearly appreciated this ability to accommodate them: among his clientele, he numbered Queen Victoria and members of her family. In 1881 she granted Thomson a coveted Royal Warrant, which permitted him to advertise as "Photographer to Her Majesty Queen Victoria."[22] Her approval and his own business acumen served him well, and he built a strong and successful studio practice.[23]

Thereafter he engaged in a few other projects, mostly building on his fashionable studio practice. Alfred de Rothschild employed him in 1884 to make a photographic record of the Rothschild family's extensive art collections.[24] In 1899 several of his studio photographs appeared, along with those of other fashionable portrait photographers of the late Victorian period, in a privately-printed book cataloguing the attendees at the Duchess of Devonshire's

1897 fancy-dress ball.[25] He apparently also made art photographs. Little is known about the latter work, but he exhibited it from time to time at salons of the Royal Photographic Society and elsewhere.[26]

He did continue his engagement with travel photography, but as instructor rather than practitioner. Beginning in 1886 and continuing into the twentieth century, he held the position of photographic instructor with the Royal Geographic Society (RGS), teaching field photography to British explorers. Photographers learned the basics of camera operation and chemical handling from Thomson, and he also taught them how to photograph human anthropological and racial types, among other subjects.[27] He took this responsibility very seriously, believing in photography as a powerful educational tool.[28]

On his death in 1921, obituaries remarked on his lengthy career in photography and commemorated his remarkable work in Asia and Cyprus, as well as his service for the RGS. Writers remarked on his photography of China and praised his skill as a technician and educator. *Street Life in London*, the work that through much of the twentieth century guaranteed him a place in histories of photography as "first photojournalist," was not mentioned.[29]

Thomson's writings

Such a biographical overview offers valuable information about Thomson, but affords little perspective into his worldview or his motivations. By examining his writings, one achieves a better understanding of his attitudes toward the world, an understanding that will become critical to analysis of *Street Life in London.* Thomson published relatively frequently, especially between the later 1860s and the end of the nineteenth century. In addition to his major, stand-alone books, he also wrote articles, sometimes in series, on travel-related or technical subjects. His writing tends to be clear and confident. His early writing is generally more casual in tone and often amusing, while from the 1880s on it becomes more serious, formal and scientific, though his enthusiasm for the medium itself remains undimmed. Perhaps most important, his writing reveals his evolving attitudes. Early in his career he often evinces a casual racism typical of Victorians looking at non-Europeans. Later his attitudes toward those of other races, classes and cultures deepen and become less markedly biased.

A representative passage from his early career appears in a six-part series on photography in the tropics for the *British Journal of Photography*, written during Thomson's return visit from Asia to Britain in 1866. In the passage, Thomson reveals his sense of humor, his confidence in his own photographic knowledge, and his Eurocentric view of the world:

> *How often have we heard it said – 'It is almost impossible to obtain fine results in photography where the climate is so hot, the atmosphere so humid, and the light so intense.' As illustrations, a series of leprous-looking prints are brought forward with blank lights and shadows. Strange to say, they are done by Jones, who succeeded so well at home, and who uses the same materials then employed... Some compassionate young lady, comparing an Indian portrait with an old home one, will exclaim – 'How frightful!... Why Harry must have grown black out in that horrid place, and turned Hindoo or Chitty, and surely that white chalk line down the ridge of his nose is the mark of his caste!' The truth is, Jones – who was never an early riser – has allowed the mild light of his Eastern mornings to pass over, and taken the bulk of his photographs under a vertical sun, and with the same old materials. Provided the right time be chosen for lighting the subject, and the chemicals are modified to suit the climate, as fine results may be obtained in the tropics as in the temperate latitudes – pictures*

possessing soft and yet brilliant lights and broad shadows, full of detail.[30]

In the remainder of the series, he delineates his own methods, exhibiting his broad understanding of the technical aspects of the medium.[31] He discusses chemical formulas, the proper construction of shipping boxes for glass negatives, and a variety of other subjects, but the articles remain relatively light in tone overall, a change from the dryness of much photographic literature of the period.

Thomson's first book, *The Antiquities of Cambodia*, appeared in 1868. A series of images of the great temple, Angkor Wat, it is illustrated with actual photographs, printed on albumen paper from wet-collodion negatives. Prior to this book, a few Thomson images had appeared as wood-engravings in published sources. After this, many of his books would contain high-quality photomechanical prints like carbon prints or woodburytypes, rather than actual photographic images. Books with real photographs were slow to produce and expensive to assemble: one could make, from a single wet-collodion negative, only three albumen prints per day.[32] Though Thomson, like other photographers, probably made copy negatives from which more prints could be taken, the process was nonetheless painstaking.

That he chose to make a photographically-illustrated book, rather than allowing his images to be rendered as wood-engravings – which permitted images and text to be printed simultaneously, a less expensive and less laborious process – demonstrates Thomson's belief that a particular accuracy was inherent in the photograph. Through his photographs he could prove that the ruins of Angkor Wat were as spectacular as his writing attested, rather than simply asserting their beauty and relying on the reader to trust him. He was not the first European to see Angkor; in the introduction to the book he states as much, crediting Henri Mouhot's prior publication with piquing his interest.[33] But the very existence of Thomson's book is a kind of gentle rebuke to Mouhot, an assertion of the primacy of Thomson's photography over Mouhot's drawings and of photography over drawing, painting and print in general.

The photographs permit readers to encounter the ruins of Angkor Wat in something like, but also unlike, Thomson's own proximity. At the start of the book, Thomson sets the scene with several pages of text, divided into brief parts, including one detailing the route of his journey and giving mention of the terrible fever he suffered *en route*, and another giving the history of the ruins as known. The latter section begins:

> *The antiquities of Cambodia, which are now found shrouded in the heart of the dense tropical forests of the country, consist of walled cities of vast extent; exquisitely built stone bridges, spanning with a multitude of arches the streams of the interior; temples more curious and extensive than those of Central America, and approaching in their classical appearance the works of the ancient Greeks or Romans; palaces of the ancient kings, adorned, like the monasteries, with the richest sculpture... The greatest of all Cambodian antiquities, and the one which this volume specially illustrates, is situated about 15 miles north of Tale Sap, and occupies a square area (measuring about three-quarters of a mile each way) surrounded by a broad ditch. Within this area are the remains existing, in wonderful preservation, of the great temple of NAKHON WAT (The Temple of the Capital).*
>
> *Regarding its origin, or the history of the people who built it, the rude races of the present day can tell us nothing. They believe it to have been the work of the gods, and their wild and fanciful traditions, which*

> *they narrate with child-like credulity, attribute its origin to a flight of Tewadah (angels), or the wish of a god, or a race of giants.*[34]

Thomson's mention of the temples of Central America cues his readers to understand that they are venturing outside the European paradigm, but then he immediately claims these ruins for the West, comparing them to temples of ancient Greece or Rome. Unlike modern-day Cambodians, Thomson is able to quantify the structures, to say how large they are, where they are located, how many miles they are from various other landmarks, and so on. Indeed, he implies that the "rude races of the present day," who make only silly, "child-like" conjectures about the buildings' origins, are not even descended from the ancient creators of the structures.

Thomson's photographs reinforce his appropriation of the ruins, divorcing them from their surroundings. Through his pictures, Thomson can present the ruins as scientifically as possible to his readers, extracted from the jungle heat and placed within the pages of his book in cool monochrome. The readers' experience with the ruins is cleaner and more clinical than Thomson's own. Unlike him, the audience has no need to imperil itself, or to trouble itself with the messy, confusing inconsistency between the grandeur of the ruins and the crudeness of present-day Cambodia.

The Antiquities of Cambodia exhibits some tendencies that persist throughout Thomson's *oeuvre*. First, here as elsewhere Thomson presents himself as image-maker and explorer, suffering privations and danger in order to bring to European armchair travelers a better understanding of the world both under and outside of their control. Second, his text, alternatively informative and performative, factual and entertaining, anchors and amplifies his images. Finally, his attitudes toward photography also demonstrate themselves here as being fully-formed. Photography allowed him to order the world he encountered, to arrange it in systematic and scientific fashion. He also believed fervently in its power to educate. The formula Thomson established in *The Antiquities of Cambodia* reappeared in publications throughout his career.

But the casual racism Thomson exhibits here diminishes in later volumes. Prior to his expedition to Angkor he had already been living in Asia for four years, but had rarely gone far beyond colonized or heavily-westernized areas. A kind of atmospheric racism, a deep mutual distrust between Europeans and Asians, had arisen in such areas. During Thomson's four-year residence in Singapore and other colonial holdings, he would have had no reason to disbelieve such ambient presumptions, and so on this first major trip beyond the boundaries of westernized Asia, he carried them with him.

But as he continued his journeys into the interior of China, across the island of Formosa, and other places in Asia, he increasingly escaped this poisonous atmosphere. In remote areas he could not rely on received wisdom, depending instead on empirical evidence. Already a man of scientific mind, Thomson began to develop a more complex understanding of Asian peoples and cultures on the basis of his own observations. The attitude that so clearly differentiates much of Thomson's photography from that of other Victorians abroad, his empathetic identification with his sitters – whether they were racially or culturally other to him, socio-economically disadvantaged, or otherwise marked as in some way different – was born of his intense interactions with the unfamiliar land and people of Asia.

The most significant evidence for this comes in his four-volume *Illustrations of China and its People*, published in 1873-74 after his return to England from Asia. The four volumes contain, collectively,

200 illustrations, again accompanied by Thomson's own writing. Thomson's text for *Illustrations of China* functions as exposition and elaboration, deftly guiding readers toward an understanding of his images that mirrored his own. It also, as in *The Antiquities of Cambodia*, details the dangers Thomson faced and the specifics of his encounters with the Chinese, building context around the pictures' content. The introduction, published with the first volume, is worth quoting at some length:

> *My design in the accompanying work is to present a series of pictures of China and its people, such as shall convey an accurate impression of the country I traversed as well as of the arts, usages, and manners which prevail in different provinces of the Empire. With this intention I made the camera the constant companion of my wanderings, and to it I am indebted for the faithful reproduction of the scenes I visited, and of the types of race with which I came into contact.*
>
> *Those familiar with the Chinese and their deeply-rooted superstitions will readily understand that the carrying out of my task involved both difficulty and danger. In some places there were many who had*

never set eyes upon a pale-faced stranger; and the literati, or educated classes, had fostered a notion amongst such as these, that, while evil spirits of every kind were carefully to be shunned, none ought to be so strictly avoided as the 'Fan Qui' or 'Foreign Devil,' who assumed human shape, and appeared solely for the furtherance of his own interests, often owing the success of his undertakings to an ocular power, which enabled him to discover the hidden treasures of heaven and earth. I therefore frequently enjoyed the reputation of being a dangerous geomancer, and my camera was held to be a dark mysterious instrument, which, combined with my naturally, or supernaturally, intensified eyesight gave me power to see through rocks and mountains, to pierce the very souls of the natives, and to produce miraculous pictures by some black art...

The superstitious influences, such as I have described, rendered me a frequent object of mistrust, and led to my being stoned and roughly handled on more occasions than one. It is, however, in and about large cities that the wide-spread hatred of foreigners is most conspicuously displayed. In many of the country districts, and from officials who have been associated with Europeans, and who therefore appreciate the substantial benefits which foreign intercourse can confer, I have met with numerous tokens of kindness, and a hospitality as genuine as could be shown to a stranger in any part of the world.

It is a novel experiment to attempt to illustrate a book of travels with photographs, a few years back so perishable, and so difficult to reproduce. But the art is now so far advanced, that we can multiply the copies with the same facility, and print them with the same materials as in the case of woodcuts or engravings. I feel somewhat sanguine about the success of the undertaking, and I hope to see the process which I have thus applied adopted by other travelers; for the faithfulness of such pictures affords the nearest approach that can be made towards placing the reader actually before the scene which is represented.

The passage continues with Thomson's statement that the order of the book reflects "as far as possible" the order in which Thomson actually visited the country; and concludes by giving some details of this order.[35]

Thomson, ever an economical writer, reveals much

in this brief introduction. In the initial paragraph he introduces the book as a specifically pictorial representation of China. He notes here that his camera served two purposes, representation of scenes and of racial types. Many images in the book do, in fact, show places and people, but to classify all the pictures in the four volumes as either landscape or racial type is reductive. It was, however, what Thomson assumed his audience would want. The concept of the racial type was familiar in nineteenth-century Europe. It connoted a representation that isolated human subjects or presented them in small groups, near enough to the camera or picture plane that their facial features and clothing were clearly visible. Such images permit the viewer to examine the subject as both specimen and spectacle. Thomson's "scenes" would then permit placement of the subject in his or her environment. In this first paragraph, Thomson demonstrates that he will cover all the necessary bases: through photography, he will satisfy readers' curiosity about the landscape and people of China.

In the next paragraph, he seems to confirm widespread western assumptions about the Chinese, noting especially their superstitious suspicion toward outsiders. He appears to mock such superstition, making it clear that he continually suffered the results of this pervasive fear. But then he immediately implies that this fear is not ingrained in the Chinese psyche. Rather, he blames the "literati, or educated classes" who encourage such superstition, taking advantage of a poor and uneducated populace. That populace itself he regards more with pity than with scorn, demonstrating a developing sensitivity to the injustices of social inequality.

Moreover, he continues, the more urban a populace, the more hostile. In rural areas he often encountered kind and hospitable people. Given his several years' experience living in both Singapore and Hong Kong, and his repeated visits to other cities like Peking where there was a significant western diplomatic presence, it seems likely that he refers here to the poisonous atmosphere of mutual mistrust between Europeans and Chinese that he found to be the norm in such places. He implies that in rural communities there was little such pervasive, atmospheric racism. He does state that where Europeans had visited previously the hospitality was greater, but not because Europeans brought the idea of hospitality. Such kindness to strangers was already ingrained in Chinese culture; it was simply more readily offered toward Europeans by people who had previously met, and liked, other Europeans.

The entire passage performs a sophisticated rhetorical reversal. First, Thomson seems to confirm his audience's assumptions with regard to Chinese hostility to outsiders, then he gently persuades the audience that such assumptions are misguided. He acts as both entertainer and educator, delivering an engaging account in words and pictures but also guiding his audience toward a more complex and less prejudicial understanding of Imperial China.

He concludes this persuasive passage by justifying his use of photography as the most "faithful" of representational media. Albumen photographs were, he acknowledges, prone to fading (and perhaps he was thinking here of his own prior publication on Cambodia). But new processes had overcome such issues. In the collotype process used for *Illustrations of China*, photographs were printed in permanent pigment rather than fugitive silver salts. Books illustrated with collotypes remained just as expensive as those illustrated with actual photographs, far more expensive than books illustrated with wood-engravings; but unlike a wood-engraving, which was an artist's rendering of a photograph and hence derivative, a collotype was created directly from a photographic negative. As such the print carried an authority ascribed only to photography, "placing the reader

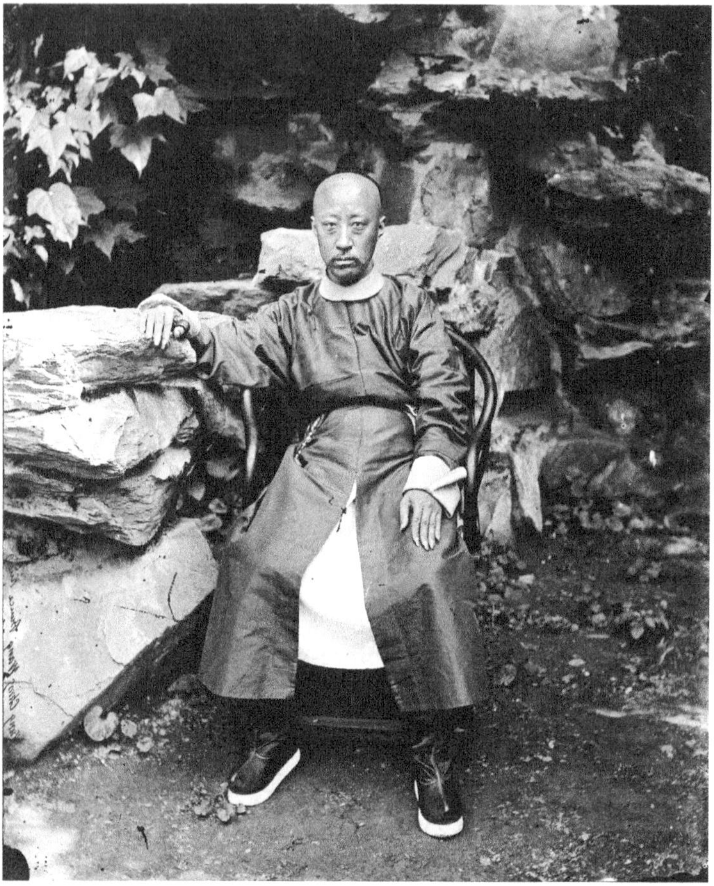

FIG 2.4: John Thomson, "Prince Kung," 1869, from *Illustrations of China and its People*, Vol. I (Sampson Low, Marston, Low and Searle, 1873). Digital positive from a wet-collodion negative. Courtesy of the Wellcome Library, London, record no. 19632i.

actually before the scene which is represented."

Thomson concludes the introduction with a promise to carry the reader through China in an order roughly equivalent to that of his own travels, starting in Hong Kong. And yet, when the reader turns the page to the first image, she finds not an image of Hong Kong but a portrait. "Prince Kung" (Figure 2.4) sits in a bentwood chair, in an outdoor courtyard next to a brick wall. He faces the camera with one arm on the wall and the other resting on his knee. A formidable-looking man, he confronts the camera directly, exhibiting none of the superstitious fear of the camera Thomson discusses in the introduction just one page before. In his descriptive text, Thomson calls the prince "quick of apprehension, open to advice, and comparatively liberal in his views..."[36] This, then, is the reader's real introduction to China-as-Thomson-sees-it: not a view of the colonial city of Hong Kong, but an image of one of the most powerful men in China, an uncle of the Emperor and a man living free from colonial control. Kung lived not in or near Hong Kong, but in Peking, a city which had a foreign presence but was by no means a colony.[37] Given that he had nothing to do with Hong Kong, and that his presence subverts the order Thomson claims to impose on his images as they appear in the book,

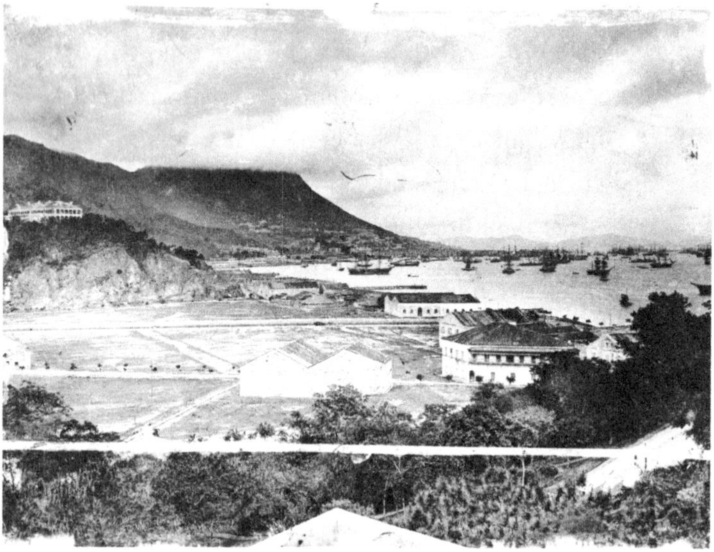

FIG 2.5: John Thomson, "Hong Kong," 1869, from *Illustrations of China and its People*, Vol. I (Sampson Low, Marston, Low and Searle, 1873). Digital positive from a wet-collodion negative. Courtesy of the Wellcome Library, London, record no. 19992i.

Thomson's choice to place him at the beginning of the book suggests a deliberate assertion of Chinese power and dignity. If Kung is the subject of the camera's gaze, he is an active subject. As the camera stares at him, he stares right back. Thomson's introductory text attempted to educate its reader gently, but with this picture he makes a more direct statement: China is formidable and powerful; it is thoughtful and intelligent; it has not been and will not be colonized.

The following plate shows a view of the Hong Kong harbor, made from a hill above the sea (Figure 2.5). It is a straightforward, informative image. The text amplifies and describes the scene, opening with facts about Hong Kong – "it is about ten miles long, by four and a-half in breadth, and of igneous formation" – then segueing into a brief history of the island.[38] One paragraph recounts an attempt by Chinese bakers in 1857 "to poison the entire foreign community" by "introduc[ing] arsenic into the bread."[39] This account supports Thomson's claim, asserted in his Introduction, that Chinese communities in urban areas deeply dislike foreigners. Yet even here, as in the Introduction, Thomson blames the incident not on culture, but on class and clout: "These bakers had, no doubt, been bribed by more influential parties; but we believe few, if any, of the offenders were punished

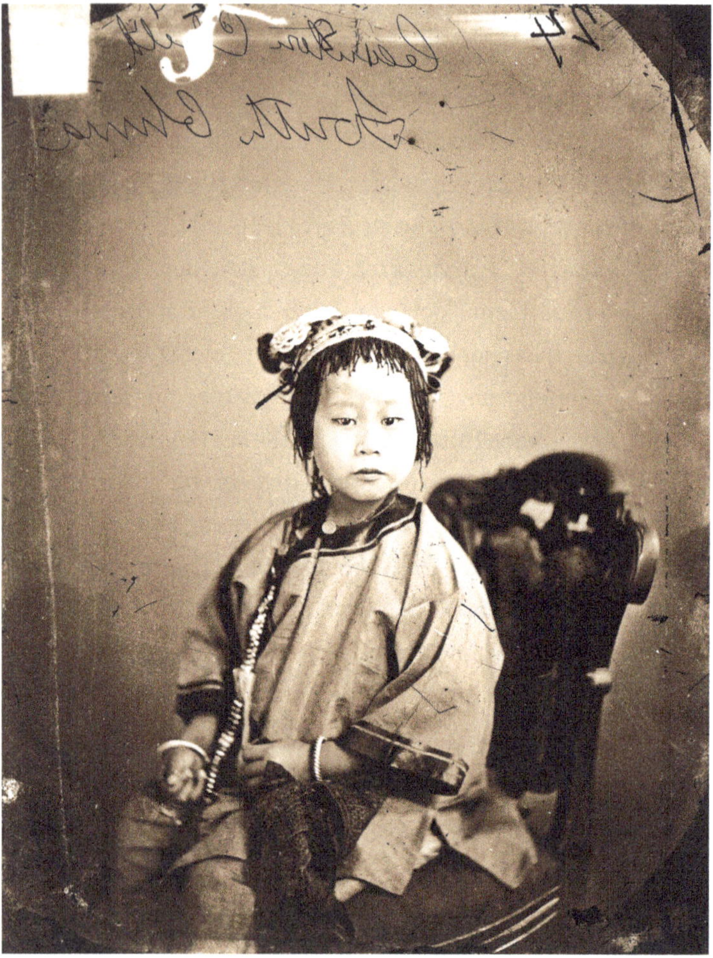

FIG 2.6: John Thomson, "A Cantonese Girl," 1869, from *Illustrations of China and its People*, Vol. I (Sampson Low, Marston, Low and Searle, 1873). Digital positive from a wet-collodion negative. Courtesy of the Wellcome Library, London, record no. 19608i.

for the crime."[40]

Next in the series of images comes a second landscape plate, again of Hong Kong harbor, made during the visit of the Duke of Edinburgh in 1869.[41] The following plate shows four images: two sedan-chair carriers in Hong Kong, photographed next to their chair in the Hong Kong streets; a fairly standard typological image of a schoolboy, made in a studio setting; another studio picture, this time of a little girl; and a portrait of a Hong-Kong artist at work (Figures 2.6, 2.7). After the rather jarringly confrontational image of Prince Kung, Thomson returns to more standard landscapes and racial types to satisfy readers' expectations. Accompanying texts explain images and humanize subjects. These texts, like Thomson's Introduction, are sometimes contradictory, first appearing to embrace racial stereotypes and then complicating them. For instance, he asserts that the sedan-chair carriers are, by and large, "happy" and "contented" with their extraordinarily difficult work, "simple [in their] habits" and enjoying an enviable freedom – all rhetoric that sounds uncomfortably like justification. And yet Thomson also praises the sedan-chair carriers as strong, proud of their ability to do difficult work, and conscientious in maintaining their equipment.[42] The image shows

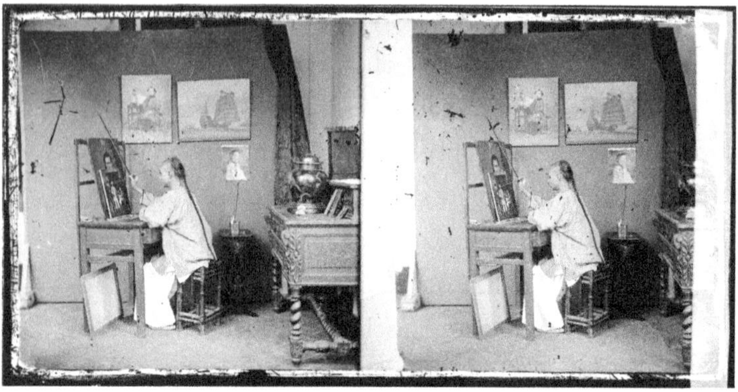

FIG 2.7: John Thomson, "A Hong-Kong Artist," c. 1868, from *Illustrations of China and its People*, Vol. I (Sampson Low, Marston, Low and Searle, 1873). Digital positive from a stereoscopic wet-collodion negative. Courtesy of the Wellcome Library, London, record no. 19840i.

them not isolated in a studio setting but embedded in the context of the street, reinforcing the impression Thomson gives in the text that their labor is real, and truly difficult.

As Thomson moves beyond Hong Kong, he maintains the initial rhythm of the book: portraits, whether single or group, strictly typological or more casual, interspersed with landscapes and other scenic views. Keen to demonstrate the diversity of Chinese society, Thomson depicted Cantonese, Mongolian and Manchu subjects (see e.g. Figures 2.8, 2.9). In Volume II, he included a series of racial types depicting the Pepohoan culture on Formosa, again alternating between straightforward, isolated typological frames and more casual images depicting people interacting with and inhabiting their dwellings and the surrounding landscape (Figures 2.10, 2.11). Unpopulated landscapes also appear, as do many images of boats and waterways.

But though Thomson frequently employs standard pictorial tropes – the artfully-composed picturesque landscape, the racial type, the seascape – the cumulative effect of these is astonishing. The multiplicity of racial types and landscapes leads the reader toward an understanding of China's land and cultures that is not simplified and scientific, but instead vital

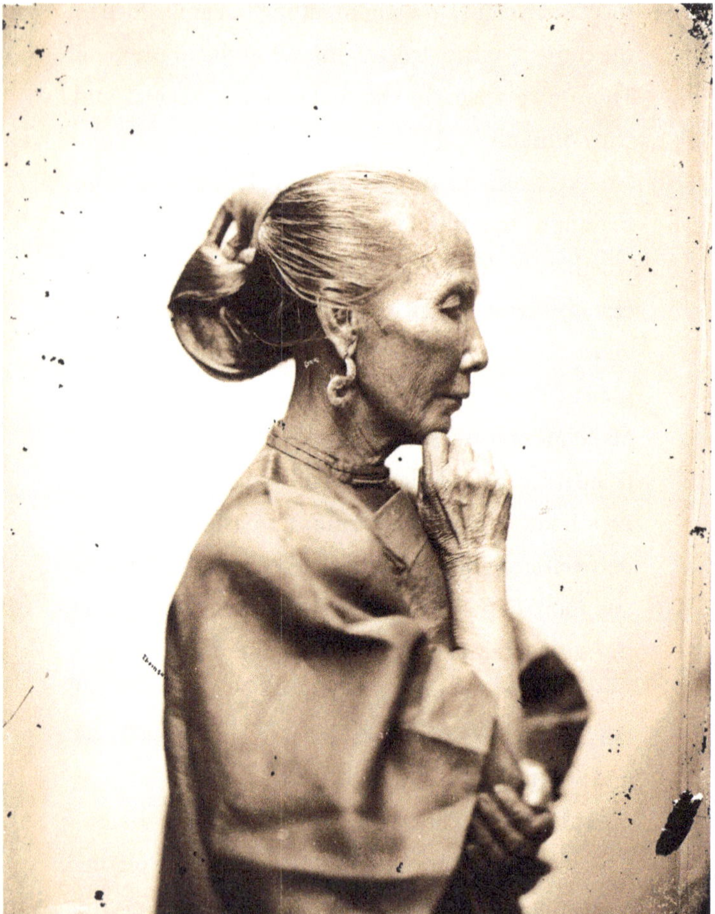

FIG 2.8: John Thomson, "A Cantonese Woman of the Working Class," 1869, from *Illustrations of China and its People*, Vol. I (Sampson Low, Marston, Low and Searle, 1873). Digital positive from a wet-collodion negative. Courtesy of the Wellcome Library, London, record no. 19578i.

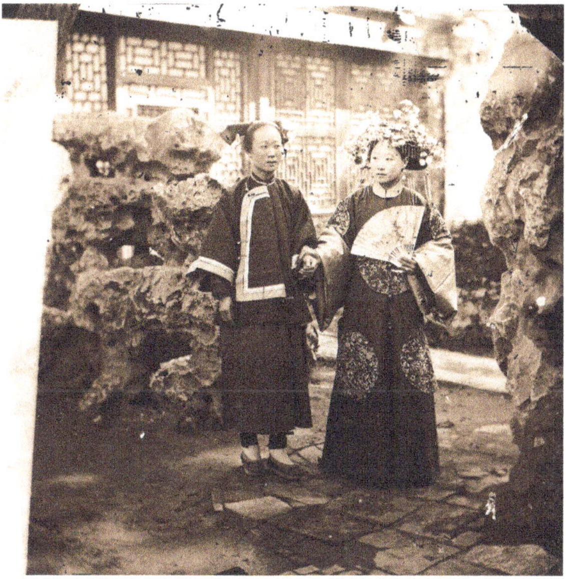

FIG 2.9: John Thomson, "Manchu Bride and Maid," 1869, from *Illustrations of China and Its People*, Vol. IV (Sampson Low, Marston, Low and Searle, 1874). Digital positive from a wet-collodion negative. Courtesy of the Wellcome Library, London, record no. 19670i.

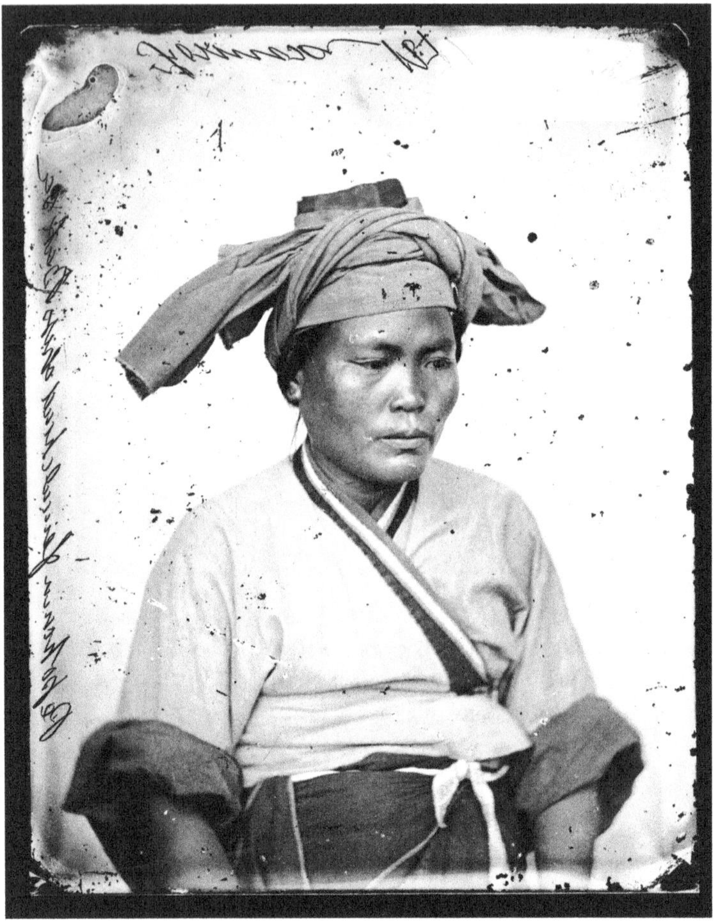

FIG 2.10: John Thomson, "Pepohoan Woman with Headscarf, Formosa," 1871, from *Illustrations of China and its People*, Vol. II (Sampson Low, Marston, Low and Searle, 1873). Digital positive from a wet-collodion negative. Courtesy of the Wellcome Library, London, record no. 19826i.

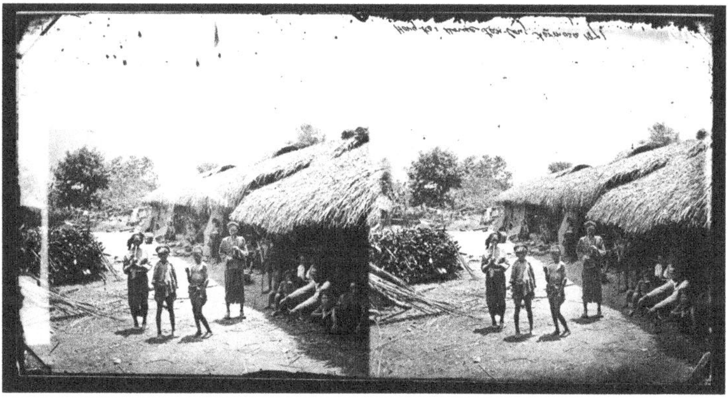

FIG 2.11: John Thomson, "Hong-Ko's House, Lan-Long, Formosa," 1871, from *Illustrations of China and its People*, Vol. II (Sampson Low, Marston, Low and Searle, 1873). Digital positive from a stereoscopic wet-collodion negative. Courtesy of the Wellcome Library, London, record no. 19806i.

and dizzyingly complex. China's enormity and diversity make it impossible, Thomson seems to say, to draw broad, crude conclusions about the country. Thomson produced not a scientific study of a strange and foreign place, but a humanist odyssey through an empire as vast and diverse, and just as resistant to classification, as the British Empire.

Published between 1873 and 1874, *Illustrations of China and its People* cemented Thomson's reputation as explorer-with-a-camera. Its publisher, Sampson Low and Co. had undertaken to become one of the premier publishers of photographically-illustrated books. Thomson's work, with a guaranteed audience of both travel and photography enthusiasts, must have seemed an excellent investment.[43]

Thomson's association with Sampson Low and Co. entailed more than photographic projects. After publication of *Illustrations of China and Its People* was underway, the photographer began contributing to other endeavors. He translated three texts from the French for Sampson Low and Co. The first, Gaston Tissandier's *A History and Handbook of Photography*, appeared in two editions in 1876 and 1878, both of which Thomson also edited. For the 1878 edition, he persuaded an aging William Henry Fox Talbot to contribute an account of the medium's English history, a feature that takes pride of place in the publisher's advertisements of the new edition.[44] Also in 1876, Thomson translated Baron Charles D'Avillier's *Spain*, a travelogue with illustrations by Gustave Doré.[45] And in 1877 he translated and edited J J Grandville's *The Public and Private Life of Animals*, a strange assortment of humorous texts, including fables and a section comparing human physiognomies to those of animals.[46]

Thomson did most of the work for *Street Life in London* in 1876 and 1877, simultaneously with these other publishing projects. Given the number of commitments he had with Sampson Low and Co., he seems to have been a kind of staff writer for them. Thomson's financial situation on his return to Britain from Asia was uncertain, and his family was growing. An affiliation with Sampson Low and Co. would have provided a reliable source of work and income for him. It could also have led the publishing house to think of Thomson when the idea of a book of street photography was first proposed, or even to conceive the project with Thomson in mind. Production of *Street Life in London* demanded a photographer with a high degree of field experience and an ability to manage the crowds that gathered whenever street photography occurred, so it is unlikely that the publishing company would seriously have considered the project unless they already had in mind a photographer with those rare skills. Thomson may well have undertaken work on *Street Life in London* not out of some deep-rooted desire to combat social injustice, but because he needed to support his family and because he already had a relationship with the publisher.

Indeed, the project for Sampson Low and Co. that took best advantage of Thomson's prior skill and experience was not *Street Life in London* but rather the Cyprus project he undertook at the end of the following year. His trip to the island, lasting several weeks in the fall of 1878, bore fruit in the quickly but lavishly produced *Through Cyprus with the Camera in the Autumn of 1878*, which appeared in mid-January 1879. Thomson's introduction for this book is not as long as the one for *Illustrations of China and its People*, but it is in some ways equally indicative of Thomson's attitude. He begins by noting his desire to present to his public, through photographs and text, a "faithful reproduction" of what he experienced during his journey. He continues:

> *Had I allowed first impressions to influence me, I should have set my face homeward soon after*

> *landing at Larnaca; for in that town I found a number of assembled immigrants bewailing the want of forethought that had brought them and their wares to an 'exhausted island,' never free from pestilence, and to a poverty-stricken people.*
>
> *Gloomy forebodings thus greeted me on all sides; but in the end I took what turned out to be the right course. I thought that, after all, I would wait and see things for myself, and pursue my original plan of exploring Cyprus with the 'camera,' taking views (as impartial as they were photographic) of whatever might prove interesting on the journey.*
>
> *...The photographs have been printed in permanent pigments, and therefore, while they supply incontestable evidence of the present condition of Cyprus, they will also afford a source of comparison in after years, when, under the influence of British rule, the place has risen from its ruins.*[47]

Thomson then laments the "maladministration" of the Turks, and expresses clear faith in British rule to bring order and prosperity to the island. His sense of British superiority is not unalloyed, however, as he expresses clear distaste for the "immigrants" who

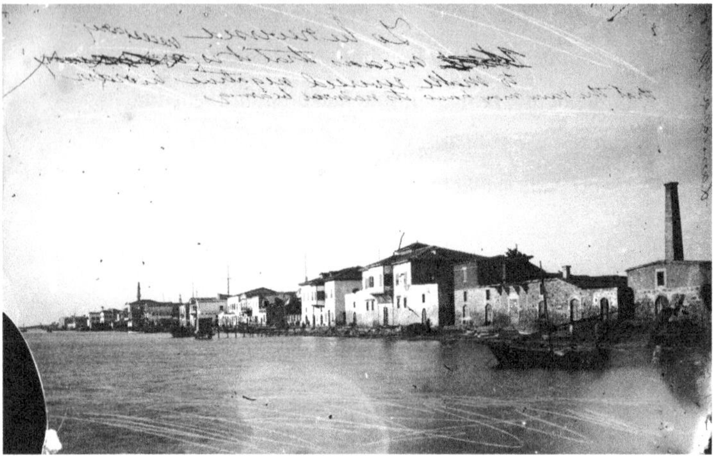

FIG 2.12: John Thomson, "Larnaca Marina Looking South," 1878, from *Through Cyprus with the Camera in the Autumn of 1878* (London: Sampson Low, Marston, Searle and Rivington, 1879). Digital positive from a wet-collodion negative. Courtesy of the Wellcome Library, London, record no. 18978i.

have arrived in hopes of taking economic advantage of the island's undeveloped state. This thinly-veiled criticism of other British travelers carries a degree of contempt: in comparison with such weak people, who wilt outside the boundaries of the British Isles, Thomson is a hardy traveler, accustomed through his years of experience to privations much greater than those he encounters on Cyprus.[48] Thomson professes faith in his own judgments over the assertions of others, and states that with his camera as his witness he will belie such "gloomy forebodings." And, as in the introduction to his *Illustrations of China*, he reassures the reader that these illustrations, while truthful because photographic, are also "permanent" in a way that albumen photographs were not.

Thomson's choice of opening image in his study of Cyprus is not as confrontational as in his *Illustrations of China*, because his purpose here was not to challenge the audience with evidence of the subject's iron will. He opens instead with unremarkable images of the marina at Larnaca (Figure 2.12). In the texts, Thomson describes the salutary effect he hopes British rule will have on the island and notes the accommodations that have already been erected for travelers. From here, he progresses away from the marina to the seashore at Larnaca, where a third image shows a young man on a rocky or shell-strewn beach next to an enormous bed of cactus. Thomson discusses in the accompanying text how the picture was made and why the vantage point was chosen. Again, he clearly understood the way text and picture interact: he states outright that his text serves "to supplement [the photograph] by personal observation." In monochrome, the scene appears bleak, but Thomson assures us this is not the case:

> *Although simple in its elements the scene is one of the most attractive in the neighborhood of Larnaca. The rich green thickets of cacti harmonize well with the warm hue of the shore, the undulating, ever-changing line of clear blue sea; while the mid-space is dotted with pale green shrubs, and distant groves of date-palms wave over the gardens of the Marina.*[49]

Text compensates for the failings of image, allowing Thomson to flesh out the bare bones of monochrome with language evoking vivid color. He thus constructs an experience for his viewer that partakes of both readership and viewership. Image and text play off one another, enriching and enlivening the audience's experience of both. Together they create a whole that is more than the sum of its parts.

The remainder of the book maintains this pattern: photograph and text augment one another to produce an experience for the viewer that is neither primarily visual nor primarily literary. Interestingly, an especially evocative image often comes accompanied by rather dry texts. This is particularly true in the case of one spectacular image, a rare photograph of an interior that must have required quite a long exposure. To make *A Rock-Cut Tomb, Famagosta* (Figure 2.13) Thomson positioned himself at the back of the tomb and photographed using only the available light pouring in from the small, debris-choked entrance to the space. A man, possibly one of the porters Thomson employed during his journey, sits in a recess in the tomb wall, visible only by the light raking across his figure. The powerfully atmospheric image evokes a kind of intrusion by the living into a space made for the dead. It offers little in the way of concrete information, however. The text, then, seems to have been designed to make up for this lack: in two brief paragraphs, Thomson speculates on dating, describes the shape and size of the tomb, and comments on its preservation.[50] Throughout the book he is concerned to maximize the total experience of the reader/viewer: if the image informs, the text evokes; if the image evokes, the text informs.

The book also incorporates a number of images of

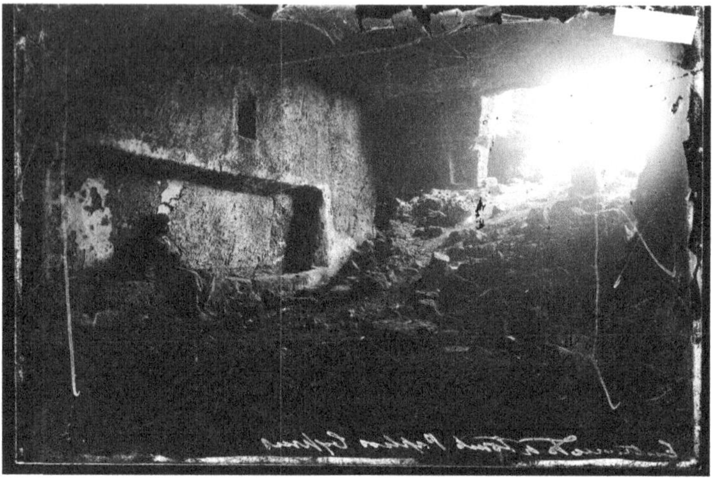

FIG 2.13: John Thomson, "A Rock-Cut Tomb, Famagosta," 1878, from *Through Cyprus with the Camera in the Autumn of 1878* (London: Sampson Low, Marston, Searle and Rivington, 1879). Digital positive from a wet-collodion negative. Courtesy of the Wellcome Library, London, record no. 19027i.

Cypriots, arranged both individually and in groups. Thomson endeavored to make the individual photographs like portraits, though he writes nothing of the subjects' identities or lives. One woman rests her chin on a carefully-placed hand; other subjects were clearly directed to look evocatively downward or off to the side. In the elegant poses and artful arrangements throughout the book one sees clearly the results of Thomson's intervention and careful direction. But if the typological photographs appear sensitive and carefully-made, accompanying texts lack the depth that characterizes his writing on China. Having spent only a few weeks in Cyprus, Thomson had no long acquaintance with the Cypriots and their country to parallel his years-long experience in Asia. His more superficial experience in Cyprus led him to produce texts that are, in the case of these typological images, rather shallow and occasionally judgmental. Female subjects, whether old or young, are accompanied by discourses on the looks of Cypriot women. Male subjects are described as physical specimens and a general impression of their disposition given. The text accompanying one image of a male sitter reads, in its entirety:

> *Another Highlander figures in this plate – a tall, bony man of a most obligingly good-natured*

> *disposition. He, however, looked a bold, determined character, whose massive hands and muscular frame would stand him in good stead in carrying out any resolve for good or evil.*[51]

In the context of Thomson's published *oeuvre* overall, these photo/text combinations are telling. With his early *Antiquities of Cambodia*, he began to develop a formula that his later *Illustrations of China and its People* honed to near-perfection. It incorporates a constant shifting between personal and (ostensibly) objective perspectives in his narratives, combined with a dialogue between text and photograph that is sometimes subtle and sometimes overt. Thomson thus invites the reader, as in *Antiquities of Cambodia*, to see and experience the environment as he did but without suffering the dangers and privations he encountered – an ideal, sanitized form of travel. But his commanding perspective is more convincing in his Asian texts than in the Cyprus travelogue. The Cambodia project and the four-volume China series were products of the ten years he spent in Asia, but creating those books was not his sole purpose and singular goal in traveling there. The Cyprus trip, by contrast, was undertaken for the very purpose of producing the book that documents it. Hence while he follows the formulas he developed in his Asian publications – alternating among landscapes, topographical views, and typological photographs – the result is a book that fits well within the conventions of the travelogue, but rarely transcends such conventions in the same way as his Asian works.

The Cyprus book was Thomson's last major publication. He continued to produce occasional articles and studies for the photographic press, but his energies after 1880 were primarily directed toward sustaining his family and growing his photographic practice. His photographs of China were occasionally republished, notably during a period at the turn of the century when England and China experienced renewed engagement and conflict, and thus his reputation as ethnographer-with-a-camera persisted to the end of his life.[52] But he never made a major journey again, and the later China publications simply repackaged his earlier material.

This overview of Thomson's *oeuvre* offers some insight into his general worldview, including his beliefs regarding the efficacy and purpose of photography and his attitudes toward human beings of different races, cultures, or socio-economic levels. Although Thomson seems to have possessed the same racial and cultural biases as the average Victorian at the outset of his travels in Asia, his attitudes shifted as his stay lengthened. Sustained contact with the Chinese led to increased respect for the culture. Travel beyond colonial centers like Hong Kong and Singapore allowed him to interact with the people of Asia in situations less suffused with colonial conflict and exploitation. As his choice of opening images for *Illustrations of China and its People* demonstrates, he saw the Chinese as a powerful, formidable force, in full command of their own history and future.

His exposure to Cyprus, being more superficial, naturally produced more superficial evaluations of its landscape, its people and its future promise. But he makes clear in his Introduction that he did not conceive of the British as a unilaterally superior master race. Indeed, he evaluated his fellow-countrymen as harshly, if not more so, than the Cypriots he encountered. Overall, Thomson's travelogues show him to have been flexible in his beliefs and comfortable with a fair degree of uncertainty. He could not ultimately escape the colonial paradigm, of course. To some extent he always served as an instrument of expansionist interests, and he operated according to a fundamentally Western mindset. But the presuppositions and prejudices of colonialism colored his experiences less than they did those of other Victorians abroad.

Toward photography, his attitude was equally progressive. Although he became a more skilled photographer over the course of his career, mastering the extreme difficulties of field photography, he regarded the medium from the start as a means of education and enlightenment and also as an art form. Educated in the fundamentals and history of art, he clearly understood the power of a well-constructed composition to persuade viewers and to convey ideology. Over the course of his publishing career, he learned to exploit the power of text-image combinations to produce an even more powerful experience for his audience. Throughout his publications, text amplifies image, image ratifies the authority of text, and careful attention to aesthetic considerations convinces audiences of the beauty, power and grace that inheres even in the unfamiliar and alien. All of this comes in to play in *Street Life in London.*

NOTES

1 Several writers have addressed the details of Thomson's life. Stephen White's 1985 *John Thomson: A Window to the Orient* was the first major monograph on the photographer. Ialeen Gibson-Cowan provided other details in a series of articles from the mid-1980s on *Street Life in London* and Thomson's 1878 publication *Through Cyprus with the Camera*. In 1997, Richard Ovenden provided the most extensive information on Thomson's life in his monograph *John Thomson (1837-1921) Photographer*. All these authors drew on the same relatively small pool of available resources: Thomson's own published writings, some archival materials, and a small amount of correspondence and other records in the possession of Thomson's descendants. Stephen White, *John Thomson: A Window to the Orient* (New York/London: Thames and Hudson, 1985); Ialeen Gibson-Cowan, "Thomson's Street Life in Context," *Creative Camera* 251 (November 1985), 10-15; Ialeen Gibson-Cowan, "John Thomson on Cyprus," *Photographic Collector* 5, no. 3 (1986), 309-19; John Thomson, *Through Cyprus with the Camera in the Autumn of 1878*, 2 vols. (London: Sampson Low, Marston, Searle and Rivington, 1879); Rpt. 1 vol. (London: Trigraph, 1985), with an essay by Ialeen Gibson-Cowan, page numbers throughout refer to the reprint; Richard Ovenden, *John Thomson (1837-1921) Photographer* (Edinburgh: National Library of Scotland/The Stationery Office, 1997).

2 Richard Ovenden, *John Thomson*, 1; Ialeen Gibson Cowan, "A Note on John Thomson," in *Through Cyprus with the Camera*, ix.

3 Richard Ovenden, *John Thomson*, 2-5.

4 Ibid., 6-7.

5 Thomson's wife Isobel writes of William's debts and drinking in her letters to John, written during their two year separation and preserved by his descendants (his replies do not survive). Isobel Thomson, letters to John Thomson, Near Suez, 4 August 1870, discussing William's drinking and spending extravagantly on credit; Port Said, 10 August 1870, discussing William's drinking; Port St. Mary House, 30 April 1871, "So you have at last got your release from William's creditors, which is a good thing."

6 See Richard Ovenden, *John Thomson*, 7-10.

7 John Thomson, *The Antiquities of Cambodia; a series of photographs taken on the spot, with letterpress description* (Edinburgh: Edmonston and Douglas, 1867), 7.

8 Ibid., 7-8; see also Richard Ovenden, *John Thomson*, 10.

9 Thomson cites Mouhot's *Travels in Indo-China, Cambodia and Laos*, among other works. Thomson, *Antiquities of Cambodia*, 7. Henri Mouhot, *Travels in the Central Part of Indo-China (Siam) Cambodia and Laos During the Years 1858, 1859, and 1860*, 2 vols. (London: John Murray, 1864).

10 Richard Ovenden, *John Thomson*, 11.

11 Ibid., 13.

12 Ibid., 11.

13 See Ibid., 12.

14 See Ibid., 13.

15 Ibid., 14-16.

16 Isobel Thomson to John Thomson, 30 June 1870.

17 "It would be a temptation to go into Mongolia. Although I am glad

the temptation of home is greater." Isobel Thomson, letter to John Thomson, Glentraugh [Isle of Man], 10 December 1871.

18 John Thomson, *Foochow and the River Min* (London: Autotype Company, 1873); John Thomson, *Illustrations of China and Its People*, 4 vols. (London: Sampson Low, Marston, Low and Searle, 1873-74).

19 Baron Charles D'Avillier, *Spain*, trans. John Thomson (London: Sampson Low, Marston, Low, and Searle, 1876); Gaston Tissandier, *A History and Handbook of Photography*, trans. and ed. John Thomson from *Les Merveilles de la photographie* (London: Sampson Low, Marston, Low, and Searle, 1876); Gaston Tissandier, *A History and Handbook of Photography*, trans. and ed. John Thomson, 2nd Rev. Ed. (London: Sampson Low, Marston, Low and Searle, 1878).

20 See Ialeen Gibson-Cowan, "A Note on John Thomson," in *Through Cyprus with the Camera in the Autumn of 1878*, viii.

21 Ibid., ix-xvii.

22 Richard Ovenden, *John Thomson*, 39.

23 Ibid., 39-40.

24 Alfred de Rothschild, *A Description of the Works of Art Forming the Collection of Alfred de Rothschild*, 2 vols., compiled and with text by Charles Davis and photographs by John Thomson (London: Chiswick Press, 1884).

25 *Devonshire House Fancy Dress Ball, July 2nd 1897: A Collection of Portraits in Costume of Some of the Guests* (Hammersmith: Privately Printed for the Committee, 1899).

26 An example, a photograph titled "Blackberrying" and depicting children – probably his own – picking berries in a bramble, appeared

in the *British Journal of Photography* in the 1880s. John Thomson, "Blackberrying," *British Journal of Photography*, 13 April 1883, n.p. and 214.

27 For general description of his service for the RGS, see Elliott S. Parker, "John Thomson, 1837-1921, RGS Instructor in Photography," *Geographical Journal* 144, no. 3 (Nov. 1978), 469. For delineation of the methods he taught for photographing human anthropological types, see John Thomson, "Photography and Exploration," *Proceedings of the Royal Geographical Society and Monthly Record of Geography* New Series 13, no. 11 (November 1891), 672.

28 "I look forward to the time when good photographs will be valued as permanent works of reference, and when they will figure in our schools and colleges in place of highly coloured diagrams." Ibid., 674.

29 J.S.K., "Obituary: John Thomson," *Geographical Journal* 58, no. 6 (December 1921), 470.

30 John Thomson, "Practical Photography in Tropical Regions," *British Journal of Photography*, 10 August 1866, 380.

31 Subsequent installments in the series appear in *British Journal of Photography*, 17 August 1866, 393; 24 August 1866, 404; 14 September 1866, 436-37; 5 October 1866, 472-73; 12 October 1866, 487.

32 See Helmut Gernsheim, *Incunabula of British Photographic Literature, 1839-1875* (London and Berkeley: Scolar Press, 1984), 8.

33 John Thomson, *The Antiquities of Cambodia*, 7.

34 Ibid., 9.

35 John Thomson, *Illustrations of China and Its People*, Vol. I (1873), n.p.

36 Thomson, "Prince Kung," *Illustrations of China and Its People*," Vol. I, n.p.

37 See also Stephen White, *John Thomson*, 26.

38 John Thomson, "Hong-Kong," *Illustrations of China and Its People*, Vol. I, n.p.

39 Ibid.

40 Ibid.

41 Thomson originally made this image for a photographic catalogue of the Duke's visit, which was published in Hong Kong shortly after the event. Rev. William Beach, *The Visit of His Royal Highness the Duke of Edinburgh to Hongkong* (Hong Kong: Noronha and Sons, 1869).

42 John Thomson, "A Hong-Kong Sedan Chair," *Illustrations of China and Its People*, Vol. I, n.p.

43 See James J. Barnes and Patience P. Barnes, "Sampson Low: Organizer of the Victorian Book Trade," *Papers of the Bibliographical Society of America* 105 (March 2011), 84. Sampson Low had various partners over the years, so the company name varies: "Sampson Low, Marston, Low and Searle," "Sampson Low, Marston, Searle and Rivington," and so on. I use "Sampson Low and Co." here and elsewhere to refer to the publishing company in a general way.

44 See, for example, an advertisement appearing in the *British Journal Almanac* for 1878, vi, in which the largest text on the page is not the book's title but the words "HENRY FOX TALBOT."

45 Baron Charles D'Avillier, *Spain*.

46 J.J. Grandville, *The Public and Private Life of Animals*, trans. and ed. J. Thomson (London: Sampson Low, Marston, Low, and Searle, 1877).

47 John Thomson, "Introduction," *Through Cyprus with the Camera, in the Autumn of 1878*, n.p.

48 An article from November 1878 summarizes a talk Thomson gave

about his Cyprus travels, in which he was more direct in his criticisms of the English travelers there: "There was but one English hotel in Cyprus, and making his way thither, Mr. Thomson found there a number of disconsolate Englishmen, whose only occupation apparently was asking each other after their health, whether they had had fever, whether they liked the place, how long they were going to stay, when they were going back, why they had come to such a place, and altogether the reception was rather dispiriting." "Mr. John Thomson, F.R.G.S.," *Photographic Journal*, 20 Nov. 1878, 20-21.

49 John Thomson, "The Sea Shore, Larnaca," *Through Cyprus with the Camera*, n.p. [image 3].

50 John Thomson, "A Rock-Cut Tomb, Famagosta," *Through Cyprus with the Camera*, n.p. [image 54].

51 Thomson, "Mountaineers," *Through Cyprus with the Camera*, n.p. [image 40].

52 John Thomson, *Through China with a Camera* (Westminster: A. Constable and Co., 1898; 2nd ed. New York / London: Harper and Co., 1899; repr. San Francisco: Chinese Materials Center, 1974).

CHAPTER THREE

ADOLPHE SMITH: LIFE AND WRITINGS

OF THE 36 TEXTS in *Street Life in London*, Adolphe Smith wrote 24, or two-thirds. Of the remaining twelve, he probably assisted in writing at least two. Smith wove much of the rhetorical net around John Thomson's photographs, and if one hopes to understand what the book attempted to accomplish, one must contend with Smith's contributions, his experiences, and his possible motivations.

Establishing the facts of Smith's life requires excavation. Prior scholarship offers little assistance here. Prolific writer, crusader for wide-ranging reforms, supporter of women's rights, and dedicated socialist, Smith has become in scholarship on *Street Life in London* little more than Thomson's sidekick. Occasionally, he does receive brief attention in other contexts, unrelated to *Street Life in London*. In 1905, for instance, he wrote a series of revealing articles on the Chicago meat-packing industry that became a key resource for Upton Sinclair's famous novel about the industry, *The Jungle*, so he shows up on occasion in discussions of that book and its impact. He also appears as a minor, ignominious character in some histories of Socialism because early in his career he made an enemy of the influential German socialist Friedrich Engels.

Apart from these brief and scattered appearances,

however, Smith is essentially invisible in secondary scholarship on any of the topics that consumed him during his life. He left no archive and, as some of his friends noted during his life, he tended toward self-effacement to the extent that he effaced himself from history. But he wrote thousands of pages during his long career as a journalist and author. His articles and books collectively constitute the single best resource for detail about his life, not only giving hard facts about his travels, his affiliations, and his experiences but also occasionally serving as eloquent statements of the philosophies and beliefs that motivated him. He wrote many of these anonymously or pseudonymously, but it is nonetheless possible to reconstruct at least a partial map of Smith's activities and experiences over the course of his life.

Of course, as a professional writer, Smith's primary motivation was not to tell his own story. Like many journalists, he worked for a variety of outlets including popular newspapers, medical and scientific journals, and pro-labor magazines catering to audiences of working men and union sympathizers. Nonetheless, when he reported on the world as he perceived it, he could not help but report on himself. Using his writings and some other documentation, this chapter constitutes the first sustained examination of Smith's life and beliefs.

In his many writings he comes across as a singular figure, seemingly interested in everything and genuinely expert on a variety of topics. He wrote about food. He wrote about travel. He wrote about hygiene, labor unionism, public works projects. He designed and executed public works projects. He testified before the House of Lords. He traveled extensively and indefatigably for nearly his entire life, attending conferences and congresses. He gave talks on subjects from women's suffrage and universal peace to battlefield medicine. He spoke and wrote fluently in both English and French. He translated professionally at conferences, a job that required him not only to deliver others' talks from time to time, but to perform real-time translation during public lectures and to serve as a kind of mediator between sometimes-hostile parties who could not understand one another without him.

He loved France, for some time his adopted home, but he seems to have thought of himself as thoroughly English, openly impatient with time-wasting continentals and fond of the British love for order and rules. If he was kind and compassionate – he made a life, after all, out of improving the lives of his fellow-humans – he also comes across in his writings as officious, perhaps a little too fond of the pomp and circumstance of congresses and conferences. One wonders how he not only survived but thrived in such a career, attending meetings his whole life! And yet one must admire how he managed, throughout this endless palavering in venues large and small, international and local, to retain his sense that such discussions *mattered*, that by reporting on and contributing to them he could help the world move forward and become more egalitarian.

Street Life in London appeared near the beginning of Smith's long career as journalist and activist. One might imagine that everything after 1878 would thus be irrelevant to the task of understanding Smith's motivations before and during the publication's production. But Smith's politics and sympathies remained remarkably consistent over the course of his life: he believed in socialism, in the value of labor unions, in the widespread need for improvements in public health policy and administration, and in the betterment of living and working conditions for laboring people worldwide. The same sympathies that motivated his texts for *Street Life in London* also compelled his work thereafter, virtually until the end of his life. Examinations of his writings and activities both before and after 1877 are thus quite valuable to understanding how and why *Street Life in London* came to exist.

Smith's life

Adolphe Smith was born in December 1846 in Headingley, Yorkshire, to Mary White Smith and her husband George Smith.[1] Assertions in some of Smith's obituaries that he had French parentage seem to have been incorrect: both of his parents, George and Mary, were from Yorkshire.[2] He had five siblings and perhaps more, at least one of whom – George, the eldest, born in 1832 – survived into adulthood. Smith's father began his marriage as a banker's clerk, but by the time of Adolphe's birth he had moved into the more exalted position of banker himself.

Little of Smith's early life or education is known. The family is absent from the 1851 census, but by 1861 Adolphe, then 14 years old, was living in Leicestershire and receiving education at a parsonage and school run by one of his relatives, Samuel Smith.[3] Thereafter Smith disappears again from the English censuses, reappearing only in 1891. It seems likely that for part of his childhood and young adulthood, he and his family lived out of the country, probably in France, though he and perhaps other family members received some education in England. This would explain how, by his adulthood, Smith had become so comfortable speaking French as to make a living at it. It would also help to explain his involvement in the defining events of his life, the Franco-Prussian War and the subsequent Paris Commune.

The Franco-Prussian War lasted less than a year, from mid-1870 to early 1871, but it proved tremendously destructive both to France's landscape and to its national psyche. It resulted from longstanding hostility between Prussia and France. Prussia might have said it was retaliating against the militarism of France's ruler, Napoleon III. France in turn feared the new-found power of the Prussian state, which had recently subjugated Austria. Napoleon III declared war on Prussia, which in turn invaded France, entering along the mountainous northeast border and progressing toward the capital. In September 1870, Napoleon III was captured after the Battle of Sedan, and a new and rather weak government came into power in France. Almost immediately, Paris itself came under siege, a condition that lasted four difficult months. In January 1871, France capitulated, agreeing among other things to cede the territories of Alsace and Lorraine to Prussia.

But many in Paris itself had no desire to surrender. During the Siege, Parisians had defended the city as members of a militia called the National Guard. When Prussian troops entered Paris to march through after the surrender, the act fomented resentment in the city. French president Adolphe Thiers, fearing the resentment could lead to violence, ordered the Guard to relinquish their weapons. When they refused, he sent French troops to confiscate the cannons. But many among the troops refused to take action against their fellow-countrymen, instead joining the rebellion they had been sent to defeat. President Thiers and his government fled Paris for Versailles, and beginning in late March 1871, the city governed itself. Almost immediately it found itself besieged again, this time not by Prussia but by the French national authority; and for the next two months the city had constantly to defend itself.

The period of the city's self-rule proved revelatory for many who believed that laborers, the poor and the disenfranchised deserved to be better served and better represented, both in France and beyond. During this period a group of elected citizens called the Commune governed the city. Some of the Council members were intellectuals; others, artisans and laborers. They put into place a series of progressive reforms that included separation of church and state and women's suffrage. Factories that had shut down when their managers and owners fled during the Commune were reopened as cooperative societies, owned by the people who worked in them. Imperial symbols were destroyed: the Chapel of Atonement, built after and as penitence for the execution of Louis XVI, was demolished; and Napoleon's Vendome Column was pulled down to much fanfare. Indeed, the very success of some of the Commune's efforts, combined with its open disdain for the trappings of power, made it terrifying to the legitimate French government, whose efforts to rout it were brutal. In late May 1871 Paris was forcibly reintegrated into the body of France. Thousands of Communards were executed in retaliation by the French government. Many more fled, were exiled, or were transported to French penal colonies.[4]

Although the details remain sketchy, it is clear that Adolphe Smith served during the Franco-Prussian War as a member of a French ambulance corps. He participated in a number of battles in and around Paris, staying in the city throughout the four-month siege. Near the end of the war he was among 90,000 men who attempted to push the Prussians back during a battle in Buzenval Park, outside the Paris city walls. The effort was unsuccessful, and the French, Smith among them, retreated. During the retreat he exhibited considerable bravery, stopping while under fire to assist an Englishman named William MacCormac (later to be knighted Sir William) who ran a non-partisan international medical operation called the Anglo-American Ambulances.[5]

After the war's end, Smith remained in Paris for the duration of the Commune. Again, his precise role is unclear. There is no question that he sympathized with the goals of the Commune and disliked the actions and governance of Thiers. But he insisted later in life that as a medic he had remained neutral throughout the event. He also made clear his distaste for the mob rule he had witnessed during the Commune. At a lecture given much later in his life he related some of his experiences during the Siege and Commune to illustrate his positions:

> *The day before the Germans entered the city I was standing in the street when I heard a noise different from ordinary noises because it was accompanied by a sort of rumbling... Then came the mob. Its nucleus was made up of women dragging the cannon of the National Guard.*[6]

Nonetheless, he went on to say, he found the French troops even more violent and threatening than the mobs of the Commune. At one point the troops fired on him while he was attempting to locate a wounded man, even though he was carrying a huge Geneva

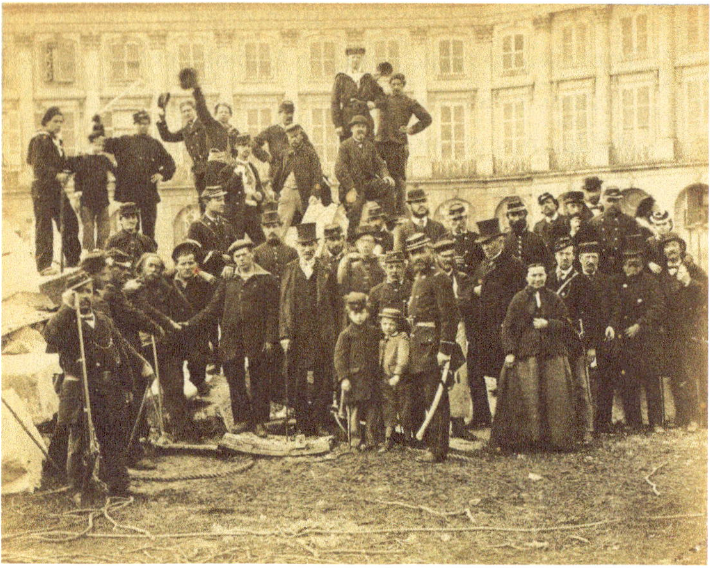

FIG 3.1: Auguste Bruno Braquehais, *Place Vendôme*, 1871, albumen print. Courtesy of the French Museum of Photography/General Council of Essonne, reference number 2003.5.9, photographed by Benoit Chain.

cross. At another point he was captured with two other Englishmen, summarily tried, and sentenced to death. The men were released only when one of them, speaking no French and having no idea what was happening, asked to go home so he could get his priestly collar.[7]

Smith claimed that in addition to this arrest, which resulted in a death sentence but not in death itself, he was detained on three other occasions.[8] He seems always to have been in the wrong place – i.e. with the Communards – at the wrong time. He certainly witnessed, and approved of, the toppling of the Vendôme Column.[9] Although later in life he proclaimed his neutrality, events such as this undoubtedly shaped Smith's attitude toward labor and laborers thereafter. During the Commune he witnessed workers freed from the boundaries placed around them by their professions, liberated to become more than cogs in the industrial machinery. Art historian Albert Boime has found in photographs of the Communards by Auguste Bruno Braquehais (Figure 3.1) a similar freedom, which he calls "social potential." Boime has noted that most of the time:

> *photographers posed laborers in their specific workaday activities and particular costume*

establishing an updated version of the picturesque social types so familiar in popular imagery. Braquehais, however, shows them emancipated from their assigned niche in the social hierarchy and proudly manifesting their amplified potential in the more egalitarian space established under the Commune.[10]

Smith felt this amplification of potential keenly; he witnessed the liberation of the French laborer not only from political subjugation but from the subjugation of social expectation. At least part of his motivation in undertaking *Street Life in London* just a few years later was to release English laborers in similar fashion from the bounds of niche, to depict them not as functionaries but as Citizens.

At the end of the Commune, Smith, like many others, fled France for England. He became a member of the expatriate socialist community in London. During this early period of his life in England, he considered himself not a man returning home but a political refugee, living among other refugees. In an article written many years later he painted an affectionate portrait of the refugees' London, radical London, detailing the houses and establishments where expatriates ate, drank, met and debated during these years just after the suppression of the Commune. His nostalgic tone revealed that he knew these places well, and as more than just a hanger-on.[11]

In the early 1870s he also gave a lecture series on the Commune and its aftermath; and starting in 1873 he published a series of articles in the London *Examiner* discussing the Commune and looking at workmen's movements in France and other European nations. He seems to have been regarded, justifiably, as an authority on such issues, a prominence permitted him in part by his command of English. Other socialists were not thrilled, however, with his pretension to speak for them all. There had never been consensus among Communards, just as there was never consensus within the socialist community. Indeed, the Commune – and Socialism in general – accommodated a wide array of beliefs, from moderate patriotic republicanism to extreme anarchism; from the desire for fair wages and just treatment of workers, to the total abolition of rents and private property. As one English observer wrote, "Some of the Communals were Communists; some were not."[12] Smith, at the end of the day, was not; and other members of the London Socialist community resented him speaking about, and for, the International Socialist movement as a whole.[13]

Such disagreements and differences of opinion tell us a great deal about the nuances of Smith's particular brand of Socialism. Understanding of such nuances is, in turn, integral to comprehending Smith's contributions to *Street Life in London*, because in so many of his essays he advocates for a specific kind of empowerment for laborers. In brief, while Smith was certainly radical by comparison with the average Victorian, he was not a particularly radical radical. He was not a Communist. And although he was a member of the International Working Men's Association, led by Karl Marx and Frederich Engels and commonly called the "First International," Smith crucially opposed one of its central doctrines, the notion that there could be a truly international laborers' movement with a centralized administration that managed conditions for workers in many nations.[14] Instead, he wrote approvingly in his series for the *Examiner* of the spread of socialism by so-called Federalist means, in which laborers organized and agitated in the ways best suited to conditions in their own home countries, administering their national movements internally rather than answering to an international body.[15]

Perhaps most important, Smith believed that the most effective workers' movements, those that would eventually lead to real social improvement, operated not through revolution but by legal means wherever possible.[16] Reform through, and compelled by, scientific principles appealed to Smith, particularly if it could be accomplished legally. He hated anarchy and reform through violence, in part because he abhorred violence in any form and in part because such measures rarely achieved any lasting change. He lamented that many European governments, unable or unwilling to tell the difference between agitation for necessary social reform and outright revolution, repressed all of it without distinction. Speaking in particular of the French Third Republic, he wrote, "[A] heavy responsibility rests on those who have not been able to distinguish between scientific genuine social reform, and the noisy clamour of ignorant rebellion."[17]

In the period after the Commune, and in part because of disagreements over just such fundamental questions, the idea of a workers' movement on a truly international scale began to fracture and the First International itself to disintegrate. Smith's calls for the restructuring of the International, and his willingness to declare his views openly, earned him the disdain of Marx and the outright hatred of Engels. The latter became essentially a lifelong foe, his anger at Smith over genuine differences of opinion about Socialist doctrine aggravated by a series of misunderstandings.

As a result of this animosity, Smith tends to appear, if at all, only as a kind of petty villain in histories of Socialism in England. Despite his sustained participation and keen interest in Socialist initiatives for the remainder of his life, he has become quite obscure. One of his friends, the socialist Ernest Belfort Bax, blamed this fate in part on Engels, and in part on Smith's own failure to seek recognition for himself:

> *Adolphe Smith… is one whose record for unostentatious and ungrudging work for the Socialist movement has been exceeded by few. Other men have got at least a certain amount of kudos and public recognition for their work. Adolphe Smith's work has been mostly of a kind unrecognized by the general public.*[18]

Smith was at least as prominent a member of the international socialist community as Bax himself and as another friend, H M Hyndman; but his failure to write a memoir, as those two men did, consigned him to a largely unsung, secondary status in English socialism. His archives also failed to find a repository at the end of his life – more the pity since he had amassed a huge and well-regarded collection of objects and documents related to the Paris Commune, the location of which is now unknown.[19]

Smith spent the years between 1871 when he arrived in London, and 1877 when *Street Life in London* began to appear, establishing himself both professionally and personally in his home country. He contributed to a number of progressive efforts, including advancement of women's suffrage.[20] His lectures and articles on the Commune fostered his reputation as an authority on international socialist matters. But he also took wider advantage of his experience as a traveler and his comprehension of politics outside England, corresponding with a variety of other papers and magazines on such subjects as the weakness of the Spanish monarchy and an industrial crisis and famine among workers in Belgium.[21] Among other journals, he wrote for *The Dark Blue*, a short-lived literary and political journal in whose pages the Pre-Raphaelite painters and poets had also appeared.[22]

In his reports on the travails of workers in France, he sometimes referred to writings by Blanchard Jerrold on the same subject.[23] He had particular reason to be acquainted with Jerrold's writings: not only were Jerrold's sympathies on such subjects similar to Smith's, but Jerrold, a progressive London journalist and newspaper publisher, was also Smith's father-in-law. In July of 1872, Smith married Alice Jerrold, Blanchard's daughter.[24] As such, he became part of a venerable journalistic dynasty. In the early nineteenth century, Alice's grandfather Douglas Jerrold had been a pioneer in the publishing of popular media. Perhaps his most enduring and influential creation was the satirical magazine *Punch*, for which he wrote continually until his death in 1857.[25] After Douglas's death, Blanchard Jerrold took over one of his father's endeavors, the editorship of *Lloyd's Weekly Newspaper*, a popular illustrated magazine with a Liberal, if not radical, stance.[26]

It would be difficult to overstate the importance of this family connection to Smith. His grandfather-in-law, Douglas Jerrold, had been an outspoken English republican, and his writing frequently gave voice – albeit often in fictional form – to the concerns of the London underclasses.[27] In his father-in-law Blanchard Jerrold, Smith encountered a fellow-journalist with a similar devotion to French politics and culture, and a commitment to liberal politics. To be sure, Blanchard was less radical than Smith: one of his best-known works is a vast, four-volume biography of – and apologesis for – Napoleon III.[28] But his social explorations, in particular his 1872 book *London: A Pilgrimage*, illustrated by French printmaker Gustave Doré, foreshadow the appearance of *Street Life in London* in 1877.[29] In fact, through Blanchard Jerrold Smith found direct connection with the prototypical social investigator, Henry Mayhew, since Jerrold and Mayhew were brothers-in-law.[30] Already a journalist and a radical, Adolphe Smith thus found his proclivity toward persuasive, activist reportage fostered and encouraged by his new family connections.

His wife, Alice, also wrote professionally. Using a variety of names (Alice Jerrold Smith, Alice Lillie Smith, even Alice Adolphe Smith) and a pseudonym (Corisande), Alice Smith produced fiction and nonfiction quite prolifically. Perhaps her best-known work is a children's book titled *A Cruise in the Acorn*, with illustrations by the famed Victorian sentimentalist Kate Greenaway.[31] She also wrote the novels *A Woman of Mind* and *Love Without Wings*; short stories; and, as Corisande, literary criticism.[32] Given this productivity on the parts of both husband and wife, the Smith household must have been alternately bustling with literary and journalistic visitors, and hushed with dual writerly absorption.

Perhaps husband and wife both worked not only

out of proclivity but out of financial need. Smith had not returned to England from France with any capital to speak of, and thereafter had only a year to establish himself prior to his marriage. Much like John Thomson, Smith found his early years after his return to England occupied by efforts to establish himself and to attain some financial stability for himself, his wife, and – after 1874 – their daughter, Rose.[33]

Street Life in London thus appears to have been for Smith, as for Thomson, not only an expression of social commitment but also a potential source of income. Given the major investment of time and energy both men put into the project, they surely desired something beyond charitable satisfaction from their efforts. Smith began work on the book sometime in 1876, if not earlier. He took primary responsibility for locating the subjects of the book and arranging appointments with them, calling upon social and professional contacts for this task. He knew at least one person in the advertising field, for instance, a useful connection since advertising provided both casual and permanent work for significant numbers of men. He also called upon employees of the city and private charitable missions. Through them, he made connections with the figures that populate the pages of *Street Life in London*. Having connected with these figures, he then had to earn their trust, arrange appointments for photographs and interviews – often returning more than once – and finally produce authoritative essays about the subjects and their professions. Given that for much of 1877 Smith and Thomson were continually interviewing and photographing new subjects, while at the same time meeting monthly deadlines for each new issue of the serial, *Street Life in London* must have kept them very busy indeed.

Street Life brought Smith more attention than he had previously received for any endeavor. In particular, publication of *Street Life in London* earned him his first appearance in the pages of *The Lancet*, in the form of a notice of its publication.[34] Shortly thereafter, he went to work for this venerable medical journal as a "special commissioner" on questions of sanitation, public health, disease control, and other topics.[35] Because most of his articles are not signed – a measure necessary to protect him and other such special commissioners from retaliation by unhappy subjects of scrutiny – it is hard to say with certainty when his tenure began or precisely how many articles he contributed, but the latter number is definitely in the hundreds and more likely in the thousands.[36] In the pages of *The Lancet* Smith undertook his most substantive and sustained journalistic investigations into a variety of issues including medical unionism and early health insurance; the unregulated and often exploitative "sweating" system of labor that dominated in tailoring and other trades; contagion and disease control in slums; and a wide variety of other topics.

The Lancet was never Smith's only employer, though. He continued to correspond with a variety of other news and information outlets throughout his career and to write independently. Shortly after publication of *Street Life in London* he began work on another major project, a biography of Charles Bradlaugh that was published during the second half of 1880.[37] Bradlaugh was an idiosyncratic radical and a deeply divisive figure at the time. He was a confirmed atheist and president of the London Secular Society, an outspoken proponent of birth control, and a supporter of women's suffrage and trade unionism; but while he sympathized with many of the social goals of socialism, he opposed its economic goals.[38] The biography is fairly straightforward, progressing through the major events of Bradlaugh's life in a linear fashion. Because the text incorporates little or no analysis, it seems likely that Smith reported on the events of his subject's life as they were narrated to him, making the book essentially an autobiography in third-person.

One aspect of the Bradlaugh biography, however, does merit sustained attention here. For its publication, Smith adopted a pseudonym: Adolphe S Headingley. Headingley is, in fact, an area in his home town of Leeds. The adoption of the name speaks to Smith's desire, this early in his career, to separate his more radical publications from those on less-controversial subjects, including his endeavors for *The Lancet*. Given that Bradlaugh was a kind of lightning rod due to his outspoken atheism, Smith's adoption of a pseudonym seems necessary to the survival of his other journalistic endeavors. Smith continued to use this pseudonym (or its variation, A S Headingley), throughout his career. Later on, however, he ceased to draw a sharp distinction between his socialistic publications and his scientific ones, and the pseudonym became a more casual appellation. Some of his articles for socialist journals in later years are signed "A S Headingley," some "Adolphe Smith." His socialist colleagues knew him interchangeably as "Smith" and "Smith Headingley." After his career as scientific journalist was well-established, then, his radical views ceased to threaten his livelihood; but at this early date, and with such a controversial subject, he trod carefully.[39]

While the Bradlaugh biography was still in production, Smith traveled with his family to France. They spent the winter of 1879-80 and perhaps longer living in the French Riviera town of Hyères, where his wife had been sent to convalesce from an illness.[40] While there he conducted research for a book, *The Garden of Hyères: A Description of the Most Southern Point of the French Riviera.* Appearing in late 1880 or early 1881, it received enough positive attention and sold well enough to merit English reprints in 1881 and a translation into French in 1882. Its cover and title page present Smith as "Author of 'Street Life in London' &c," but this was the last time that Smith would use *Street Life* in this manner. The substance of *The Garden of Hyères* represented his interests far better, auguring his subsequent career as an expert in sanitation and health-related matters. Indeed, while an abridged version of *Street Life*, titled *Street Incidents*, also appeared in 1881, it seems to have had little or no impact on Smith's life and career, through which it passed unmentioned.[41] *The Garden of Hyères*, by contrast, established Smith as a powerful writer both of travelogues and health reportage.

Thereafter, Smith and family remained in France at least until 1882, a year that proved eventful for Smith in ways both good and bad. If the town of

Hyères had brought him success, it also became the site of tragedy: his wife, Alice, died there in March. Her death, though given as "sudden," was not entirely a surprise, as she had been in delicate health.[42] Indeed, the Smiths had been living in Hyères largely because it was a health resort with an ideal climate, knowledgeable doctors, and a significant English clientele.

Lack of correspondence makes it impossible to say how Smith felt about her passing. But the fevered activity in which he engaged for the remainder of that year, and for the remainder of his life, speaks volumes. The decade of their marriage was his only truly settled period, a time during which he remained for a fairly long stretch in London. The year of her death marks the beginning of near-constant activity, of engagements in travel and demonstration and translation and writerly production on an extraordinary scale that would last nearly the rest of his life.

Among other activities, Smith and a French socialist and friend, Dr. Paul Brousse, organized a series of workers' agitations and demonstrations in Paris in 1882. Brousse had been an anarchist in earlier years, but in the early 1880s he became less radical and began to favor policies of gradualism. He was a founder of the Federation of Socialist Workers of France (FTSF, in French), also known as the "possibilists" because they favored working for reform within, rather than against, the existing bourgeois state.[43] Smith, possessed of similar ideas, acted for many years as a kind of go-between for the "possibilists" and the English labor movement. He translated the texts of the FTSF and other moderate French socialists into English, delivered talks on their ideas, and promoted the spread of similar ideas in the English labor movement.[44]

The workers' demonstrations Smith organized with Brousse took advantage of widespread dissatisfaction over the suspension of plans to build a tunnel connecting France to England below the English Channel. "Under the pretext of supporting the Channel tunnel scheme," Smith later wrote, "we held magnificent Anglo-French labour demonstrations in Paris," part of a larger attempt to resuscitate the Workers' International after its demise ten years before.[45] The attempt succeeded – although later Internationals never had the impact of the First – and beginning in 1882 Smith also acted as official French-English translator at the conferences of the Second International, a position he occupied well into the twentieth century. This in turn launched a secondary career as official translator at many other congresses and conferences.[46]

By 1883, Smith had returned to England. He would continue to travel widely and constantly for the remainder of his life, but hereafter he would do so from his native country. He elected to formalize his interest in health and medical issues, matriculating as a student of Chemistry at Charing Cross Hospital and becoming a Fellow of the Chemical Society, a distinction which permitted him to sign himself "FCS" although he rarely did so.[47] The year 1883 also saw publication of a pamphlet in which Smith maintained his interest in and explication of public sanitation technologies, *Pneumatic Drainage: A Description of the "Berlier System."*[48] In addition, a second edition of the Bradlaugh biography appeared.[49]

Throughout, and long afterward, Smith also worked steadily for *The Lancet*. It is worth pausing to examine his work for the journal in some detail here. By 1878 he had begun his endeavors as a *Lancet* "Special Commissioner," investigating the form of subcontract labor known as "sweating," among other things. Sweating was most common in the tailoring trades but also appeared in other professions. Official regulations for governance of laboring conditions in these trades did exist, but they were difficult to enforce because many workers labored not in factories but at home, receiving their pay per piece rather than per hour. Without oversight, abuse of workers and employment of children ran rampant, and laboring conditions were frequently atrocious. In such conditions disease spread easily among the workers and could be carried, via the clothing being tailored and laundered, into the community at large. In one of Smith's first articles, he drew public attention to the contamination of Army uniforms with diseases including smallpox and scarlet fever.[50] He would continue examining this subject for years, gathering information and statistics that permitted him to compare conditions in a wide variety of trades and environments.

By the late 1880s the House of Lords had taken up the "sweating" system of labor as an object of inquiry, their investigation driven in part by Smith's scathing exposes in *The Lancet*. In March of 1889 Smith testified before the Select Committee formed to investigate the system. His testimony, like his writing, reveals him to have been a deft but judicious user of facts and statistics – deploying them when necessary and useful, avoiding their use if he did not understand them fully. "Figures are very treacherous," he observed at one point, "and I do not like to give [them] without having specially studied the subject."[51] His statements before the committee centered on the terrible conditions and extraordinarily high child mortality rates among workers in a village district, Cradley, associated with the nail-making trade. Throughout, he demonstrated his thorough research methods, his genuine depth of knowledge, and his devotion to investigation even at cost to himself. He understood Cradley's water system and its sewage disposal methods (such as they were); he had been inside its poorly-ventilated subterranean workshops; he had visited its overcrowded and disease-filled houses; he had seen typhoid fever sufferers with his own eyes.[52]

Smith's careful restraint in the face of such injustices speaks volumes, making his testimony on sensational or horrifying subjects that much easier to believe. In all his investigations, this quality comes through. For instance, if he wrote, as he did when visiting Chicago's meat-packing district in the early twentieth century, that he witnessed pigs slaughtered cruelly and haphazardly, that their blood caked the walls of rooms "to the height of five feet" and that they were plunged into scalding water to have their bristles removed while they were still alive, he doubtless actually saw this.[53] If he encountered conditions he deemed a bright spot or a positive development, such as the large and well-ventilated houses for Chicago meat-packing workers, he made a point of mentioning this as well.[54] Indeed, in his lengthy investigation of the Chicago slaughterhouse system, conducted in late 1904 and published as a series in *The Lancet* in January 1905, he continually evinced just such attitudes: disgusted at the ill treatment of men and animals or conditions rife for the spread of disease; impressed and pleased with properly sterile, sanitary, scientific, and/or humane developments.[55] He would report outrages if he saw them, but not if he didn't. He was a muckraker, but not a liar.

His reports on the conditions of the Chicago slaughterhouses contrast with the infamous novel partially inspired by them, Upton Sinclair's *The Jungle*. Smith acted as Sinclair's guide on one occasion, accompanying him through the slaughterhouses, but where Smith was dispassionate, Sinclair sensationalized, exaggerating the poor conditions in the slaughterhouses to the extent that even other reformers denied the novel's accuracy. Nonetheless, Smith inspired Sinclair, who in turn inspired a massive public outcry over sanitary and labor conditions in the American meat-packing industry – a development leading directly to the establishment of the Food and Drug Administration in 1907.[56]

Smith's other major investigations for *The Lancet* included an extended tour of the European continent from 1892-94 when he followed and reported on the progress of a cholera epidemic, advancing epidemiologists' understanding of how the disease spread; and a years-long series called "The Battle of the Clubs," which dealt with the strengths and weaknesses of early medical cooperative societies in England and on the continent.[57] In these cases and others, his investigations performed a genuine public service, spurring legal reforms or scientific developments and leading to real change.[58] All in all, Smith's work for *The Lancet* proved by far the most substantive of his career. Through it, he exerted real influence on the systems he hoped to improve with his careful investigations and his dramatic-yet-reliable revelations.

At the same time, he undertook work for *The Lancet* and for many other outlets that was perhaps more pedestrian but no less demanding of his time and energies. He traveled continually, visiting and reporting on hundreds of international congresses and conferences on a wide variety of subjects. Many of these coincided with world's fairs, on which he also reported: the Paris *Exposition Universelle* of 1889; the 1904 World's Fair in St. Louis, and others.[59] Over the years he attended – to name just a few – various annual meetings of the International Congress of Hygiene; the International Congress on the

Intervention of the State in Labour Contracts; the International Congress on Free Education (of which he was elected President in 1889); the International Congress on Climatology and Hydrology; the International Congress of Hygiene and Demography; the Federation of the Medical Unions of France; the Congress of Deontology (i.e. medical ethics); and various congresses for members of the medical press.[60] Indeed, on his death in 1925, one newspaper notice cited him as expert not in public health or sanitation, but in "international societies"![61]

Smith also continued to observe and participate in socialist endeavors both in England and abroad. He maintained a moderate, anti-revolutionary position, but even as he repudiated political upheaval, he actively campaigned for dramatic overhaul of public health laws. For Smith, socialism and public health reform went hand in hand: such reform, in his view, *required* the increased participation of the state in matters of personal and collective health and well-being.[62]

His membership in the Fabian Society exemplifies his center-left, bourgeois brand of socialism. Founded in the mid-1880s, the Society advocated advancement and social equalization on a gradualist, rather than a radical, basis. Fabians welcomed members from the intellectual and socially-successful classes as well as from among the downtrodden, believing that "not only those who suffer from the present system, but also many who personally benefit by it, recognise its evils and will welcome a remedy."[63] Attending early Fabian society meetings, Smith encountered a variety of other intellectual lights in late-Victorian society, including Annie Besant and George Bernard Shaw.

He also worked as an official translator for the International Trades Union Congress (ITUC), among other international bodies. The pamphlets he published in 1886 and 1888, summarizing the proceedings of the Congress in those years, function as cogent statements of Smith's own personal positions.[64] Ostensibly explaining to his English audience the goals of the French trade unions and the relationship of unionism to socialism in France, the pamphlets actually promote the moderate, "possibilist" school of French socialist thought over other, more radically Marxist veins. The later pamphlet, in particular, explicitly lauds the 1888 ITUC for "endors[ing], not the Socialism of the barricade, but the Socialism of the ballot box."[65]

But though his brand of socialism was moderate, his defense of his beliefs and his dislike for more radical socialism proved immoderate. The enemies he had gained in the early years after the Commune, among them Friedrich Engels, Karl Marx, and Marx's children, remained enemies for life. One poignant story illustrates this enmity. H M Hyndman, another English socialist, relates in his biography that a group of Danish Social Democrats persuaded Smith to accompany them on a visit to Engels. Smith agreed to go, though he doubted Engels would be pleased to see him. "They were all received very well at first," Hyndman writes, "Smith passing in unnoticed among the rest." But Engels soon recognized him. "He jumped up, rushed up to Smith saying, 'What, are you Smith, Smith-Headingley? You are! Then get out of my house. I am amazed you should have had the impudence to come here.'"[66] Engels's hatred of Smith, born of the two men's disagreements in the wake of the Commune and the dissolution of the First International, continued unabated until the end of the elder man's life.

Outside of Smith's public engagements with socialism and science, details of his life remain hazy. Official records give glimpses here and there of his personal and family arrangements. From the early 1880s, he maintained a home base in England. Census records indicate that after the death of his wife Alice he lived with his unmarried daughter, Rose Hester, until he died in 1925.

Somewhat more perplexing is his relationship with a second Rose, a woman named Rose E S Wenham. By 1891 he and Rose E S had married, and she is listed as his wife, Rose E S Smith, in the census for that year. Indeed, her entire family, including both of her parents and two sisters, lived in the household as well.[67] A lifelong atheist, Smith apparently found himself prevailed upon by his new wife to have his daughter baptized, at the very least; and so Rose Hester was baptized (as Rose Esther) in 1892, at age 17.[68] By 1901, however, Rose E S Wenham was no longer living with Smith as his wife, although she and her family remained in his household. Oddly, census records give her as Smith's "boarder," and indicate that she had returned to use of her maiden name. Rose Wenham remained by his side until the end of his life, nursing him during his final illness, but – in public, at least – he referred to her not as his wife but as "Mrs. Wenham."[69] Even more oddly, travel records from after the time of Smith's second marriage list him as a "widower," though his second wife (if Rose E S remained that) was still very much alive.[70]

In 1911, he traveled to Monaco to visit a model hospital that had been opened ten years before, meeting with Prince Albert to discuss the new facility.[71] The following year, he published a book on the principality, *Monaco and Monte Carlo*.[72] A history and travelogue of the country of Monaco and its capital city, the book was written for a broad audience and concentrated only a single chapter on medicine. It was quite lavishly illustrated, incorporating both photographic illustrations and color plates by the artist Charles Maresco Pearce. Easily Smith's most popular book, it received a fair amount of attention in England and abroad, with largely favorable reviews.[73]

The later years of Smith's life brought increased attention to the wartime events of his youth. In part this was due to French governmental initiatives aimed at commemorating the Franco-Prussian War. Beginning in 1911, 40 years after the war, the French government began issuing commemorative medals to individuals who had served during the war, whether in combat, medical or service capacities. Smith received his medal in 1913.[74] As the decade progressed, his experiences became all the more relevant, given the imminence of a new conflict. Before and during the First World War, Smith drew on his experience as a wartime medic and his expertise in sanitation and public health in a series of speaking engagements. In March of 1915, for instance, he gave a lantern-slide lecture on "The War and the Wounded, 1870-71,

1914-15" to an audience of health professionals and concerned volunteers.[75] During the lecture he focused in particular on those fatalities during the Siege of Paris that had resulted from lack of food, urging British authorities to think of such circumstances when planning for the possibility of a siege of London. His lantern slides illustrated the advances in battlefield medicine, but he stressed that cholera and typhoid were still widely present among the various European armies and called for attention to sanitation both on and beyond the battlefield.[76]

Later in 1915, Smith and a British MP named John Hodge embarked together on a tour of French cities, lecturing on the British Socialist movement. The tour, sponsored by the British Socialists, was intended to explain to French working people the dominant trends in British Socialism and to demonstrate British socialists' fraternity and solidarity with their French counterparts. Conducted during WWI, it seems also to have been designed to show broader British support for French interests in the war – a position clearly of interest to the French government, as Smith and Hodge met with French president Raymond Poincaré himself while planning the tour.[77]

Smith and Hodge hoped to dispel widespread impressions that British socialists were anti-war or that they supported pacifist efforts. The advent of the war had caused a kind of collective anxiety among socialists, not least due to a widespread fear that the dominance of Germany on the European continent could include its dominance of international socialist dialogues – or, conversely, that its dominance of socialism could lead to its dominance of Europe in general. Indeed, although several years before Smith had participated in at least one international pacifist congress, by the advent of WWI he and others had come to believe that pacifism among socialists in Allied countries had been encouraged by German socialists as part of a conspiracy to diminish opposition to German domination.

After the end of the war, Smith remained involved in a kind of personal battle against Germany. He had come to see his early disagreements with Marx and Engels not as differences over doctrine but as his own lifelong defense of socialism against its "autocratic" domination by Germans.[78] He feared that pro-German elements were influencing decision-making in the young Labour party.[79] He argued that Germans at international congresses on a wide variety of topics behaved in a uniformly high-handed fashion, and he railed with almost martial vehemence against the dominance of Germany in medicine, in the war against tuberculosis, in medical ethics, and so on.[80] His views, though controversial, were not regarded as extreme, paranoid, or marginal: a series of articles on socialist history, in which he expressed these ideas quite clearly, appeared in the mainstream and popular London *Times*.[81]

Right up to his death, Smith remained engaged with the issues that had interested him all his life. He traveled and spoke publicly about a variety of topics into his late 70s. Increasingly, however, ill health made this difficult.[82] In late November 1925, Smith died of arteriosclerosis after several weeks of illness.[83] Obituaries, among them a laudatory piece appearing in the pages of his longtime employer *The Lancet*, discussed his commitment to the health and well-being of the masses and his dedication to justice and fairness in labor practices. The *Lancet* obituary asserted that "among the host of nameless contributors to our columns none can have had wider influence on broad social conditions than Adolphe Smith."[84] The London *Times* also praised Smith's lifelong dedication to the public good. "During his long life Mr. Smith came to know much of men and cities, and especially of labour conditions. As special commissioner of the *Lancet* for more than 40 years, Mr. Smith was instrumental in detecting many defects in social machinery."[85] Notably, however, no obituary mentions the activity for which Smith is now best-known, his co-authorship of *Street Life in London.* His present-day legacy is based on an activity that, in his own life, was little more than a footnote.

Smith's writings

The wide-ranging diversity and the functional character of many of Adolphe Smith's writings, like those of John Thomson, prevent us from regarding his body of work as an *oeuvre.* But the writer's intent to discuss particular topics – public health initiatives, child labor, the Paris Commune, socialist conspiracies, and so forth – does not preclude us from seeking other meanings in the text as well. I turn now to look more closely at the writing itself.

This view is necessarily fragmentary, since the anonymous nature of many of Smith's publications and the sheer volume of his output prevent any but an incomplete view. Still, one can discern trends and tendencies in his writing that in turn illuminate and contextualize his work for *Street Life in London.* Some I have already touched on: Smith's dedication to a moderate, gradualist form of socialism; his interest in public health and sanitation; his careful, discerning use of fact and statistic. All of these figure into his texts for *Street Life in London.* But there are other discoveries to be had from an examination of his body of work. Here and there one gets a sense that Smith was possessed of a *joie-de-vivre* that he suppressed in much of his writing. He was also irrepressibly curious about other people – their habits, their happinesses, their miseries. Even prior to 1876 when Smith and Thomson began work on *Street Life in London*, Smith had clearly "traveled much in London," to paraphrase Thoreau. His forays into the slums and byways of the city for *Street Life* were doubtless not his first. Smith also demonstrated in his writings his inclusive, generally egalitarian attitudes toward people of other races or creeds. Finally, he occasionally revealed a surprising belief or assumption: a faith in the pseudo-sciences of physiognomy and phrenology, for instance, at least in the earlier part of his life; or some later dalliances with spiritualism. All of these help to build an idea of Smith as a person and as a writer, and from there to understand what he hoped to accomplish when he and Thomson undertook *Street Life in London*.

Prior to *Street Life in London*, Smith's productions were brief and varied. He wrote a series of articles for the London *Examiner* about the progress of socialism internationally, but he also concentrated on subjects closer to home, smaller and less overtly political.

Among other publications, he wrote for *The Food Journal*, which concentrated on food in a wide variety of contexts. Smith's curiosity, his experiences as a traveler both in his own city and in the world beyond, and his enjoyment of the company of others come through quite clearly here. He was something of an epicure, in the classic sense that he reveled in simple pleasures and the society of others. In one piece from 1873, he delineates the benefits of leading a "bohemian" lifestyle. He begins by noting that readers might have an idea of "Bohemia" as connoting filth, laziness and dissipation, since "Bohemianism means emancipation from the laws of etiquette... and a sole desire to do that which is the most convenient."[86] But while it is true that for some that means letting oneself go to seed, for others it indicates doing the best they can in straitened circumstances and taking real pleasure in simplicity. He describes a young married couple he knows. In lieu of expensive furniture they have surrounded themselves with books and evidence of their travels. Rather than eating in cheap-but-terrible restaurants, they cook for and serve themselves:

> *A little glass of real Vermouth... prepares the palate and sharpens the appetite. The cost of this rare and extravagant luxury for the two amounts*

> *to [sixpence]. Then the finest slice of Lyons or Mortadella sausage is cut and eaten with olives, of which a retail supply can be bought at the French grocer's for [threepence]... Everything had... to be cooked on a small frying-pan over a little spirit-lamp; yet the chops, the steaks, the veal kidney and cutlets had a special taste of their own, given to them by these amateur cooks. The smallest speck of green herb... gives the whole a relish and refined taste which is something like civilisation when compared to the cannibalism of the half raw steak drawn from the English gridiron and eaten without any attempt to alter or modify its carnivorous flavour.*[87]

Far from simply lauding the superiority of French cooking over English, the article argues for the possibilities to be had in poverty, the joys of a life lived in the moment. Even when not writing explicitly about socialism, Smith clearly conceived his purpose as both didactic and class-oriented, part of his overall endeavor to laud the dignity of those who must do for themselves.[88]

Smith also wrote about international politics for a variety of outlets. In addition to his *Examiner* series on international socialism, he contributed among others a piece for the literary journal *The Dark Blue* about the former king of Spain, Amadeo. An Italian by birth, Amadeo had not been raised or educated to rule, and certainly not in Spain. Ultimately he could not manage Spain's complex politics, and after just two years he abdicated, in 1873. The problem, Smith argues, was not the wrong king but the wrong sort of governance entirely: only a Republic could alleviate Spain's political confusion. Amadeo, he notes, was basically an honorable man but unsuited to rulership. Interestingly, he supports this assertion by resorting to physiognomy:

> *...[in general] the political conduct of Amadeo was remarkable for its modesty and moderation. Indeed, his very appearance marked him as a frank, intelligent, good-natured gentleman, but nothing more... Amadeo is, it is true, rather tall, and height is always marked as a kingly attribute; but his features are irregular, his forehead is high and narrow, his nose rather long; his eyes are good, but his mouth much too prominent.*[89]

Although Smith does not use the word, he indicates that Amadeo does not fit the "type" of a king. In this article Smith's generally progressive ideology comes up against widely accepted, fundamentally retrograde assumptions about the correspondence of physical attributes to intellectual capabilities and suitability for particular social roles. His thinking reveals a fundamental tension between the rhetoric of self-determination and the ossification of social hierarchies that underlies much of Victorian dialogue about social mobility.

Far more frequently, however, he expresses his general egalitarianism. His belief in classlessness and social equality extended both to women and to members of other creeds and races, both in Europe and beyond. Such sentiments were not shared by many Victorians, including many of his fellow socialists. Although Smith certainly had his pro-England biases, his extensive travels seem to have made him comfortable with a wide variety of races, customs and religions. In particular, his admiration for what he considered rational, scientific, and/or especially effective sanitary practices and measures knew no national boundaries. During a cholera epidemic in 1892-94, when he traveled widely through Europe, he found the best measures for checking the spread of the disease in Constantinople, where he praised the Sultan for strictly quarantining sufferers while at the same time providing them with ample food and otherwise treating them very humanely.[90] On later visits to the city, he noted with approbation the near-total absence of alcoholism and other vice-related diseases, and consistently praised Turkish and Muslim hygienic practices.[91]

Likewise, he evinced concern for people who were ill-treated because of race or religion. Visiting St. Louis during the 1904 World's Fair, he deplored conditions in parts of town primarily inhabited by African-Americans.[92] Later that same year, while still in America, he lectured in New York on the Dreyfus Affair, which he decried as an anti-Semitic plot. Dreyfus, he said, was "martyred" by Jesuits attempting to control political and military power in France.[93]

Smith's concern extended to many who simply could not defend themselves, including children. A key aspect of his engagement with labor and sanitary reform throughout his career was his campaigning for the abolition of child labor, which he did at many international congresses and in the pages of *The Lancet*. When he found children being mistreated in other ways, as well, he was quick to say so. A notable instance occurs in his reports from the 1904 St. Louis World's Fair, at which one of the most popular and frequently-mentioned entertainments was a display of live babies in incubators. Smith found it disgusting and deemed it inhumane, unsanitary, and potentially deadly for the children.[94]

He was almost as vocal about mistreatment or suffering of animals. In 1882 he reported on a lecture by Louis Pasteur about the creation of vaccines for diseases of livestock. Although fully supportive of Pasteur's work, Smith was deeply moved that so many animals had to die in Pasteur's laboratories for the doctor to arrive at a successful vaccine. These animals, Smith wrote, ought to be regarded as martyrs.[95] He was less sentimental and more condemnatory about the appalling treatment of animals in American slaughterhouses. Pigs were scalded alive to remove their bristles, and the treatment of cattle was just as horrifyingly wanton. "Here the evident desire," he wrote:

> *is to treat living animals as if they were bales of cotton, of wool, or of any other kind of raw material... The sole object seems to be to convert each animal into saleable product in the quickest and cheapest manner possible.*[96]

He implied that the mistreatment of animals and the mistreatment of workers in Chicago's packing plants went hand-in-hand. Cattle that failed to fall unconscious after being stunned with a mallet sometimes had to be shot while they ran about inside the plant, even at risk of the bullet ricocheting. After the cattle were strung up, the men had to run alongside the line to cut their throats and catch their blood in buckets, getting covered in it all the while. Since workdays were long and much of this work happened in windowless underground rooms, many men never saw the sun in winter.[97] Smith believed that the mistreatment of both man and animal in the meat-packing plants ultimately endangered the public health, greatly increasing the potential that spoiled or diseased meat might find its way into the general food supply. Social problems, he implied, tended to be intertwined: any form of injustice was sure to be tied to other injustices. Combating maltreatment of both animals and men, then, would ultimately benefit the public interest.

But alongside such clear, far-seeing comprehension of the issues confronting an industrialized society, Smith occasionally expressed beliefs that seem surprisingly unscientific. Simultaneously with his studies of epidemiology, sanitation and labor conditions, for instance, he engaged from at least the late 1890s in "constant practical experimentation" with spiritualism and séances. He makes it clear that he did not believe that mediums could channel spirits, but he thought instead that the phenomena frequently seen at séances – mediums' fantastic ability to divine very personal details about attendees, or to channel spirits that said precisely what attendees wanted to hear – could be attributed to "telepathy, thought reading, ...conscious or unconscious suggestion, ...clairvoyance, and even... the gift of prophecy."[98] Throughout these experiments he maintained scientific method, keeping "minute books" in which he detailed his experiments with spiritualism and their results.

For the most part, however, Smith's scientific and journalistic productions treated subjects of more immediate and practical import. His skills as a reporter on science, politics, travel and other matters for a popular audience are perhaps best displayed in his book-length productions. I focus on one of these in particular, *The Garden of Hyères*, because he wrote it just a couple of years after *Street Life in London*. Extolling the virtues of a French Riviera town frequented by invalids but less well-known than Cannes or other such places, it functions as both travelogue and informational guide for the sick and their caregivers.

In it one finds confirmed much of what one divines

from Smith's other writings. He begins by reporting on the difficulties of Channel crossing and the options available to English travelers, then describes the French countryside one encounters when traveling to the south by train. In the process, he reveals again his enjoyment of good food and simple pleasures, as well as his considerable knowledge of French wines. Glancing mentions of "the memory of good dinners, and hard fighting against the Germans" in Chablis and Nuits confirm both his own intimacy with this countryside and his experiences within it during the 1870 war.[99] In describing Lyons, he entreats his reader to seek out not fashionable districts and sights but artisans and workers who, he claims, are better-read and better-educated in the principles of socialism and republicanism than their Parisian counterparts.[100] Even in this travelogue for a popular audience, then, he promotes the advancement of socialism and the interests of the worker, as though he simply could not turn off his political voice.

He continues with this combination of the scientifically specific and the broadly general, the universal and the personal. He demonstrates that the weather in the town of Hyères is indeed mild by giving a table of daily temperature records for February and March 1867, one of many such straightforwardly factual elements in the book. But he also claims that the women of the town of Arles, all beautiful, may be divided into "three distinct types, the Roman, the Greek, and the Saracen."[101] He assures the reader that the town doctors in Hyères are utterly trustworthy, then notes – in mid-paragraph, and almost in passing – that "to the climate of Hyères, and to the untiring attention and skill of our two resident English doctors, is due the preservation of a life that was more dear to me than my own existence," that is, his wife's.[102] A chapter on the flora of the town, both native and cultivated, demonstrates his encyclopedic knowledge of plant life, among many other things.[103] But in the next chapter, on the resources available in the town for the student of the natural sciences, he again reveals himself, if unintentionally: "...I would earnestly advise anyone who is condemned by circumstances or by his doctor to spend a winter or several winters at Hyères, to select a science and devote himself to its study."[104] Smith's very book itself was, I think, the product of such selective study: he undertook it both because there was no such resource already extant, and because he was "condemned by circumstance" – by the illness of his wife – to stay there for an extended period.

In a chapter on the history of Hyères, he openly

displays his own aversion to organized religion. While he expresses true respect for the deep and apparently genuine Christian faith of King Louis IX – Saint Louis – who landed at Hyères after a crusade in Palestine, he relates with disgust another episode, driven by "religion and superstition," in which two innocent women were burned at the stake for performing witchcraft that caused a married couple to quarrel. He also deplores how the French coast was beset by the "depredations" of Muslim invaders, and thereafter enveloped in the "wars of religion" provoked by the Reformation.[105]

At the same time, he again surprises by revealing a considerable knowledge of, and strong opinions about, art and architectural history. The town's ancient Church of St. Louis, he asserts, stands as a transitional monument between the Romanesque and Gothic architectural styles, its arches being neither perfectly rounded nor sharply arched and its windows, while filled with stained glass, being small.[106] In giving a tour through the old town of Hyères, he notes other architectural remnants on churches and private houses, discussing their various styles and revealing the settlement's long past.[107] He knows enough of art to critique the products of the folk tradition lining the walls of a local church, the votive Ermitage above

Hyères. Devotional paintings there depict people surviving the effects of lighting-strikes, storms at sea and other calamities. One painting, showing a child surviving a fall out a window, depicts a recent event at which one of Smith's doctor-friends attended. While Smith appreciates the quality of this particular painting over the others, he again discounts its subject-matter, implying that the presence of the doctor, and not the intervention of God or prayer, accounted for the child's survival. "Indeed," he continues, "it has been suggested that an opposition chapel might appropriately be built where trophies and pictures of all persons who have not escaped from some special danger might be hung; and it is further urged that this new collection would soon become the more numerous of the two."[108]

Up to the end of the book he continues in similar fashion to reveal simultaneously his knowledge of the subject and his own thoughts about it, which prove at once deeply personal and intensely political. The final passage meditates on a proposed hospital for children at Hyères, which would be dedicated to treatment of all children, rich and poor alike. He concludes:

> *It will be, indeed, a sign of real prosperity and real greatness when, side by side with the luxurious*

> *residences where the middle and upper classes prolong their existence and modify the suffering entailed by their diseases, asylums will be built for the benefit of the poorer and industrial classes, whose labour is the foundation of all wealth.*[109]

Despite its claim to serve as a guide for invalids and their families and its myriad discourses on the plants, landscape and climate of Hyères, the book is at its base a plea for equal treatment of suffering people of all classes. Tired of being surrounded in Hyères by the coddled, sick rich, Smith used his book as a means to plead for a different paradigm, and to remind his readers – the same weak, ill people by whom he found himself beset in the south of France – that their pain was not the only pain to be had in this world. Indeed, Smith's entire body of work, from beginning to end, functioned in much this same way: always targeting a comfortable, middle-class audience, it reminded them over and over of the suffering and hard work on which their comfort was built, and begged them to remember the very thing with which he closes here: "labour is the foundation of all wealth."

NOTES

1 Certified Copy of an Entry of Birth Given at the General Register Office, Hunslet, sub-district Kirkstall, County of York, 11 January 1847. See also "Births March 1847," General Register Office Index, citing Hunslet records Vol. 13, 305.

2 Their own marriage certificate attests to this: Marriages solemnized in the Parish Church of Leeds, in the County of York, in the Year 1831, 407. West Yorkshire Archive Service, reference P 68/4/19.

3 1861 Census, Leicestershire county, Parish Thringstone, Registration district Ashby de la Zouch, subdistrict Whitwick, 23. Public Record Office reference R.G. 9/2271. The English census was conducted every ten years.

4 For accounts of the Franco-Prussian War and the Commune, see Robert Tombs, *The Paris Commune 1871* (London/New York: Longman, 1999); David A. Shafer, *The Paris Commune: French Politics, Culture and Society at the Crossroads of the Revolutionary Tradition and Revolutionary Socialism* (New York: Palgrave, 2005); Colette E. Wilson, *Paris and the Commune, 1871-78: The Politics of Forgetting* (Manchester/New York: Manchester University Press, 2007). For accounts of iconoclasm during the Commune, see especially John Milner, *Art, War and Revolution in France 1870-71: Myth, Reportage and Reality* (New Haven/London: Yale University, 2000).

5 A number of Smith's obituaries mention this incident. See e.g. "Mr. Adolphe Smith," *Times* (London) no. 44118, 13 Nov. 1925, 14, col. E. For MacCormac, see William MacCormac, "Recollections of Work in an Ambulance," in 9 parts, *British Medical Journal*, 5 Nov. 1870, 483; 12 Nov.

1870, 525-26; 19 Nov. 1970, 548-49; 26 Nov. 1870, 575-76; 3 Dec. 1870, 601-02; 17 Dec. 1870, 652-53; 14 Jan. 1871, 33-34; 4 Feb. 1871, 113-14; 11 Mar. 1871, 249-50. See also "Obituary: Sir William MacCormac, Bart., K.C.B., K.C.V.O.," *British Medical Journal* 2, no. 2137, 14 Dec. 1901, 1771-75.

6 "Tales of the Paris Commune," *New Castle News* (New Castle, PA), Friday, March 17, 1905, 2.

7 Ibid.; see also "Tales of the Paris Commune: Delegate to the Peace Congress Lectures on his Experience in the Siege," *Sun* (New York), 28 November 1904, 10.

8 On one of these Smith actually witnessed one of the Commune's central events, the deaths of two Versaillais generals, Jules LeComte and Clement Thomas. After the suppression of the Commune the legitimate French government, anxious to vilify the Communards and the mutineers, propagated the story that the generals were killed by their own mutinous troops. But Smith's account complicates the accepted narrative. At first, soldiers commanded by the two men actually protected their leaders from what was essentially a lynching by an enraged mob. But then Thomas was shot by someone in the crowd, and thereafter a few soldiers seized LeComte as well, pushing him up against a wall and executing him. Later, Smith heard that the anonymous killer of Thomas, firing from the crowd, had actually been seeking revenge for the deaths of his parents, killed on the barricades years earlier during the revolution of 1848. See Sylvanus Urban, Gentleman [pseud.?], "Table Talk," Gentleman's Magazine 16 (February 1876), 252. The situation under the Commune vacillated between attempts by elected Commune officials to maintain order and outbursts

of mob rule, with interventions by individuals pursuing their own agendas. The attempts of Thiers's government, after the Commune, to attribute to it a wide variety of atrocities – some true, some fictional, some exaggerated – only complicate this situation.

9 Ibid., 256.

10 Albert Boime, "Introduction," *Art and the French Commune* (Princeton: Princeton University Press, 1995), 17.

11 Adolphe Smith, "Political Refugees," in Walter Besant, *London in the Nineteenth Century* (London: A. & C. Black, 1909), 399-406.

12 Dr. J.H. Bridges, "The Late Commune of Paris," *Bee-Hive*, 22 July 1871, quoted in Royden Harrison, "Marx, Engels, and the British Response to the Commune," *Massachusetts Review* 12, no. 3 (Summer 1971), 470.

13 E. Belfort Bax gives an account of Smith's lecture series, and how it helped to sow dissent especially between him and Engels, in his autobiography. See Ernest Belfort Bax, *Reminiscences and Reflexions of a mid and late Victorian* (London: G. Allen and Unwin, 1918), http://www.marxists.org/archive/bax/1918/ autobiog/ch02.htm (accessed 11 July 2011).

14 See e.g. A. [Adolphe Smith], "Federalism and Solidarity," *Examiner* (London) no. 3413, 28 June 1873, 658-59, in which he calls such centralized governance "despotism."

15 See e.g. A. [Adolphe Smith], "Spanish Socialism," *Examiner* (London) 3397, 8 March 1873, 245-46.

16 In France, for instance, he believed that workers' cooperative organizations posed the greatest threat to Thiers's Third Republic after the Commune. See A. [Adolphe Smith], "The Co-operative Movement in

France," *Examiner* (London) 3404, 26 April 1873, 430-31.

17 Adolphe Smith, "Co-operation Under the Septennate," *Examiner* 3455, 18 April 1874, 397-98.

18 Ernest Belfort Bax, "Reminiscences and Reflexions."

19 Passing mention of this archive is made from time to time in articles about Smith. See e.g. "Tales of the Paris Commune: Delegate to the Peace Congress Lectures on his Experience in the Siege."

20 In 1873, Smith spoke at a meeting of the London National Society for Women's Suffrage. Advertisements, *Examiner* 3399, 22 March 1873, 316.

21 For the former subject, see Adolphe Smith, "Amadeo," *Dark Blue* 5, no. 1 (March 1873), 1-8. For the latter, see A. [Adolphe Smith], "The Industrial Crisis in Belgium," *Examiner* (London) no. 3407, 17 May 1873, 498-500.

22 Volumes 1 and 2 of *The Dark Blue* were published by Sampson Low, Son, and Marston (later publishers of *Street Life in London*); the last three, including Volume 5 to which Smith contributed, were published by the British and Colonial Publishing Co. See Walter E. Houghton et. al., *The Wellesley Index to Victorian Periodicals 1824-1900*, Vol. IV (Toronto: University of Toronto Press/London: Routledge and Kegan Paul, 1987), 178-82 and 192.

23 A. [Adolphe Smith], "Prud'hommes in Difficulty," *Examiner* (London) 3391, 25 January 1873, 85-86.

24 "Certified Copy of an Entry of Marriage Given at the General Register Office," citing GRO records for 1872, Quarter S, volume 1a, page 1084. The marriage took place in Marylebone district, Middlesex county,

and was solemnized in the Register Office before two witnesses: George Smith, Adolphe Smith's eldest brother (Smith's father, also named George Smith, was deceased) and Joseph A. Bonnert. See also "MARRIAGES registered in July, August, and September 1872," General Register Office Index, citing Marylebone records, 219.

25 Michael Slater, "Jerrold, Douglas William (1803–1857)," *Oxford Dictionary of National Biography*, Oxford University Press, 2004, http://www.oxforddnb.com/view/article/14789 (accessed 28 July 2011).

26 Michael Slater, "Jerrold, (William) Blanchard (1826–1884)," *Oxford Dictionary of National Biography*, Oxford University Press, 2004, http://www.oxforddnb.com/view/article/14790 (accessed 27 July 2011).

27 Michael Slater, "Jerrold, Douglas William," *Oxford Dictionary of National Biography*.

28 See Michael Slater, "Jerrold, (William) Blanchard," *Oxford Dictionary of National Biography*.

29 Gustave Dore and Blanchard Jerrold, *London: A Pilgrimage* (London: Grant & Co., 1872).

30 See Ialeen Gibson-Cowan, "Thomson's Street Life in Context," *Creative Camera* 251 (November 1985), 10.

31 Alice Jerrold (Mrs. Adolphe Smith), *A Cruise in the Acorn* (London: Marcus Ward and Co., 1875).

32 Mrs. Adolphe Smith [Alice Jerrold Smith], *Love Without Wings*, 3 vols. (London: Tinsley Brothers, 1877); Mrs. Adolphe Smith [Alice Jerrold Smith], *A Woman of Mind*, 3 vols. (London: Sampson Low, Marston, Searle and Rivington, 1879); see also Willert Beale (Walter Maynard), *The Light of Other Days Seen Through the Wrong End of an Opera Glass*,

Vol. II (London: Richard Bentley and Son, 1890), 282; Adrian Room, *Dictionary of Pseudonyms*, 5th ed. (Jefferson, NC / London: McFarland, 2010), 117.

33 Certified Copy of an Entry of Birth given at the General Register Office, 6 November 1874, Registration district Saint George Hanover Square, sub-district St. Margaret, County of Middlesex.

34 "Annotations: London Street Life," *Lancet* 109, no. 2789 (10 February 1877), 213.

35 In testimony before the House of Lords Select Committee on the Sweating System in 1889, Smith stated in response to a question that he had been working for the *Lancet* for "about 12 years," or since about 1878. Adolphe Smith, Testimony before the House of Lords Select Committee on the Sweating System, 22 March 1889, *House of Commons Papers: Reports from Committees: Vol. 5: Sweating System: Third Report from the Select Committee of the House of Lords on the Sweating System, With the Minutes of Evidence and Appendix* (London: Henry Hansard & Son), 1889, 397 no. 22610.

36 For a mention of the need for anonymity, see "The Last Thirty Years," *Lancet* 202, no. 5223 (6 October 1923), 750.

37 Adolphe S. Headingley [Adolphe Smith], *The Biography of Charles Bradlaugh* (London: Remington, 1880).

38 See Smith's biography of Bradlaugh; also Edward Royle, "Bradlaugh, Charles (1833-1891)," *Oxford Dictionary of National Biography* (Oxford: Oxford University Press, 2004; online edn, Jan 2011), http://www.oxforddnb.com/view/article/3183 (accessed 19 July 2012).

39 A few modern-day references continue to assert, erroneously, that

"Adolphe Smith Headingley" was Smith's real name, and "Adolphe Smith" the pseudonym. See e.g. Walter Houghton et. al., "Pseudonyms and Initials," *The Wellesley Index to Victorian Periodicals*, Vol. IV, 744.

40 Smith states in *The Garden of Hyères* that someone close to him weathered an illness there. Since Alice Smith later died there, it seems likely that she, rather than their young daughter Rose, was the reason for the visit. See Adolphe Smith, *The Garden of Hyères: A Description of the most Southern Point of the French Riviera* (London: Fleet Print Works/ J. Evans & Co., 1881), 32.

41 Adolphe Smith and John Thomson, *Street Incidents: A Series of Twenty-One Permanent Photographs with Descriptive Letter-Press* (London: Sampson Low, Marston, Searle & Rivington), 1881.

42 For remarks on the suddenness of her death see the brief obituary in the *Union and Advertiser* (Rochester, NY), 57, no. 102, 1 May 1882, 1; for the state of her health see the *Daily Courier* (Syracuse, NY), 8 May 1882, n.p.

43 "It was not necessary to destroy the bourgeois State before… reforms could be achieved. Within contemporary capitalist society public services were developing of their own accord – for example, railways and postal services… [I]t was the function of the Socialist Party to accelerate the general trend and to control it, especially in those areas where the bourgeoisie showed little concern directing it towards socially beneficial results. Eventually society would become one in which the public services satisfied the needs of all on a Communist basis…" David Stafford, *From Anarchism to Reformism: A Study of the Political Activities of Paul Brousse within the First International and the*

French Socialist Movement 1870-90 (Toronto: University of Toronto Press, 1971), 186. See also 134-50.

44 Ibid., 332 fn. 37.

45 Adolphe Smith, "The International: German Domination and the Trade Unions," Letter to the Editor, *Times* (London) no. 41885, 3 Sept. 1918, 4 col. E.

46 Adolphe Smith, "The Old and the New International, A Reminder of Facts," Letter to the Editor, *Times* (London) no. 41568, 28 August 1917, 5 col. E; Smith here calls himself "Interpreter at all the International Socialist conferences and congresses held since 1882."

47 Chemical Society Certificate of a Candidate for Election, dated April 19, 1883 and June 21, 1883. Archives of the Chemical Society, London. On this Certificate a number of well-known chemists of the day attested to personal knowledge of Smith's character. These included Thomas Bolas, an active and productive researcher in the chemistry of photography whose research frequently appeared in the photography-related press of the period.

48 Adolphe Smith, *Pneumatic Drainage: A Description of the "Berlier System"* (London: E & F. Spon, 1883).

49 Adolphe S. Headingley [Adolphe Smith], *The Biography of Charles Bradlaugh*, 2nd ed. with an appendix by W. Mawer (London: Freethought), 1883.

50 [Adolphe Smith], "Report of the Lancet Special Commission on the Contamination of Uniforms Provided by the Army Clothing Depot," *Lancet* 111, no. 2841 (9 Feb. 1878), 217-19.

51 Adolphe Smith, Testimony before the House of Lords Select Committee on the Sweating System, 403 entry 22662.

52 Ibid., 397-407.

53 [Adolphe Smith], "Chicago: The Dark and Insanitary Premises Used for the Slaughtering of Cattle and Hogs – the Government Inspection," *Lancet* 165, no. 4246 (14 January 1905), 120-23.

54 [Adolphe Smith], "Chicago: The Stockyards and Packing Town: Insanitary Condition of the World's Largest Meat Market (From our Special Sanitary Commissioner)," *Lancet* 165, no. 4245 (7 January 1905), 49-52.

55 See also [Adolphe Smith], "Chicago: Tuberculosis among the Stockyard Workers – Sanitation in Packingtown – The Police and the Dumping of Refuse – Vital Statistics," *Lancet* 165, no. 4247 (21 Jan. 1905), 183-85; [Adolphe Smith], "Chicago: Unhealthy Work in the Stockyards – Shameless Indifference to the Insantiary Condition of the Buildings and the Cattle Pens – Pollution of the Subsoil – The Need for Legislative Interference," *Lancet* 165, no. 4248 (28 Jan. 1905), 258-60.

56 For information regarding Sinclair, *The Jungle*, and his consultations with Smith, see Louise Carroll Wade, "The Problem with Classroom Use of Upton Sinclair's The Jungle," *American Studies* 32, no. 2 (Fall 1991), 79-101.

57 See [Adolphe Smith], "The Cholera in France," *Lancet* 140, no. 3605 (1 Oct. 1892), 792-96; Adolphe Smith, "Are We Prepared to Resist a Cholera Epidemic?" *New Review* 9, no. 53 (October 1893), 353-61. The "Battle of the Clubs" series ran from 1895 to about 1908; see e.g. [Adolphe Smith], "The Battle of the Clubs at Brussels," *Lancet* 146, no. 3756 (24 August 1895), 476-77; [Adolphe Smith], "The Battle of the Clubs," *Lancet* 154, no. 3961 (29 July 1899), 304-06; [Adolphe Smith], "The Battle of the Clubs: A Five Years' Struggle at Shipley," *Lancet* 170, no. 4400 (28 Dec. 1907), 1876-77; [Adolphe Smith], "The Battle of the

Clubs," *Lancet* 171, no. 4417 (25 April 1908), 1240-42.

58 His obituary in *The Lancet* provides the best information on the lasting impact of "The Battle of the Clubs," while his obituary in *The Times* discusses his reportage on the cholera outbreak. See "Adolphe Smith," *Lancet* 206, no. 5333 (14 Nov. 1925), 1033; "Mr. Adolphe Smith," *Times* (London) no. 44118 (13 Nov. 1925), 14, col. E.

59 See e.g. [Adolphe Smith], "The Paris Universal Exhibition," *Lancet* 133, no. 3435 (29 June 1889), 1324-25; [Adolphe Smith], "The Paris Universal Exhibition," *Lancet* 134, no. 3437 (13 July 1889), 89-91; [Adolphe Smith], "The Paris Universal Exhibition," *Lancet* 134, no. 3451 (19 Oct. 1889), 813-17. Overall, Smith wrote "nearly a hundred columns" about the 1889 Paris Exhibition alone. See "The Paris Universal Exhibition of 1889," *Lancet* 134, no. 3453 (2 Nov. 1889), 924. Smith visited St. Louis in November 1904 just before his explorations of the Chicago slaughterhouses. He was unimpressed with sanitation there. See [Adolphe Smith], "The World's Fair at St. Louis," *Lancet* 164, no. 4239 (26 Nov. 1904), 1527-29; [Adolphe Smith], "The World's Fair at St. Louis," *Lancet* 164, no. 4241 (10 Dec. 1904), 1681-83; [Adolphe Smith], "Sanitation at St. Louis, Missouri," *Lancet* 164, no. 4242 (17 Dec. 1904), 1753-54.

60 For specific reference to Smith's election to the presidency of the Congress on Free Education, see [Adolphe Smith], "The Paris Universal Exhibition (From our Special Correspondent)," *Lancet* 134, no. 3449 (5 Oct 1889), 713-15. References to his attendance at other meetings are taken from articles, some signed by Smith and some unsigned, in which Smith made comments or contributions that merited mention. Given that Smith probably also wrote most of the unsigned articles,

he may have given weight to his comments in the reports that was not merited by their real impact. At any rate, these reports do serve as a record of Smith's physical presence at these many meetings and congresses. For reference see the following (among others): [Adolphe Smith], "The Sixth International Congress of Hygiene (From our Special Correspondent)," *Lancet* 130, no. 3344 (1 October 1887), 683-85; "The International Congress of Hygiene and Demography," *Lancet* 134, no. 3547 (22 Aug. 1891), 441-58; [Adolphe Smith], "Federation of the Medical Unions of France," *Lancet* 138, no. 3561 (28 November 1891), 1250-51; "The First International Congress on Medical Ethics or Deontology, Held at Paris, July, 1900," *Lancet* 156, no. 4013 (28 July 1900), 275-79; [Adolphe Smith], "The First International Congress of the Medical Press, Held at Paris, July, 1900," *Lancet* 156, no. 4015 (11 Aug. 1900), 454-56; "The Eleventh International Congress of Hygiene and Demography," *Lancet* 162, no. 4178 (26 Sept. 1903), 913-17; "The International Association of the Medical Press Committee Meeting at Berne," *Lancet* 165, no. 4262 (6 May 1905), 1230-32; "The Third International Congress of the Medical Press," *Lancet* 174, no. 4495 (23 October 1909), 1242-46; "The International Congress on Tuberculosis at Rome," *Lancet* 179, no. 4628 (11 May 1912), 1301-05.

61 "Wills and Bequests," *Times* (London) no. 44144, 14 Dec. 1925, 17 col. E.

62 See, for instance, [Adolphe Smith], "The Paris Universal Exhibition," *Lancet* 134, 89-91, where he argues for the universal need for state intervention into matters concerning child labor.

63 "The Fabian Society and Socialist Notes," *Our Corner* 8 (July 1886), 60.

64 Adolphe Smith, "Report of the International Trades Union Congress,

Held at PARIS from August 23rd to 28th, 1886" (London: Foulger and Co., 1886); Adolphe Smith, "A Critical Essay on the International Trade Union Congress, held in London, November, 1888, by Adolphe Smith (Interpreter to the Congress)" (London: Published by the Author, 19 Barclay Road, Walham Green, SW, 1889).

65 Adolphe Smith, "A Critical Essay on the International Trade Union Congress" (1888), 14.

66 H.M. Hyndman, *The Record of an Adventurous Life* (New York: Macmillan, 1911), 231-32.

67 1891 Census, Administrative County of London, Civil Parish Leeds, Borough Fulham, Parish St. John's, 11.

68 "Baptisms Solemnized in the Parish of St. John's Fulham in the County of London in the Year 1892," 270. London Metropolitan Archives, St. John, Walham Green, Register of Baptisms P77/JN Item 003.

69 The latter two details come from a small cache of letters written by both Smith and Wenham to the English socialist J.L. Mahon and preserved at the Labour History Archive and Study Centre, People's History Museum, Manchester, UK, file CP/IND/MISC/2/10.

70 La Provence Passenger Manifest, September 14, 1912. www.ellisisland.org/search/FormatPassRec. asp?ID=100986090120&BN=P00098-6&sship=La%20Provence&lineshipid=487 (accessed 7 June 2011). One can only speculate about the reasons for this situation: perhaps Rose Wenham objected to Smith's atheism to the extent that she could not be married to him. Perhaps the arrangement had some pedestrian, fiscal explanation – taxes or some such matter. I am tempted to ascribe this unorthodox (at least on paper) arrangement to some progressiv-

ism on Smith's part: an objection to the social requirement that his wife take his last name, for instance, or a refusal to regard her as his legal property. Certainly this would be in keeping with his general forward-thinking tendencies with regard to women and gender roles. But because the details of Smith's personal situation are unknown – missing, like all his personal effects – such explanations must remain, at least for now, conjectural.

71 [Adolphe Smith], "Monaco's Model Hospital," *Lancet* 177, no. 4575 (6 May 1911), 1229-31; [Adolphe Smith], "The Drainage Problem at Monaco," *Lancet* 177, no. 4577 (20 May 1911), 1384-85.

72 Adolphe Smith, *Monaco and Monte Carlo* (London: Grant Richards Ltd./Philadelphia: J.B. Lippincott, 1912).

73 See e.g. "Reviews and Notices of Books: Monaco and Monte Carlo, by Adolphe Smith," *Lancet* 181, no. 4671 (8 March 1913), 693-94; "Monaco and Monte Carlo [Book review]," *Bookman* 43 no. 255 (December 1912), 64; "Monaco and Monte Carlo [Book review]," *Academy and Literature* 2124 (18 January 1913), 80. Interestingly, in one section of the book Smith introduces a series of statistics – intended to refute assertions that legal gambling in Monaco led to higher suicide rates – derived in part from correspondence with French criminologist and anthropometrist Alphonse Bertillon. If not friends, the two men knew one another professionally at least.

74 "Medical News," *Lancet* 181, no. 4687 (28 June 1913), 1840. This was probably the "Médaille commémorative de la guerre 1870-1871."

75 "The War," *Lancet* 185, no. 4776 (13 March 1915), 575.

76 "The War: A Lecture on the War," *Lancet* 185, no. 4777 (20 March 1915), 629.

77 "English Lecturers Touring France," *Bismarck Daily Tribune* (Bismarck, ND), 13 November 1915, 2.

78 Adolphe Smith, "The Old and the New International, A Reminder of Facts."

79 Adolphe Smith, "Direct Action: Labour and Foreign Affairs: Propaganda of Kaiserism," Letter to the Editor, *Times* (London) no. 42140, 1 July 1919, 8 col. A.

80 [Adolphe Smith], "Science as Made in Germany," *Lancet* 194, no. 5006 (9 August 1919), 258.

81 Adolphe Smith, "The Pan-German Internationale: I – Marx and his Successors," *Times* (London) no. 42164, 29 July 1919, 14 col. C; Adolphe Smith, "The Pan-German Internationale: II – Trade Unionists Abroad," *Times* (London) no. 42165, 30 July 1919, 14 col. C; Adolphe Smith, "The Pan-German Internationale; III – the Capture of the Machine," *Times* (London) no. 42166, 31 July 1919, 10 col. F. It is worth noting that unlike many conspiracy theorists of the time, Smith did not express any anti-Semitic sentiment in his writings.

82 Smith discusses his illness and his heart problems in his letters to J. Mahon, Labour History Archive and Study Centre.

83 Smith left behind a modest sum of money, just over £600. This sum went not to his daughter, Rose, nor to Rose Wenham, but to "Grace Marian Wilson (wife of William Mortimer Wilson), and the said William Mortimer Wilson gentleman." See "Smith Adolphe," Probate Calendar, Index of Wills and Administrations, 1925. Grace was probably Smith's niece, who lived in Derbyshire and was "a leading resident in the place and member of the Unionism party." See Adolphe Smith, letter to J.

Mahon, 9 May 1924, Labour History Archive and Study Centre, People's History Museum, Manchester, UK, file CP/IND/MISC/2/10. While it is of some interest that he left her his money, I am more concerned with the idea that he might have sent to her, a woman with political interests similar to his own, his archival materials. Mentions are repeatedly made of the wealth of documentation he had gathered on the Commune and the Siege of Paris. But Grace Marian Wilson proves a cipher, and her fate – and the fate of any materials Smith might have willed to her – remains unknown.

84 "Adolphe Smith [obit.]," *Lancet* 206, 1033.

85 "Mr. Adolphe Smith," *Times* (London), 13 Nov. 1925, 14.

86 Adolphe Smith, "Bohemia Beautified," *Food Journal* (London) 4 no. 58 (1 March 1873), 67-70.

87 Ibid.

88 One suspects, based on his intimate knowledge of their eating and housekeeping habits, that the young Bohemian couple he described were himself and his wife, Alice.

89 Adolphe Smith, "Amadeo," 3.

90 Adolphe Smith, "The Present Menace of Cholera," *Fortnightly Review* 92, no. 548 (August 1912), 348-49.

91 [Adolphe Smith], "The Eighth International Congress of Hygiene and Demography: The Excursion to Constantinople," *Lancet* 144, no. 3711 (13 October 1894), 884-86.

92 [Adolphe Smith], "Sanitation at St. Louis, Missouri," *Lancet* 164, 1753.

93 "Calls it a Jesuit Plot: Adolphe Smith Tells of Persecution of Dreyfus," *New York Daily Tribune*, 28 November 1904, 5.

94 [Adolphe Smith], "The World's Fair at St. Louis," *Lancet* 164, 1681-83. Smith was right about the exhibit: at one point nearly half the babies died from infectious disease.

95 Adolphe Smith, "The Science of Health: The Fourth International Congress of Hygiene [From our Special Correspondent]," *Phrenological Journal* 76, no. 1 (January 1883), 40-45.

96 [Adolphe Smith], "Chicago: The Dark and Insanitary Premises Used for the Slaughtering of Cattle and Hogs," *Lancet* 165, 120.

97 Ibid., 121-23.

98 Adolphe Smith, "A Spiritist Revival," *Contemporary Review* 98 (July-December 1910), 315.

99 Adolphe Smith, *The Garden of Hyères*, 12.

100 Ibid., 15-16.

101 Ibid., 20, 27.

102 Ibid., 36.

103 Ibid., 42.

104 Ibid., 54.

105 Ibid., 66-68.

106 Ibid. 73.

107 Ibid., 74-77.

108 Ibid., 89.

109 Ibid., 122.

CHAPTER FOUR

WE ARE NOT THE FIRST ON THE FIELD

AS JOHN THOMSON and Adolphe Smith acknowledged from the outset, *Street Life in London* emerged into a literary and artistic landscape already crowded with endeavors to depict, catalogue, classify, explain, assist and reform the denizens of urban streets and their environs. *Street Life in London* sits at the confluence of various literary genres and ways of thinking about public poverty: sociological studies of street life and culture; technical and scientific attempts to address sanitation and living conditions in slums and tenement housing; visual catalogues of poverty; sensationalistic, touristic exposes of "low life"; literary journeys through the urban underbelly, both fictional and nonfictional. In order to determine how *Street Life in London* both inherited and rejected such prior models, how it attempted to revolutionize the representation of poverty, one must understand what Smith and Thomson believed they were updating.

This chapter does not attempt a comprehensive catalogue of the literature of the London streets and slums. Rather, it provides an overview of the literary and pictorial milieu into which *Street Life in London* emerged and it identifies some notable precursors to and/or foils for *Street Life*. This will permit better understanding of Smith's and Thomson's pictorial and textual innovations. The chapter considers a selection of earlier street studies, examining first literary, then visual models. It examines most closely those prior models that Smith and Thomson themselves either allude to or cite outright: Henry Mayhew's *London Labour and the London Poor*; some sensationalist works by journalist James Greenwood; and the various collections of pictorial "street types" and "street cries" popular for centuries prior to the Victorian era.[1] The chapter also identifies certain tendencies and characteristics that reappear throughout the literature of urban exploration. Many of these *Street Life* shares with its predecessors; others it partially or wholly rejects.

Ultimately, *Street Life in London* appears as a relatively restrained example of this type of literature. Although it falls roughly into a category of concerned popular journalism – neither a scientific study nor sensationalist slumming – I will argue that its very innovation and its distinguishing feature, the photographic illustrations of street scenes, act as a kind of constraint on its content. Smith and Thomson simply could not confront controversial or indelicate topics, because photographic illustrations of certain subjects would have been too real for their Victorian audiences. They could not risk a charge of indecency, so they excluded some topics that other studies of the London streets did confront – prostitution, for instance. Their study thus avoids titillation, but it also proves unable to confront some difficult truths.

Existing scholarship provides some helpful systems for understanding and categorizing the vast literature of urban exploration. For the purposes of this study, fictional precedents prove less useful than non-fiction, although there is admittedly some overlap between the two – something of the concrete even in the works of Charles Dickens, for instance, and something of the mythic even in the journalistic work of Mayhew.[2] Even disregarding the literature of fictional London, however, what remains is an unwieldy mass. One helpful system of organization appears in H J Dyos's article "The Slums of Victorian London," in which he identifies five loose categories into which Victorian works on the city could be classed.[3] The first, "reports of poor law commissioners, select committees, and royal commissions," and second, sociological studies for more general audiences, are the most dryly factual. The third category, to which Dyos assigns Mayhew's *London Labour and the London Poor,* is more colorful and humanistic, but also more superficial: "essentially a form of higher journalism, not of social analysis."[4] Similar to this, but without the reforming impulse, is the fourth category, popular journalism that simply gawks at the spectacle of poverty: "better than stark ignorance," Dyos notes, but hardly authoritative. Notably, he places James Greenwood in this category.[5] The fifth, broad category includes philanthropic- and religious-minded literature.[6]

Other authors identify reoccurring tropes and themes in street literature: the streets' kinetic quality; the feeling of being caught in the crowd; the dramatic contrasts of wealth and poverty in the London streets; assertions that Londoners know more of the inhabitants of other continents than they do of other classes within their own city. James Winter notes how frequently bodily metaphors appear in reference to the city: streets like blood vessels, for instance, or the polluted city as a diseased lung.[7] Julian Wolfreys finds repeated references to secret or hidden alleys, passages, views and even entire structures, unknown to all but the few most familiar with the vicinity, and standing in for the city's mysterious, constantly changing character.[8] In his introduction to *The Moving Pageant*, a sourcebook of London street literature, Rick Allen identifies sub-genres within the more popular literature: a "round-the-clock" genre, in which the author gives account of a specific 24- or 48-hour period in the city; or works blending "topographical documentary and comic fiction" by inventing foreign travelers or country rubes who go about the city, gawking at its wonders.[9] Allen also notes that street literature changed over time:

> *For much of the eighteenth century, writers mostly treated "low life" (an elastic term covering anything disreputable as well as of humble status) with a mixture of amusement and contempt... However, by the era of the French Revolution... the tone of writing about the poor has typically become more serious: thereafter, their condition variously invokes pity, indignation, apprehension, but, above all, a sense of responsibility on the part of the writer to leave the reader better informed about it.*[10]

This sense of responsibility persists, and by the later Victorian era most such works proclaim this desire to inform the reader as among their primary motivating factors – even when, as in the case of some of the most sensationalist street studies, the actual end is not to edify but to titillate.

I have identified a few other recurring tropes and tendencies. First, authors often assert the accuracy or authenticity of their testimonies, pointing out how natural and unaffected their portrayals are and sometimes emphasizing the superiority of their own reports over other writers' more questionable claims.[11] Direct quotations provide the most common means for authors to bolster their assertions of accuracy. Some quote informants who knew they were being interviewed, others overheard conversations. Sometimes this quoted testimony rings true, while at other times it appears rather questionable. Second, since the goal of much of this literature was reform, writers were generally unafraid to recommend actions they believed might change or alleviate their subjects' unfortunate conditions. These run the gamut from suggestions for philanthropic engagement or directed giving, to recommendations for policy changes.

Third, one might also place this literature on a scale of euphemism and/or politeness, the relative frequency with which it references unpleasant or unseemly subjects. It is possible to divine a work's intended audience based on when and how it brings up indelicate or potentially offensive subject-matter. Scientific studies, for instance, tend to use direct but dryly scientific language, particularly as it concerns issues of sanitation and the presence of untreated waste in living areas. Works aimed at broader and more "polite" audiences, by contrast, avoid references to unseemly subjects unless necessary, and then use common euphemisms, gloss over the most difficult aspects of an issue, or treat the subject with a palpable disgust mirroring the reader's anticipated reaction. Sensationalist literature swings back toward openness about vice and filth, but where scientific works are dryly factual in their confrontation of difficult subject-matter, slumming literature tends to be coy, falsely modest or even cruel in its directness.

Finally, much street literature tends to be motivated at least in part by a classificatory impulse, a desire to catalogue the various kinds of people and/or labor one might encounter in the streets. The impulse is to make the streets more legible and comprehensible to the middle-class observer. Attempts range from simple inclusion of "Flash" (street slang) dictionaries and lists of criminal types to the more complex – e.g., the entirety of Mayhew's *London Labour and the London Poor*, which purports to catalogue and classify the various forms of street labor and poverty.

In particular, one finds a tendency to foreground single figures, usually referred to as types. The Oxford English Dictionary defines "type," in part, as:

> *The general form, structure, or character distinguishing a particular kind, group, or class*

> *of beings or objects... A person or thing that exhibits the characteristic qualities of a class; a representative specimen; a typical example or instance; A person or thing that exemplifies the ideal qualities or characteristics of a kind or order; a perfect example or specimen of something; a model, pattern, exemplar.*[12]

A "type," then, is an individual – for the purposes of this study, a human being – who represents and/or serves as the very model of a particular class or group, and who embodies the characteristics associated with that group. These individuals thus become complex signifiers, at once being simply themselves and standing in for entire categories, sometimes multiple categories. The many typological studies of urban labor in the nineteenth century employed such systematization in attempts to make sense of the overwhelming variety of labor. Typological studies symbolically tame the working classes, rendering them comprehensible and manageable by dividing and subdividing them, fixing them in place.

The literature of the London streets: an overview

A brief and necessarily limited survey of street literature permits us to see some of these tropes and tendencies in action, the better to understand where *Street Life in London* might fit within them. To begin, one should understand that not all literature of the London streets focuses entirely on poverty. A case in point is Charles Dickens' *Sketches by Boz*, 1833-36. An inveterate wanderer of the streets, Dickens observed and reported in this series of essays on a wide variety of situations he encountered. Scenes of poverty and degradation appear, but they alternate with and often take a secondary role to humorous observations on modern middle-class city life. In "The Streets – Night," for example, Dickens describes a "dark, dull, murky winter's night," alternating amusing descriptions of suburban preparations for teatime with a description of the wrenching desperation one encounters on such nights:

> *That wretched woman with the infant in her arms, round whose meagre form the remnant of her own scanty shawl is carefully wrapped, has been attempting to sing some popular ballad, in the hope of wringing a few pence from the compassionate passer-by. A brutal laugh at her weak voice is all she has gained. The tears fall thick and fast down her own pale face; the child is cold and hungry, and its low half stifled wailing adds to the misery of its*

wretched mother, as she moans aloud, and sinks despairingly down on a cold damp doorstep.[13]

In another of the sketches, "Gin Shops," Dickens contrasts the opulent interiors of such shops with the terrible conditions of the neighborhoods surrounding them. Here he criticizes philanthropic temperance endeavors for trying to quash drinking without addressing the misery lying at its root, suggesting that a shift in focus would produce far better results.[14]

Nonetheless, as one scholar has noted, "the dominant attitude of 'Boz' in these sketches is one of delighted and sympathetic observation," not of social criticism.[15] While the London of the sketches is more realistic than that of his novels, the aim is still primarily to entertain, rather than to inform or reform. To that end, Dickens lightly fictionalized some vignettes by profiling types of figures one might find at a theater or in a gin-shop, assigning them names and imagining conversations between them – thus blending documentary with fiction, a trope identified by Allen as common in such literature.[16]

James Grant's *The Great Metropolis*, from 1837, provides a similarly comprehensive vision of both polite and desperate London.[17] Grant begins by describing a London social club called Almack's, progresses into a lengthy discussion of political opinions and the potential effects of universal male suffrage, then moves on to characterize the London publishing industry. A mention of the poor Irish neighborhood of St. Giles's is followed by expositions on the workings of the Bank of England, the Stock Exchange, and the Old Bailey.[18] Grant does address some difficult subject matter, particularly when he discusses Newgate prison. Though reformed considerably by the time of Grant's writing, Newgate remained notorious for corrupting rather than reforming the youths confined there. Grant states his opinion that prison will never be a place of true rehabilitation for prisoners as long as the inmates continue to associate with, and thus corrupt, one another. To remedy the issue he recommends certain policy changes, a tendency one often finds in such street literature. But overall Grant's work, like *Sketches by Boz*, exists mainly to entertain and falls roughly into the category of popular journalism.

By contrast, physician and reformer Hector Gavin's 1848 sociological study of the Bethnal Green slum district in London's East End, *Sanitary Ramblings*, combined eyewitness reportage with extensive statistics.[19] Gavin "rambled" into seemingly every street, warren and court in the district, reporting in unvarnished language on what he saw and augmenting his assertions, where possible, with statistics. Already in 1848 one of the city's most depressed areas, Bethnal Green gave rise to epidemics, had notoriously high death-rates, and boasted extraordinary accumulations of filth. Pigs were still kept in some courts; houses alternated with dairies, stables and lead-works; and there were no controls in place for water contamination or the positioning of wells and pumps relative to cesspools and privies. In relating such conditions, Gavin resorts to euphemism or elision only rarely. His text makes open reference to manure, cesspools, and other accumulations of effluvia. More than once he refers to "night soil," or human waste, and more than once he admits to being overpowered by nausea.[20] In one passage, he criticizes the presence of graveyards in residential areas, noting that graves were often opened and used repeatedly as repositories for multiple bodies, resulting in an overpowering stench of decomposition.[21]

But Gavin uses unvarnished language in the interest of accuracy, not salaciousness. He directs his attention almost solely at the conditions of the edifices, roadways and open spaces of Bethnal Green, mentioning the inhabitants of the neighborhood only to relate the physical effects of their environs on their health. Though he clearly sympathizes with their misery, he expresses no interest in their personal lives or their morals, as so many urban reformers might have. His lack of euphemism and strict focus on the built environment virtually guaranteed that interest in his work would come largely from serious sanitary reformers, engineers, and governmental entities with an interest in sponsoring urban improvement projects, rather than from moralizing philanthropists or common gawkers.

Another publication from the same year, 1848, presents a very different vision of London's "low life." *The Sinks of London Laid Open*, by an anonymous author and incorporating a few images by famed illustrator George Cruickshank, is more populist than Gavin's *Sanitary Ramblings*, but simultaneously more sensationalist, more interested in "character and crime."[22] In addition to its text, the book includes a dictionary of "flash," or street slang, terms, and "a list of the sixty orders of prime coves."[23] The list includes no explanation, just a litany of enigmatic terms: "cloak twitchers," "ginglers," "lully priggers," and "bloods," among others. It serves to establish the anonymous author's credentials, but does not perform any useful, informative function.[24]

The bulk of the text is given over to an account

of the anonymous author's 24-hour sojourn in a low lodging-house, where he seems to have spent most of the time watching the inhabitants drink in the common room. He quotes extensively from conversations he overheard. These conversations, most concerning criminal activities or peppered with bawdy remarks, reflect badly on their participants and by extension on the poor as a whole. The quotes seem, however, to come from subjects who clearly did not know anyone was listening. This prompts one to wonder how the author recorded them in the first place, if he had no notebook in hand. Thus the accuracy of these quotes, and by extension the accuracy of the author's entire damning testimony on the character of the poor, comes into question.[25]

Overall the text is chatty and anecdotal. The author makes coy, pseudo-euphemistic references to sensational topics, exhibiting the pretense of sparing his audience's sensibilities while in fact titillating them. In addition, the work actively buys into typological notions that one could read a man's character in his face, and that physiognomy was destiny. One character, the author asserts, has "a countenance by far too dark and sinister-looking to be honest." Another has a "villainous" head and is "the very type of a hedge-ruffian... The very sight of this model of his tribe brought vagrancy, with all her train, before our eyes, mugger's carts, tinker's wives, bull-dogs, donkeys, creels, kail pots, and all the trumpery of a gipsey's [*sic*] camp."[26]

Throughout, the author makes obvious his disdain for the figures he encounters. All of them seem dangerous, or cunning, or beyond the reach of assistance, and he openly mocks them for it. He calls one woman "a happy compound between the slut and the sot."[27] Overall, he makes it seem as though the poor have arrived at poverty of their own volition. At the same time, he implies, they do not really have it that bad: as far as he could tell, all the "cadgers" had butter and good coffee at meals.[28]

With its "flash dictionary" and its "list of the sixty orders of prime coves," the book seems designed as a kind of guide to the London underworld; but the author describes such repugnant society that one wonders who would desire to keep it after reading this book. The book, then, has no value other than as entertainment. In Dyos's scheme, it would fall into the category of popular sensationalism. It exhibits a number of characteristics often found in works of street literature: a "round-the-clock" vision given from an outsider's point of view; repeated proclamations of its own unvarnished veracity. "[T]he cadging house," the author writes, "is the very spot for the pourtrayer [*sic*] of life, who wishes to lay claim to anything like originality; here Nature has her full scope, and affectation rarely shows her face."[29]

Here, then, we have a sense of the range of such literature: scientific reform like Gavin's study at one end, vulgar entertainment like *The Sinks of London Laid Open* at the other, a wide variety of popular-journalistic endeavors in between. Myriad other street-studies fall somewhere within this spectrum, some largely hewing to the patterns exhibited by these examples, others deviating from them to a greater or lesser extent. Henry Mayhew's *London Labour and the London Poor* is in some ways the very model of a popular-journalistic study.[30] But the enormity of its scope also demanded of it a degree of flexibility not present in briefer street-literature endeavors.

A journalist, playwright and satirist, Mayhew began his endeavors to profile poverty in the London streets in 1849. Originally his essays appeared in the London *Morning Chronicle;* later he collected, expanded and reworked them into a series of pamphlets, and finally into a massive, minutely-printed four-volume series, published in 1861-62.[31] Assisted by his brother Augustus and others, Mayhew interviewed hundreds of informants in every imaginable profession and/or condition, from well-fed and well-paid skilled laborers to desperate homeless people, prostitutes and professional pickpockets.[32] He gathered information on the nature of their work, its profitability and its stability, and on their living, familial and social conditions.

The work attempts, in effect, to catalogue the poor of London. Volume I profiles street-sellers of a wide variety of items: groceries, prepared foods, drinks, household goods, books and stationery, art, and so forth. Chapter 13, for instance, focuses on "Street-sellers of Manufactured Articles," with several dozen sub-sections on sellers of rat-poison, blacking, matches, fly-papers, corn-salve, walking-sticks, and more. Volume II includes more discussion of street-sellers, including sellers of live animals; it also profiles buyers and finders, street performers and other laborers. Volume III first examines "destroyers of vermin," then a variety of entertainment-related professions including clowning, music-playing, and photography, then labor on the Thames, and finally vagrancy. Volume IV or the "extra volume" profiles, as Mayhew wrote on the title page, "Those That Will Not Work. Comprising. Prostitutes. Swindlers. Thieves. Beggars."

Throughout, information comes in a variety of formats. Mayhew's own reporting often alternates with extensive, often pages-long, quotes from informants. He bolsters his assertions with statistics, often in the form of tables or charts. He quotes or references other authorities. And all four volumes are illustrated with images, which appear every twenty pages or so. Overall, the reader staggers under the sheer weight of information in Mayhew's study. Page 131 of Volume I, to give just one example, bears a "Table showing the quantity of trees, shrubs, flowers, roots, and branches sold annually, wholesale, at the metropolitan markets, and the proportion retailed in the streets." It relates, for several dozen types of shrubs, potted plants, roots and cut flowers, the proportion sold to retailers in Covent Garden and Farringdon versus to costermongers for resale in the streets.[33] There are many more such tables throughout the four volumes. He provides history lessons, too, and information about a wide variety of professions. In Volume III, for instance, he gives a lesson on the background of Guy Fawkes Day parades. Later in the same volume he interviews a series of photographers who provide fascinating details of how the business was practiced in the 1850s.[34] Mayhew's own racial prejudices certainly appear, and he makes no secret of his revulsion at common practices among the poor like their tendency to live together while unmarried. At the same time, the texture and the particularity of his reports testify to a general sense of trustworthiness in his narratives.

His extensive passages of quotation provide a good illustration of how these qualities coexist. Mayhew clearly compiled the quotations from interviews he conducted, omitting his interventions and questions but transcribing the answers they prompted. For instance, one scavenger in a dust-yard – a garbage dump – discusses a brief period during which he was apprenticed to make (presumably ceramic) pots for honey:

> *...I was sent to help at and larn [sic] honey-pot and other pot making, at Deptford; but honey-pots was a great thing in the business. Master's foreman married a relation of mine, some way or other. I never tasted honey, but I've heered [sic] it's like sugar and butter mixed. The pots was often wanted to look like foreign pots; I don't know nothing what was meant by it; some b------ dodge or other. No, the trade didn't suit me at all, master, so I left. I don't know why it didn't suit me; cause it didn't.*[35]

Mayhew obviously asked the boy a series of questions: Had he ever had honey? Why did they make the pots foreign-looking? Did the trade suit him? Why not? As throughout Mayhew's study, the questions themselves do not appear. Mayhew acts as interlocutor, then writes himself out of the picture.

We also find Mayhew doing in this passage something he does throughout the study, transcribing not only the words but the grammar, the accent, and any patois the informant used. One wonders at times about the accuracy of these reports: how would he have transcribed an accent, for instance? If he took reports in shorthand, which he probably did, was it possible to be completely accurate? And yet the variation among informants, the distinctions between their voices, testifies that the quotations were accurate to at least some extent.[36] In Volume III the reader encounters back-to-back interviews of two Italian street-performers, a clarinet-player and a monkey-trainer. Mayhew transcribes their words and conveys a sense of their accented English, but the monkey-trainer's language is so much less polished than the clarinet-player, so much more heavily accented, that one gets a sense Mayhew was drawing not on stereotype but on reality for these reports.[37]

Mayhew's study incorporates many of the tropes common to such literature. He begins, for instance, with a meditation on the anthropology of nomadism, contending that England's tribes of beggars, outcasts and vagabonds are to the British as the nomadic tribes of Africa and Asia are to their host nations:

> *It is curious that no one has as yet applied the above facts to the explanation of certain anomalies in the present state of society among ourselves. That we, like the Kafirs, Fellahs, and Finns, are surrounded by wandering hordes... paupers, beggars, and outcasts, possessing nothing but what they acquire by depredation from the industrious, provident, and civilized portion of the community; – that the heads of these nomades are remarkable for the greater development of the jaws and cheekbones rather than those of the head; –and that they have a secret language of their own – an English "cuze-cat" or "slang" as it is called – for the concealment of their designs: these are points of coincidence so striking that, when placed before the mind, make us marvel that the analogy should have remained thus long unnoticed.*[38]

Mayhew thus employs the common tendency to draw parallels between conditions among the poor in England and conditions for ethnic others in far-flung places. Although the trope does not persist throughout Mayhew's study – indeed, he is more likely to draw distinctions, rather than parallels, between native English paupers and foreigners in London's streets – its presence here at the start of the study imparts a pseudo-anthropological flavor to Mayhew's entire undertaking.

Perhaps more than any other author we have discussed so far, Mayhew openly encouraged his readers' philanthropic endeavors and proposed policy reforms where he saw a need for them. Profiles of needy individuals in his columns frequently brought them relief in the form of directed donations, whether Mayhew had called for these or not. Of more long-term impact were his overviews of entire corrupt or broken work systems, for which he frequently suggested necessary changes. In Volume II, during a lengthy discussion of the business of rubbish-disposal, he devotes a section to the problems of casual labor, which he felt engendered feelings of disconnectedness from one's work. Various work systems fell under this heading, including the "middleman" or "sweating" systems of labor, in which piecework was done not by employees of a factory or other controlled work environment but by contractors working out of their own homes or small, unregulated workshops, often in terrible conditions. His deep criticisms of such systems come alongside suggestions for official inquiry and reform.[39] Similarly, during his explication of the omnibus- and cab-driving professions and their various problems, he devotes an entire section to suggestions for regulation of the cab-driving trade.[40]

One way in which Mayhew deviates rather dramatically from the standard for popular-journalistic works is in his tendency to confront, usually head-on, the more unpleasant aspects of street life. Indeed, given his study's aspirations to comprehensiveness, he could hardly have done otherwise: too many street professions dealt, either directly or indirectly, in dirt, filth, vice and decay. To give just one example, the transport, sorting and disposal of trash, sewage and other waste in London employed thousands of people, so in discussing these professions he had of course to confront directly the nature of their work. He delineates at various points the specific substances contained within a dust-heap; the constitution and texture of the mud scraped away from various types of road surface; the gross weight of horse- and cattle-dung deposited in the streets of London; and the estimated amount, in both weight and gallons, of "wet house-refuse," i.e. sewage and slaughterhouse waste, produced in the London metropolitan area.[41] His language is decidedly not euphemistic. In another place, while describing the use of meat from dead horses, he notes that one use for horsemeat was as a breeding medium for maggots, to be used as chicken-feed.[42] Although he frequently quotes other authorities as sources for these findings, giving his account the authenticity of a scientific study, he nonetheless confronts over and over again throughout the four volumes subject-matter that his polite audience might have found difficult to stomach.[43]

This consistent willingness to confront all the realities of poverty is, in the end, what raises Mayhew's study above other pseudo-journalistic undertakings. He approached poverty systematically, rather than as a series of colorful vignettes. As such, writes scholar Eileen Yeo, "Mayhew completely transcended the London low life genre."[44] Yeo notes that Mayhew certainly aimed to classify the poor. At the same time, he willingly adjusted his classification system to suit his findings as he progressed.[45] Still, the pressures of publication took a toll on the project overall: "The relentless schedule of... deadlines virtually forced [Mayhew] to publish his notebooks as he went," generating a more organic, less systematic treatment of the subject than Mayhew himself desired.[46] Nonetheless, he confronted in a manner not previously found in low-life sketches the true variety of street life. While he did profile the standard picturesque street figures, he devoted ample space as well to the streets' more difficult problems and, most notably, to a variety of mundane trades, less interesting than street selling but ultimately more representative of the conditions of the laboring classes overall.

Perhaps the manner in which Mayhew's study most clearly fails to rise to the occasion of modernity is in its use of illustrations. The four volumes incorporate several dozen illustrations in total, all of them wood-engravings done after sketches or photographs. In comparison with the sheer weight of text, the illustrations provide relatively little information and constitute only a small portion of the overall content of the books. But because each image occupies a full page, and because they provide a sometimes-refreshing break from the closely-printed text, they make a strong impression on the reader. Some of them incorporate only a title, others have a notation beneath the title, usually given in square brackets: "From a Sketch," "From a Photograph," or sometimes "From a Photograph by Beard." The last notation refers to the famed London photographer Richard Beard, the first and for a long time the only person in England to have a patent to practice daguerreotypy and thus the first well-known English society portraitist.[47]

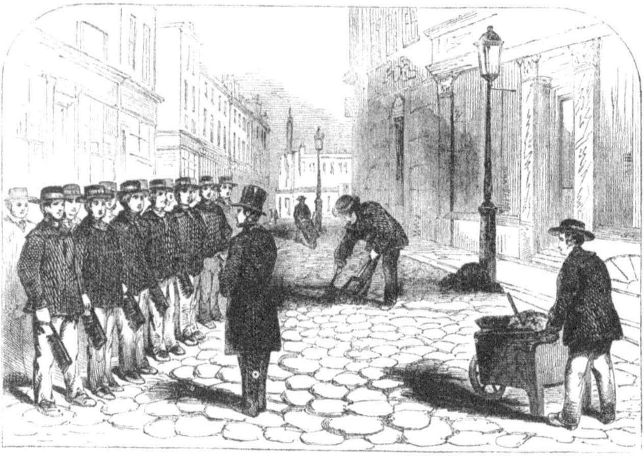

STREET ORDERLIES.

FIG 4.1: *Street Orderlies*, from Henry Mayhew, *London Labour and the London Poor*, Vol. 2 (London: Griffin, Bohn, 1861), 226-27. Private collection.

Images without a notation presumably draw on the printmaker's own imagining of the scene.

The images in Mayhew's study by and large appear quite retrograde, being generally static and providing little of the complexity conveyed by the texts. They tend to revert, in general, to the standards of traditional typological imagery, rather than partaking of the multivalent vision of labor Mayhew provides in his written accounts. Images conceived from the artist's imagination collapse various stages or postures involved in a particular type of labor into one scene, a standard technique for rendering a comprehensive vision of one's subject-matter. In *Street Orderlies* (Figure 4.1), for example, we see a scene of the orderlies (employees of charitable organizations that provided work for otherwise-unemployed men) standing at attention before an overseer, while others around them demonstrate the various attitudes taken by a street-sweeper while at work.

But even in images derived from photographs, pictorial convention comes into play. For Beard's camera the figures pretended to labor, not in their accustomed locales but almost certainly in Beard's studio. Each posed in such a manner as to make the nature of the work and the tools of his or her trade clearly visible in the image, just like a traditional

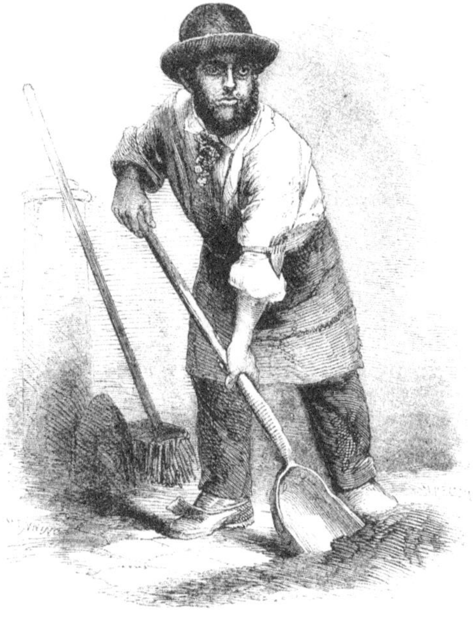

THE LONDON SCAVENGER.

[From a Daguerreotype by Beard.]

FIG 4.2: *The London Scavenger*, from Henry Mayhew, *London Labour and the London Poor*, Vol. 2 (London: Griffin, Bohn, 1861), 226-27. Private collection.

street type. Then the printmaker drew on, but did not precisely copy, the photographic images, instead vignetting the central figure against an anonymous street-like setting, littered here and there with some of the tools the subject might use in his trade. Beard's *London Scavenger* (Figure 4.2) poses with shovel in hand, looking at the viewer while pretending to go about his work. The printmaker sketches in a broom and post behind the scavenger and cobblestones under his feet, giving the impression that he stands in a city street rather than in Beard's photography studio. Certainly there is no way Beard could have photographed in the darkness of a sewer; so *The Sewer-Hunter* (Figure 4.3) too must have posed in the studio and not in his accustomed environs.

Overall, the images convey a sense of a static London. The vignetting employed in many images, and the white of the page around each picture, convey a sense that the Londoners labor in a void, disconnected from the city around them. The images give a very different impression from the text, which tends to be driven throughout by a sense of interconnectedness drawn from Mayhew's willingness to follow where his informants led him as they guided him through their lives. Follow a chimney-sweep in Mayhew's text and you may be taken into a discourse

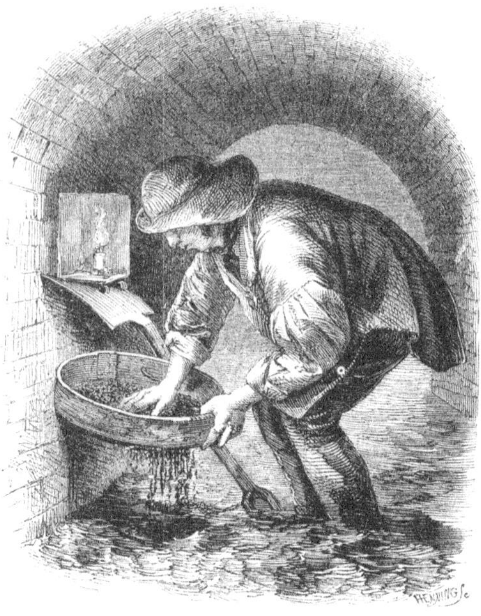

THE SEWER-HUNTER.

[From a Daguerreotype by BEARD.]

FIG 4.3: *The Sewer-Hunter*, from Henry Mayhew, *London Labour and the London Poor*, Vol. 2 (London: Griffin, Bohn, 1861), 388-89. Private collection.

on the evils of alcoholism or a discussion of May-Day festivities. Sweeps in the book's images, however, appear to be going nowhere in particular, stuck in the eternal present.

In some ways, journalist James Greenwood's work resembles Mayhew's. Certainly Greenwood was, as scholars have acknowledged, a member of the post-Mayhew generation of social investigators.[48] He fervently believed, as did Mayhew, in the need for overarching social and legal reform, not only for charitable solutions to the problems of poverty. But more than Mayhew, Greenwood aimed for journalistic vividness, rather than scientific accuracy. He preferred "searching out the interesting, the colorful and curious, thieves' slang and beggars' dodges, human interest stories and lively anecdotes."[49] And where Mayhew aimed for comprehensiveness, Greenwood provided quick-and-dirty exposés or broad overviews. His most sensational publication, and the one that generated the most commentary, was "A Night in a Workhouse," a series of articles and later a pamphlet originating from a night Greenwood spent, in disguise, in Lambeth workhouse in 1866.[50] In comparison with Mayhew's four-volume *London Labour*, Greenwood's longest studies amounted to one volume each. And where Mayhew profiled everything he encountered, good and bad, sensational and mundane, Greenwood focused his attentions only on the bad. The night he spent in the workhouse was, as one might imagine, not a particularly pleasant one. Likewise, in 1869 he titled his first book on working life in London *The Seven Curses of London*, aiming to delineate specifically the problems faced by the poor. His books of the 1870s – including *In Strange Company* (1873), *The Wilds of London* (1874), and *Low-Life Deeps* (1876) – continue this trend.[51]

Just one of Greenwood's publications, *The Seven Curses of London* (1869), aims to systematize in any way the examination of poverty. Like Mayhew he provides a system of classification, but unlike Mayhew's semi-taxonomic system Greenwood's delineates in seven categories the "curses" that perpetuate poverty in London: I. Neglected Children; II. Professional Thieves; III. Professional Beggars; IV. Fallen Women; V. The Curse of Drunkenness; VI. Betting Gamblers; VII. The Waste of Charity.[52] Each section, divided into subchapters, discusses specific outrages perpetrated on or by the poor of London. The system originates in and satisfies Greenwood's own aims, rather than arising in some measure out of an inherent logic in street labor itself.

Certainly on a continuum of attitudes toward

poverty, with extreme sympathy at one end and a belief in the innate degeneracy of the poor at the other, Greenwood's would fall toward the sympathetic end. Like Mayhew he searches for the root causes of social ills, often finding them not in poverty itself but in systems of unjust or unfair labor compensation, exploitation, and public indifference to which the poor are subject. But unlike Mayhew's relatively measured reporting, Greenwood's overall tone tends toward constant indignation if not total outrage. In the first chapter of *Seven Curses*, "Neglected Children," he devotes a section to "baby farming," the practice of wet-nursing or temporarily adopting children for a fee, an unregulated profession rife with horrors: for instance, so-called baby-farmers had been known to kill children when the money allotted for their keep ran out. Discussing public reaction to one such murder trial, he condemns the middle class for caring about the subject only when bombarded by public revelations in the newspapers:

> *It was only while our tender feelings were suffering excruciation from the harrowing story of baby torture that we shook in wrath against the torturer. Considering what our sufferings were (and from the manner of our crying out they must have been truly*

> *awful) we recovered with a speed little short of the miraculous. Barely was the trial of the murderess concluded and the court cleared, than our fierce indignation subsided from its bubbling and boiling, and quickly settled down to calm and ordinary temperature.*[53]

Londoners could summon up anger over the horror of a child murder already committed, he implies, but they could not sustain the effort necessary to solve the problems that led to the neglect of children in the first place. The tone of indignation and the sarcasm fairly characterize Greenwood's writing. Overall, although he condemns Londoners for their susceptibility to the sensational, his books themselves seethe with sensationalistic righteous outrage.

He dedicated himself to alleviating the conditions he profiled, but his descriptions often drip with titillating condescension, resembling far more the language of low-life slumming than of scientific social investigation. In a passage in *The Wilds of London*, he derides the notion that, for a sailor, seeing a prostitute constituted a pleasant diversion from his otherwise-dangerous job. "Pleasure!" he writes. "Perilous indeed must be the ordinary occupation of the man who can find delight and relaxation in being bullied and contemptuously treated by a brawny-armed, big-knuckled wretch, whose breath is pestilence and her language poison."[54] Although his purpose in investigating the "hunting grounds" of the women he called "tigresses" was to examine and expose conditions in the prostitutes' district of London, his account of their degradation does not seem calculated to garner sympathy for them but rather to satisfy audiences' desire for scandal.[55]

Greenwood was not over-fond of quoting directly from his informants. Quotations come from other authors, and occasionally he imagines what a vagrant or child-thief or some other such figure *might* say, if given the freedom to speak.[56]

The exception is his first major contribution to the literature, *A Night in a Workhouse*, throughout which he reports on conversations in which he participated and those he overheard. But from the start one wonders how, if at all, he was able to write down his reports, given that the first thing he does on reaching the workhouse is have a bath and relinquish his clothing for the night, being left only with a workhouse-issued nightshirt. Exchanges such as this, in which Greenwood gives half his allotted bread to a young boy nearby, he presumably reproduced from memory:

> *"Did you 'ear that, Punch?" one of them asked.*
>
> *"'Ear what?" answered Punch, sleepy and snappish.*
>
> *"Why, a cove forgot his toke! Gordstruth! you wouldn't ketch me a forgettin mine."*
>
> *"You may have half of it, old pal, if you're hungry." I observed, leaning up on my elbows.*
>
> *"Chuck it here, good luck to yer!" replied my young friend, starting up with an eager clap of his dirty hands.*
>
> *I "chucked it here," and, slipping the other half under the side of my bed, lay my head on my folded arms.*[57]

A Night in a Workhouse continues this way throughout, snippets of conversation alternating with Greenwood's own observations on his miserable night. Greenwood having no resources with which to note his observations, the "quoted" nature of this and other language must be regarded as, fundamentally, a fiction. Indeed, Greenwood continued to refer to his experience, and to "quote" from it, in his later works as well, so the fiction persisted even into his later and more straightforwardly journalistic writings.[58]

A Night in a Workhouse obviously partakes of the "day-in-the-life" trope present in some of this literature, although Greenwood's other works do not.

Greenwood also displays other common tendencies, like comparisons of his own activities to anthropological or even zoological observation. Remarking on how frequently the men got up during the night to drink, Greenwood notes that his bed was near the water-pail, a vantage point that afforded him "peculiar opportunities of study as one after another of my comrades came to the fountain to drink; just as the brutes do in those books of African travel."[59] Likewise, in *A Night in a Workhouse* and other pieces, Greenwood consciously positions himself as an outsider, looking in – or rather, looking from the inside, since he was often in disguise – at the spectacle of poverty.[60]

Despite his sensationalism, Greenwood was decidedly euphemistic – even squeamish – in his treatment of unseemly subject-matter. "When discussing street children, for instance," observes Jeffrey Richards, "he never once alludes to their 'extraordinary licentiousness' and 'unnatural precocity' as noted by Henry Mayhew."[61] Although he devotes a chapter of *Seven Curses* to prostitution, he makes clear his own reluctance in treating the subject and his intention to avoid addressing the most indelicate aspects of it: "[T]he writer hastens to confess... that it is not his intention to expose this terrible canker that preys on the heart and vitals of society in all its plain and bare repulsiveness."[62]

He essentially averts his eyes; most of his chapter consists of quotes from other social investigators. In "A Visit to 'Tiger Bay,'" one of his newspaper columns later collected in *The Wilds of London*, he openly shudders to think that in order to observe prostitutes' behavior with their clients he might have to go into their "dens." He is much happier to find that he can see them in the act of seduction, prior to the final "picking and plucking" of the "game," at one of the nearby pubs.[63] Other indelicacies of poverty, too, receive only glancing, and often shuddering, mention: lice become "certain little animals which shall be nameless," for instance.[64] Greenwood, unlike Mayhew, has no rotting horseflesh, no maggot breeding, no scientific breakdown of the constitution of "dust."

Smith and Thomson do not mention the last work of social investigation profiled here, but it was just as powerful a precursor to *Street Life in London* as the works of Mayhew and Greenwood. *London: A Pilgrimage* appeared in 1872, with text by Smith's father-in-law Blanchard Jerrold and images by the great French illustrator Gustave Doré. Like *Street Life*, the 1872 work incorporated images not as subsidiary illustrations but as a vital aspect of the content, more important even than the text. Text and image occupy the same pages, Doré's pictures appearing in a variety of sizes alongside text that sometimes, but not always, relates. Text generally does not caption the image; rather the text and image address the same subject-matter in two forms. In format at least, *London: A Pilgrimage* can claim perhaps the most direct relationship with *Street Life in London*.

London: A Pilgrimage takes an approach rather more like Dickens' *Sketches by Boz* or James Grant's works than like the social investigation of Gavin, Mayhew or Greenwood, addressing both rich and poor London rather than focusing exclusively on the lower classes. The authors admitted from the outset the difficulty of such comprehensiveness: "It is impossible," wrote Jerrold in the Preface, "to put a world in a nutshell. To the best of our judgment we have selected the most striking types, the most completely representative scenes, and the most picturesque features..."[65] Doré's illustrations do indeed include fully realized scenes of city streets and other locations populated with a variety of figures, as well as traditional street types.

Jerrold indicates that he and Doré wandered through the city together, Doré with sketchbook and Jerrold with notebook, and that to some extent he acted as Doré's guide, Doré choosing the locations they visited on any given day.[66] As such, although the images and text seem to have a kind of equal

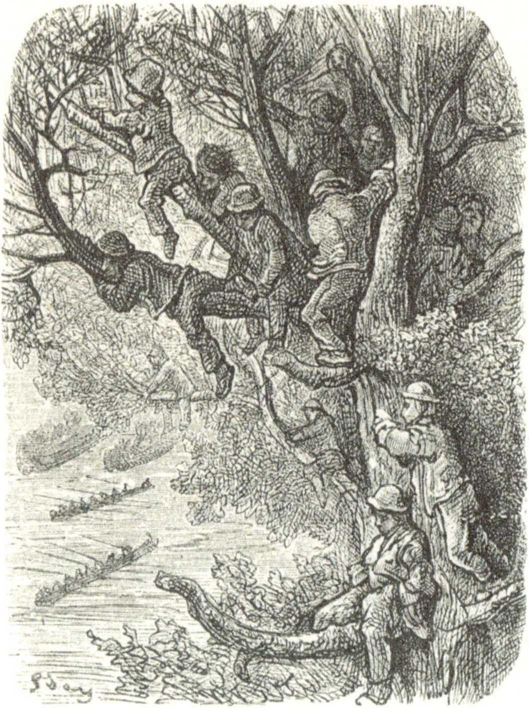

FIG 4.4: Gustave Doré, *Perched in the Trees*, from *London: A Pilgrimage* (London: Grant and Co., 1872), 50. Collection of Iowa State University Library.

weight, Doré's images ultimately take precedence over Jerrold's writing. The two wandered methodically, to some extent, or at least present their wanderings in a methodical order: the book begins with London Bridge, then gradually moves up and away from the river.

Scenes of poverty are concentrated by and large in the final sections of the book, as the two authors make their way east toward and through Whitechapel. Prior to these final sections, the poor do appear here and there, but in a relatively picturesque, decontextualized manner. At the boat-races, poor children crowd into trees along the water (Figure 4.4), and flower-selling Irishwomen do brisk business with spectators.[67] Jerrold presents a well-known fly-paper vendor in writing as a living relic and a nostalgic reminder of the past glory of Piccadilly, while Doré depicts him nostalgically too, as a street-type (Figure 4.5).[68] Only with Chapter XIV, "Work-a-Day London," do Jerrold and Doré begin to focus in a sustained manner on the city's laborers.

Both Doré and Jerrold take a sympathetic view of labor and poverty, overall. Indeed, Jerrold puts the continued forward movement of London as an industrial center squarely on their shoulders:

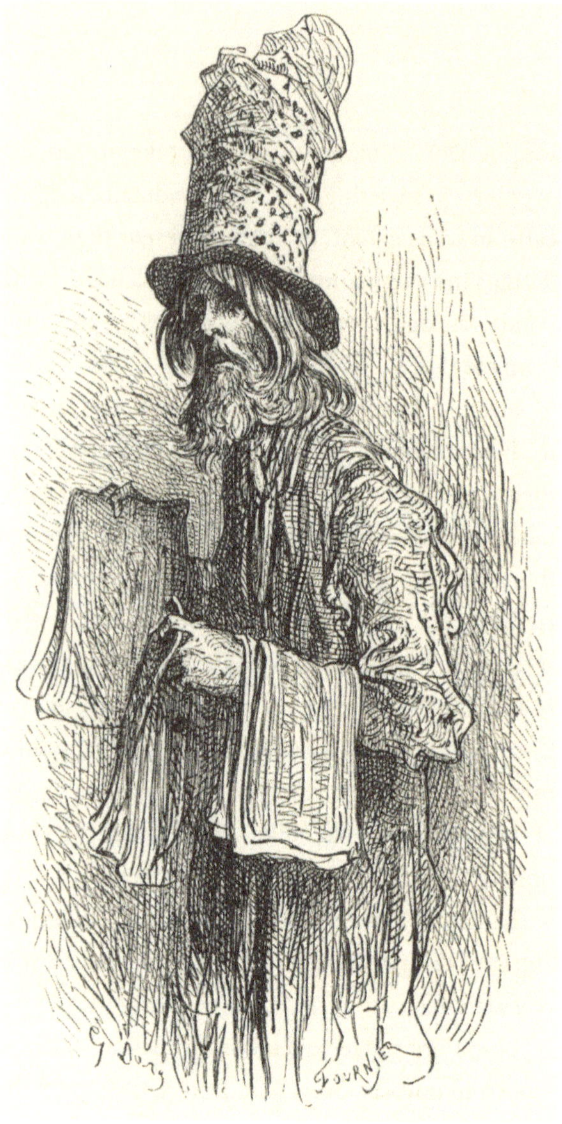

FIG 4.5: Gustave Doré, *The Fly Paper Merchant*, from *London: A Pilgrimage* (London: Grant and Co., 1872), 84. Collection of Iowa State University Library.

> *[The early risers] are the vanguard of the army of Labour, who are to carry forward the marvelous story of London industry another step before sundown: to add a new story to a new terrace; the cornerstone to another building; bulwarks to another frigate; another station to another railway; and tons upon tons of produce from every clime, to the mighty stock that is for ever packed along the shores of the Thames.*[69]

He treats the Irish flower-girls with sympathy, too. He contrasts them with another flower-seller, a Frenchwoman whom he describes as "the bold, daintily attired damsel who decorated the button-holes of the Paris Jockey Club under the Empire," before noting the London flower girls' moral superiority to this degraded counterpoint.[70] His mention of the French flower-seller is particularly notable because Adolphe Smith later makes the identical comparison in a *Street Life in London* entry titled *Covent Garden Flower Women*, expounding at greater length on the Covent women's honesty in comparison with "Isabelle," the Jockey Club's flower-seller. Smith clearly had read, and admired, his father-in-law's work.

In *London: A Pilgrimage* both Doré and Jerrold only observe, by and large. They rarely speak to the people they profile, and most of their subjects appear more typical than individual. There are a few exceptions – a maker of cardboard railway carriages for children, "an intelligent New Cut dealer" of vegetables who laments how necessities get more expensive every year while luxuries like ginger-beer and penny ices get cheaper.[71] Overall, however, Doré and Jerrold treat the poor as objects for observation, even as they advocate for "education on the spot" in the streets as the best way to understand the problems and the nature of poverty.[72] Jerrold quotes from literature more frequently than from any other source; second to that he quotes the policemen who guide him through the slums.[73] The poor themselves tell little, if any, of their own story.

Jerrold does, unlike some other social investigators, give account of how his and Doré's own intrusions into the slums altered the environs: how they were observed by the poor, how the policemen carefully guarded them, how the denizens of the slums recognized and were recognized by the officers. He notes that they could not have gone in unguarded. At one point he recounts how he and Doré accompanied the police to an arrest in a public-house. When their group arrived, the entire bar fell silent and the music stopped. In another place they were assailed by demands for money for gin, "not so much because they had any hope that their prayer would be granted, as humoring a savage rebellious spirit that stirred in them to mock at us for lamenting their woe-begone condition."[74] Jerrold and Doré do not give the poor much opportunity to speak for themselves, and they were not interested, as Mayhew was, in a systematic description of poverty and laboring life in all its forms. Still, *London: A Pilgrimage* does acknowledge to some extent the effects of social observation on those who are observed.

Because the book was calculated to reach a polite audience, and to appeal to its readers with picturesque and sentimental renderings of London, Doré and Jerrold largely avoid indelicate subject-matter. They gesture at poverty's injustices and depict the destitute as ragged and desperate, but they do not discuss in any meaningful way the issues of prostitution, the precise nature of the "filth" they see in streets and back-courts, or the content of the rough language they encounter. Certainly in both text and image Jerrold and Doré demonstrate tremendous sympathy, but their depictions are ultimately just that, sympathetic rather than specific. Doré's illustrations, in particular, turn the hard scenes he encountered into a series of vignettes. Those illustrations that do not draw on the street type for inspiration refer instead

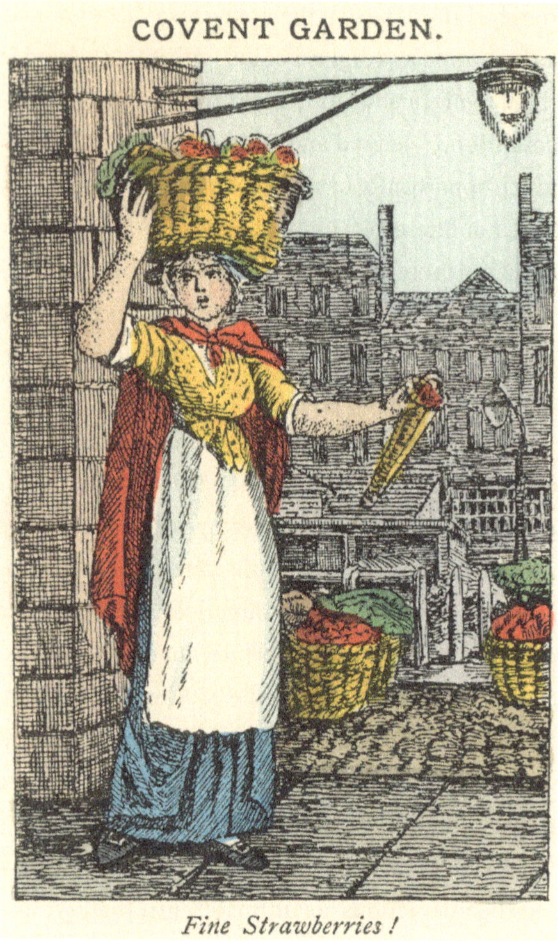

FIG 4.6: After W.M. Craig, *Fine Strawberries!* 1805. Reprinted in Andrew White Tuer, *London Cries with Six Charming Children*… (London: Field and Tuer, [1883]), 28. Collection of Iowa State University Library.

to the venerable tradition of genre painting, with its broad pathos and dependence on narrative legibility.

Visual typology

Combining text and image, Doré and Jerrold's work is *Street Life in London's* nearest progenitor. Having examined the standards and tropes common in literature of the London streets, I turn now to a similar overview of images concentrating on the same subject-matter. Doré and Jerrold's *London: A Pilgrimage*, like Mayhew's *London Labour and the London Poor* before it, drew on a centuries-old tradition of typological depictions of the poor. Perhaps the most venerable form of such typological representation was the "street cry." These prints depicted street merchants and other characters shouting out their presence and advertising their goods or services for sale. Their cries appear as captions within or below the images, often transcribed phonetically to reproduce the seller's accent or street patois (Figures 4.6, 4.7). Such images were predicated on the notion that exterior markers such as physiognomy and clothing served as indices of the character of the individual and, by extension, of the group being represented. In a collection of street types, figures tend to be isolated against neutral backgrounds, either completely white backdrops or

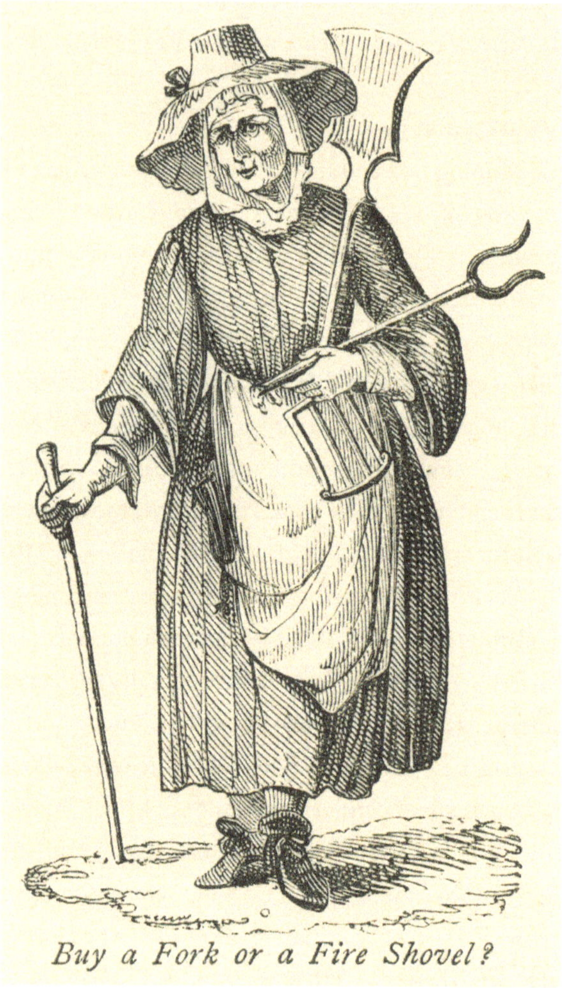

FIG 4.7: After Marcellus Laroon, *Buy a Fork or a Fire Shovel?* 1687. Reprinted in Andrew White Tuer, *London Cries with Six Charming Children…* (London: Field and Tuer, [1883]), 4. Collection of Iowa State University Library.

anonymous urban settings. Viewers desired clarity, above all: figures should stand facing the viewer or in profile, and the tools of their particular trade, if any, should be easily visible.

Collections of such prints began to appear in France in the early sixteenth century, quickly becoming popular throughout Europe and persisting as a recognizable visual form into the nineteenth century. As Sean Shesgreen writes in *Images of the Outcast*, his excellent study of the London "street cries" tradition, wealthy print collectors prized such images of the poor even as they rejected the actual people represented in such imagery. The prints served as a form of entertainment and they satisfied buyers' curiosity about the dark realities of poverty; but, Shesgreen notes, they also "aestheticize[d], regulate[d] and order[ed] on paper the collective lives of city streets with their burgeoning commerce and carnivalesque turmoil," rendering poverty more comprehensible by erasing its chaotic, unpredictable and even its potentially-rebellious aspects.[75]

At least at first, Shesgreen writes, street cries and other street types were fairly straightforward. After the late eighteenth century they frequently took on satirical undertones or some degree of innuendo (see, for example, Figure 4.8).[76] By the late 1840s the

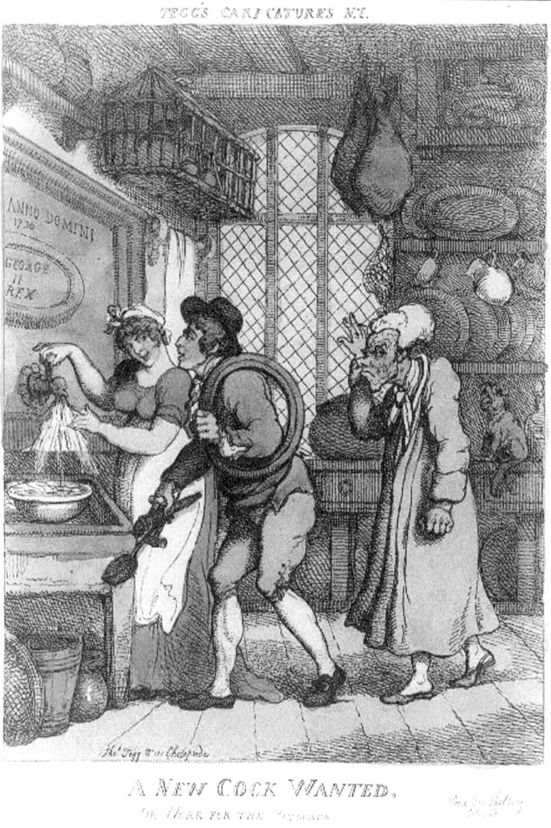

FIG 4.8: Thomas Rowlandson, *A New Cock Wanted*, from the *Tegg's Caricatures* series. London: Thomas Tegg, 1810. British Cartoon Prints Collection, Prints and Photographs Division, Library of Congress, LC-USZ62-22413.

form had nearly run its course.[77] When street laborers appeared in illustrations for Mayhew's study, isolated against sketched-in backdrops, the images were deliberately retrograde. By the time of *Street Life in London*, in 1877, any evocation of the form – particularly if the street-figure's characteristic cry were reproduced alongside the image – was self-consciously nostalgic.

Photography, though it appeared in 1839, did not offer viable alternatives for depicting the poor until several decades later. Lengthy exposure times demanded static poses, so early photographs of street laborers partook to some extent of the same pictorial language as street cries, or of the broadly sentimental genre scenes beloved by Victorians. Indeed, early "street" photography took inspiration from art more than from life: one well-known image, Oscar Rejlander's *Poor Jo*, 1860, is named after a character from Dickens's *Bleak House*, and depicts not an actual crossing-sweeper but a studio model.[78]

But even such constructed street photographs were not particularly common. Into the 1870s, when the photographic press wrote of "street photography," it meant photographs of buildings and city streets, pursued as part of an overarching interest in antiquarianism – not photographs of people. Indeed, one article reassured photographers that if they proceeded carefully, no human figures would appear in the image:

> *Where for any special purpose great delicacy of detail is desired, a small stop is necessary then, of course, instantaneous exposures are impossible, and the best plan is to expose and let the pedestrians pass by. They will scarcely perceptibly show in the picture, though if a white-bloused workman should come within the field of view it would be well to cap the lens till he had gone by.*[79]

The idea that one might go out into the city and photograph the people one encountered there remained an unusual one, even into photography's third and fourth decades of existence.

A few famous exceptions do exist. D O Hill and Robert Adamson photographed Newhaven fishermen and fishwives in the mid-1840s. Between 1868 and 1871, Thomas Annan occasionally captured images of the denizens of the slums of Glasgow, Scotland. But Hill and Adamson were not aiming to make social-documentary images, and Annan's primary purpose was to document not the people but the environs of the Glasgow slums for urban improvement projects.[80] None of these photographs were widely seen, at any rate. Thomson may have known of Hill and Adamson's experiments, but Annan's more than likely escaped his awareness. As far as he knew, the street photographs that served most clearly as precedents for his *Street Life* images were his own earlier images made in the streets of China.

This is in keeping with overall trends. Prior to the 1870s, when photography was called upon to catalogue people, the subjects were of anthropological, not sociological, significance. Indeed it was within anthropology that the type-photograph came into its own in the nineteenth century. By the early 1860s photographs of human beings, particularly human beings from recently-colonized parts of the world, appeared regularly in both popular exhibitions and the collections of scholars. Photography played a critical part in the emerging science of anthropology, as historian Elizabeth Edwards explains:

> *The methodological need for contemporary scientists to classify material in the biological sciences required a typological conception of humankind... In bald terms, the stress was on the physical nature of humankind which could be classified, quantified, and placed appropriately in the evolutionary framework.*

Photography served as the ideal means of representing that physicality. The "type" specimen, Edwards continues, "was not a new concept" in the nineteenth century, but:

> *[b]y the mid-nineteenth century 'racial type'... became regarded as something real and concrete. In broad nineteenth century anthropological usage, the 'type' represented the general form or character which distinguishes a given group and was accepted as standard; it was also the person or thing which exhibits these qualities, at least some of them... Although many anthropologists did in fact acknowledge that the 'type' represented an essence of race, not every feature being present in every specimen, they felt the 'type' established the parameters of a race... The 'reality' of photography, the actual visual representation of the 'type,' only strengthened this perception.*[81]

Type overtook individual identity; "[t]he stress was on the generality as represented in one specimen."[82] When a "specimen" did retain his or her individual identity, there was generally an overwhelming reason why this should be so. The name of Trucanini, a native Tasmanian woman, remained attached to her photographs only because she was the last representative of her race.[83]

Not all type-photographs were dryly scientific. Indeed, the majority, in the 1860s and 70s, were "portrait-types," partaking of the visual language of the portrait studio but intended to depict the subject not as individual but as specimen.[84] John Thomson himself produced myriad portrait types while living in Asia. In these photographs, made either in the studio or in a makeshift street-studio, figures pose in thoughtful manner; but they pose as representatives of a class, not as individuals (see, for example, Figures 2.6, 2.8, 2.9, 2.10). As his comfort with field photography advanced and his attitudes toward his subjects matured, he began making increasingly naturalistic street photographs (Figures 4.9, 4.10). But many are still clearly constructed tableaux, and still partake of the standards of typology.

In the late 1860s, type-photography began to become more scientific and rationalized, as a result of systems devised by John Lamprey and T H Huxley. Lamprey proposed posing naked subjects in front of a gridded backdrop which would serve as a universal system of measurement. Huxley designed a similar system, with subjects holding a measuring stick instead. Both systems specified how far the subject

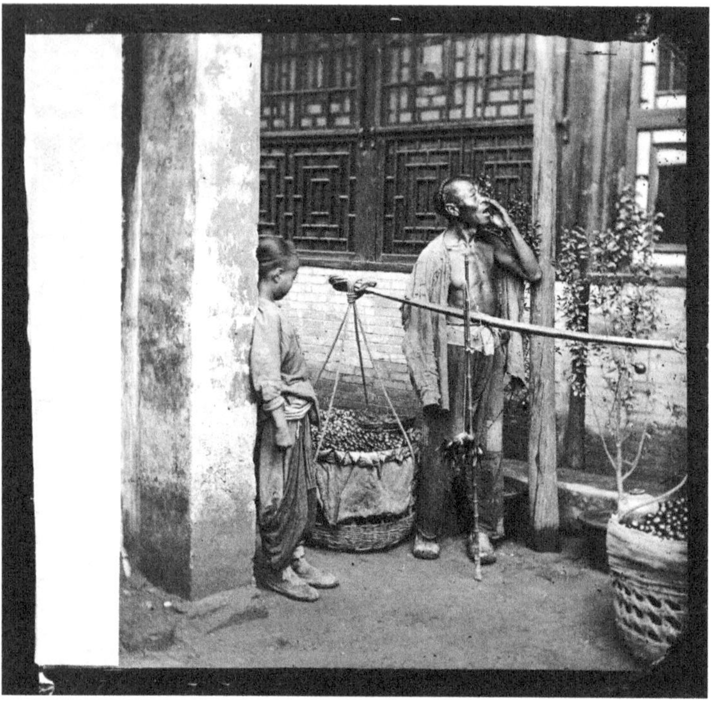

FIG 4.9: John Thomson, *A Travelling Fruit-Seller, Peking*, 1869, from *Illustrations of China and Its People*, Vol. IV (London: Sampson Low, Marston, Low and Searle, 1874). Digital positive from a wet-collodion negative. Courtesy of the Wellcome Library, London, record no. 19710i.

should stand from the camera, but Huxley's system was more rigid than Lamprey's with regard to the subject's pose. The appearance of these systems marks the beginning of an increasingly scientific approach to type-photography. The camera became not just a passive recording device but an active participant in the quantification of the subject. Huxley's system, in particular, was deployed to catalogue the racial types specifically living under British rule, and thus became an active part of the colonialist endeavor.[85] In 1877 Thomson was not yet employing such systems, though he almost certainly knew of them. By the time he had become an Instructor in Photography to the Royal Geographic Society in the later nineteenth century, he understood scientific type-photography well enough to instruct others in its practice.

Categorizing *Street Life in London*

Adolphe Smith and John Thomson saw *Street Life in London*, correctly, as a contribution to street-exploration literature and the representation of poverty. The schemata laid out by scholars for ordering and classifying the literature of the London streets like that of Dickens, Mayhew, Greenwood and others apply to *Street Life in London* as well. Positioning *Street Life* in relation to its predecessors gives one a sense of why

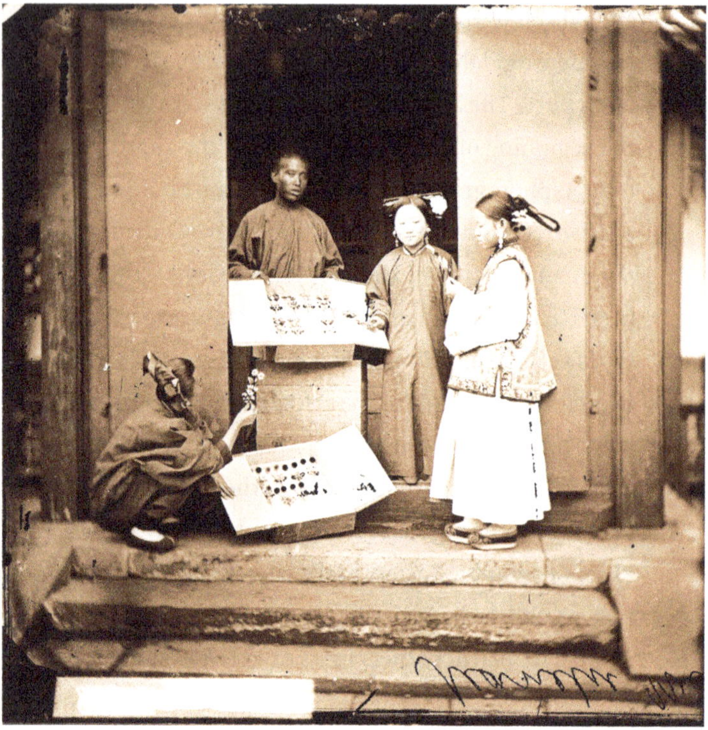

FIG 4.10: John Thomson, *Manchu Women Buying Hair Ornaments, Peking*, 1869, digital positive from a wet-collodion negative. Courtesy of the Wellcome Library, London, record no. 19654i.

the book failed, why the authors' and publisher's ambitions for it so outstripped its performance.

Within H J Dyos's five broad categories, *Street Life in London* belongs in the third, "higher journalism," along with the work of Henry Mayhew: not a government project, nor as dryly factual as some of the sociological studies Dyos examines; but also not a sensationalistic examination of so-called "low life." *Street Life* does not purport to present a "round-the-clock" vision of the city, like Greenwood's *A Night in a Workhouse* or *The Sinks of London Laid Open.* It does not invent rubes to marvel at London, and although both Smith and Thomson were outsiders to the slums they portrayed, the book does not make a point of presenting itself from an outsider's point of view. It does, however, concern itself in some entries with the dramatic contrasts of wealth and poverty to be found in the street, concentrating in particular on the competing interests that arise between parties of different classes. And in its opening passages it does echo a refrain found in other works of street literature and particularly in Mayhew, the notion that the London streets are like an unknown land, their inhabitants' habits less well-understood than those of peoples in faraway parts of the empire.

Street Life in London, like many studies,

incorporates assertions as to the authenticity of its contents. Indeed, in the Preface, the accuracy of photography's "testimony" is given as the very justification for the book's existence. Throughout the book, too, we find quoted testimonials from street figures, and in a footnote in one entry Thomson asserts, "The quotations were jotted down as they were uttered," testifying both to their accuracy and to the means by which he procured them.[86] Although one wonders at his ability to transcribe both word and accent, rendering informants' conversations and the patois in which they were conducted, *Street Life in London* here follows in the footsteps of Mayhew, so its quotations may be regarded in a similar light, as generally trustworthy. These transcribed conversations also serve to ground *Street Life* in an empirical world similar to the one Mayhew occupied, and to differentiate Smith and Thomson's study from those of Greenwood and Jerrold/Doré, who rarely allowed their subjects to speak.

But Smith and Thomson's study does not impress the reader, in the same way that Mayhew's does, with the sheer weight of information it provides. Although Smith provides litanies of fact about a variety of professions including cabdriving and military recruitment, they cannot compare with Mayhew's myriad tables and charts. Smith and Thomson clearly interviewed many informants, but they augment a description of a particular trade or occupation with reports from only one or two practitioners, not the dozens Mayhew sometimes quoted. And although *Street Life in London* was organized according to an internal logic, its monthly installments often revolving around a single theme, Smith and Thomson did not attempt to provide a comprehensive taxonomy of street professions.

In that manner, its relative lack of any organizing principle, *Street Life in London* more closely resembles the work of James Greenwood than that of Mayhew. Greenwood offered an organizational system in just one of his books, *The Seven Curses of London*, and in that book the system was his own, not arising out of any native logic he encountered or perceived in the streets. The studies he published in 1873 and 1874 were less systematic, and in their rambling quality they foreshadow *Street Life's* general lack of overarching logic or system. Indeed, *Street Life* does not even have the spatial logic that drives *London: A Pilgrimage*, which comes into the city via the Thames, moves up and away from the river, and then progresses from the wealthy West to the poorer East End.

As scholar Rick Allen has noted, works of social

exploration or slumming were expected at least to gesture toward sympathy for the subjects depicted within, so all of these works call for reforms or philanthropic interventions to at least some degree.[87] *Street Life in London* followed suit. At first, both Smith and Thomson enthusiastically recommended social and political reforms whenever they saw a need. Smith called for restructuring of the class-based system of military rank (and, by extension, for the restructuring of a class-based society as a whole) in "Recruiting Sergeants at Westminster;" and Thomson wrote in "Street Floods in Lambeth" of the desperate need for urban improvement to prevent future tidal flooding of low-lying areas around the Thames and to contain outbreaks of disease in the affected areas.[88] As the serial publication progressed, however, they moved increasingly toward gentler suggestions for intervention aimed not at politicians and reformers but rather at philanthropists. This was part of the overall trajectory toward conventionalism that I trace in the final chapters of this book.

Mayhew, too, advocated for both systemic reform and individual involvement. He sometimes found himself at odds with powerful interests over his relatively radical sympathy for the poor, but at the same time was able to elicit directed philanthropic giving by revealing particularly bad working conditions in a profession or profiling especially pathetic individuals.[89] Erring on the side of pathos in *London: A Pilgrimage*, Jerrold and Doré illuminated the sacrifices of some dedicated philanthropists in their final chapter, presumably encouraging readers to follow suit, but overall made few suggestions for more widespread official reform. *Street Life in London* emulates Mayhew's approach more than that of Jerrold and Doré.

The final system of classification this chapter has proposed is a kind of continuum of euphemism, from the dryly frank language of scientific studies like Gavin's *Sanitary Ramblings*, through the relative delicacy of James Greenwood's studies, to the brazen and vulgar sensationalism of slumming works like *The Sinks of London Laid Open*.[90] Here, *Street Life in London* sits at a near-extreme of politeness. In its rejection of any unpleasant subject-matter it surpasses even the quite restrained *London: A Pilgrimage*. The word "prostitute," for instance, never appears in *Street Life*. "Girls on the street are my best customers," says one street seller, and this is as close to an appearance as prostitutes ever make.[91] Adolphe Smith remarks in another text that "It is most revolting to think" about children being born in the confines of a waterman's barge-home, but he does not address the issue further.[92] Even the authors' collaborative discussion of the various means of sorting and salvaging "dust" – again, a common euphemism for everything refuse-related – in the entry "Flying Dustmen" is remarkably restrained. They do not address the content of dust-piles except to note how various consistencies of refuse may be reused. This enthusiasm for recycling acts, indeed, as a sort of purifying agent in itself; they portray dust-piles primarily as a resource, not as a threat.[93] The only potentially indelicate subject on which they expend much energy is the abuse of alcohol, and they are careful always to express disdain for excess and admiration for any efforts toward temperance – hardly a controversial position.

Street Life in London was partially done in, I contend, by this middling position. It embraced Mayhew's semi-scientific tone, but not his all-encompassing vision, so it could not pretend to comprehensiveness. James Greenwood compensated for this lack by increasing the pitch of his plea, presenting readers with a first-person account of his night in a workhouse and assailing them with his anger; but Smith and Thomson shrank away from such fury. They patronized their subjects less than Greenwood, and were more willing than either Greenwood or

Jerrold/Doré to permit their subjects to speak for themselves. But in their careful navigation of the streets, they tread too softly for readers to hear what they had to say.

What drove *Street Life in London* to this polite irrelevance was the presence of Thomson's photographs, the very feature designed to distinguish the publication. Victorian viewers saw photography as equivalent to reality, absolutely faithful to what it represented. They did not accord paintings, or even prints made carefully and accurately from photographs, the same respect they accorded to photographs themselves. The images in Henry Mayhew's books, even those made from daguerreotypes, showed viewers a saddening, pathetic reality; but they spoke the language of art, not of life, and as such they permitted viewers a degree of distance. Photographs, even if a creator openly admitted to heavy alteration, simply belonged to a different paradigm. Photographers H P Robinson and O G Rejlander famously came under fire for their composite art photographs, even though they explained quite clearly how the images were created. Audiences were simply horrified by the nude bodies in Rejlander's *Two Ways of Life*, despite their comfort with nudity in paintings. And a painting of a dying girl, even if made from life, would have felt more appropriate to Victorian audiences than Robinson's *Fading Away*, though Robinson created it from multiple negatives and employed actors to play the parts in the charade.

Simply put, Thomson and Smith could not have presented photographs of prostitutes, or piles of street filth, or the packed and slimy interiors of slum courts in their book. Even a mention of such horrors alongside a photograph of another subject would have occasioned a kind of uncomfortable proximity. The authors and the publisher wanted Thomson's photographs to distinguish *Street Life in London* from its progenitors; but the photographs became, in the end, the element binding the project and holding it back.

Indeed, *Street Life in London* trod its middle ground so assiduously that up to the present, scholars of anything other than the history of photography have generally ignored it. It is remarkable how infrequently scholarly overviews of street literature mention *Street Life in London*. H J Dyos seems to have been unaware of its existence, making no reference to it in "The Slums of Victorian London" even though he does examine the works of Mayhew and Greenwood and even various works of fiction. Rick Allen's "sourcebook" of London street literature likewise ignores *Street Life* completely, though it incorporates many excerpts and illustrations from other works of the same time period on the same subject-matter.[94] The magisterial two-volume collection *The Victorian City* incorporates dozens of articles on subjects including sanitation, prostitution, architecture, the growth of suburbs, and depictions of the Victorian city in image and literature; but only one of its many authors refers to *Street Life*, and then only to its images, not to its texts.[95] Most recently, Tony Seaton omitted *Street Life in London* from his survey of literary and artistic representations of slums through the early twentieth century, part of a larger volume on slum tourism.[96]

As a hybrid text-image production, *Street Life in London* is inherently liminal. This in-between quality has led, I believe, to the publication's persistently low profile and to its continuous disregard by scholars outside of the history of photography.[97] In some ways, *Street Life in London* still suffers from the same problems that dogged it in the nineteenth century and prevented it from becoming financially successful. Its hybrid nature, privileging neither text nor image, damned it to a marginalized existence in the world of both.

NOTES

1 Notably, this chapter does not consider Friedrich Engels's 1844 study *The Condition of the Working Class in England*. Despite its clear importance as an example of this class of literature and its prominence as an early entry in the literature of Socialism, it did not appear in English until 1885, long after publication of *Street Life in London*.

2 In *Writing London*, Julian Wolfreys draws a helpful distinction between literature set in London, and that set in "London." That is, he identifies a division between those writers who shape a kind of mythic city that fits the scale and scope of their narratives – William Blake and Charles Dickens being his prime examples here – and those for whom "London" is simply London: a real place in which the actions in their narratives, whether fictional or non-fictional, unfold. Wolfreys draws this distinction in order to eliminate, for his own purposes, the latter category, being more interested in how authors construct a mythic London. For my purposes the former category, literature taking place in a London that really existed and that one could attempt to navigate even today, has more relevance for *Street Life in London*. Julian Wolfreys, *Writing London*, Vol. I, *The Trace of the Urban Text from Blake to Dickens* (London: MacMillan / New York: St. Martin's Press, 1998), 7-12.

3 H.J. Dyos, "The Slums of Victorian London," *Victorian Studies* 11, no. 1 (September 1967), 5-40.

4 Ibid., 11-13.

5 Ibid., 15.

6 Ibid., 17.

7 James Winter, *London's Teeming Streets 1830-1914* (London / New York:

Routledge, 1993), 1, 153-54.

8 Julian Wolfreys, *Writing London*, vol. 1, 20-21.

9 Rick Allen, "Introduction," *The Moving Pageant* (London / New York: Routledge, 1998), 2-27.

10 Ibid., 11.

11 See e.g. Anonymous, *The Sinks of London Laid Open* (London: J. Duncombe, 1848), 40. The work's very title implies that the slums of London have never been quite so visible to outside examination before, that they are being exposed for the reader's examination and also opened to the salutary effects of light and air.

12 "type, n.," *Oxford English Dictionary Online*, Second edition, 1989, on-line version June 2012, http://www.oed.com.ezproxy1.library.arizona.edu/view/Entry/208330 (accessed 20 July 2012), see entries 5, 7.

13 Boz [Charles Dickens], "The Streets – Night," *Bell's Life in London*, 17 January 1836. Reprinted in *Sketches by Boz and Other Early Papers 1833-39*, ed. Michael Slater (Columbus: Ohio University Press, 1994), 55-60; quotes on 55, 58.

14 Boz [Charles Dickens], "Gin-Shops," *Evening Chronicle* (London) (7 February 1835), reprinted in *Sketches by Boz and Other Early Papers*, 185.

15 Michael Slater, "Introduction," *Sketches by Boz and Other Early Papers*, xiv.

16 Rick Allen, "Introduction," *The Moving Pageant*, 2-27.

17 James Grant, *The Great Metropolis*, 2 vols. (London / New York: Saunders and Otley, 1837).

18 See especially Grant, *The Great Metropolis*, Vol. I Ch. 3 and Vol. II Ch. 1-3.

19 Hector Gavin, ***Sanitary Ramblings: Being Sketches and Illustrations of***

Bethnal Green, A Type of the Condition of the Metropolis and Other Large Towns (London: John Churchill, 1848).

20 See e.g. Ibid., 9, 21, 47-48, 56, 72-73.

21 Ibid., 85-86.

22 Anonymous, *The Sinks of London Laid Open*, 4.

23 "Cove" was a slang term for a man or a fellow – like "chap" or "guy."

24 Ibid., 131. Just one of these "orders of prime coves," "gypsies," really constitutes a particular ethnic group, although their appearance here in this list of criminal types indicates the perceived criminality of the entire group.

25 Ibid., 28-31.

26 Ibid., 27-28.

27 Ibid., 28.

28 Ibid., 38-39.

29 Ibid., 40.

30 Henry Mayhew, *London Labour and the London Poor: A Cyclopaedia of the condition and earnings of those that will work, those that cannot work, and those that will not work*, 4 vols. (London: Griffin, Bohn and Co., 1861-62, repr. New York: Dover Publications, 1968).

31 E.P. Thompson, "Mayhew and the Morning Chronicle," in Eileen Yeo and E.P. Thompson, *The Unknown Mayhew* (New York: Pantheon, 1971), 41.

32 See Anne Humpherys, "Mayhew, Augustus Septimus (1826–1875)," *Oxford Dictionary of National Biography*, Oxford University Press, 2004, http://www.oxforddnb.com/view/article/18432 (accessed 20 July 2012). Ialeen Gibson-Cowan states that Mayhew was also assisted by

his brother-in-law Blanchard Jerrold, later father-in-law to Adolphe Smith. See Ialeen Gibson-Cowan, "Thomson's Street Life in Context," *Creative Camera* 251 (November 1985), 10.

33 Henry Mayhew, *London Labour and the London Poor*, vol. I, 131.

34 Henry Mayhew, *London Labour and the London Poor*, vol., III; for Guy Fawkes Day, see 64-72; for street photography, see 204-210.

35 Henry Mayhew, "Statement of a 'Regular Scavenger,'" *London Labour and the London Poor*, Vol. II, 224.

36 Eileen Yeo posits that Mayhew worked with a standard, rehearsed questionnaire, beginning with questions about employment and wages including seasonal shifts, then progressing into questions about changes in the trade over time. Eileen Yeo, "Mayhew as a Social Investigator," *The Unknown Mayhew*, 63-64.

37 Henry Mayhew, *London Labour and the London Poor*, Vol. III, 177-81.

38 Henry Mayhew, *London Labour and the London Poor*, Vol. I, 2.

39 Henry Mayhew, *London Labour and the London Poor*, Vol. II, 297-338. It should be noted that reform of the sweating system of labor did not begin in earnest until the 1880s. Adolphe Smith, among others, investigated sweating in the clothing trades, acting as witness before a House of Lords committee on the subject.

40 Henry Mayhew, *London Labour and the London Poor*, Vol. III, 354.

41 Henry Mayhew *London Labour and the London Poor*, Vol. II: for the constitution of a dust-heap, see 171; for street-surface soil, see 185-89 and 198-99; for horse and cattle dung, see 195; for "wet house-refuse," see 385.

42 Henry Mayhew, *London Labour and the London Poor*, Vol. II, 8-9.

43 For instance, Mayhew quotes a Report to the Metropolitan Commission of Sewers in discussing the means by which "Wet House-Refuse" is removed and the possibility of this substance as a means for the transmission of Cholera. See ibid., 385-86.

44 Eileen Yeo, "Mayhew as a Social Investigator," 68.

45 Ibid., 69-70.

46 Ibid., 68-69.

47 See John Ward, "Beard, Richard (1801–1885)," *Oxford Dictionary of National Biography Online* (Oxford: Oxford University Press, Oct 2006), http://www.oxforddnb.com/view/article/66897 (accessed 20 July 2012).

48 Jeffrey Richards, "Introduction," in James Greenwood, *The Seven Curses of London* (London: Stanley Rivers and Co., 1869; repr. Oxford: Basil Blackwell, 1981), v.

49 Ibid., viii.

50 James Greenwood, *A Night in a Workhouse* (London: F. Bowering, 1868).

51 James Greenwood, *In Strange Company* (London: Henry S. King, 1873); James Greenwood, *The Wilds of London* (London: Chatto and Windus, 1874; repr. New York/London: Garland, 1985); James Greenwood, *Low-Life Deeps* (London: Chatto and Windus, 1876).

52 James Greenwood, *The Seven Curses of London*, xxii-xxvi.

53 Ibid., 21-22.

54 James Greenwood, The Wilds of London, 8.

55 *The Wilds of London* collected columns Greenwood wrote for a variety of newspapers. In the Preface, Greenwood asserted that "It is only by

perseveringly and persistently proclaiming the existence of evils that one may hope to rouse those who hold the power to apply proper remedies," but the sensationalist tone he employs in many of the pieces belies his desire to see these problems reformed. See Ibid., vi.

56 "It is all very fine for you to sit there," Greenwood imagines one child-thief saying to a magistrate after his arrest, "...it is all very fine for you to preach to me that I never shall do any good, but one of these days come to something that's precious bad, if I don't cut the ways of thieving, and take to honest ways.... but how am I to get into them sorts of honest ways? Will you give me a hist up to 'em? Will you give me a leg-up – I'm such a little cove, you see – on to the bottom round of the ladder that leads up to 'em? If it ain't in your line to do so, p'raps you could recommend me to a lady or gentleman that would? No! Then, however am I to get into honest ways?" James Greenwood, *The Seven Curses of London*, 83.

57 James Greenwood, *A Night in a Workhouse*.

58 To give one example, he quotes from a conversation he overheard at the workhouse when discussing begging "dodges" or tricks in *The Seven Curses of London*. One boy tells others how to gain admittance to the casual ward of the workhouse even after having exceeded his allotted monthly admittances (seeking admission three nights or more in a row was prohibited): "Swear God's truth; stop at nothing. They're bound to believe you. There ain't nothing else left for 'em. They think that there's an end somewhere to lyin' and cheekin', and they're ---- fools enough to think that they can tell when that end shows itself. Don't let your cheek have any end to it. That's where your right, my

lads." James Greenwood, *The Seven Curses of London*, 155.

59 Greenwood, *A Night in a Workhouse*.

60 Greenwood also disguised himself to go into the prostitutes' district known to the newspapers as "Tiger Bay." See Greenwood, "A Visit to 'Tiger Bay,'" in *The Wilds of London*, 1. He does not say that he was incognito for the theater entertainments he saw in "An Evening at a Whitechapel 'Gaff,'" but in planting himself among the audience he was able to observe not only the activities on stage but also the behavior of the audience, again observing as an outsider. Greenwood, "An Evening at a Whitechapel 'Gaff,'" *The Wilds of London*, 12-20.

61 Jeffrey Richards, "Introduction," in *The Seven Curses of London*, xvi and fn. 19; Richards quotes here from Mayhew, vol. I, 477.

62 James Greenwood, *The Seven Curses of London*, 173.

63 James Greenwood, "A Visit to 'Tiger Bay,'" in *The Wilds of London*, 3-4.

64 James Greenwood, *A Night in a Workhouse*.

65 Blanchard Jerrold, "Preface," in Jerrold and Gustave Doré, London: *A Pilgrimage* (London: Grant & Co., 1872; repr. New York/London: Benjamin Blom, 1968), xi.

66 See e.g. Ibid., 23, 88.

67 See Ibid., 50, 54.

68 Ibid., 84. Doré's image of a sandwich-board-man receives even less explanation, appearing only at the end of a chapter on Hyde Park to introduce the subject of the next chapter, theatrical entertainment.

69 Ibid., 114.

70 Ibid., 117.

71 See ibid., 126-28.

72 Ibid., 138-39.

73 See e.g. ibid., 139-40.

74 Ibid., 149.

75 Sean Shesgreen, *Images of the Outcast: The Urban Poor in the Cries of London* (New Brunswick, NJ: Rutgers University Press, 2002), 1.

76 Ibid., 1-8.

77 Ibid., 12.

78 See "Poor Jo," in Robert A. Sobieszek, *Masterpieces of Photography from the George Eastman House Collections* (New York: Abbeville Press, 1985), 182-83.

79 See e.g. "Street Photography," *British Journal of Photography* 25, no. 942 (24 May 1878), 241-42: "By [street photography] we refer to the photographing of views of the streets, and street architecture generally, of our cities and towns…"

80 The Newhaven pictures, writes Roy Strong, "all are conceived according to the notion that the working classes are picturesque. The pictures are not at any point animated by a social conscience…" Roy Strong, "D.O. Hill and the Academic Tradition," in Colin Ford, ed., *An Early Victorian Album: The Photographic Masterpieces (1843-1847) of David Octavius Hill and Robert Adamson* (New York: Knopf, 1976), 58. Anita Ventura Mozley writes of Annan that he "was no John Thomson …He did not interview the people who crowd the narrow alleys… Their presence in his photographs, while evidently not unwelcome to him, does not seem, either, to have been especially sought, and was probably occasioned by the imposing presence of this tall man and his cumbersome photographic apparatus from the world outside the

closes." Anita Ventura Mozley, "Introduction to the Dover Edition," in Thomas Annan, *Photographs of the Old Closes and Streets of Glasgow 1868/1877, with a Supplement of Fifteen Related Views* (New York: Dover, 1977), vii.

81 Elizabeth Edwards, "Photographic 'Types': the Pursuit of Method," *Visual Anthropology* 3 (1992), 240.

82 Ibid., 241.

83 Peter Hamilton, "Policing the Face," in Peter Hamilton and Roger Hargreaves, *The Beautiful and the Damned: The Creation of Identity in Nineteenth Century Photography* (London: Lund Humphries / National Portrait Gallery, 2001), 87.

84 Elizabeth Edwards, "Photographic 'Types,'" 242.

85 See Ibid., 244-48.

86 [John Thomson], "The Dramatic Shoe-Black," *Street Life in London*, 55, fn.

87 Rick Allen, "Introduction," *The Moving Pageant*, 2-27.

88 See Adolphe Smith, "Recruiting Sergeants at Westminster," *Street Life in London*, 19-22; John Thomson, "Street Floods in Lambeth," *Street Life in London*, 23-27.

89 See e.g. E.P. Thompson, "Mayhew and the Morning Chronicle," in Yeo and Thompson, *The Unknown Mayhew* (New York: Pantheon, 1971), esp. 24-32.

90 Mayhew broke with this tendency, addressing unpleasant subjects openly as part of his endeavor to catalogue and explain everything he encountered in the London streets.

91 [John Thomson], "Dealer in Fancy-Ware," *Street Life in London*, 50.

92 Adolphe Smith, "Workers on the 'Silent Highway,'" *Street Life in London*, 95.

93 [John Thomson], "Flying Dustmen," *Street Life in London*, 133-35.

94 Rick Allen, *The Moving Pageant* (London/New York: Routledge, 1998).

95 Raphael Samuel, "Comers and Goers," in H.J. Dyos and Michael Wolff, eds., *The Victorian City*, Vol.I (London / Boston: Routledge and Kegan Paul, 1973), 123-60. Another study in the book which concentrates explicitly on photographic depictions of the urban poor ignores *Street Life* entirely.

96 Tony Seaton, "Wanting to Live with Common People…? The Literary Evolution of Slumming," in Fabian Frenzel, Ko Koens, and Malte Steinbrink, eds., *Slum Tourism: Poverty, Power and Ethics* (London/New York: Routledge, 2012), 21-48.

97 Certainly there has been nothing to match the scale of the exposure received by, for instance, the deeply personal photographs and diaries kept by the mid-Victorian barrister A.J. Munby and his servant/wife Hannah Cullwick. Munby and Cullwick's semi-sadomasochistic relationship, catalogued in their diaries and alluded to in photographs they commissioned, has warranted myriad studies in history, gender studies, art history and other fields, despite the fact that it represents an aberrance in Victorian culture and that it is questionable whether any of the "lessons" it teaches may be extrapolated beyond Munby and Cullwick themselves. *Street Life in London* arguably incorporates similar – albeit less titillating – hints at gender inequity, class imbalances, and social exploitation, and it too couples photograph with text, allowing them to inform and to play off one another; yet

one hardly finds a similar massing of scholars at its trough. See e.g. Leonore Davidoff, "Class and Gender in Victorian England," in *Worlds Between: Historical Perspectives on Gender and Class* (New York: Routledge, 1995), 103-150.

CHAPTER FIVE

MAKING STREET LIFE IN LONDON

CLOSE EXAMINATION of *Street Life in London*, as of any work of art, affords considerable insight into its genesis. Its appearance, the several formats in which it was issued, even the advertisements inside its covers provide valuable clues to its intended audience and its publisher's aspirations. Given the lack of archival evidence connected to the publishers or authors, one could conclude that questions about the conception of *Street Life in London*, its success or failure as a commercial endeavor, or the methods the authors employed in producing it are unsolvable. But in truth the publication itself – alongside some external evidence, including reviews of *Street Life in London* and information about the publishing company – is an authority on its own creation.

This chapter first examines the physical publication in order to establish, among other things, the extent of the publisher's role in shaping it. Sampson Low and Co. determined the book's physical appearance, packaging and marketing – and its pricing – with little input from the authors. Next, the chapter examines the mixed critical reviews of the publication, then addresses the timeline on which the book was made, the methods employed by Smith and Thomson, and the locations in which Smith and Thomson worked.[1] It closes with a consideration of

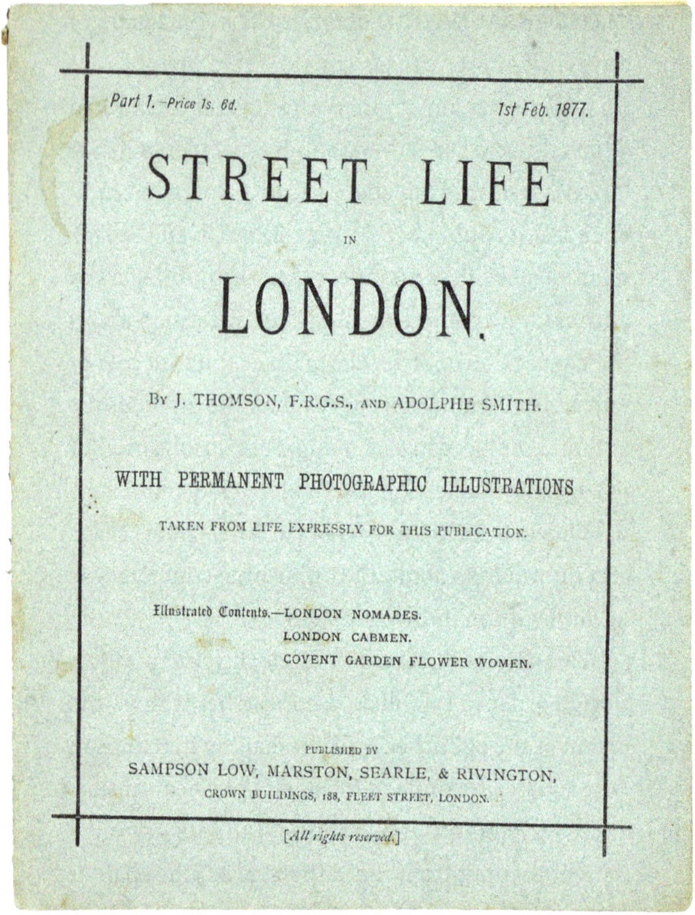

Part 1.—Price 1s. 6d. 1st Feb. 1877.

STREET LIFE

IN

LONDON.

By J. THOMSON, F.R.G.S., and ADOLPHE SMITH.

WITH PERMANENT PHOTOGRAPHIC ILLUSTRATIONS

TAKEN FROM LIFE EXPRESSLY FOR THIS PUBLICATION.

Illustrated Contents.—LONDON NOMADES.
LONDON CABMEN.
COVENT GARDEN FLOWER WOMEN.

PUBLISHED BY
SAMPSON LOW, MARSTON, SEARLE, & RIVINGTON,
CROWN BUILDINGS, 188, FLEET STREET, LONDON.

[*All rights reserved.*]

FIG 5.1: Cover, *Street Life in London*, Part 1 (London: Sampson Low, Marston, Searle and Rivington, February 1877). Copyright Museum of London.

the audience that the publisher and authors imagined for their work.

Physical appearance of the publication

Street Life in London appeared in three formats: a twelve-month serial, a single-volume book, and an abbreviated version titled *Street Incidents*. The serial ran from February 1877 to January 1878, appearing at the start of each month. Every issue contained three entries, each consisting of an essay and a photograph (or, in one instance, two photographs) about a particular type of London street labor, a location associated with labor or street life, or a specific individual. The first installment in February 1877, for instance, includes the entries *London Nomades*, about itinerant salespeople; *London Cabmen*; and *Covent Garden Flower Women*, about flower-sellers in London's theater district.

The serialized *Street Life in London* had covers of pale blue paper, with black lettering inside a black border. Front covers listed the price, title, authors' names, contents, and publisher's information (Figure 5.1), and back covers bore full-page advertisements (Figure 5.2). Other commercial notices appeared inside both front and back covers (Figures 5.3, 5.4). *Street Life*'s text was printed on cream-colored paper

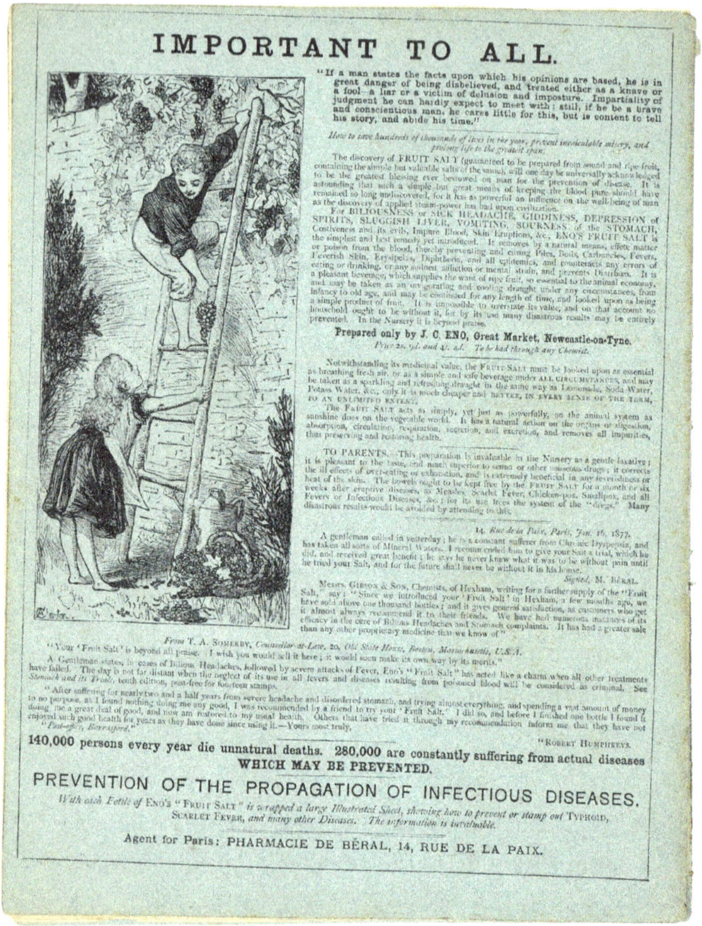

IMPORTANT TO ALL.

"If a man states the facts upon which his opinions are based, he is in great danger of being disbelieved, and treated either as a knave or a fool—a liar or a victim of delusion and imposture. Impartiality of judgment he can hardly expect to meet with; still, if he be a brave and conscientious man, he cares little for this, but is content to tell his story, and abide his time."

How to save hundreds of thousands of lives in the year, prevent incalculable misery, and prolong life to the greatest span.

The discovery of FRUIT SALT (guaranteed to be prepared from sound and ripe fruit, containing the simple but valuable salts of the same), will one day be universally acknowledged to be the greatest blessing ever bestowed on man for the prevention of disease. It is astounding that such a simple but great means of keeping the blood pure should have remained so long undiscovered, for it has as powerful an influence on the well-being of man as the discovery of applied steam-power has had upon civilization.

For BILIOUSNESS or SICK HEADACHE, GIDDINESS, DEPRESSION of SPIRITS, SLUGGISH LIVER, VOMITING, SOURNESS of the STOMACH, Costiveness and its evils, Impure Blood, Skin Eruptions, &c., ENO'S FRUIT SALT is the simplest and best remedy yet introduced. It removes by a natural means, effete matter or poison from the blood, thereby preventing and curing Piles, Boils, Carbuncles, Fevers, Feverish Skin, Erysipelas, Diphtheria, and all epidemics, and counteracts any errors of eating or drinking, or any sudden affliction or mental strain, and prevents Diarrhoea. It is a pleasant beverage, which supplies the want of ripe fruit, so essential to the animal economy, and may be taken as an invigorating and cooling draught under any circumstances, from infancy to old age, and may be continued for any length of time, and looked upon as being a simple product of fruit. It is impossible to overstate its value, and on that account no household ought to be without it, for by its use many disastrous results may be entirely prevented. In the Nursery it is beyond praise.

Prepared only by J. C. ENO, Great Market, Newcastle-on-Tyne.

Price 2s. 9d. and 4s. 6d. To be had through any Chemist.

Notwithstanding its medicinal value, the FRUIT SALT must be looked upon as essential as breathing fresh air, or as a simple and safe beverage under ALL CIRCUMSTANCES, and may be taken as a sparkling and refreshing draught in the same way as Lemonade, Soda Water, Potass Water, &c., only it is much cheaper and BETTER, IN EVERY SENSE OF THE TERM, TO AN UNLIMITED EXTENT.

The FRUIT SALT acts as simply, yet just as powerfully, on the animal system as sunshine does on the vegetable world. It has a natural action on the organs of digestion, absorption, circulation, respiration, secretion, and excretion, and removes all impurities, thus preserving and restoring health.

TO PARENTS.—This preparation is invaluable in the Nursery as a gentle laxative; it is pleasant to the taste, and much superior to senna or other nauseous drugs; it corrects the ill effects of over-eating or exhaustion, and is extremely beneficial in any feverishness or heat of the skin. The bowels ought to be kept free by the FRUIT SALT for a month or six weeks after eruptive diseases, as Measles, Scarlet Fever, Chicken-pox, Smallpox, and all Fevers or Infectious Diseases, &c.; for its use frees the system of the "dregs." Many disastrous results would be avoided by attending to this.

14, *Rue de la Paix, Paris, Jan. 16, 1877.*

A gentleman called in yesterday; he is a constant sufferer from Chronic Dyspepsia, and has taken all sorts of Mineral Waters. I recommended him to give your Salt a trial, which he did, and received great benefit; he says he never knew what it was to be without pain until he tried your Salt, and for the future shall never be without it in his house.

Signed, M. BÉRAL.

Messrs. GIBSON & SON, Chemists, of Hexham, writing for a further supply of the "Fruit Salt," say: "Since we introduced your 'Fruit Salt' in Hexham, a few months ago, we have sold above one thousand bottles; and it gives general satisfaction, as customers who get it almost always recommend it to their friends. We have had numerous instances of its efficacy in the cure of Bilious Headaches and Stomach complaints. It has had a greater sale than any other proprietary medicine that we know of."

From T. A. SOMERBY, *Counsellor-at-Law,* 20, *Old State House, Boston, Massachusetts, U.S.A.*

"Your 'Fruit Salt' is beyond all praise. I wish you would sell it here; it would soon make its own way by its merits."

A Gentleman states, in cases of Bilious Headaches, followed by severe attacks of Fever, Eno's "Fruit Salt" has acted like a charm when all other treatments have failed. The day is not far distant when the neglect of its use in all fevers and diseases resulting from poisoned blood will be considered as criminal. See *Stomach and its Trials,* tenth edition, post-free for fourteen stamps.

"After suffering for nearly two and a half years from severe headache and disordered stomach, and trying almost everything, and spending a vast amount of money to no purpose, as I found nothing doing me any good, I was recommended by a friend to try your 'Fruit Salt.' I did so, and before I finished one bottle I found it doing me a great deal of good, and now am restored to my usual health. Others that have tried it through my recommendation inform me that they have not enjoyed such good health for years as they have done since using it.—Yours most truly,

"ROBERT HUMPHREYS.

"*Post-office, Barrasford.*"

140,000 persons every year die unnatural deaths. 280,000 are constantly suffering from actual diseases WHICH MAY BE PREVENTED.

PREVENTION OF THE PROPAGATION OF INFECTIOUS DISEASES.

With each Fotile of ENO'S "FRUIT SALT" *is wrapped a large Illustrated Sheet, showing how to prevent or stamp out* TYPHOID, SCARLET FEVER, *and many other Diseases. The information is invaluable.*

Agent for Paris: PHARMACIE DE BÉRAL, 14, RUE DE LA PAIX.

FIG 5.2: Back Cover, *Street Life in London*, Part 1 (London: Sampson Low, Marston, Searle and Rivington, February 1877). Copyright Museum of London.

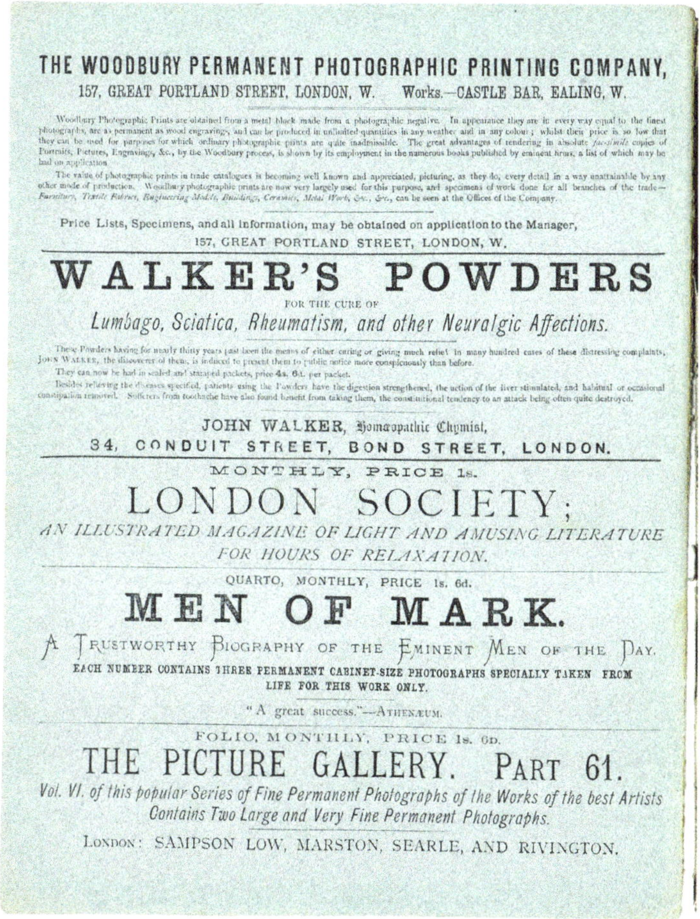

THE WOODBURY PERMANENT PHOTOGRAPHIC PRINTING COMPANY,
157, GREAT PORTLAND STREET, LONDON, W. Works.—CASTLE BAR, EALING, W.

Woodbury Photographic Prints are obtained from a metal block made from a photographic negative. In appearance they are in every way equal to the finest photographs, are as permanent as wood engravings, and can be produced in unlimited quantities in any weather and in any colour; whilst their price is so low that they can be used for purposes for which ordinary photographic prints are quite inadmissible. The great advantages of rendering in absolute *fac-simile* copies of Portraits, Pictures, Engravings, &c., by the Woodbury process, is shown by its employment in the numerous books published by eminent firms, a list of which may be had on application.

The value of photographic prints in trade catalogues is becoming well known and appreciated, picturing, as they do, every detail in a way unattainable by any other mode of production. Woodbury photographic prints are now very largely used for this purpose, and specimens of work done for all branches of the trade—*Furniture, Textile Fabrics, Engineering Models, Buildings, Ceramics, Metal Work, &c., &c.*, can be seen at the Offices of the Company.

Price Lists, Specimens, and all information, may be obtained on application to the Manager,
157, GREAT PORTLAND STREET, LONDON, W.

WALKER'S POWDERS
FOR THE CURE OF
Lumbago, Sciatica, Rheumatism, and other Neuralgic Affections.

These Powders having for nearly thirty years past been the means of either curing or giving much relief in many hundred cases of these distressing complaints, JOHN WALKER, the discoverer of them, is induced to present them to public notice more conspicuously than before.

They can now be had in sealed and stamped packets, price 4s. 6d. per packet.

Besides relieving the diseases specified, patients using the Powders have the digestion strengthened, the action of the liver stimulated, and habitual or occasional constipation removed. Sufferers from toothache have also found benefit from taking them, the constitutional tendency to an attack being often quite destroyed.

JOHN WALKER, Homœopathic Chymist,
34, CONDUIT STREET, BOND STREET, LONDON.

MONTHLY, PRICE 1s.
LONDON SOCIETY;
AN ILLUSTRATED MAGAZINE OF LIGHT AND AMUSING LITERATURE FOR HOURS OF RELAXATION.

QUARTO, MONTHLY, PRICE 1s. 6d.
MEN OF MARK.
A TRUSTWORTHY BIOGRAPHY OF THE EMINENT MEN OF THE DAY.
EACH NUMBER CONTAINS THREE PERMANENT CABINET-SIZE PHOTOGRAPHS SPECIALLY TAKEN FROM LIFE FOR THIS WORK ONLY.
"A great success."—ATHENÆUM.

FOLIO, MONTHLY, PRICE 1s. 6D.
THE PICTURE GALLERY. PART 61.
Vol. VI. of this popular Series of Fine Permanent Photographs of the Works of the best Artists Contains Two Large and Very Fine Permanent Photographs.

LONDON: SAMPSON LOW, MARSTON, SEARLE, AND RIVINGTON.

FIG 5.3: Inside Front Cover, *Street Life in London*, Part 1 (London: Sampson Low, Marston, Searle and Rivington, February 1877). Copyright Museum of London.

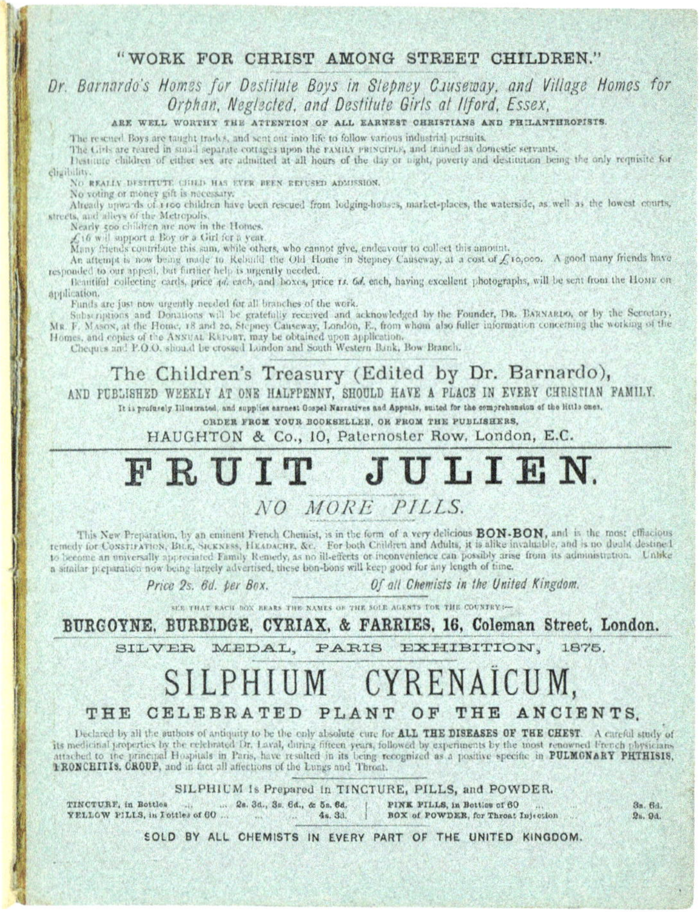

"WORK FOR CHRIST AMONG STREET CHILDREN."

Dr. Barnardo's Homes for Destitute Boys in Stepney Causeway, and Village Homes for Orphan, Neglected, and Destitute Girls at Ilford, Essex,

ARE WELL WORTHY THE ATTENTION OF ALL EARNEST CHRISTIANS AND PHILANTHROPISTS.

The rescued Boys are taught trades, and sent out into life to follow various industrial pursuits.

The Girls are reared in small separate cottages upon the FAMILY PRINCIPLE, and trained as domestic servants.

Destitute children of either sex are admitted at all hours of the day or night, poverty and destitution being the only requisite for eligibility.

NO REALLY DESTITUTE CHILD HAS EVER BEEN REFUSED ADMISSION.

No voting or money gift is necessary.

Already upwards of 1100 children have been rescued from lodging-houses, market-places, the waterside, as well as the lowest courts, streets, and alleys of the Metropolis.

Nearly 500 children are now in the Homes.

£16 will support a Boy or a Girl for a year.

Many friends contribute this sum, while others, who cannot give, endeavour to collect this amount.

An attempt is now being made to Rebuild the Old Home in Stepney Causeway, at a cost of £10,000. A good many friends have responded to our appeal, but further help is urgently needed.

Beautiful collecting cards, price 4*d.* each, and boxes, price 1*s.* 6*d.* each, having excellent photographs, will be sent from the HOME on application.

Funds are just now urgently needed for all branches of the work.

Subscriptions and Donations will be gratefully received and acknowledged by the Founder, DR. BARNARDO, or by the Secretary, MR. F. MASON, at the Home, 18 and 20, Stepney Causeway, London, E., from whom also fuller information concerning the working of the Homes, and copies of the ANNUAL REPORT, may be obtained upon application.

Cheques and P.O.O. should be crossed London and South Western Bank, Bow Branch.

The Children's Treasury (Edited by Dr. Barnardo),

AND PUBLISHED WEEKLY AT ONE HALFPENNY, SHOULD HAVE A PLACE IN EVERY CHRISTIAN FAMILY.

It is profusely Illustrated, and supplies earnest Gospel Narratives and Appeals, suited for the comprehension of the little ones.

ORDER FROM YOUR BOOKSELLER, OR FROM THE PUBLISHERS,

HAUGHTON & Co., 10, Paternoster Row, London, E.C.

FRUIT JULIEN.

NO MORE PILLS.

This New Preparation, by an eminent French Chemist, is in the form of a very delicious **BON-BON**, and is the most efficacious remedy for CONSTIPATION, BILE, SICKNESS, HEADACHE, &c. For both Children and Adults, it is alike invaluable, and is no doubt destined to become an universally appreciated Family Remedy, as no ill-effects or inconvenience can possibly arise from its administration. Unlike a similar preparation now being largely advertised, these bon-bons will keep good for any length of time.

Price 2s. 6d. per Box. *Of all Chemists in the United Kingdom.*

SEE THAT EACH BOX BEARS THE NAMES OF THE SOLE AGENTS FOR THE COUNTRY:—

BURGOYNE, BURBIDGE, CYRIAX, & FARRIES, 16, Coleman Street, London.

SILVER MEDAL, PARIS EXHIBITION, 1875.

SILPHIUM CYRENAÏCUM,

THE CELEBRATED PLANT OF THE ANCIENTS.

Declared by all the authors of antiquity to be the only absolute cure for **ALL THE DISEASES OF THE CHEST**. A careful study of its medicinal properties by the celebrated Dr. Laval, during fifteen years, followed by experiments by the most renowned French physicians attached to the principal Hospitals in Paris, have resulted in its being recognized as a positive specific in **PULMONARY PHTHISIS, BRONCHITIS, CROUP**, and in fact all affections of the Lungs and Throat.

SILPHIUM Is Prepared in TINCTURE, PILLS, and POWDER.

TINCTURE, in Bottles	2s. 3d., 3s. 6d., & 5s. 6d.	PINK PILLS, in Bottles of 60	3s. 6d.
YELLOW PILLS, in Bottles of 60	4s. 3d.	BOX of POWDER, for Throat Injection ...	2s. 9d.

SOLD BY ALL CHEMISTS IN EVERY PART OF THE UNITED KINGDOM.

FIG 5.4: Inside Back Cover, *Street Life in London*, Part 1 (London: Sampson Low, Marston, Searle and Rivington, February 1877). Copyright Museum of London.

in black letterpress, and images were mounted on thin, cream-colored card stock inside orange borders, with their titles printed beneath in black. Images were interleaved with their accompanying texts. The serial's page numbers ran consecutively throughout the twelve issues, indicating that the publishers regarded the series as a unified endeavor, destined for single-volume binding on its conclusion.

In November 1877 a second version appeared, collecting all 36 entries into a single volume that was marketed as a Christmas book.[2] The book had at least three possible covers: embossed red fabric with gold and black accents (Figure 5.5); embossed green fabric with gold and black accents, identical to the red in all but color (Figure 5.6); and plain blue cloth over cardboard, with dark blue binding and gold lettering (Figure 5.7). Inside the covers, however, all single-volume copies of *Street Life in London* are identical. The single-volume book, in all three bindings, precisely reproduces the page layout and order of the serialized *Street Life*, with just one exception. This concerns the placement of the Preface, in which Smith and Thomson spell out their goals for the project. In the serial, the Preface appeared not with the first monthly issue of February 1877, but with the second, in March 1877. In single-volume versions the Preface appears

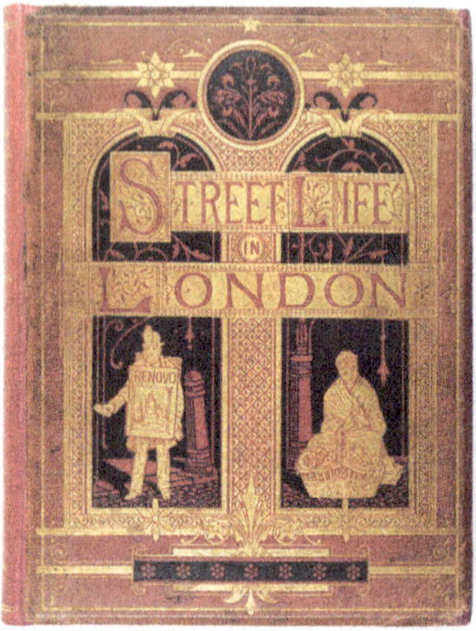

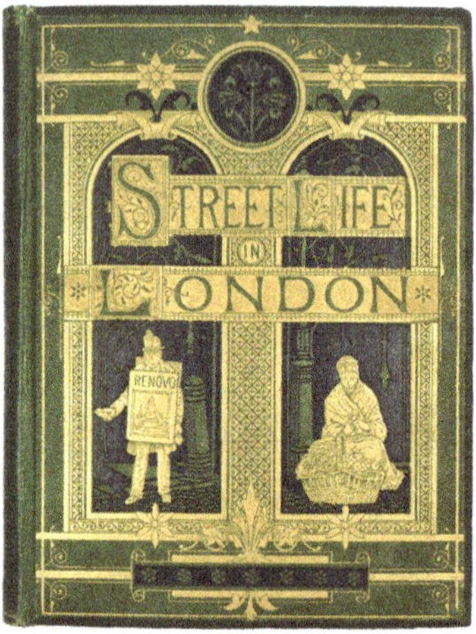

FIG 5.5: Red Embossed Front Cover, *Street Life in London* (London: Sampson Low, Marston, Searle and Rivington, 1877). Private Collection (top left).
FIG 5.6: Green Embossed Front Cover, *Street Life in London* (London: Sampson Low, Marston, Searle and Rivington, 1877). Copyright Museum of London (top right).
FIG 5.7: Plain Front Cover, *Street Life in London* (London: Sampson Low, Marston, Searle and Rivington, 1877). Private Collection (bottom right).

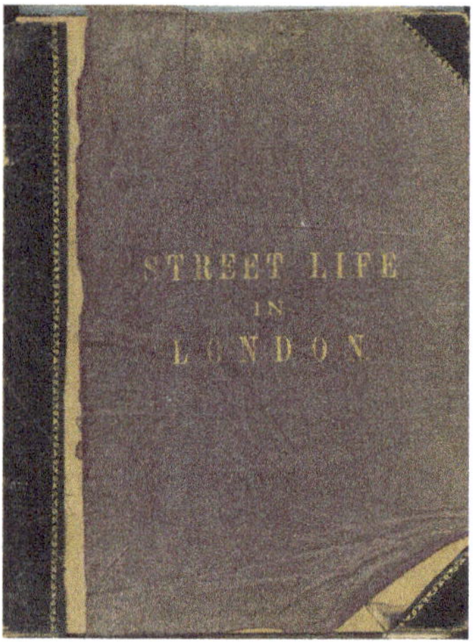

instead at the start of the book, after the contents page and before the first entry, *London Nomades*.[3]

But if the interiors of single-volume copies of *Street Life* are identical to the serialized publication, the embossed red- and green-fabric covers on many single volumes tell a different story. Indeed, they promise a different kind of publication entirely, a collection of traditional "types" of street laborers. On these covers, an elaborate framing device encloses the book's title and, below it, pictures of two of the people profiled within: the *London Boardman* at left, and one of the *Covent Garden Flower Women* at right (see Figures 5.5 and 5.6). The *Boardman*, a sandwich-board carrier profiled on page 69 of the text, is arguably the book's most pathetic figure. In Thomson's photograph (Figure 6.26) the man is filthy, and Smith writes in his accompanying essay that sandwich-board-carrying frequently served as a job of last resort for otherwise-unemployable alcoholics, elderly former laborers with broken bodies, and other men in dire straits. Here on the cover, however, the boardman gleams, his face and body gilded and the brand name on his sign, *Renovo*, shining. Likewise, although depicted alone here on the cover, the flower-seller is actually one of four people shown in Thomson's photograph *Covent Garden Flower Women* (Figure 6.3).

The cover of the single-volume *Street Life in London* thus misrepresents its own contents. The gilded cover promises a book filled with colorful characters and romantic tropes, a simplified taxonomy of the London streets, whereas the publication really depicts London street life in a bleaker, less picturesque manner. The horrifyingly pathetic London Boardman becomes here a kind of tragicomic jester; the flower-seller, eking out a meager existence by selling products cast off by professional florists, becomes a Dickensian street-ornament.

The publication appeared in its third format, as *Street Incidents*, in 1881. Whereas *Street Life in London* incorporates 36 entries, *Street Incidents* includes only 21. Strictly speaking, *Street Incidents* is not an abridgement but an abbreviation, since it collects under one cover only those entries published in the last seven months of the publication's serial run. In external appearance it exactly resembles *Street Life in London*, embossed cover and all; only the title changes.

The Woodburytype

Photographs in *Street Life in London* appear as woodburytypes. The choice to use this process lay ultimately with the publisher, but John Thomson doubtless supported it wholeheartedly as the best way to render his photographs in print. Indeed, for a book promoted, as *Street Life in London* was, on the strength of its photographic content, the woodburytype would have been the most logical choice of process.

The woodburytype, writes Barret Oliver, "marks the turning point in technology between prints made by hand on a small scale and prints made with the aid of machinery as part of mass production."[4] Named for its inventor, Walter Woodbury, the woodburytype was one of the finest mass-produced, photomechanical print processes. Woodburytypes are among the most perfect photographic reproductions ever made, resulting in continuous-tone images nearly indistinguishable from actual photographs. Indeed, woodburytypes were in some ways superior to photographic processes of the late nineteenth century. Above all, because they were printed in ink, woodburytypes did not fade, whereas albumen and other photographic prints did.

To make a woodburytype, one first creates, from a photographic negative, a relief print in a gelatin medium. After hardening, the gelatin medium in turn is placed in contact with a lead sheet and put into a special press capable of exerting tremendous pressure. Under pressure, the hardened gelatin relief creates a reverse impression on the lead sheet, which becomes the printing plate. A special, semi-transparent ink is poured on the plate and the paper is then laid on. Thereafter, very little pressure is applied to the plate, just enough to transfer the ink to the paper. Due to the relief quality of the plate, the ink varies in thickness, giving the finished woodburytype itself the quality of a very low relief – one of the hallmarks of the process. The ink, being semi-transparent, "allows the white paper base to show through the pigment more or less depending on [the density of] the ink," producing a continuous range of middle tones.[5] The ink could vary in color, but printers frequently used a deep, purplish-brown tint – as throughout *Street Life in London* – to approximate the tone of a fresh, unfaded albumen photograph.[6]

The making of a woodburytype, though essentially a mechanized process, still required the presence of a skillful operator and could result in prints with individual idiosyncrasies. For instance, in some single copies of individual images in *Street Life in London*, areas of deep black display crackling or crazing, indicating that the printer used too much ink. Also, individual woodburytypes could be hand-finished after printing, as we see when we look at one particular image from *Street Life*, titled *An Old Clothes' Shop, Seven Dials* (Figure 6.16). In all extant copies of the publication, this image has rounded corners, whereas all other images in the publication have square corners. Because the photograph is otherwise roughly the same size as others in the book (4.5 x 3.5 inches), one suspects that the corners were rounded to remove some blemish. Both of the top corners reveal irregularities, probably flaws in the negative. Although they could not be completely trimmed out, the corners were rounded to minimize their interference with the image, indicating that the printers working for Woodbury engaged in some hand finishing, probably at Thomson's direction.

The role of the publisher

Though Thomson would have had at least some control over the production of the prints, the ultimate decision to use woodburytypes came from the publisher, Sampson Low and Co.[7] *Street Life in London* was not Low and Co.'s first work with John Thomson. The firm had already published the work Thomson considered his masterpiece, the four-volume *Illustrations of China and its People*. Illustrated with "permanent photographs" printed with the collotype process, the publication fit well within a genre in which the publishing firm had recently become interested, travel literature. The company's principal, Sampson Low, had "a reputation as a prominent publisher of travel literature," and his firm had published travelogues of Africa, the Hebrides, the Himalayas, New Guinea, India and other places within and beyond the British Empire's borders.[8]

Low and Co. was an early adopter of photography as a means of illustration for its publications. Prior to the appearance of *Illustrations of China*, the firm had used the medium largely for authors' frontispiece portraits, although at least one photographic catalogue of artworks had also appeared.[9] Thomson's publication strengthened Low's reputation as a publisher of photography, and thereafter many other photographically-illustrated books appeared in the firm's catalog, "over one hundred [such] works prior to 1890."[10]

Low and Co. also employed Thomson as a translator. Between 1872 and 1876, he worked on several publications for the company, all translated from French: Baron Charles D'Avillier's travelogue *Spain*, 1876; Gaston Tissandier's *History and Handbook of Photography*, 1876, with a second edition in 1878; and a translation of J.J. Grandville's *The Public and Private Life of Animals*, 1877.[11] Hence *Street Life in London* was born at least in part out of a preexisting relationship between the publisher and the photographer.

No documentation exists to show how their relationship developed, the publisher's records having been destroyed, along with those of many other firms, during a Second World War air attack on London's Paternoster Row.[12] Still, it is easy to imagine how the publication could have come together, Low and Co. either conceiving the idea of a photographically-illustrated serial on London street life or being persuaded, perhaps by the authors themselves, to consider the idea. Given the difficulties of street photography in 1876-77, only a photographer with considerable technical expertise and extensive experience in field photography – i.e. only John Thomson and perhaps a few others at the time – could have managed such a difficult endeavor and returned with consistently compelling images. Hence it seems likely that Thomson was on board with the publication as it was being developed. Given *Street Life's* reformist agenda, Smith, too, probably had an active hand in conceiving the project.

Certainly the firm, not the authors, conceived of the publication's format, a series of twelve installments published monthly for a year and then collated into a single volume. This format precisely matches that of Low's other photographically-illustrated monthly publications, *Men of Mark: A Trustworthy*

Biography of Eminent Men of the Day, and *The Picture Gallery*. Each monthly installment of *Men of Mark* included three cabinet-sized woodburytypes of prominent citizens, and each issue of *The Picture Gallery* included between two and four photographs of works of art.[13] Both publications ran for several years, and in both instances the twelve serial installments for a given year were gathered at year's end into a single volume.

Moreover, Low and Co., not the authors, determined the price of the serial, eighteenpence per monthly issue.[14] This was the publisher's standard price for its photographically-illustrated serials: each issue of *Men of Mark* and *The Picture Gallery* cost the same.[15] Likewise, Low and Co. determined the price for the single-volume book, twenty-five shillings, again the same as the bound version of *Men of Mark* for 1877 and just a little less than the price of the 1877 volume of *The Picture Gallery*.[16]

Critical reception of *Street Life in London*

From the outset, reviews of *Street Life in London* were mixed. Some critics liked the publication, apprehended its purpose and appreciated its innovations; others misunderstood or outright disliked it. For every critic who perceived the publication as an attempt at photographic social exploration, another saw it as a series of studies for artists or a failed collection of street types. Before it had even appeared, one member of the photographic press – a constituency one might expect to have welcomed such a project – anticipated *Street Life's* failure, asserting in the *Photographic News* that "We hardly see how such a periodical can possibly live a long time, for street-types in London are not very numerous, or, at any rate, such as would interest are not..."[17] From the start, then, reviewers expected a book of traditional types, not realizing that *Street Life in London* aimed to break away from this mode of depiction.

After *Street Life* began its run, the *Photographic News* reversed its earlier position, asserting that the book's "aim is full of interest" and noting that only through photography might one capture "the actual verisimilitude of such scenes."[18] But the critic for the *British Journal of Photography* was more ambivalent. He appreciated the difficulty of Thomson's achievements, given the challenges of street photography in 1877; but he did not see the photographs as particularly innovative.[19] Indeed, he criticized two photographs precisely for their innovations, disdaining *Halfpenny Ices*, one of the book's livelier and more spontaneous-seeming photographs (Figure 6.20), because it represented too accurately the rabble-ish groups of boys one might find in the London streets; and quibbling with the manner in which subjects in *Cheap Fish of St. Giles's* (Figure 6.22) seem too aware of the camera's presence.[20] By contrast, *London Boardmen*, one of the most traditionally typological images in the publication (Figure 6.26), received praise for being "thoroughly characteristic," and the reviewer liked *The Water Cart* (Figure 6.27) another relatively traditional image, because the horse was "well rendered."[21]

A critic from *Lloyds Weekly London Newspaper* offered a similar appraisal. The critic praised the authors' intrepid ventures into "shad[y] and... dangerous" areas and found the texts impressively informative, but complained that the figures in the photographs were neither large enough nor frontal enough:

> *[W]e want to see the faces of the street-folk, not the streets or alleys in which they stand. For example, one photograph presents the back view of a hansom cab and cabman – now the typical cabman is the picture wanted. A series of single figures would be best...*[22]

Some reviewers did appreciate the publication's

advancements. An insightful notice in the medical journal *The Lancet*, for example, hailed *Street Life* as a new sort of endeavor, in the vein of Mayhew's *London Labour and the London Poor* but "rather more ambitious" than Mayhew's project.[23] Instead of a book of street types, the reviewer saw the publication as an effort "to throw light on the haunts and ways of life, the hardships and struggles, of the lower strata of society," predicting that it would prove useful "to the sanitarian, the citizen, and the philanthropist."[24]

Likewise, the *Westminster Review* perceived *Street Life* as having both immediate value as an endeavor in social exploration, and the potential for future value to historians. "It is well for us," the reviewer wrote, "to get such vivid little pictures of how whole classes of our fellow-citizens live, while we are considering how to spread comfort and health and moral light around, and to workers and writers of a future day such a collection as this will be of incalculable value."[25] The reviewer continued by remarking that, refreshingly, the publication refrained from caricaturing or patronizing its subjects. In later months, this critic continued to praise monthly issues of *Street Life*, noting the clarity of the texts and the "intelligent sympathy" with which they presented both "drunken and incapable" subjects and "exemplary" ones.[26] The reviewer understood the book's calls for reform, as well, agreeing with the wisdom of some of Smith's suggestions for legal action.[27]

The praise accorded the serialized *Street Life*, however, all but evaporated when the book-length version appeared in late 1877. Although one reviewer appreciated the work, calling it "an attempt to let half the world know how the other half lives" and finding its subjects deeply affecting, others roundly criticized it.[28] *The Athenaeum's* critic found that the book did not live up to its potential: "The idea of illustrating life in the metropolis by photographs seems, on the face of it, excellent," but *Street Life's* pictures lacked artfulness, instead having a "'dead and alive' look" and lacking "the magic we call 'spontaneity.'"[29]

Reviewers were especially confused by the packaging and marketing of the single-volume version. The lavish, gilt cover promised a series of traditional street types, but reviewers were disappointed by the contents. And they found the timing of the book's appearance particularly perplexing: appearing in November 1877, the book was marketed as a gift volume for the Christmas season. A reviewer in the London *Times* confessed his confusion that such a book would be released at Christmas-time. Charles Dickens had treated similar subject-matter with humor and pathos, making it more appealing. By comparison *Street Life* was dry and unmoving, and the critic predicted poor sales: "The taste for this style of literature, when unembellished by an ingenious fancy and peculiar powers of description, is not, perhaps, a very general one."[30]

The critic's prediction about *Street Life's* appeal seems to have been correct: neither the serialized nor the single-volume publications sold. Unlike Low and Co.'s other photographically-illustrated monthly productions, *Men of Mark* and *The Picture Gallery*, which ran for several years, the publisher suspended *Street Life* after just one year, indicating that it did not perform as expected. This explains why, on the contents page of single-volume copies of *Street Life in London*, the heading reads "Illustrated Contents of Vol. I" (Figure 5.8). If there are no other volumes, why designate this one as the first? Clearly the publisher regarded the project, at least initially, as a multi-year endeavor. Low and Co. presumably pinned high hopes on the single-volume *Street Life*, hoping that as a Christmas book it might counter poor sales of the serial installations. But when reviewers panned the book and the public appeared indifferent to it, the publisher decided instead to cancel the series.

Street Incidents appeared four years later, and

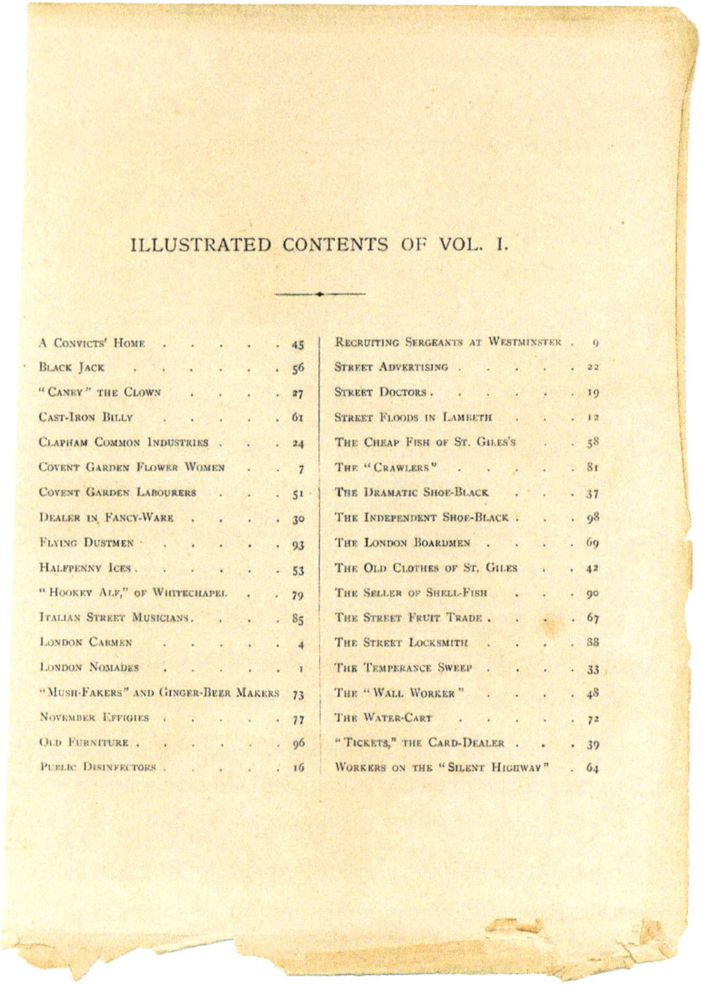

ILLUSTRATED CONTENTS OF VOL. I.

FIG 5.8: Contents Page, *Street Life in London* (London: Sampson Low, Marston, Searle and Rivington, 1877). Private collection.

marks the publisher's attempt to recoup losses on remaining copies of the serial by repackaging unsold material. But the first five months' installments of *Street Life in London* apparently sold better than the final seven months' issues, leaving Low and Co. with excess copies only of the issues from July 1877 through January 1878. Thus *Street Incidents* incorporates only the last 21 entries from *Street Life in London*. *Street Incidents* almost certainly appeared with no participation by or input from the authors, being solely the publisher's endeavor to recoup expenditures on this unsold material.

Establishing a timeline

Visual and textual evidence in *Street Life in London* itself permits the establishment of a rough timeline for its creation. Smith and Thomson began working on it in late summer of 1876. Thomson made a number of images in the fall of that year, fewer over the winter of 1876-77. He continued photographing through the spring and summer, finishing sometime in autumn 1877. Thereafter, he continued to assist in writing texts until November 1877. Smith, for his part, participated in production of the serial throughout its run. He played a critical role in establishing contact with the book's subjects, and he wrote texts from the beginning of the publication also until November 1877. At that time the publication had to be completely ready, as the single-volume version of *Street Life* appeared in mid-November 1877, in time for the Christmas season. Monthly issues of the serial appearing in December 1877 and January 1878 were thus prepared well ahead of time.

Serial issues of *Street Life in London* appeared at or even slightly ahead of the start of each month, so they had to have been ready to print about two weeks ahead of their release, or by the middle of the prior month. Thomson always made the photographs first, before he and/or Smith wrote the accompanying texts. Indeed, with the exception of the December and January issues, both authors tended to write texts just before they appeared in print, sometimes several months after the creation of their accompanying photographs.

Images appear in the serial not in the order they were made, but in accordance with thematic or even seasonal demands of the individual installments. For instance, the first issue in February 1877 was designed to give the audience a broad overview of the London streets, to serve as an advertisement for what would follow. The three images appearing within – *London Nomades*, *London Cabmen*, and *Covent Garden Flower*

Women" (Figures 6.1-6.3) – were made during late summer and autumn 1876. For *London Cabmen*, the timeline is based on visual evidence: given the subjects' heavy clothes and the presence of just a few, solitary leaves clinging to the branches of trees in the background, Thomson clearly took the picture in late autumn.[31] For *Covent Garden Flower Women*, textual evidence suggests that the photograph must have been created no later than the early autumn, but that Smith did not interview the subjects or write the essay until late 1876 or very early 1877.[32]

For the other February entry, *London Nomades*, Thomson took the picture and wrote the text. He provides quite a few clues as to time frame. He clearly made the picture on a bright, warm day, probably in early autumn.[33] But when he returned to interview the subjects, he discovered that one of them had been murdered, as he relates in his essay. In subsequent research, Thomson learns that the inquest for the murder, occurring shortly after the woman's death, was "the 18th of November last," or November 18, 1876, so he made the picture prior to that date and conducted the interview after, just a few weeks before the image and essay appeared in print in February 1877.[34]

Subsequent monthly issues similarly incorporate

some entries for which a concrete timeline may be established, alongside others for which one may only guess at dates. For March 1877, the entry *Street Floods in Lambeth* (Figure 6.5) profiles a group of people affected by seasonal tidal flooding of the Thames. The floods came annually in the winter. Thomson indicates that he photographed the aftermath of the floods of early 1877, producing the image no more than five weeks prior to its publication and writing the text immediately thereafter.[35] But for the other two entries in March 1877, timing may only be approximated through visual clues. In *Recruiting Sergeants at Westminster* (Figure 6.4), the sun shines brightly, the trees in the background have leaves, and the subjects wear no heavy overcoats, all signs pointing to a warm day in late summer or early fall 1876. In *Public Disinfectors* (Figure 6.6), the subjects' heavier clothing and the indistinct shadows suggest a chilly and overcast day, probably in later fall 1876.

Thomson made a number of photographs over the summer of 1877 just before their publication. Many show warm-weather labor or activities: peddling of strawberries, which only happened during the short, early-summer growing season (Figure 6.25); making and selling of Italian ices and ice creams (Figure 6.20); hawking of ginger-beer (Figure 6.28). He continued into early-to-mid autumn 1877, photographing a shell-fish seller (Figure 6.34) on a day warm enough to merit rolled-up sleeves, but late enough in the year to fall within the autumn oyster season. By late autumn 1877, he had finished photographing for the book, his famous image *The Crawlers* (Figure 6.31) being among the last he made.[36]

Old Furniture (Figure 6.36), published in the last installment of *Street Life in London* in January 1878, was almost certainly among the first photographs Thomson took for the book in summer or autumn 1876. By the time it appeared in print, the scene it depicted had disappeared, a casualty – as Smith writes in the text – of one of London's many "improvement" projects. By the time Smith wrote his text the shop had been gone for nearly a year.[37]

The authors' methods

Examining the photographs and texts also affords insight into the authors' methods. First, of course, they located and established relationships with their subjects, a task for which Smith had primary responsibility. Second, after the authors made preliminary contact with a subject, most image/text entries required at least two visits, one to make the photograph and one or more to collect information for the text. Smith did not necessarily accompany Thomson when the photographer made his pictures, nor did the two men always work together to conduct interviews or gather other information for their texts. Third, Thomson and Smith offered modest compensation to at least some of their subjects, sometimes in the form of a copy of their photograph or a free dinner. Finally, the authors wrote some texts individually and others collaboratively, often months after the creation of the photographs.

In making connections with subjects, Smith sometimes relied on professional contacts from business or philanthropic organizations. A "Mr. Smith, of the City Mission" introduced him to one subject, the cabdriver called Cast-Iron Billy.[38] He met another subject, a Frenchman who went by the nickname Tickets, through another philanthropist named George Moore.[39] Occasionally a contact introduced him to more than one potential subject. A contact in the advertising business, for instance – a trade that offered employment to many otherwise-unemployable men – connected Smith with subjects profiled in three separate entries: *Street Advertising* (April 1877), *The Wall Worker* (July 1877) and *The London Boardmen* (October 1877). The texts for these entries, all by Smith, cross-reference one another, suggesting that the subjects were photographed and the research and interviews conducted at around the same time.

In other instances, subjects profiled in one of *Street Life's* entries introduced him and/or Thomson to other friends and associates, who then became subjects for the book. Thomson cites the primary subject of the entry and photograph *The Dramatic Shoe-Black*, Jacobus Parker, as a source in another text, *The Wall-Worker.*[40] And the subject of the final profile, a boot-black, is the son of a woman who appears in one of the very earliest profiles in the publication, *Covent Garden Flower Women*. In his text for the latter entry, published in February 1877, Smith discusses one woman whose son contributes substantially to the household income, "bring[ing] his share of grist to the mill by earning pence as an 'independent boot-black.'"[41] The boy in the final entry also works as an "independent shoe-black," practicing the profession because his mother – just like the Covent Garden flower-seller – "has to nurse an invalid husband."[42]

Thomson also photographed multiple subjects in the same location. The *Dealer in Fancy-Ware* and *The Temperance Sweep* stood at the same spot on the sidewalk, probably on the same day, with the same graffiti on the wall behind them (Figures 6.12, 6.13).[43] Another location likewise appears as the background for both the strawberry-peddlers in *The Street Fruit Trade* and the driver in *The Water-Cart* (Figure 6.25, 6.27).

Street Life in London clearly did not result from a series of random encounters, but rather grew organically out of a kind of network of street figures, the philanthropists who served them, and the companies and individuals who employed them. It presents the London streets not as a hodgepodge of desperation and disconnectedness, but as a real and vital community, in which innumerable individual links are forged into a complex network. Angela Vanhaelen writes that "the book works to organize disparate individuals into neighbourhoods of co-workers, friends and kin."[44]

Once they had contacted an informant, Thomson and Smith generally made multiple visits. In the book's first entry, *London Nomades*, Thomson states that he returned at least once after making his photograph.[45] In *Covent Garden Flower Women* Smith notes that he saw the subjects again in order to collect information for the text.[46] In writing about *The Crawlers*, published in November 1877 near the end of the serial's run, Smith makes clear that taking the picture and collecting information were two separate endeavors. He interviewed one woman whose circumstances he discusses at length; but, he notes, she did not make it to her appointment with Thomson and thus does not appear in the image.[47]

The authors also compensated many informants in some manner. Smith bought dinner for his informant in *The Crawlers*.[48] For *London Nomades*, and probably in other instances, Thomson brought the subject a copy of his photograph on a return visit. In *London Nomades*, Thomson reports, the subject regarded the gift as an unexpected surprise and one he did not ask for, indicating that Thomson and Smith gave subjects copies of their photographs routinely, not just on request.[49] Thomson also reported that from one street-seller, the "dealer in fancy-ware," he "bought several articles," a purchase that functioned, practically, as a form of ingratiation if not outright compensation.[50]

Clearly, the authors interacted with their subjects in ways more meaningful than simply posing them, photographing them, and disappearing. In *A Convicts' Home* Smith writes that he not only went to the restaurant and halfway-house as journalist, but ate there as customer:

> *I have had the pleasure of sitting down to [the restaurant owner's] table with half-a-dozen of the best behaved and most inoffensive men (who were, I*

was informed, convicts) that I have met in the course of Street Life study. In their conversation, these men displayed an earnest determination to work, they alluded but charily to the time when they 'got into trouble,' and did not resort to any hypocritical cant. Indeed, those who assume a pious tone, quote the bible, and talk about 'being saved,' and 'God's help,' and so forth, are generally the least to be trusted.[51]

The detail he gives about these men's attitudes lends an authenticity and journalistic vividness to his account. The execution of *Street Life in London* involved a significant degree of interaction, even negotiation, between the authors and their subjects, who thus become not merely objects for our examination but participants in their own representation.

Finally, the authors shared the labor of writing texts for the publication. For the first two months of the serial's run, either Thomson or Smith signed every text with his initials at the end, Smith contributing two essays for each one of Thomson's. But beginning with the third monthly installment in April 1877, Thomson never again claimed authorship of an essay. Thereafter, most monthly installments included two texts signed by Smith, and one with no signature. In all, Adolphe Smith signed 24 texts; Thomson signed two; and ten remain unattributed.

Gibson-Cowan believes Thomson wrote the ten unsigned essays, but left off signing them to distance himself from the venture: [52]

> *One can conceive of several reasons why this might be: loss of confidence in the enterprise; concern over the damage that the critics' misconceptions of his intentions would do to his reputation; dissatisfaction at the way things were working out with his collaborator and possibly the surfacing of ideological difference which may have been a source of tension.*[53]

Among other factors that might have contributed to Thomson's ambivalence, she cites a photography-related scandal of the previous year in which a reformer, Dr. John Barnardo, was found to have posed and falsified photographs of street urchins in order to generate philanthropic revenue for his rehabilitative housing for street children. Gibson-Cowan proposes that this scandal so tarnished the reputation of socially-conscious photography that it affected perception of *Street Life in London.*

There are some problems with her explanation, however. For one, the "harm caused by the Barnardo

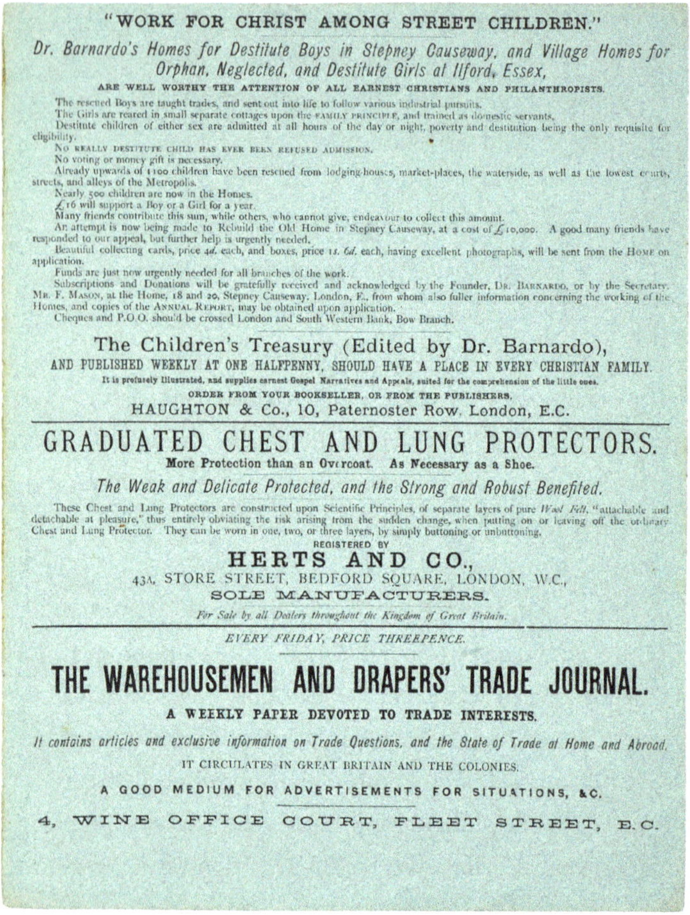

"WORK FOR CHRIST AMONG STREET CHILDREN."

Dr. Barnardo's Homes for Destitute Boys in Stepney Causeway, and Village Homes for Orphan, Neglected, and Destitute Girls at Ilford, Essex,

ARE WELL WORTHY THE ATTENTION OF ALL EARNEST CHRISTIANS AND PHILANTHROPISTS.

The rescued Boys are taught trades, and sent out into life to follow various industrial pursuits.

The Girls are reared in small separate cottages upon the FAMILY PRINCIPLE, and trained as domestic servants.

Destitute children of either sex are admitted at all hours of the day or night, poverty and destitution being the only requisite for eligibility.

NO REALLY DESTITUTE CHILD HAS EVER BEEN REFUSED ADMISSION.

No voting or money gift is necessary.

Already upwards of 1100 children have been rescued from lodging-houses, market-places, the waterside, as well as the lowest courts, streets, and alleys of the Metropolis.

Nearly 500 children are now in the Homes.

£16 will support a Boy or a Girl for a year.

Many friends contribute this sum, while others, who cannot give, endeavour to collect this amount.

An attempt is now being made to Rebuild the Old Home in Stepney Causeway, at a cost of £10,000. A good many friends have responded to our appeal, but further help is urgently needed.

Beautiful collecting cards, price *4d.* each, and boxes, price *1s. 6d.* each, having excellent photographs, will be sent from the HOME on application.

Funds are just now urgently needed for all branches of the work.

Subscriptions and Donations will be gratefully received and acknowledged by the Founder, DR. BARNARDO, or by the Secretary, MR. F. MASON, at the Home, 18 and 20, Stepney Causeway, London, E., from whom also fuller information concerning the working of the Homes, and copies of the ANNUAL REPORT, may be obtained upon application.

Cheques and P.O.O. should be crossed London and South Western Bank, Bow Branch.

The Children's Treasury (Edited by Dr. Barnardo),

AND PUBLISHED WEEKLY AT ONE HALFPENNY, SHOULD HAVE A PLACE IN EVERY CHRISTIAN FAMILY.

It is profusely Illustrated, and supplies earnest Gospel Narratives and Appeals, suited for the comprehension of the little ones.

ORDER FROM YOUR BOOKSELLER, OR FROM THE PUBLISHERS,

HAUGHTON & Co., 10, Paternoster Row, London, E.C.

GRADUATED CHEST AND LUNG PROTECTORS.

More Protection than an Overcoat. As Necessary as a Shoe.

The Weak and Delicate Protected, and the Strong and Robust Benefited.

These Chest and Lung Protectors are constructed upon Scientific Principles, of separate layers of pure *Wool Felt*, "attachable and detachable at pleasure," thus entirely obviating the risk arising from the sudden change, when putting on or leaving off the ordinary Chest and Lung Protector. They can be worn in one, two, or three layers, by simply buttoning or unbuttoning.

REGISTERED BY

HERTS AND CO.,

43A, STORE STREET, BEDFORD SQUARE, LONDON, W.C.,

SOLE MANUFACTURERS.

For Sale by all Dealers throughout the Kingdom of Great Britain.

EVERY FRIDAY, PRICE THREEPENCE.

THE WAREHOUSEMEN AND DRAPERS' TRADE JOURNAL.

A WEEKLY PAPER DEVOTED TO TRADE INTERESTS.

It contains articles and exclusive information on Trade Questions, and the State of Trade at Home and Abroad.

IT CIRCULATES IN GREAT BRITAIN AND THE COLONIES.

A GOOD MEDIUM FOR ADVERTISEMENTS FOR SITUATIONS, &C.

4, WINE OFFICE COURT, FLEET STREET, E.C.

FIG 5.9: Inside Back Cover, *Street Life in London*, Part VIII (London: Sampson Low, Marston, Searle and Rivington, September 1877). Copyright Museum of London.

scandal" cannot have been "considerable," as Gibson-Cowan suggests, because many monthly installments of *Street Life*, even later installments in the series, carried advertisements for Barnardo's homes inside their covers (Figure 5.9). They would hardly have done so if Barnardo's actions had truly tarnished photography's reputation. In addition, Thomson probably was not put off by Smith's radicalism. Smith was fairly moderate for a radical; and Smith's earlier publications had made his politics quite obvious, so they would not have come as a surprise to Thomson. Finally, it seems unlikely that Thomson redacted his signature due to embarrassment at the serial's poor sales. *Street Doctors*, the first unsigned text, appears in just the third installment of *Street Life in London*, in April 1877, too early for Thomson to have concluded that sales of the serial were poor.

It seems most likely that from April 1877 Thomson no longer signed the texts he contributed because he regarded them as collaborative efforts. In a few instances his collaborator was Smith, but most frequently Thomson collaborated with his informants, permitting them to tell their own stories. The latter essays consist in large part of quotations, knit together by brief authorial comments. We see this, for instance, in the text for *Street Doctors*: after a short introduction, the remainder of the essay consists almost entirely of direct reports from such doctors and the patients they serve. A similar pattern occurs in other unsigned texts: *Dealer in Fancy-Ware*, *The Dramatic Shoe-Black*, *The Wall Worker*, *Black Jack*, *The Water-Cart*, and *The Seller of Shell-Fish*. Thomson removed his signature from these because he could not consider himself the "author" of a text written – or spoken – primarily by another.

Thomson and Smith probably collaborated to produce the other three unsigned texts: *Cast-Iron Billy*, *The Street Fruit Trade*, and *Flying Dustmen*. They have the stylistic hallmarks of each author: from Smith, a detailed attention to fact and frequent use of statistics; from Thomson, use of direct quotations (something Smith only rarely did), a tendency to discuss the London street-dwellers in ethnographic terms as a kind of separate culture, and occasional reference to his experiences in China.[54] The text for *Cast-Iron Billy*, for instance, incorporates lengthy quotations throughout, typical of Thomson's contributions. But it also incorporates statistics about cab use and fares in London, a tendency more typical of Smith. Most tellingly, the text deplores the lack of retirement benefits or other resources available to an aged man too sick to work any longer, an issue that greatly concerned Smith.[55] Hence the two authors must have worked together to produce this essay, as they also did for *The Street Fruit Trade* and *Flying Dustmen*.

The London of *Street Life in London*

Smith and Thomson photographed their subjects in a variety of locations throughout London. However, they tended to return to some places more frequently than others. The Covent Garden/Seven Dials/Drury Lane area, for instance, appears in many entries. Seven Dials was so named because it centers on an intersection of seven streets at a small roundabout with a sundial in the middle. The seven streets, radiating outward from the intersection, housed shops and slums in the nineteenth century, and the triangular plots of land between them were shot through with a warren of tiny side-alleys. Thomson made many of the images in *Street Life in London* in the Seven Dials neighborhood, or between Seven Dials and the area of Covent Garden not far away. *An Old Clothes' Shop, Seven Dials*, for instance, depicts a shop on a tiny street called Lumber Court (Figure 6.16). *Cheap Fish of St. Giles's* (Figure 6.22) was made nearby. *A Convicts' Home* (Figure 6.17) depicts a shop in Drury Lane, near Seven Dials; and *The Crawlers* (Figure 6.31) shows a woman sitting on the steps of a workhouse in Short's

Gardens, one of the seven streets radiating out from the center at Seven Dials.

Smith and Thomson worked in a number of areas south of the Thames. They visited Lambeth, a South London neighborhood, at least twice.[56] Street flooding drew Thomson there in early 1877 to photograph the *Sufferers from the Floods* (Figure 6.5) and examine the damage to their homes.[57] And both *The Water-Cart* and *Strawberries, All Ripe! All Ripe!* (Figures 6.25, 6.27), were made in Lambeth Borough, specifically in the district of Brixton.[58] In the Battersea area, just south of and adjoining the river, Thomson photographed the *London Nomades*. Straight south of Battersea, they went to Clapham Common to find the subjects shown in *Clapham Common Industries* and *Mush-Fakers and Ginger-Beer Makers*.

Smith and Thomson also visited the East End, then rising in importance as a working-class neighborhood. They concentrated their efforts on a major commercial thoroughfare, Whitechapel Road. In *The Street Locksmith* Smith writes that many such locksmiths' stalls stood in Whitechapel. And in his text for *Hookey Alf of Whitechapel*, also made in the area, he writes that the region had been fields, but in the past two centuries a "huge suburb... [had] sprung into existence all around."[59] The widening road had overtaken, but not consumed, an odd little pub in existence since 1693, the location depicted in *Hookey Alf*.[60]

In a few instances it is possible to pinpoint the precise location in which the image was created. The title of *Covent Garden Flower Women*, for instance, gives the general location, but Smith's text is even more specific: the group stands before "those ugly Tuscan pillars which Inigo Jones designed to ornament the church of St. Paul."[61] This is not Christopher Wren's massive St Paul's Cathedral but a smaller and more modest structure, designed by Jones and known as "the Actors' Church" for its proximity to London's Theater District. Thomson photographed the women to the right of the church's façade, before a fence that no longer exists. Although the arched window over the side door in the background of Thomson's photograph has been replaced by a circular plaque, we can still identify Jones's Tuscan pillars, which support the church's portico (Figure 5.10). Later in 1877, Thomson returned to Covent to photograph the *Covent Garden Labourers* just yards from where he depicted the women in the earlier image (Figure 5.11).[62]

Thomson made *Recruiting Sergeants at Westminster* near Westminster Abbey, which is visible in the background. Specifically the picture was taken from

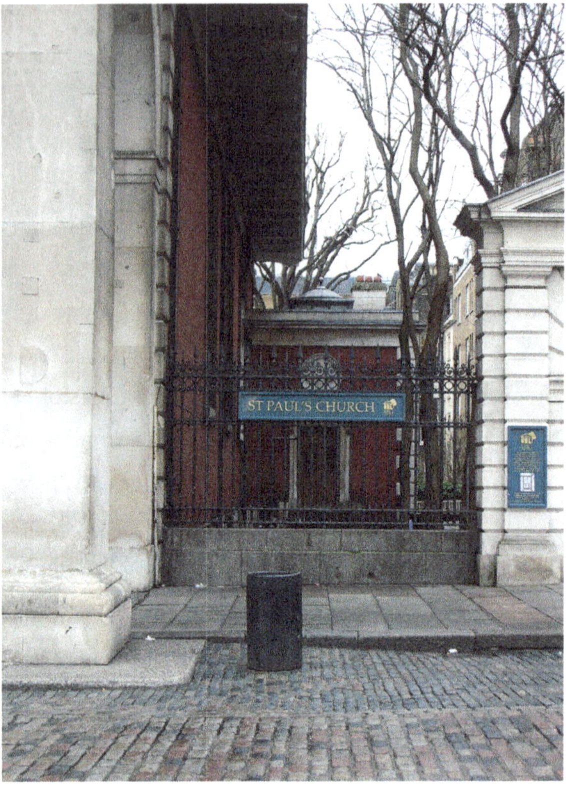

FIG 5.10: Location of *Covent Garden Flower Women*, St. Paul's Church, Covent Garden, London. Photograph by the Author.

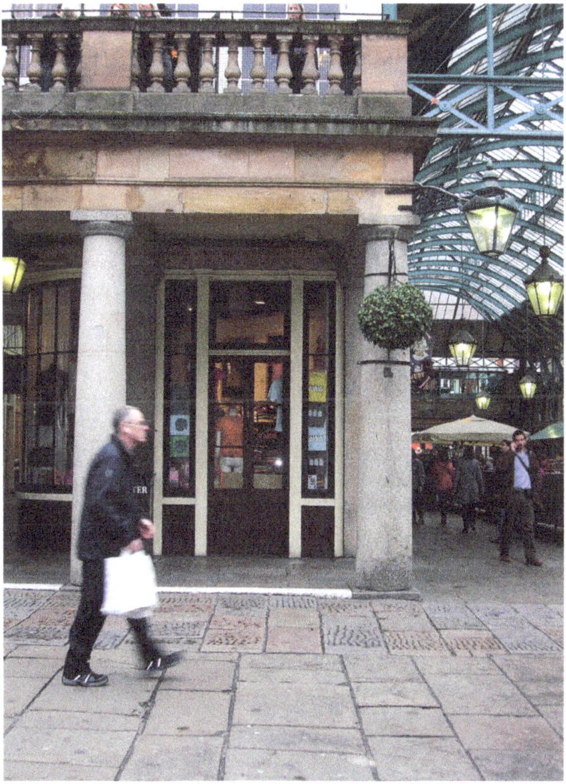

FIG 5.11: Location of *Covent Garden Labourers*, Covent Garden, London. Photograph by the Author.

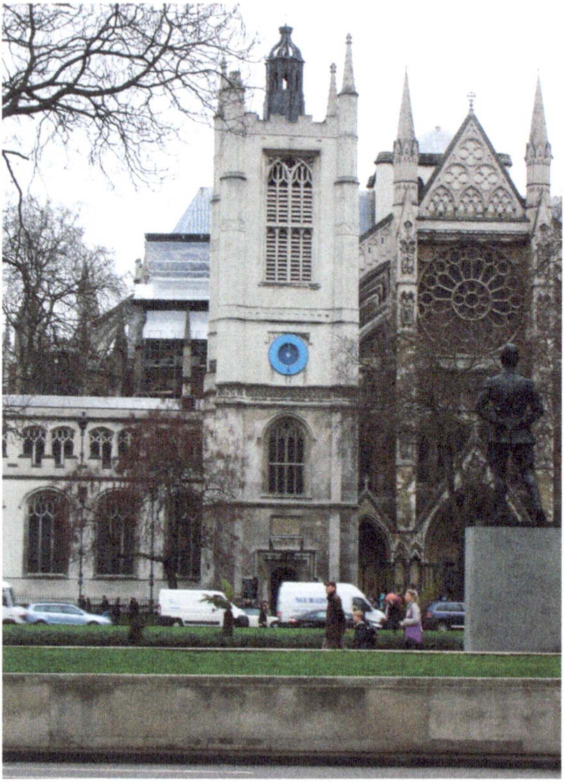

FIG 5.12: Westminster North Transept Portal and St. Margaret's Church, London, photographed from the approximate location of *Recruiting Sergeants at Westminster*, next to the former Mitre and Dove pub. Photograph by the Author.

the north, looking south toward the Abbey's north transept portal. The clock tower visible in the image actually belongs to another structure, the Church of St. Margaret just next to the Abbey. Thomson photographed the recruiters outside a pub called the *Mitre and Dove*, where they habitually waited for and courted recruits. Smith notes that this was "at the corner of King Street and Bridge Street." King Street no longer exists, and HM Treasury now stands on the former spot of the Mitre and Dove (Figures 5.12, 5.13).[63]

Street Life in London also documented areas of the city destined to disappear or to change drastically in the short term. *Old Furniture*, appearing in the last issue in January 1878, paid homage to a London that had already disappeared, "improved" out of existence after Thomson photographed it, but before the picture appeared in print. The shop shown in the photograph (Figure 6.36), Smith writes, stood "at the corner of Church Lane" in the central London district of Holborn, near New Oxford Street, again not far from Covent Garden.[64] Church Lane "was not certainly one of the worst streets in the neighbourhood," Smith writes, "but... the tax-payers of [New Oxford Street] had to be conciliated."[65]

Occasionally, Smith and Thomson mention a location in their texts that does not appear in the book,

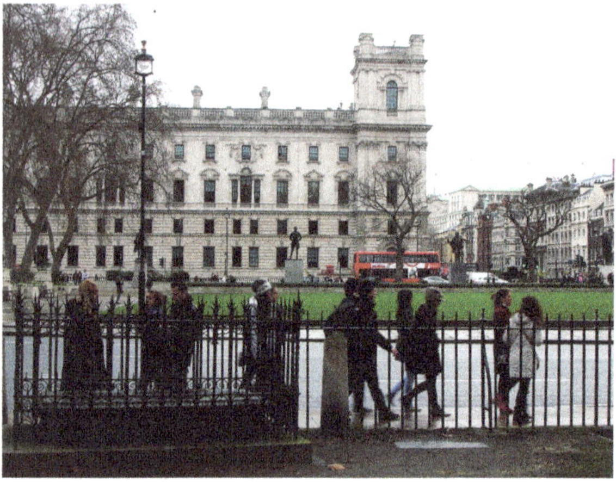

FIG 5.13: Former location of the Mitre and Dove, now HM Treasury, London, photographed from Westminster Abbey North Transept. Photograph by the Author.

but that constituted an important locus of street trade and street life in the city. One such location is Petticoat Lane, discussed in *Old Clothes of St. Giles* as a street market specializing in inexpensive and secondhand clothing.[66] Located in East London not far from Whitechapel Road, it never appears in *Street Life in London* but receives mention on more than one occasion. We might think of it as part of a network of secondary locations, not part of the fabric of the book itself but absolutely and integrally part of the fabric of London's vibrant street life and culture.[67] Saffron Hill, home to a large Italian community, is another such location. Italian subjects who lived in the district appear in *Halfpenny Ices* and *Italian Street Musicians* (Figures 6.20, 6.32) but they are shown in the neighborhoods where they plied their trade, not in the one where they lived.[68]

The question of audience

Street Life in London required intensive effort from its authors. They visited subjects repeatedly to establish rapport, make photographs and collect interviews; traveled to all parts of London; researched and wrote essays about a wide variety of street professions and roles; and engaged in all the labor necessary to turn their activities into a cohesive publication. They clearly believed that their effort would bear fruit in a publication with significant power to reach and to persuade its audience. But the authors did not necessarily agree with one another as to whom this audience would be.

Thomson and the publisher, Low and Co., seem to have had relatively similar ideas about the potential audience for the serial. The publisher clearly directed *Street Life in London* at the same audience already purchasing its other serialized publications, *Men of Mark* and *The Picture Gallery*. The company priced *Street Life* similarly, eighteenpence per monthly issue of the serial and twenty-five shillings for the bound volume; and they advertised it alongside and identically to these other publications in their various printed notices in newspapers and magazines. Low and Co. seems to have imagined that its audience would purchase *Street Life in London* out of simple loyalty to the publisher's brand. Indeed, they probably imagined even wider appeal for *Street Life* because it carried Thomson's name, and thus would also interest people who had previously purchased Thomson's *Illustrations of China and Its People*.

But the audience for Thomson's volumes on China – readers interested in travel, ethnography, and photography – found less to interest them in a series of views of familiar London. Devotees of photography may have been willing to pay for the series, but the other constituencies were not. And the respectable, upper-middle-class Victorians who happily purchased biographies of eminent men and photographs of famous works of art with which to edify themselves proved less willing to spend their money on pictures of street rabble. What they found off-putting was not the subject-matter of the photographs *per se* – street characters – but rather how the subject-matter was presented. Viewers of the photographs expected a series of traditional street-types, but they saw something very different. Due to John Thomson's innovative, contextual presentations of street labor they found instead a series of pictures they could not "read," a presentation of poverty that made little visual sense.

Adolphe Smith envisioned a potential audience for *Street Life* simultaneously more realistic and more idealistic than the one envisioned by Thomson and the publisher: he imagined the publication would be read by people just like him. Possessed of a degree of public-spiritedness and reformist drive, they would not just stare voyeuristically at images of poverty but do something about the conditions they saw. In participating in *Street Life in London* he both revealed the conditions of poverty to the imagined audience, and modeled behavior that he hoped they would emulate. But Smith's constituency of middle-class philanthropists proved no more likely to purchase the publication than Thomson's armchair ethnographers. Many were doubtless deterred by the price of the publication. Others may have found Smith's calls for systemic reform too strident, too revolutionary. At the end of the day, the audience Smith imagined – bourgeois socialists like him, philanthropists with disposable income, people who viewed reading as an active rather than a passive experience – proved illusory.

As the public's relative apathy to the publication and the consequent poor sales became clear, Smith and Thomson scrambled to alter their work, attempting to increase interest and generate sales. Thomson began with a desire to reject the strictures of visual typology, but increasingly embraced those strictures as the project progressed. Smith started out promoting systemic social reform, but suppressed his radicalism in later months, replacing it with suggestions for smaller-scale, individual philanthropic interventions. In the final chapters I will examine the trajectory of these alterations, demonstrating how the publication changed over time. From a collaboration between two authors – and, to some extent, the publisher – *Street Life in London* expanded, becoming in effect a collaboration with its audience, as well.

NOTES

1 In prior literature on *Street Life in London*, two authors have provided the most concrete evidence regarding *Street Life's* background, conception and execution: Ialeen Gibson-Cowan, in a series of articles she wrote during the mid-1980s; and Richard Ovenden, in his 1997 monograph on John Thomson's life and work. Other authors have tended to build on the scholarship of these two. A few authors refer to evidence within the publication itself and also to published reviews of the book to make their cases. Angela Vanhaelen, for instance, discusses in a 2002 article how the authors' use of preexisting systems of relationships among their informants imparts to the London streets sense of communitarian interconnectedness. In a 1993 study, Jeff Rosen notes – but overstates – the critical flavor of contemporary reviews of the publication. In what follows, I employ similar strategies of close reading of the object and, where available, documentary evidence, to give a more complete sense of how *Street Life in London* was packaged and marketed, and how it might have been conceived and executed. Ialeen Gibson-Cowan, "Thomson's Street Life in Context," *Creative Camera* 251 (November 1985), 10-15; Ialeen Gibson-Cowan, "John Thomson on Cyprus," *The Photographic Collector* 5, no. 3 (1986), 309-19; Richard Ovenden, *John Thomson (1837-1921) Photographer* (Edinburgh: National Library of Scotland/ Stationery Office, 1997); Angela Vanhaelen, "Street Life in London and the Organization of Labour," *History of Photography* 26, no. 3 (Autumn 2002), 191-204; Jeff Rosen, "Posed as Rogues: The Crisis of Photographic Realism in John Thomson's Street Life in London," *Image* (Rochester, NY) 36, nos. 3-4

(Fall/Winter 1993), 8-39.

2 "Sampson Low, Marston, Searle and Rivington's List of New Books" places *Street Life in London* under the "Books for Christmas Presents" heading. Advertisement, *Athenaeum* 2616 (15 Dec. 1877), 785.

3 Oddly, even in these single-volume copies the contents for March 1877 appear on the verso of the Preface page, out of order. This indicates that single-volume copies of *Street Life* simply collate and re-bind pages originally printed for publication in serialized format.

4 Barret Oliver, *A History of the Woodburytype: The First Successful Photo-mechanical Printing Process and Walter Bentley Woodbury* (Nevada City, CA: Carl Mautz Publishing, 2006), 11.

5 Ibid., 25.

6 Ibid., 24.

7 The name of Low's company varied as new business partners arrived and departed; *Street Life in London* and *Street Incidents* both appeared under the imprint of Sampson Low, Marston, Searle and Rivington. For the sake of brevity, I refer to the publishing company as "Low and Co."

8 James J. Barnes and Patience P. Barnes, "Sampson Low and the Victorian Book Trade," *Journal of the Bibliographical Society of America* 105 (March 2011), 83.

9 Ibid., 84.

10 Ibid.

11 Baron Charles D'Avillier, *Spain*, Trans. J. Thomson (London: Sampson Low, Marston, Low, and Searle, 1876; rpt. Bickers and Son, 1881); Gaston Tissandier, *A History and Handbook of Photography*, trans. and ed. J. Thomson (London: Sampson Low, Marston, Low, and Searle, 1876;

New York: Scoville Manufacturing Co., 1877); Gaston Tissandier, *A History and Handbook of Photography*, trans. and ed. J. Thomson, 2nd Rev. Ed. (London: Sampson Low, Marston, Searle, and Rivington, 1878); J.J. Grandville, *Public and Private Life of Animals*, trans. and ed. J. Thomson (London: Sampson Low, Marston, Searle, and Rivington, 1877).

12 James J. Barnes, Interview with the author, telephone, 23 June 2011, not recorded.

13 Advertisements for *Men of Mark*, along with notices of other Low publications and paid advertisements for patent medicines and other items, ran inside the front and back covers and on the outside back cover of each monthly installment of *Street Life in London*.

14 Eighteenpence equals one shilling sixpence, each shilling containing twelve pence; it would be written 1s. 6d., as it was on the cover of monthly issues of *Street Life in London*.

15 *The Picture Gallery*, too, is advertised inside the front cover of individual issues of *Street Life in London*.

16 See advertisement, *Atheneum* 2616, 785.

17 "Photography in and out of the Studio: More Photographic Publications," *Photographic News* (26 January 1877), 37.

18 "Our Editorial Table: Street Life in London," *British Journal of Photography* (16 February 1877), 80; "Critical Notices: Street Life in London," *Photographic News* (8 June 1877), 271.

19 See "Our Editorial Table: Street Life in London. Part II," *British Journal of Photography* 24, no. 878 (2 March 1877), 104; "Street Life in London," *British Journal of Photography* 24, no. 896 (6 July 1877), 324; "Our Editorial Table: Street Life in London," *British Journal of Photography* 24, no.

919 (14 December 1877), 595.

20 "Our Editorial Table: Street Life in London," *British Journal of Photography* (10 August 1877), 382.

21 "Our Editorial Table: Street Life in London. Part IX," *British Journal of Photography* 24, no. 910 (12 October 1877), 489.

22 "Literature: Street Life in London," *Lloyd's Weekly London Newspaper*, 11 March 1877, 5.

23 "Annotations: London Street Life," *Lancet* 109, no. 2789 (10 February 1877), 213.

24 Ibid.

25 "Politics, Sociology, Voyages, and Travels," *Westminster Review* (July 1877), 116.

26 "Politics, Sociology, Voyages, and Travels," *Westminster Review* (January 1878), 254.

27 "Politics, Sociology, Voyages, and Travels," *Westminster Review* (April 1878), 515.

28 "Christmas Books," *Saturday Review* 44, no. 1153 (1 December 1877), 694.

29 "Gift-Books," *Athenaeum* 2616 (15 December 1877), 778.

30 "Christmas Books," *Times* (London) no. 29115, 3 December 1877, 3.

31 The weather was not oppressively bad but just overcast: shadows, albeit with indistinct edges, are visible beneath the cab and on the sidewalk. Their length and angle indicate that Thomson took the picture either in early morning or later afternoon; the absence of other people on the street or sidewalk argues for morning as the more likely time.

32 Adolphe Smith, "Covent Garden Flower Women," *Street Life in London* (London: Sampson Low, Marston, Searle, and Rivington, 1877-78), 18.

33 Raphael Samuel writes that the Battersea gypsies' camp, where these people likely lived, was occupied all the time, but that only in the winter months would a caravan with a group this large have been there. The horse would have been sold over the winter, to save the cost of its care. T.W. Wilkinson, "Van Dwelling London," in G.R. Sims, ed., *Living London*, Vol. III (1903), 321-22, referenced in Raphael Samuel, "Comers and Goers," in H.J. Dyos and Michael Wolff, eds., *The Victorian City*, Vol. I (London/Boston: Routledge/Kegan Paul, 1973, 130-31.

34 John Thomson, "London Nomades," *Street Life in London*, 10.

35 Near the end of his essay, Thomson writes that one of the children of the "skilled lace-maker" at the center of the picture was so sickly it would probably not "survive to witness the probable floods of 1878." John Thomson, "Street Floods in Lambeth," *Street Life in London*, 27.

36 The November 1877 issue incorporates one photograph showing the Guy Fawkes celebration of 5-7 November, but this must have been made at the prior year's parade, in 1876.

37 Adolphe Smith, "Old Furniture," *Street Life in London*, 136.

38 [Adolphe Smith and John Thomson], "Cast-Iron Billy," *Street Life in London*, 91.

39 Adolphe Smith, "'Tickets' the Card-Dealer," *Street Life in London*, 61.

40 See [John Thomson], "The Dramatic Shoe-Black," *Street Life in London*, 55; [John Thomson], "The Wall Worker" *Street Life in London*, 70.

41 Adolphe Smith, "Covent Garden Flower Women," *Street Life in London*, 18.

42 Adolphe Smith, "The Independent Shoe-Black," *Street Life in London*, 142.

43 Angela Vanhaelen observes that Thomson and Smith use this location more than once as a deliberate mechanism to reinforce "community ties between people" in the London streets, out of a desire to "visually convey the notion of cooperative communities of workers." Angela Vanhaelen, "Street Life in London and the Organization of Labour," 199.

44 Ibid.

45 John Thomson, "London Nomades," *Street Life in London*, 10.

46 Adolphe Smith, "Covent Garden Flower Women," *Street Life in London*, 18.

47 Adolphe Smith, "The Crawlers," *Street Life in London*, 119-20.

48 Ibid.

49 John Thomson, "London Nomades," *Street Life in London*, 10.

50 Ibid., 47.

51 Adolphe Smith, "A Convicts' Home," *Street Life in London*, 70.

52 Ialeen Gibson-Cowan, "Thomson's Street Life in Context," 14.

53 Ibid.

54 Thomas Prasch also identified Thomson as the author of the unsigned texts based on his "distinctive stylistic tendencies… a greater inclination to discuss the circumstances that produced the photograph itself… a strong commitment to direct quotation of street people's own words, usually with deliberate stilting of language to reflect the speaker's accent and style… and a habit of comparing London to China…" See Thomas Prasch, "Fixed Positions: Working-Class Subjects

and Photographic Hegemony in Victorian Britain," Ph.D. Diss., Indiana University, 1994, 193, fn. 5. I agree with Prasch generally, although I find that Thomson does not always reference the making of the photograph, and that for three of these unsigned texts he did collaborate with Smith.

55 [Adolphe Smith and John Thomson], "Cast-Iron Billy," *Street Life in London*, 89-91.

56 Lambeth is across the Thames and slightly south from the Houses of Parliament.

57 John Thomson, "Street Floods in Lambeth," *Street Life in London*, 23-27. Later, Thomson may have photographed both the *Dealer in Fancy-Ware*"and the *Temperance Sweep* in Lambeth, since the sweep "lives in a house near Lambeth Walk." See Adolphe Smith, "The Temperance Sweep," *Street Life in London*, 54.

58 In the first image, a sign on the side of the cart identifies the driver as Richard Mayo, and his district as Brixton. Thomson depicts Mayo in the center of a street lined with well-built, new-looking, middle-class homes. These same homes appear in the background of Thomson's photograph *Strawberries, All Ripe! All Ripe!* which accompanies the entry titled *The Street Fruit Trade*.

59 Adolphe Smith, "'Hookey Alf,' of Whitechapel," *Street Life in London*, 113.

60 Ibid.

61 Adolphe Smith, "Covent Garden Flower Women," *Street Life in London*, 17.

62 One might be tempted to claim that Thomson made the two photographs at the same time. But atmospheric conditions clearly indicate

not only different days but different seasons: in the photograph of the women there are no sharp shadows and everyone is heavily bundled up, whereas the laborers stand in Covent Garden on a bright, sunny day, without scarves or other protective clothing.

63 Adolphe Smith, "Recruiting Sergeants at Westminster," *Street Life in London*, 19.

64 Adolphe Smith, "Old Furniture," *Street Life in London*, 136.

65 Ibid.

66 Adolphe Smith, "The Old Clothes of St. Giles's," *Street Life in London*, 65.

67 Henry Mayhew profiles the Petticoat Lane district in some detail in *London Labour and the London Poor*, particularly in Vol. II. See Henry Mayhew, *London Labour and the London Poor*, Vol. II (London: Griffin, Bohn, 1861), esp. 10-30. His extensive description of the area may have convinced Thomson and Smith that they did not need to revisit the place, although it seems equally likely that the area was omitted from *Street Life in London* because its crowded and narrow streets would have been difficult to photograph.

68 Smith clearly visited Saffron Hill, because he gives a relatively vivid description of the unpleasantly dirty, unsanitary interiors of the milk-shops where the ice-cream makers bought their supplies; but he seems not to have interviewed any of the Italian ice-men themselves.

CHAPTER SIX

TRUE TYPES OF THE LONDON POOR

STREET LIFE IN LONDON was the product of a variety of forces, interests and pressures. It was not a monolithic production resulting from the vision of one individual. Instead, its two authors brought their separate agendas, John Thomson's pictorial and Adolphe Smith's political. The influence of the past, of literary and pictorial tradition for the representation of poverty, also shaped the publication, as did external pressures. These various interests and pressures competed for space in the book's pages, sometimes coming together to produce a document of remarkable power and complexity, other times clashing with or simply looking past one another. As a serial, *Street Life in London* evolved over time. This chapter analyzes monthly installments of the serial, demonstrating what Thomson and Smith were hoping to accomplish with them and how those hopes shifted over the course of the serial's publication. Their aspirations are embodied in the Preface, the first subject discussed here. The chapter then progresses into examination of the publication's structure, specifically the themes and internal logic uniting (partially or wholly) individual entries in each monthly installment.

The Preface as mission statement

Comprised of 36 texts and 37 photographs, *Street Life*

in London appeared in twelve monthly installments, three entries at a time, from February 1877 through January 1878. The authors declared their goals for the publication in a Preface, which serves as a coherent statement of Smith and Thomson's initial aspirations for the work:

> *In presenting to the public the result of careful observations among the poor of London, we should perhaps proffer a few words of apology for reopening a subject which has already been amply and ably treated. We are fully aware that we are not the first on the field. "London Labour and London Poor" is still remembered by all who are interested in the condition of the humbler classes; but its facts and figures are necessarily ante-dated. In later times Mr. James Greenwood has created considerable sensation by his sketches of low life, but the subject is so vast and undergoes such rapid variations that it can never be exhausted; nor, as our national wealth increases, can we be too frequently reminded of the poverty that nevertheless still exists in our midst.*
>
> *And now we also have sought to portray these harder phases of life, bringing to bear the precision of photography in illustration of our subject.*

> *The unquestionable accuracy of this testimony will enable us to present true types of the London Poor and shield us from the accusation of either underrating or exaggerating individual peculiarities of appearance.*
>
> *We have selected our material in the highways and the byways, deeming that the familiar aspects of street life would be as welcome as those glimpses caught here and there, at the angle of some dark alley, or in some squalid corner beyond the beat of the ordinary wayfarer. It also often happens that little is known concerning the street characters who are the most frequently seen in our crowded thoroughfares. At the same time, we have visited, armed with note-book and camera, those back streets and courts where the struggle for life is none the less bitter and intense, because less observed. Here what may be termed more original studies have presented themselves, and will help to complete what we trust will prove a vivid account of the various means by which our unfortunate fellow-creatures endeavour to earn, beg, or steal their daily bread.*[1]

Smith and Thomson assert at the outset their

familiarity with the literature of urban spectatorship and reform, implicitly positioning their own study within it. The works in this immense body ranged widely: from governmental reports detailing the need for sanitary reforms in slums, to books like the anonymously-written *The Sinks of London Laid Open* that gawped bald-facedly at the spectacle of misery; from dryly technical studies to moralizing lamentations; from scientific tracts like Hector Gavin's *Sanitary Ramblings* to diaristic meditations to works of fiction.[2] Smith and Thomson cite in particular Henry Mayhew's *London Labour and the London Poor* and the sensationalist works of James Greenwood. In so doing they identify their work with a narrower subset of urban studies, those reaching a popular, non-specialist audience that was broadly humanistic in its outlook toward poverty but not clamoring for revolution or social upheaval.

But if *Street Life in London* aimed to reach the same constituency, it would nonetheless provide a different experience. Thomson and Smith note that they brought a new means of representation, photography, to the table. Using it they would not follow Mayhew slavishly but examine his precedent thoughtfully, update and revise it. Likewise, where Greenwood offered only "sketches of low life," their photographs would provide more than just a rapid and cursory glance. The presence of photography made their project ontologically different from its predecessors, in the same way that any photograph differs from a sketch or painting of the same subject. They evoke the popular understanding of photography not as a mere representation of its subject but an emanation from it. The photograph not only shows the subject, but proves its existence. Their use of the medium in this publication thus serves a dual function. First, because its use in such a popular nonfiction study of poverty is novel, it sets the publication apart. Second and more important, because of its ring of truth, its presence demonstrates the publication's unassailable accuracy.

Thomson and Smith conclude the Preface by noting that readers will find in *Street Life in London* both "familiar aspects of street life" and scenes "less observed." That is, the publication will both tread recognizable ground and make new contributions to its genre. The literature of urban spectatorship tended to visit and revisit the same groups: street sweepers, flower-sellers, costermongers. *Street Life* does address some such subjects, but it also adds new figures, groups not usually seen as street laborers even though they conducted much of their business in public: advertising-bill-pasters, painters of shop signs, military recruiters. Smith and Thomson maintain a kind of rhythm of tradition and novelty, offering both "familiar" and "less observed" subject-matter for much of the publication's run.

In the second paragraph of the Preface, they state that the "accuracy" of the photographic medium "will enable us to present true types of the London poor." This concept of the "true type" indicates a critical break with past modes for representing the poor, whether in image or in text. A "true type" did not indicate simply a typological photograph, but rather a new mode for representation of poverty: socially-conscious, context-dependent, and reform-minded. Whereas a traditional "street type" was a patent construction, Thomson's photographs would present subjects naturalistically, casually posed and integrated into their surroundings. And Smith's texts, rather than simply captioning and explaining the photographs, would serve to round out the images, giving readers a sense of the subject as individual and of the nature of his or her work. Their study would thus improve upon the broad generalizations of its predecessors. Its photographs and texts would satisfy readers' hunger for information, but in ways that deviated from prior models. Photographs would show street laborers and other figures embedded in the physical landscape of London and enmeshed within their respective social milieus. They would depict not only individuals but locations and relationships. Texts would deepen this contextualization through descriptions of street industries, provision of facts and figures, discussions of pressing social problems, and pleas for reform. As we will see in the next chapter, however, the authors amended these aims as the project unfolded.

February and March 1877: setting the stage

A new installment of *Street Life in London* appeared every month from February 1877 to January 1878. Each included three entries, and each entry comprised a text and a photograph (or, in a single instance, two photographs). Most installments operate according to an internal logic that is sometimes thematic, sometimes syntactic.

Ialeen Gibson-Cowan has argued that "later issues show a lessening of the same strong editorial direction" that had been exhibited in the first monthly issue, and that after February 1877, organization of the serial became increasingly haphazard.[3] Gibson-Cowan identifies the theme of the first issue, which includes the entries *London Nomades*, *London Cabmen*, and *Covent Garden Flower Women* (Figures 6.1-6.3), as

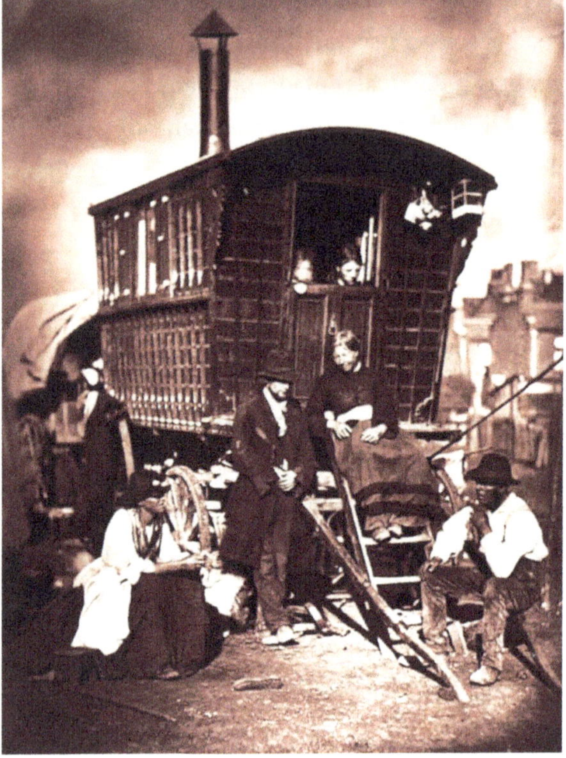

FIG 6.1: John Thomson, *London Nomades,* from Adolphe Smith and John Thomson, *Street Life in London* (London: Sampson Low, Marston, Searle and Rivington, 1877-78). Woodburytype.

mobility versus stability. She calls the nomadic street-sellers "wanderers by inclination," while the Cabmen are "vocationally mobile" but do not live their entire lives on the move, and the Covent Garden Flower Women represent stability and sameness, standing as "permanent fixtures outside St. Paul's Church" and even passing their accustomed spots down to their daughters.[4]

Though compelling, Gibson-Cowan's explanation does not address the crucial link between the serial's first two issues. Together, the February and March 1877 issues function to fulfill the promise Thomson and Smith make in their Preface to present both "the familiar aspects of street life" and "more original studies." With the first two monthly issues they demonstrate how the serial will both satisfy the audience's existing assumptions and expectations regarding urban poverty and street life, and expand knowledge, offering novel characters and a novel view of the London streets and their denizens. Taken together, the two issues demonstrate Thomson and Smith's initial aims for the project quite clearly.

The February issue opens with *London Nomades*, with text signed by Thomson. He organized the photograph (Figure 6.1) with an eye to both informational clarity and compositional balance. A caravan occupies the center of the image. The six subjects – four adults outside the wagon, and two children peering out from within – have clearly posed for their picture, aware of Thomson's presence and complicit in the making of the image. Thomson arranged them more or less in a triangle, a harmonious arrangement conveying stability and order and implying that these people, though poor, hardly rise up in rebellion or threaten the status quo.[5] Even the wagon, emblem and instrument of their mobility, stands still, the horses unhitched from the traps and absent from the image.[6] The image is balanced and artful. Even so, it does not conform to the static standards of a "street type": it is too complex, and its figures too varied in their appearances.

Thomson's accompanying text starts with a pseudo-anthropological examination of nomadism and ends, rather startlingly, with an account of a murder. The essay sits neatly between the informative and the sensational – between Mayhew and Greenwood. Thomson begins not in the streets of London, but in Africa and Formosa:

> *In his savage state, whether inhabiting the marshes of Equatorial Africa, or the mountain ranges of Formosa, man is fain to wander, seeking his sustenance in the fruits of the earth or products of*

the chase. On the other hand, in the most civilized communities the wanderers become distributors of food and of industrial products to those who spend their days in the ceaseless toil of city life. Hence it is that in London there are a number of what may be termed, owing to their wandering, unsettled habits, nomadic tribes. These people, who neither follow a regular pursuit, nor have a permanent place of abode, form a section of urban and suburban street folks so divided and subdivided, and yet so mingled into one confused whole, as to render abortive any attempt at systematic classification... The class of Nomades with which I propose to deal makes some show of industry. These people attend fairs, markets, and hawk cheap ornaments or useful wares from door to door. At certain seasons this class 'works' regular wards, or sections of the city and suburbs. At other seasons its members migrate to the provinces, to engage in harvesting, hop-picking, or to attend fairs...[7]

Nomads in other places spend their lives seeking sustenance, whereas in London they serve a useful purpose, delivering food and other goods to those who toil in the cities, far from the open fields where their food is cultivated. Unlike those in "savage" lands,

London's nomads cater to the needs and desires of others. Part of a web of urban activity, they are motivated by more than just the simple, animal desire to fill their own bellies.

The passage reinforces the connection between *Street Life in London* and Mayhew's *London Labour and the London Poor.*[8] Mayhew, too, opened his study with a passage considering the status of nomadism and comparing conditions in Africa to those in London:

> *Of the thousand millions of human beings that are said to constitute the population of the entire globe, there are – socially, morally, and perhaps even physically considered – but two distinct and broadly marked races, viz., the wanderers and the settlers – the vagabond and the citizen – the nomadic and the civilized tribes.*[9]

After considering the physical characteristics of members of various nomadic tribes worldwide, Mayhew continues, "Moreover it would appear, that not only are all races divisible into wanderers and settlers, but that each civilized or settled tribe has generally some wandering horde intermingled with, and in a measure preying upon, it."[10] If this is true in Africa then it must be true in Europe, as well, so Mayhew proposes to undertake a study of the nomadic tribes of his own home city, "[using] the moral characteristics of the nomade races of other countries, as a means of comprehending the more readily those of the vagabonds and outcasts of our own."[11]

Since Thomson and Smith state their debt to Mayhew in the Preface, it makes sense that they would open with a similar gambit, evoking the example of Darkest Africa as a parallel to Darkest London. This trope, what one scholar calls a "tendency to assimilation" of distinct cultures, appears frequently in the literature and journalism of the colonial era, including the literature of the London streets.[12] Mayhew's opening evokes this common analogy, which "tends to collapse the distinction" between non-European cultures and the poor of England.[13]

Unlike Mayhew, however, Thomson recognizes the problems inherent in the analogy. As such, while he appears to pay homage to the common trope, he actually problematizes Mayhew's formulation, just as his photograph problematizes the "street type" model. The African model of nomadism, Thomson notes, applies only imperfectly to the wanderers of England. English nomads provide a valuable service, making them integral to English culture, rather than – like Mayhew's "vagabonds and outcasts" – auxiliary, even burdensome to the fixed culture about whose borders they skulk. Also, unlike Mayhew's nomads, who fall into "two distinct and broadly marked races," each with "its peculiar and distinctive physical as well as moral characteristics,"[14] Thomson's nomades are "so mingled into one confused whole, as to render abortive any attempt at systematic classification."[15] Where Mayhew asserts the possibility that one can come to a true understanding of the nomadic "tribes" of London through systems of ordering and classification, Thomson rejects such schemata as impossible. As such, he rejects one of the central tenets of Mayhew's study.

Thomson does feel confident in rendering a few blanket assertions regarding these homegrown wanderers. "As a rule, they are improvident, and, like most Nomades, unable to follow any intelligent plan of life. To them the future is almost as uncertain, and as far beyond their control, as the changes of wind and weather."[16] But he points out that this is not a racial characteristic: these people do not self-identify as gypsies, who are "a distinct class." Many of the London nomades do have gypsy heritage, which "may be noted in their appearance as well as in their mode of life," but in general the subjects of his image and others like them are "careful to disclaim what they deem a discreditable relationship" with Romany people.[17] Again, if some of the London nomades are genetically Roma, they are nonetheless, in sentiment and in the way Thomson treats them, fundamentally part of and necessary to English life. He attributes their wandering habits not to any genetic or constitutional determinacy but to a general "lack of education other than that picked up in the streets and highways."[18] If these people's failure to plan for the future and their consequent improvidence constitute social problems, they are thus solvable: whereas racially- or genetically-attributable characteristics could not be overcome, access to education would encourage the nomades toward self-sufficiency, rendering them less burdensome to English society at large.

But Thomson did not devote the entire entry to educating his public. He also provided some entertainment in the form of a murder. Some months after making the photograph he returned to the subjects to gather information for his essay and to give them a print of the photograph. When he presented the van's owner – William Hampton, shown standing in the picture – with the image, the man exclaimed that one of the people shown in the image with him was "'old Mary Pradd... wot was murdered in the Borough, middle of last month.'"[19] Thomson recounts

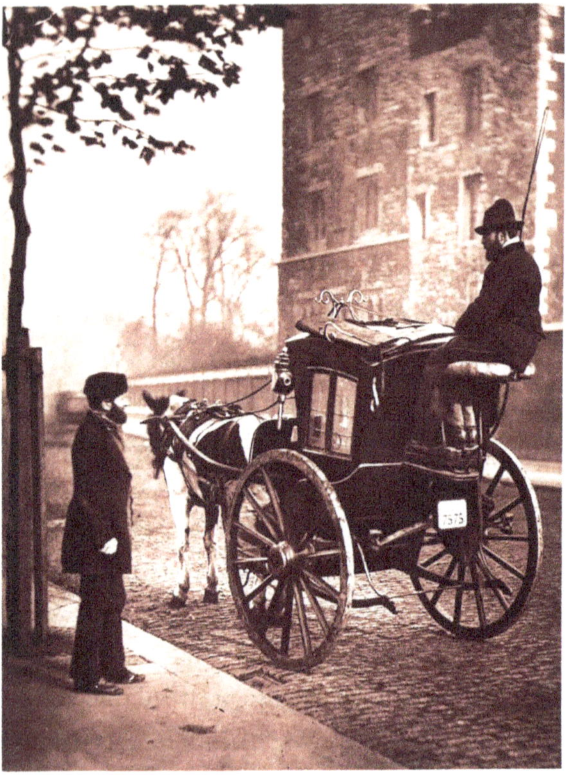

FIG 6.2: John Thomson, *London Cabmen*, from Adolphe Smith and John Thomson, *Street Life in London* (London: Sampson Low, Marston, Searle and Rivington, 1877-78). Woodburytype.

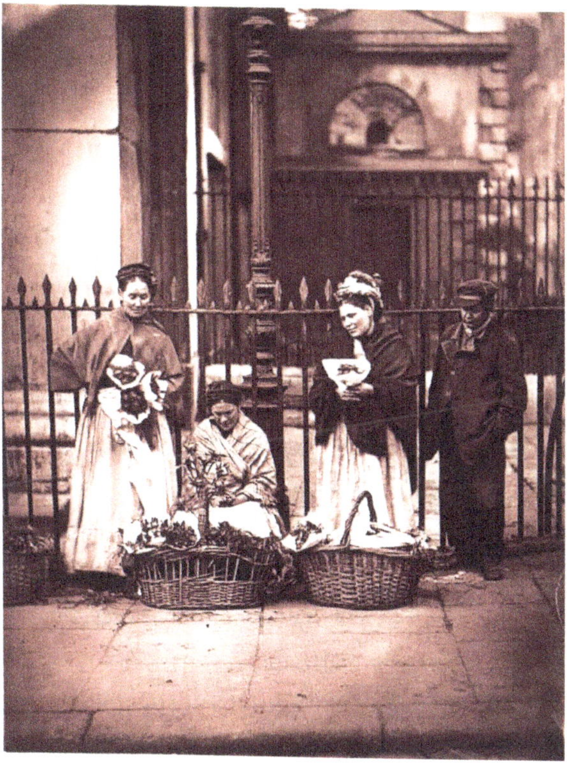

FIG 6.3: John Thomson, "Covent Garden Flower Women," from Adolphe Smith and John Thomson, *Street Life in London* (London: Sampson Low, Marston, Searle and Rivington, 1877-78). Woodburytype.

the story of the murder, drawing both on Hampton's telling and on his own subsequent research into the subject.[20] Pradd, an alcoholic, was found dead on the floor next to a bed on which two drunk men were asleep. She had bled to death, but the inquest jury returned an indeterminate verdict since there was no way to ascertain how the injury occurred, or who had caused it.[21]

So far, the February 1877 installment of *Street Life in London* promises to satisfy readers expecting a Mayhevian view of London. At the same time, it does question Mayhew's legacy. Likewise, if the image itself does not entirely satisfy viewers' desire to gawk at a "street type" specimen, the text proves sensational enough, à la Greenwood. The second entry, *London Cabmen*, similarly updates but does not significantly complicate the traditions of street literature. Even the minor changes it does make to the paradigm, however, were enough to disturb some critics.

Thomson's image (Figure 6.2) depicts two men, one in the driver's seat of a small cab and the other standing nearby on a sidewalk. They look at one another as if in conversation. The image is well-balanced and nicely composed, but at least one critic found it lacking. "We would suggest that the figures in the photographs be on a larger scale – we want to see the faces of the street-folk, not the streets or alleys in which they stand," the reviewer complained. The photograph "presents the back view of a hansom cab and cabman – now, the typical cabman is the picture wanted."[22] No matter how well composed the image overall, a back view simply would not do.

This critic did praise the apparent courage with which the authors pursued their subjects, and the "careful original descriptive matter" that accompanied the photographs.[23] Smith's text for *London Cabmen* does indeed showcase his facility with fact and statistic, his generally redemptive attitude toward the poor and laboring classes, and his warm feelings toward labor unionism and other forms of empowerment for laborers. Here, for instance, he defends cabbies against accusations that they were rough and dishonest:

> *There is no better abused set of men in existence than the London Cabmen; but... [d]espite the traditional hoarse voice, rough appearance, and quarrelsome tone, cab-drivers are as a rule reliable and honest men, who can boast of having fought the battle of life in an earnest, persevering, and creditable manner.*[24]

Smith contends that most drivers are honest men, persuading readers to shift blame for the shady nature of the industry onto the large cab and bus companies that employ many of them. Cabmen see little of the money they take in from customers, because they are milked or sweated for profit by so many others. Without the burden of such systematic exploitation, cabmen would prove a generally honest, admirable lot.

As proof of this, Smith offers "the cab-driver who furnishes the subject of the accompanying illustration."[25] In his early career, this driver began receiving regular commissions from a most unlikely patron, "a bricklayer [who had] inherited a sum of £1300..."[26] The lucky laborer and his wife, once a washerwoman, "engaged [the cabdriver] day after day" to drive them about while they "threw out handfuls of money to the street urchins who followed and cheered in their wake," and to wait for them while they took friends out for benders at brewpubs. Eventually the bricklayer went mad, and spent all his money.[27]

The consistent income these characters had provided, however, permitted the cabdriver to buy his own cab and horse and thus to become a fully independent operator, owing no rent or cut of his pay to any overseer or employer. Being free of the system within which most other cabmen labored, he had no need to overcharge his customers. He also eventually felt comfortable enough to marry and start a family. Corruption, Smith implies, inheres in the system, not in the individual laborer. Workers who succeed on their own ultimately become better and more productive citizens, buying into the same institutions and values – like marriage – that middle-class readers held dear.

The cabbie tells a strange tale, at once his own and someone else's. His story of success through perseverance, diligent savings, and luck comes at the expense of the bricklayer's story of failure through profligacy and lack of foresight. This is in keeping with *Street Life in London's* consistent tendency to place directly before the reader, closest at hand, those characters who either deserve pity or who have, through thrift and self-control, already saved themselves. When the book raises the specter of the undeserving poor person whose own faults and failings have brought about his downfall, it tends to keep that figure at arm's length. Here, the thrifty, providential character gives account of the laughably, ruinously oblivious one. This narrative device serves to keep the vices of the undeserving poor at a remove while foregrounding the virtues of the deserving, hardworking poor. "The elusive pauper," scholar Angela Vanhaelen writes, "acts as a foil for the moral labourers portrayed by

Thomson and Smith."[28]

Hereafter Smith shifts into factual mode, presenting numerous statistics to support his assertion that drivers are, overall, a worthy group:

> *Altogether there are 4142 Hansom cabs, and 4120 Clarence, or four-wheel cabs, in London. These are managed by 10,474 drivers, and the honesty of these men is best proved by the fact that whereas 1912 articles forgotten in the cabs were given up to the Lost Property Office in 1869; this number had increased in 1875 to 15,584.*[29]

Smith concludes by noting the profession's efforts to organize: a Cab-drivers' Society formed in 1874, and by December 1875 "it numbered thirteen branches, had enrolled 1658 members, and possessed funds amounting to nearly £800."[30] It had achieved recognition at the Trades' Union Congress and had strong negotiating powers.[31] From the outset of *Street Life in London*, then, we find Smith promoting the interests of labor and arguing for its right to organize. We find him also implicitly condemning capitalism through his critique of the corrupt system under which the vast majority of cab drivers labored, a system which kept them impoverished and subject to a cycle of high rents and debts to overseers.

The third entry in the February 1877 installment is the most conventional. To begin with, the subjects themselves – the flower-women of Covent Garden – would have been familiar to readers both from their frequent appearance in collections of street typology and from life, by virtue of their constant presence before St. Paul's Church in London's theater district.[32] Among the poorest of poor people, they were certainly needier than either the Nomades or the Cabmen presented in the two prior entries. They were also more romantic figures, and in both picture and text the authors fall back fairly heavily on trope and convention.

The photograph (Figure 6.3) depicts four people, three women and a man, in a row parallel to the picture plane. Three of the figures stand while the fourth sits or kneels, but all face the photographer. The picture clearly mimics a traditional "street type." The flower woman was a figure of some romantic freight in London life, appearing frequently in street typology, and Thomson seems unable or unwilling to rid himself of such freight.[33] Indeed, when packaging the single-volume version of *Street Life in London*, the publisher seized on the resemblance of this photograph to traditional street types, selecting out one of these women and incorporating an image of her with her flower basket into the cover design (see Figures 5.5 and 5.6). In so doing they packaged the book as a collection of street types rather than a nuanced exploration of London's social landscape.

In describing these women and their profession in his text, Smith – normally not given to sentiment in his treatment of the ravages of poverty – follows Thomson's lead, also retreating into romance:

> *[T]here seems to be something inexpressibly touching in the tendency of the poor to fall back on nature's gifts when reduced to the last extremity. The familiar sight of a poor woman holding a pale child in her arms and offering modest violets to the pedestrian, is pregnant with a poetry which rags and dirt fail to obliterate. In exchange for nature's gifts, she seems to challenge human compassion; and shall the heart of man remain cold where the produce of field and garden are so bounteous and beautiful? Unfortunately, with the spread of civilization, nature seems to lose its hold, and artifice gains on almost every sphere of human endeavour. The fruits, which the earth gives gratuitously, have been converted into the property of a privileged few; and the pauperized street vendor*

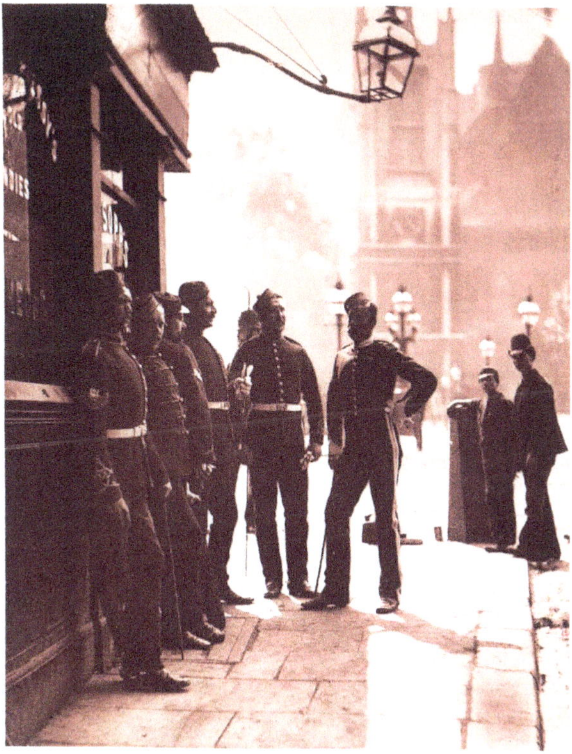

FIG 6.4: John Thomson, *Recruiting Sergeants at Westminster,* from Adolphe Smith and John Thomson, *Street Life in London* (London: Sampson Low, Marston, Searle and Rivington, 1877-78). Woodburytype.

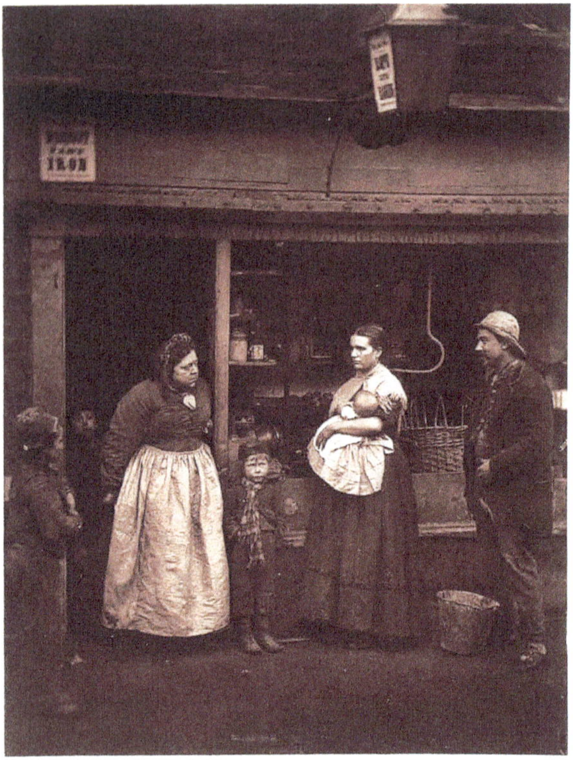

FIG 6.5: John Thomson, *Sufferers from the Floods*, from Adolphe Smith and John Thomson, *Street Life in London* (London: Sampson Low, Marston, Searle and Rivington, 1877-78). Woodburytype.

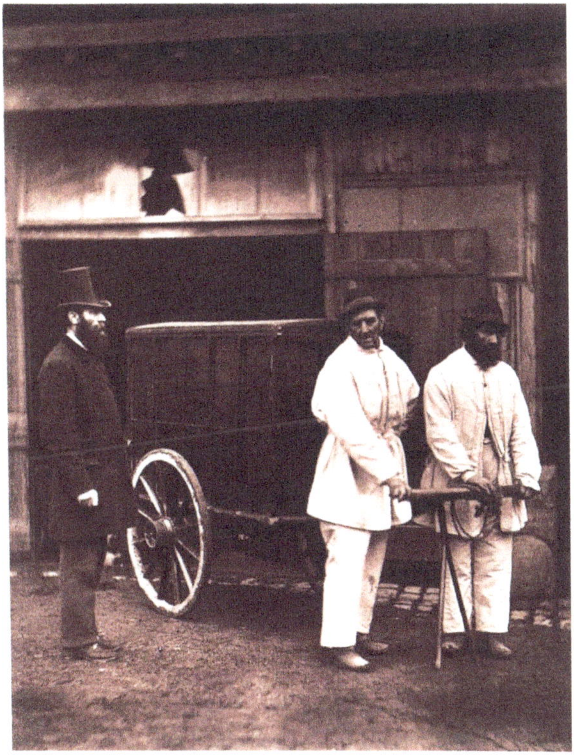

FIG 6.6: John Thomson, *Public Disinfectors*, from Adolphe Smith and John Thomson, *Street Life in London* (London: Sampson Low, Marston, Searle and Rivington, 1877-78). Woodburytype.

> *must bargain and haggle before she can obtain the refuse flowers disdained by fashionable dealers. Even such simple flowers as the primrose and violet are now governed by the inexorable and iron laws of supply and demand.*[34]

The passage presents the women's condition as parallel to that of nature in general, which has been forced to conform to the "inexorable and iron" laws of capitalism. Laden with socialist feeling, the text nonetheless fails to recognize the women as laborers. Instead, they become symbols. They are literal child-bearers, accompanied by their babies as they ply their trade; and they create a scene "pregnant with poetry." It becomes difficult to tell whether Smith refers to the women or to nature itself. The women *are* nature itself.

As such, their identity as individuals matters relatively little to Smith. Indeed, they go unnamed, even as he does pay such attention to their male companion, a man called "Corduroy." Smith treats the women, on the other hand, as largely of a piece, one standing in for another. He presents them explicitly as eternal: like the church building behind them, "rebuilt after the old model" after a fire destroyed it in 1795, these women pass down not only their professions but their very physical positions from one generation to another.[35]

Just one of the women merits Smith's brief attention as an individual. He describes her work as vital to the support of her family, since her husband is an invalid. Though her son assists in supporting the family through his work as an "independent bootblack," she is the primary provider.[36] Smith notes in passing that the typical income for a flower-seller ranges from "more than a pound net profits... in a week" in summer to "less than a shilling" per day in bad weather," but he gives no precise details or figures like those in *London Cabmen*.[37]

Right up to the end, he emphasizes the women's symbolic function. In the final passage, he introduces another flower-woman, one "Isabelle, the favourite flower-girl of the Paris Jockey Club."[38] The official flower seller of this fashionable Second Empire club, Isabelle served as a kind of mascot.[39] A kept woman, she lived "in a most luxurious apartment, endowed with a fine collection of diamonds, besporting herself in a neat little brougham" and given an allowance of £400 per year. Recently, however, she had fallen from grace, due to her miserly (and, in France, illegal) refusal to help her destitute mother, something the London flower women would never do:

"The flower-women of Covent Garden are not gifted with the artistic instinct and coquettish charms of Isabelle, but warmer hearts beat beneath their hoddin-grey than ever stirred the black and yellow satin of the Jockey Club."[40] To the romantic character of the English flower-woman, Smith counterposes the feminine wiles of a Parisian courtesan.[41] The Covent Garden women play Madonnas to the notorious Isabelle's whore.[42] Like Thomson, Smith buys in to the traditions of the street type genre here. While he and Thomson desired to present "true types" of the London poor, faced with a group of workers so frequently represented in prior art and literature they proved themselves unable to disengage with stereotype.

In this initial issue, *Street Life in London* promised a largely familiar vision of the London streets. Readers fond of Mayhew, Greenwood and their ilk could feel comfortable here. The February 1877 issue does question some common assumptions about the streets, but the issue as a whole presents the streets as known and knowable, existing in a kind of non-threatening stasis. It reassures readers, presenting a London whose social ills were not intractable but comprehensible and even solvable, and encouraging a compassionate attitude toward the poor.

The March 1877 issue continues this encouragement of compassion, but at the same time it fulfills the authors' promise from the Preface to present "more original studies." The March issue broadens the definition of street life to include some figures not traditionally considered among the masses of the public poor, and in both text and image Smith and Thomson push boundaries. Texts emphasize street life not as eternal and picturesque but as difficult and changeable, and Thomson's three photographs are among the most compelling in the entire publication.

The March installment includes *Recruiting Sergeants at Westminster*, *Street Floods in Lambeth*, and *Public Disinfectors* (Figures 6.4-6.6): military recruiters, flood victims, and public health officers, all figures that readers would not immediately have associated with street labor. Each entry pairs a well-composed, striking image with a forceful and informative text. Here, Smith and Thomson do not simply report on the conditions of the streets, but campaign overtly for reform. If the February 1877 issue serves as a kind of promise to the reader of what *Street Life in London* has in store, the March issue aims to make the reader complicit, to activate and motivate him to engage with the politics of the streets. Together, the two issues unite to introduce readers to what Smith and Thomson hoped would follow: a vision of the London streets both familiar and novel, comfortable and compelling.

Through his images, Thomson declares from the start that he will reject the standards of the street type. His picture of the Westminster recruiting sergeants (Figure 6.4) demonstrates the inscrutability of the London streets and sublimates the demands of descriptive clarity to those of style. Photographing in the mid-morning, he places the men with the sun at their backs, a decision that creates pleasing shadows and dramatic contrasts of light and dark but suppresses the details of their faces and clothing, silhouetting them instead against a bright background. Little of their physiognomies or of their uniforms, i.e. little of the detail expected of a typological image, appears clearly here. And rather than resorting to the stiff postures of a traditional street type, Thomson permits the men to pose themselves. Three lean against the pub's wall, two stand casually, and one presents himself jauntily, hand on hip, as though defying expectations of military rigor. Thomson also masses dark forms at the left margin of the composition, while light floods in from the right. All in all he creates a breathtaking departure from the standards of street typology, seeming to thumb his nose at such rigidly hieratic images.

The tonal and spatial imbalances of this image recall the Japanistic compositions of the Impressionists. Though Thomson almost certainly had heard nothing of Impressionism in 1876-77, he worked within a similar matrix of influences: in addition to having extensive experience of the art and architecture of Asia, he also understood intimately the unconventional, dispassionate machine aesthetic of the camera. Indeed, his expertise as an optician made him a connoisseur of the distortions of photographic lenses. If this image does not inform us of the typical physiognomy of a recruiting sergeant or the details of his dress, it conveys atmosphere in spades through its defiantly dramatic, almost radical arrangement. Rather than conforming to the standards of popular print culture, it embraces the innovations of high art.

Smith's *Recruiting Sergeants* essay also incorporates a complexity not usually found in profiles of street figures. The essay begins innocuously enough by filling in the details the image has suppressed: the names, ranks and military affiliations of the six recruiters depicted, the location of the pub, and so on. Smith also explains that the pub shown here essentially functions as the recruiters' office. Their usual practice is to ply a potential recruit with beer while persuading him to enlist. On his agreement to join, they then pay him a shilling. Smith uses this information to justify including these men in a book about street poverty, since military recruiting is hardly a lucrative career. The shilling paid to the recruit, and the cost of beer to persuade him, come out of the recruiter's own pocket and are repaid only once the recruit reports for duty. Because some recruits never report, the recruiters frequently lose this money. In addition, the recruiters receive inadequate living expenses from the military and must augment these with their own funds to survive. No man gets rich as a recruiter.[43]

But Smith's primary reason for including the recruiters is not to argue that they should be counted among the poor. Rather, he uses them as entrée to an argument about the injustices of class-based inequality. In 1877 military ranking was primarily a matter of class and family position, rather than of merit. Officers bought their positions and could be removed only if demonstrating gross incompetence. Worthy recruits from the lower social orders had almost no chance of becoming officers, no matter how competent. "Will the day never dawn," Smith cries, "when some patriotic reformer shall... throw the army open to all, render its rewards accessible to sterling merit alone, without regard for wealth, position or family influence...?"[44] It becomes quite clear that he is using the military as a metonym for the whole of British society. He questions not only class-based rank and promotion within the military, but social class itself. Although the literature of urban spectatorship often did propose reforms designed to ameliorate the conditions of poverty, they were rarely so radical as this; and thus Smith's text breaks with its literary antecedents just as Thomson's picture does with its pictorial ones.

Thomson's image for the next entry, *Sufferers from the Floods*, shows a group of people from Lambeth, an overcrowded area of London that was swamped every winter by the tidal flooding of the Thames. The picture affords the viewer little insight into what constitutes a "typical" flood victim, as the subjects are of all ages, both genders, and a variety of builds (Figure 6.5). Worry and misfortune, not physical characteristics, unite them.

Thomson made *Sufferers from the Floods* under less-than-ideal conditions: January weather, narrow streets that admitted little sunlight. But he clearly did his best given the circumstances. Despite the overall darkness, there are blazes of white in the clothing of two women shown here; and the faces of three children – usually the most likely subjects to move during a long exposure – are clear and sharp, indicating that Thomson made the exposure as brief as possible despite the limited light. Still, the scene appears dark and squalid, this place hardly penetrated by even the smoggiest ray of sunshine.[45] In the shallow space, seven figures – three adults, three children, and an infant – stand more or less in a line parallel to the picture plane. But the lighting and the squalid environs prevent the image from achieving the clarity of a street type. Instead, it conveys an atmosphere of deprivation and despair.

This sense befits the tone of the text. The floods brought misery in two forms: the immediate destruction of property, and the late-arriving specter of contagious disease. That the floods occurred in deepest winter only compounded the wretchedness of the situation. Thomson calls on authorities to take measures to control the flooding:

> *A dangerous experiment is being tried with the health of the community at a time when epidemic disease is only held in check by the most vigilent* [sic] *efforts of modern science. It would be difficult to conceive conditions more favourable to the growth of disease than those at present existing in the low-lying, densely populous quarters of*

Lambeth, that have been invaded by the floods.[46]

In this text, Thomson also gives readers a glimpse of the private, indoor world of poverty *beyond* the London streets, providing a rare account here of the interiors of two houses in the area to show how they and their inhabitants were affected by the floods. In one small rented room he found an entire family: a young husband and wife, their child, and the wife's mother. The husband, out of work since the floods had destroyed his nearby place of business, could not find more than two days' worth of labor in a week. Thomson writes that he was "much struck with the bright, cheerful appearance of the comely young wife, and the success of her efforts to maintain a clean, comfortable, and attractive home to cheer her husband on his return after his wanderings in search of work."[47] None of them were yet sick, but the wife worried that the lack of work would begin to "break down" her husband.[48]

In contrast to this house was "another, a few paces further on, occupied by a widow, her son, and her daughter."[49] Astonishingly squalid, it still bore evidence of the most recent flooding as the widow had little time to clean. In addition to the filthy little girl who lived with her mother, another daughter came home periodically to take advantage of the poor woman, even beating her when she refused to give up her last shreds of clothing for pawn. Her son, who made "good wages in the mason's yard," was her only comfort, but "'since the floods he has been troubled by a hacking cough; I don't like to hear it, and it don't leave him, sir.'"[50] As often in *Street Life in London*, those Thomson meets close-at-hand, like the widow herself, appear hardworking and honest. Those with blemished character or unsavory habits, like the widow's violent daughter, are introduced and discussed secondhand, remaining in the background where they seem less threatening.

In one passage, Thomson meditates on his experiences in China. There, he writes, people have adapted to the constant threat of flooding:

> *The Chinese, some of them, construct their houses to meet emergencies. I have heard a Chinaman boast that a mud cabin was the fittest abode for man. In case of flood it settles down over the furniture, keeps it together, and forms a mound upon which the family may sit and fish until the flood abates.*[51]

In London conditions are far worse, the people have not adapted as well, and there are no fish to eat while one waits for the waters to recede. The implication of the passage is clear: if conditions in heathen China are superior to those in London, then London is having serious trouble indeed. The passage typifies Thomson's ethnographic approach to the London streets: a world deserving of his sympathy and his concern, to be sure, but a world ultimately apart from his own.

For the third entry in March 1877, *Public Disinfectors*, Thomson photographs and Smith describes a pair of quite new professions involving the inspection and disinfection of houses where infectious disease has been found. In one way these men are like the *Recruiting Sergeants* profiled in the first March entry: while they appear *in* the streets, they are not *of* the streets. Certainly they would have been unexpected characters in a book devoted to street types, since they did not sell any product or service. Indeed, one would hardly desire to interact with them professionally, since they dealt exclusively in disease. Here, again, Thomson and Smith prove that their book will show not only the old but the new: familiar types, as well as people and places "beyond the beat of the ordinary wayfarer," as they state in the Preface.[52]

Thomson's photograph (Figure 6.6) depicts three men. Two stand together on the right side of the picture, the third on the left side facing toward, but not looking at, the pair. The man at left, heavily bearded, wears a dark coat over dark pants and shoes. His hat is tall and flat-crowned, a gentleman's hat. His clothing cannot be said to constitute a uniform, unless we consider it the Baudelairean "uniform" of the modern middle class.[53] The other two men, by contrast, wear identical quilted white jackets over white pants – laborers' clothing. Both also have on sturdy shoes and low-crowned hats with brims.

The most notable difference between the two groups, however, is not of clothing but of attitude. The man at left stands in hieratic profile, his hand clenched in a fist at his side. While a side view is sometimes found in typological imagery, here the pose derives from another paradigm, that of the portrait studio. This man has had his picture made before, perhaps more than once; directed to stand still by Thomson, he assumed an attitude familiar to him from prior experience. The other two men, by contrast, had probably never been photographed. Certainly their poses here do not possess the same rigid, programmatic dignity of the other man's. One of them looks at the camera with his mouth open, while the other stares down almost dejectedly. They stand behind the push-bar of a handcart bearing a large, dark, paneled box. Their hands on the bar, they appear ready to haul the vehicle away, like draft animals.

The three men stand in a dirt courtyard possessed of a few scattered cobblestones. Behind them is a wooden building, its wide barn doors flung open to reveal a dark interior. Above the doorway, the jagged edges of a broken window form a counterpoint to the rectilinear forms of the structure. Thomson uses these rectangles and their varied gray tones to advantage: the building serves as a kind of proto-modernist backdrop for the group before it, its overlapping rectangles again recalling Japanist and Impressionist formal elements.

In the text, Smith identifies the three men as members of a team dedicated to seeking out and eradicating infectious disease. The man on the left is "Mr. Dickson, the Inspector of Nuisances for the Parish or Union of St. George's." Those on the right are the nameless disinfectors, public employees elevated from service on road crews to what Smith calls "the dignity of disinfection."[54] This dangerous but well-paid business involved sterilizing private homes after someone among their inhabitants either died of or fully recovered from an infectious disease. The collective profession of these three men, disease control, was new in 1877, the result of legislation less than a decade old. The public had not yet learned to regard their services as absolutely necessary. Indeed, people often lied about the presence of disease in their homes, in part because they had to pay the expenses associated with disinfection. Hence much of the work of the Inspector of Nuisances involved seeking out cases of disease. Without power to force entry, he sometimes resorted to subterfuge, questioning neighbors, servants, and children to find out where disease was present.[55]

After the inspector performed the intellectual labor of locating disease, the disinfectors would enter the home to engage in their physical labor. This involved going into the sickroom, now emptied of its former inhabitant, and removing everything. Smith describes the process:

> *Once in the sickroom, no prying eyes are allowed to watch the disinfectors at work. They have strict orders to exclude everyone from their dangerous presence. Alone and unseen, they remove, one by one ... all textile materials they can find in the room, carefully place them in the hand-cart, and drag them off to the disinfecting-oven... Few persons care to be present on these occasions; and, but for their own honesty of purpose, the disinfectors might*

> *often make away with various objects which in all probability would not at first be missed. The men chosen for this work are therefore carefully selected, and have generally been known for many years to the Vestries by whom they are appointed.*[56]

In the passage, Smith takes pains to persuade his audience that these men, among the few members of the working class allowed unsupervised access to the houses of the wealthy, deserve not fear but admiration. The disinfectors endanger themselves on a daily basis precisely because disease operates without consideration for class. As disease functions invisibly and inexorably, crossing barriers of class and culture to invade the houses of rich and poor alike, so too must the work of disease control happen everywhere, unimpeded by inter-class misunderstandings or ill-will. Smith acknowledges the potentially "sinister" quality of such pervasive surveillance, but contends that the public health depends on the inspectors' ability to oversee every household in their districts, rich or poor; and on the disinfectors' ability to penetrate into and excise pockets of disease wherever they might arise.[57]

The March 1877 issue broadens and deepens definitions of "street life." Hereafter, however, the

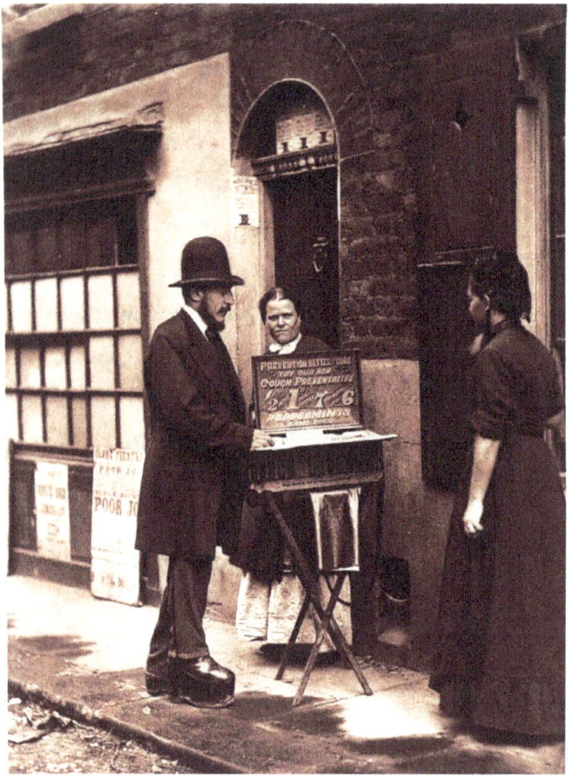

FIG 6.7: John Thomson, *Street Doctor*, from Adolphe Smith and John Thomson, *Street Life in London* (London: Sampson Low, Marston, Searle and Rivington, 1877-78). Woodburytype.

publication begins to succumb to external pressures and, in the process, to change. While subsequent issues do not, as Gibson-Cowan argued, entirely lose thematic unity or editorial direction, the neat contrapuntal order exhibited in the first two issues does begin to break down. Thomson's images trend toward the typological, in response to criticisms such as those leveled at *London Cabmen*. Thomson's texts cease to bear his signature, becoming more collaborative and incorporating extensive quotes from his informants in an attempt to render them more like the street "characters" readers expected. Smith's texts also change, incorporating – possibly at the publishers' insistence – more emphasis on philanthropy, less on reform. Smith begins to exhibit on occasion, too, a lack of sympathy toward his subjects, an attitude for which women in particular often serve as the target. The entire publication, in both text and image, becomes more like the publications on which it was modeled, and whose tropes and traditions it had originally intended either to reject or to remodel.

April 1877 to January 1878: thematic unity and variety

Individual issues of the serial are generally organized around a particular theme or with a particular narrative logic. The April 1877 installment, for instance,

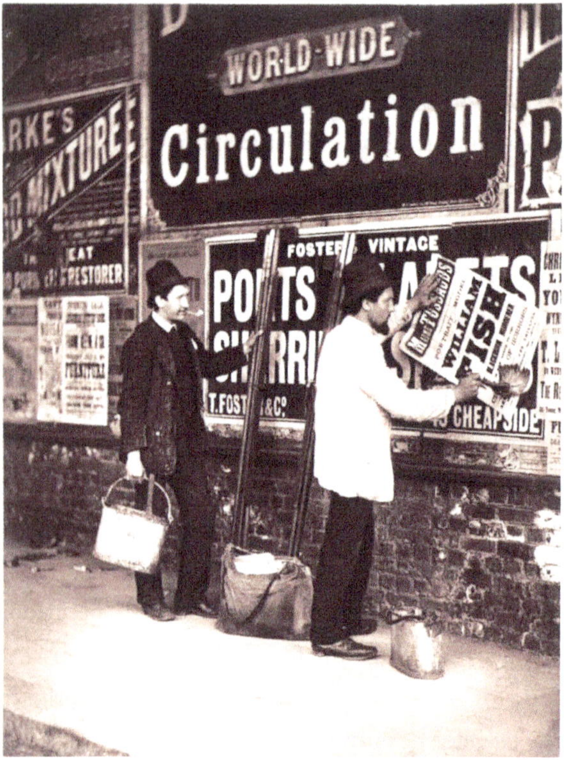

FIG 6.8: John Thomson, *Street Advertising,* from Adolphe Smith and John Thomson, *Street Life in London* (London: Sampson Low, Marston, Searle and Rivington, 1877-78). Woodburytype.

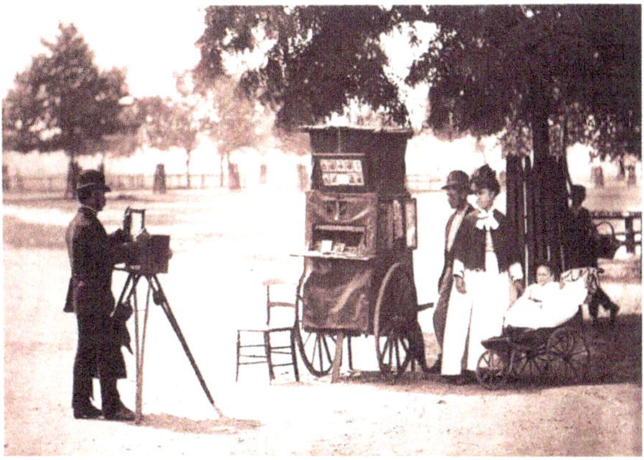

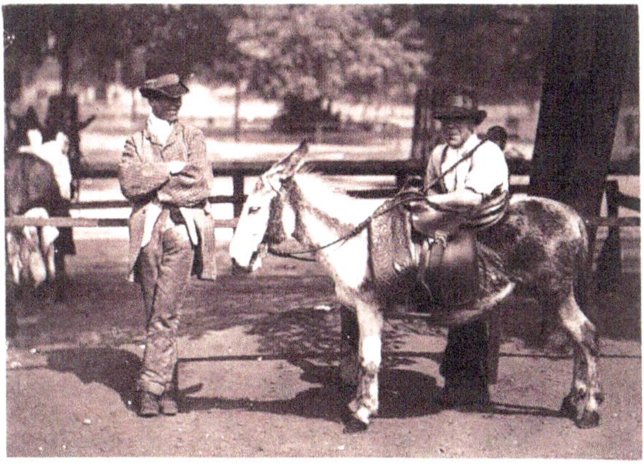

FIG 6.9: John Thomson, *Photography on the Common*, from Adolphe Smith and John Thomson, *Street Life in London* (London: Sampson Low, Marston, Searle and Rivington, 1877-78). Woodburytype. **FIG 6.10:** John Thomson, *Waiting for a Hire*, from Adolphe Smith and John Thomson, *Street Life in London* (London: Sampson Low, Marston, Searle and Rivington, 1877-78). Woodburytype.

continues the combination of familiar and novel exhibited by the first two monthly issues, and one of its entries has seasonal relevance. It profiles a *Street Doctor* (Figure 6.7) much like the quacks and "patterers" who appear regularly in Mayhew's first volume, but it also includes an entry devoted to members of the advertising trade, a new addition to the compendium of street labor.[58] Advertising firms provided many jobs to seasonal, semi-skilled, and otherwise underemployed workers, and *Street Advertising* (Figure 6.8) is the first of three separate entries in *Street Life in London* focusing on the advertising industry. The third entry, *Clapham Common Industries*, profiles members of two professions, a portrait photographer and a seller of donkey-rides, in separate photographs (Figures 6.9, 6.10). Both of these workers began appearing regularly on the Clapham Common around Easter, in late March or early April, so their appearance in this particular issue accords with seasonal appeal.

The May 1877 installment exhibits both thematic and literal relationships among its three entries: *Caney the Clown*, *Dealer in Fancy-Ware*, and *The Temperance Sweep* (Figures 6.11-6.13). The issue concerns itself in large part not with the labor of the poor, but their diversions. "Caney" was formerly a circus clown prior

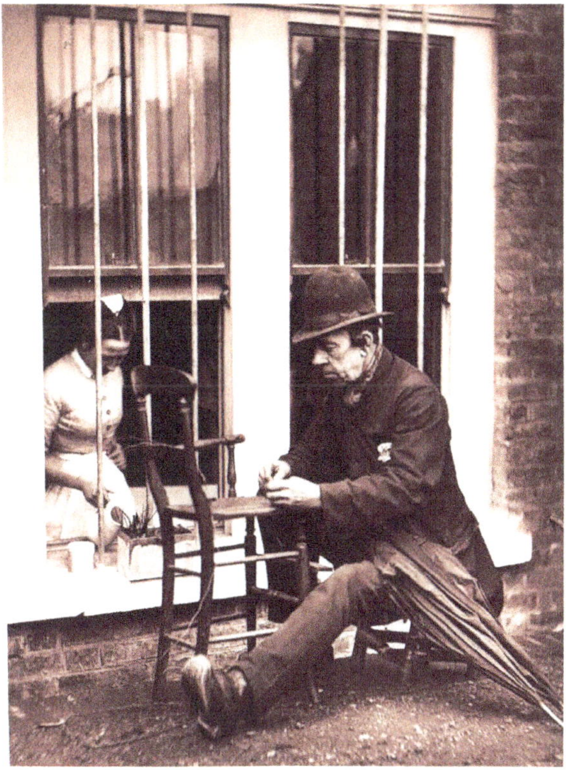

FIG 6.11: John Thomson, *Caney, the Clown*, from Adolphe Smith and John Thomson, *Street Life in London* (London: Sampson Low, Marston, Searle and Rivington, 1877-78). Woodburytype.

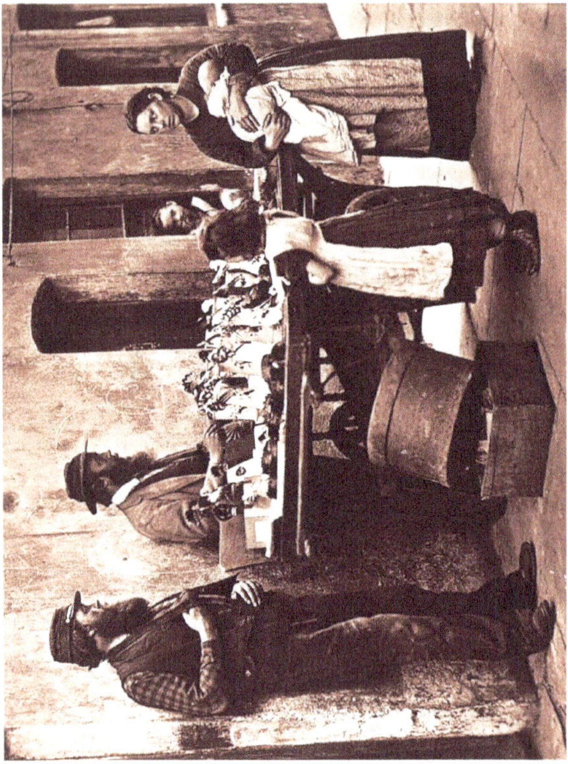

FIG 6.12: John Thomson, *Dealer in Fancy-Ware,* from Adolphe Smith and John Thomson, *Street Life in London* (London: Sampson Low, Marston, Searle and Rivington, 1877-78). Woodburytype.

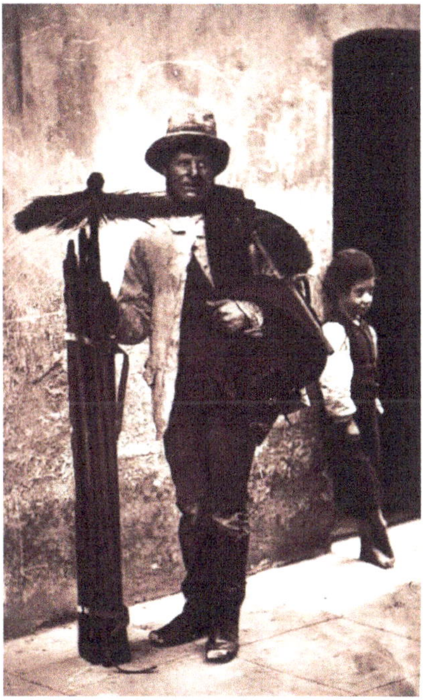

FIG 6.13: John Thomson, *The Temperance Sweep,* from Adolphe Smith and John Thomson, *Street Life in London* (London: Sampson Low, Marston, Searle and Rivington, 1877-78). Woodburytype.

to his current profession of chair-mending, and his act appealed primarily to a poor and working-class audience, among whom he achieved widespread fame. The Dealer in Fancy-Ware sold frivolous, decorative items to workers out strolling on their days off. And although some of the *Temperance Sweep* entry focuses on the alcoholism and recovery of the title character, much of the text examines the May Day traditions of the chimney sweeps, a subject also treated extensively in Mayhew.[59] More compellingly, physical and concrete ties also unite the three narratives in the May issue. Caney, hero of the first entry, is mentioned again in the third, performing as a clown in the May-Day parades overseen by the chimney sweeps. And for the second and third entries, Thomson used the same physical space as a setting, photographing the bric-a-brac dealer and the chimney sweep on the same sidewalk, with the same graffiti-covered wall in the background (Figures 6.12-6.13).[60] The May 1877 installment thus presents the London streets not as chaotic, unknowable, and uncontrollable, but as logical, continuous, and narratively sensible. Together, the three stories contribute to a sense of the London streets as home-like and communitarian, their inhabitants part of a network or even a family that not only works but plays together.[61]

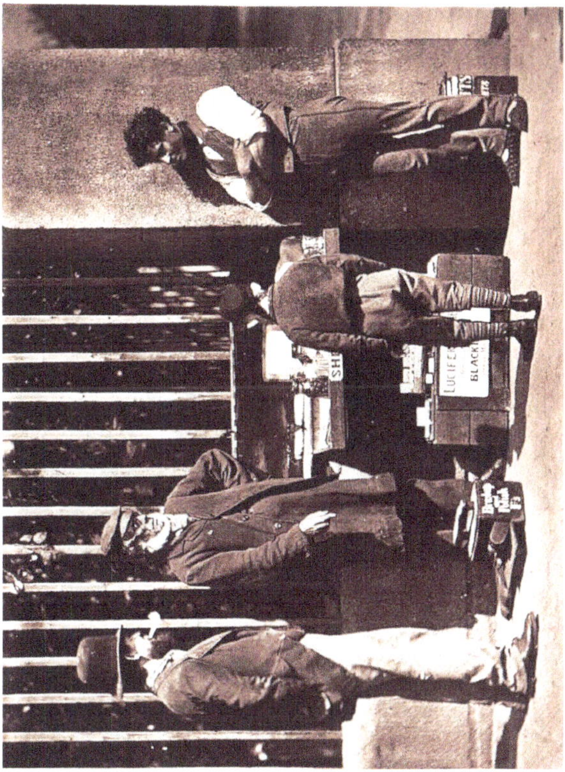

FIG 6.14: John Thomson, *The Dramatic Shoe-Black,* from Adolphe Smith and John Thomson, *Street Life in London* (London: Sampson Low, Marston, Searle and Rivington, 1877-78). Woodburytype.

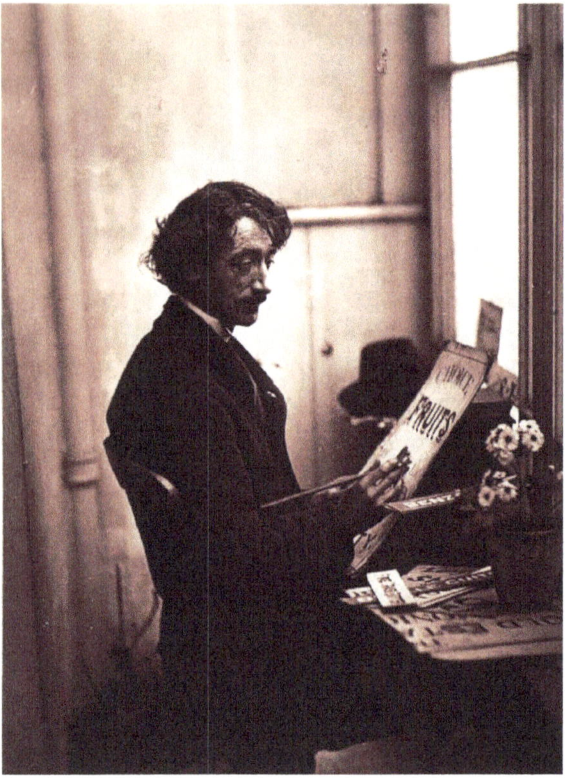

FIG 6.15: John Thomson, *Tickets the Card-Dealer*, from Adolphe Smith and John Thomson, *Street Life in London* (London: Sampson Low, Marston, Searle and Rivington, 1877-78). Woodburytype.

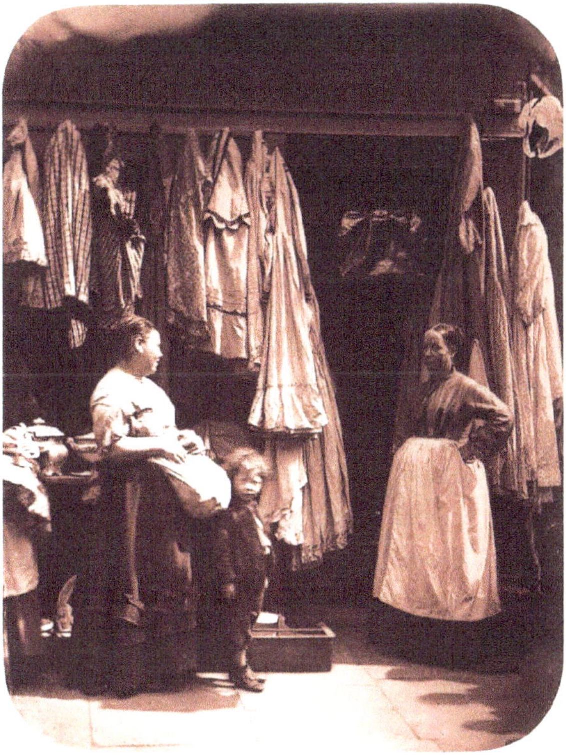

FIG 6.16: John Thomson, *An Old Clothes' Shop, Seven Dials*, from Adolphe Smith and John Thomson, *Street Life in London* (London: Sampson Low, Marston, Searle and Rivington, 1877-78). Woodburytype.

June 1877 profiles an assortment of unusual characters: in *The Dramatic Shoe-Black*, a well-educated former actor and skilled worker who now shines shoes; in *Tickets the Card-Dealer*, a widely-traveled Frenchman who labors in London as a peddler of shop-signs; and in *The Old Clothes of St. Giles*, the female owner of a secondhand shop (Figures 6.14-6.16). In July 1877, *A Convicts' Home* profiles a benevolent man who, after a knockabout childhood and a stint as a police officer, now runs a restaurant for the poor and halfway-house for criminals. Also in July, *The Wall Worker* is the second of the *Street Life* entries to focus on an advertising-related job; and *Covent Garden Labourers* introduces a group of porters who work in the Covent Garden fruit-and-flower markets (Figures 6.17-6.19).

In August 1877 each entry addresses to some extent the cultural and racial diversity of the streets. *Halfpenny Ices* (Figure 6.20) profiles traveling Italian sellers of ices and ice creams, discussing their cultural identity at length.[62] *Black Jack* (Figure 6.21) focuses on a costermonger whose other nickname is "Darkie," introducing questions about his race.[63] In *Cheap Fish of St. Giles's* (Figure 6.22) Smith addresses and to some extent challenges questions of racial stereotype in discussing the fish vendor's culturally mixed clientele.[64]

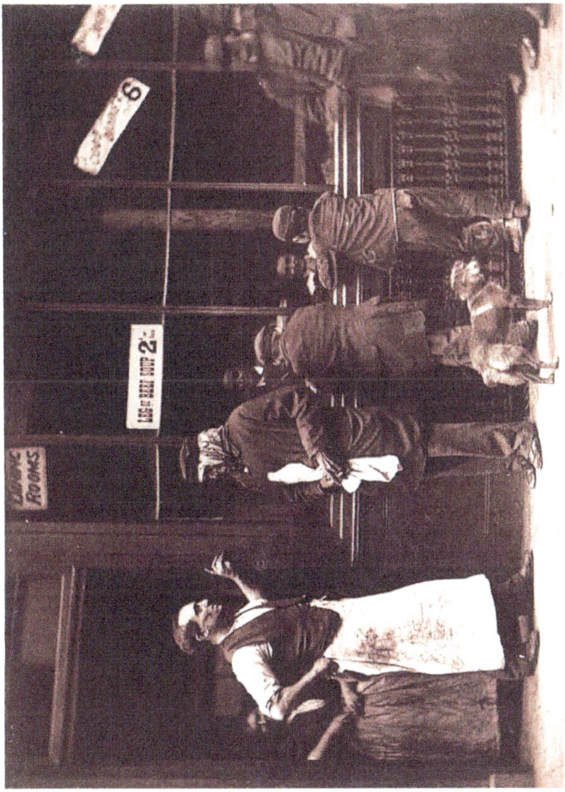

FIG 6.17: John Thomson, *A Convicts' Home*, from Adolphe Smith and John Thomson, *Street Life in London* (London: Sampson Low, Marston, Searle and Rivington, 1877-78). Woodburytype.

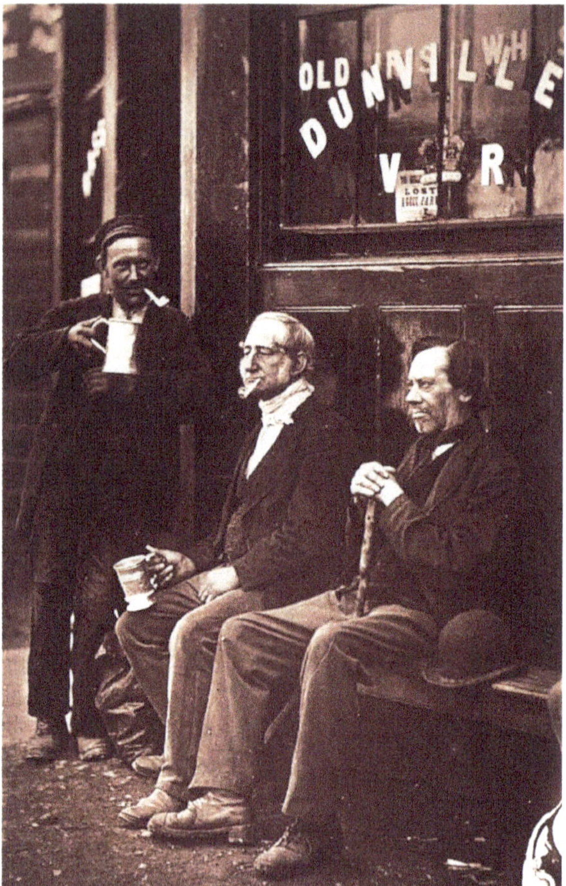

FIG 6.18: John Thomson, *The Wall Worker,* from Adolphe Smith and John Thomson, *Street Life in London* (London: Sampson Low, Marston, Searle and Rivington, 1877-78). Woodburytype.

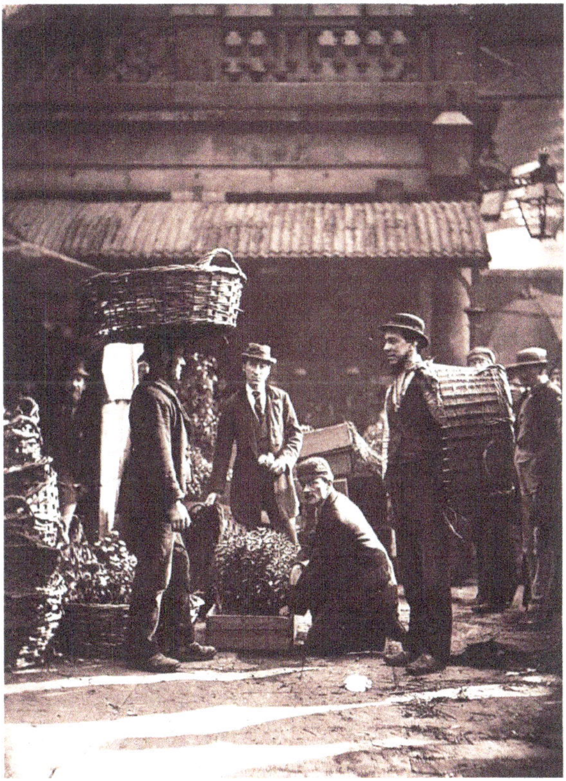

FIG 6.19: John Thomson, *Covent Garden Labourers*, from Adolphe Smith and John Thomson, *Street Life in London* (London: Sampson Low, Marston, Searle and Rivington, 1877-78). Woodburytype.

Entries for September 1877 are united by comparisons between past and present, whether nostalgic or forward-looking. *Cast-Iron Billy* (Figure 6.23) profiles a former omnibus driver whose career began before the advent of the railroad and has continued well into the age of steam power, making him a kind of living relic. The bargemen profiled in the second entry, *Workers on the Silent Highway* (Figure 6.24), find their livelihood impaired by a bureaucratic morass, since the water-shipping trade is regulated by three separate entities of varying ages, at least one quite ancient. And the third entry, *The Street Fruit Trade*, self-consciously references the bygone genre of the street cry. Indeed, Thomson titles the accompanying photograph *as* a street cry: *Strawberries! All Ripe! All Ripe!* (Figure 6.25).[65]

October 1877 includes three quite straightforwardly typological images: *The London Boardmen*, *The Water-Cart*, and *Mush-Fakers and Ginger-Beer Makers* (Figures 6.26-6.28). It seems here as though Thomson gave in completely to the external pressures and expectations being placed on the publication. By November, Adolphe Smith had clearly followed suit, as the texts for that issue – *November Effigies*, *Hookey Alf of Whitechapel*, and *The Crawlers*, all written by Smith – foreground acts of charity,

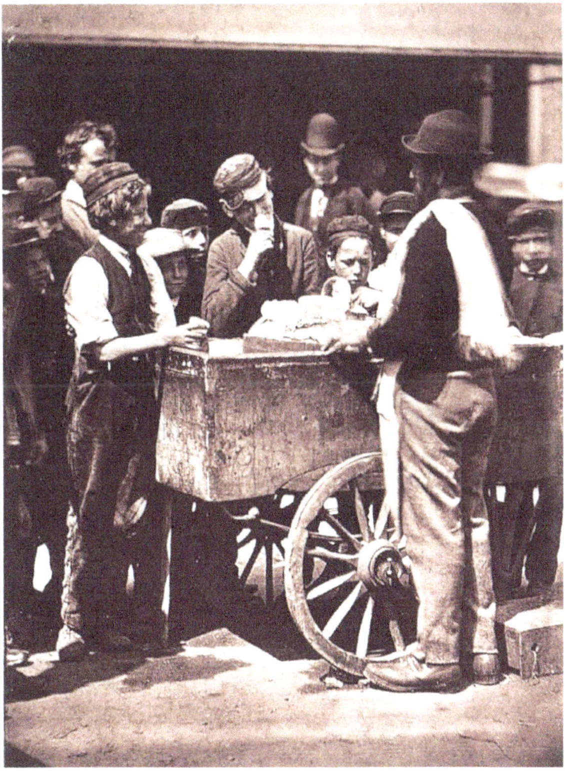

FIG 6.20: John Thomson, *Halfpenny Ices*, from Adolphe Smith and John Thomson, *Street Life in London* (London: Sampson Low, Marston, Searle and Rivington, 1877-78). Woodburytype.

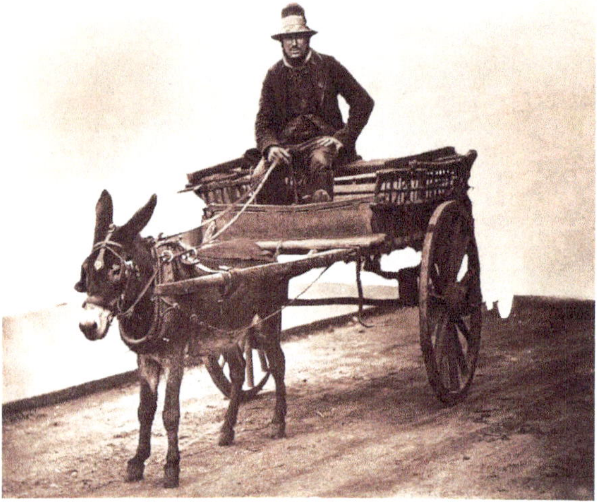

FIG 6.21: John Thomson, *Black Jack*, from Adolphe Smith and John Thomson, *Street Life in London* (London: Sampson Low, Marston, Searle and Rivington, 1877-78). Woodburytype.

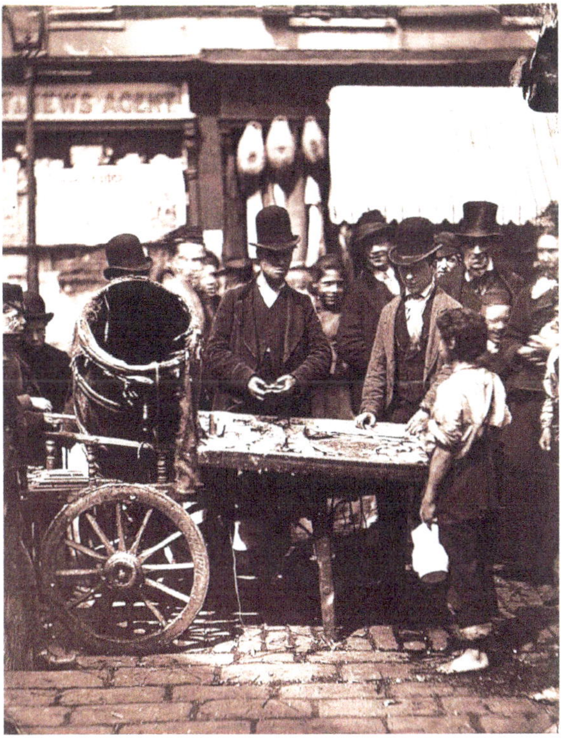

FIG 6.22: John Thomson, *The Cheap Fish of St. Giles*, from Adolphe Smith and John Thomson, *Street Life in London* (London: Sampson Low, Marston, Searle and Rivington, 1877-78). Woodburytype.

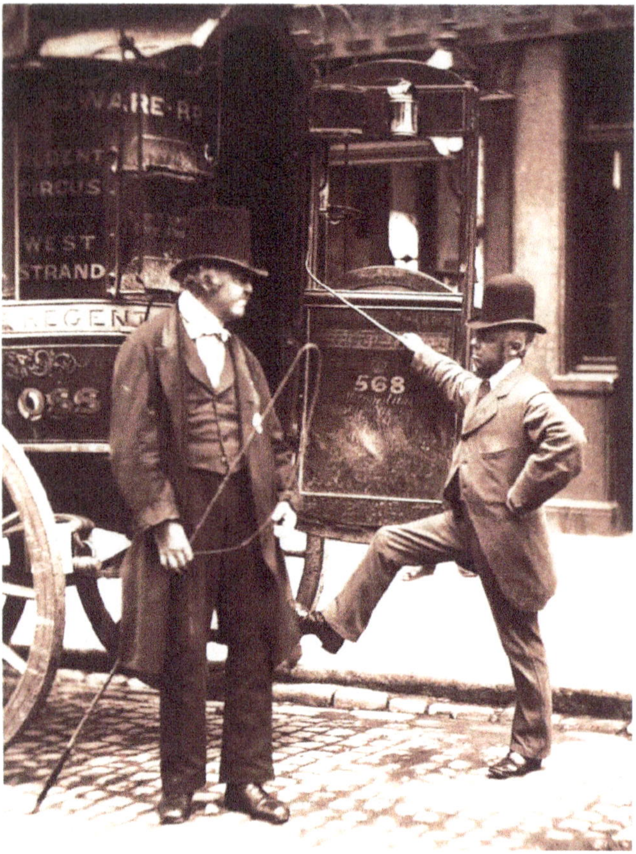

FIG 6.23: John Thomson, *Cast-Iron Billy*, from Adolphe Smith and John Thomson, *Street Life in London* (London: Sampson Low, Marston, Searle and Rivington, 1877-78). Woodburytype.

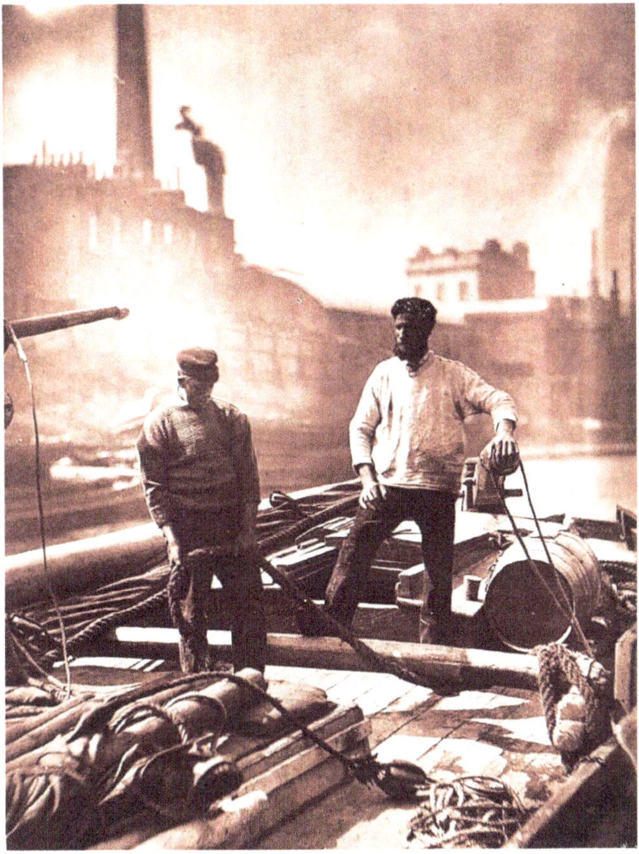

FIG 6.24: John Thomson, *Workers on the Silent Highway,* from Adolphe Smith and John Thomson, *Street Life in London* (London: Sampson Low, Marston, Searle and Rivington, 1877-78). Woodburytype.

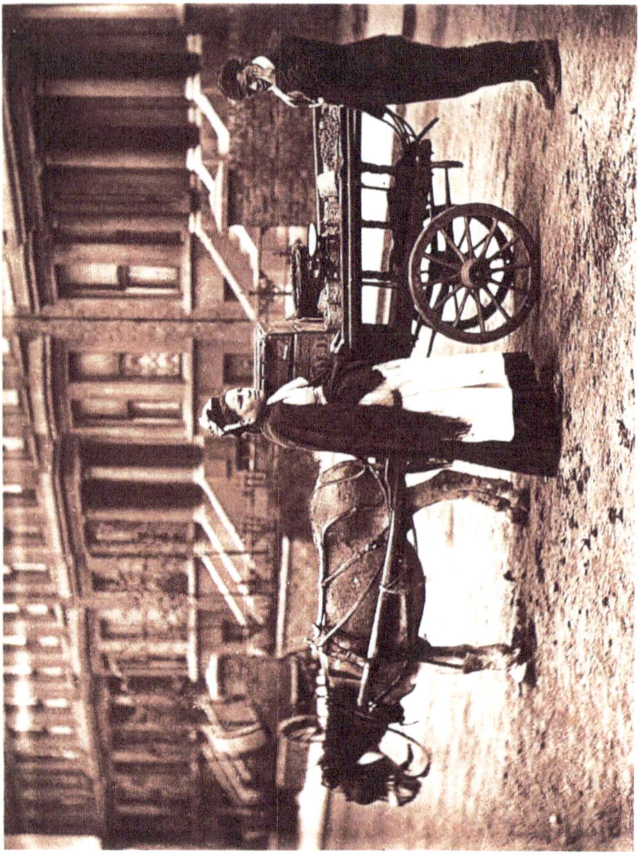

FIG 6.25: John Thomson, *Strawberries! All Ripe! All Ripe!*, from Adolphe Smith and John Thomson, *Street Life in London* (London: Sampson Low, Marston, Searle and Rivington, 1877-78). Woodburytype.

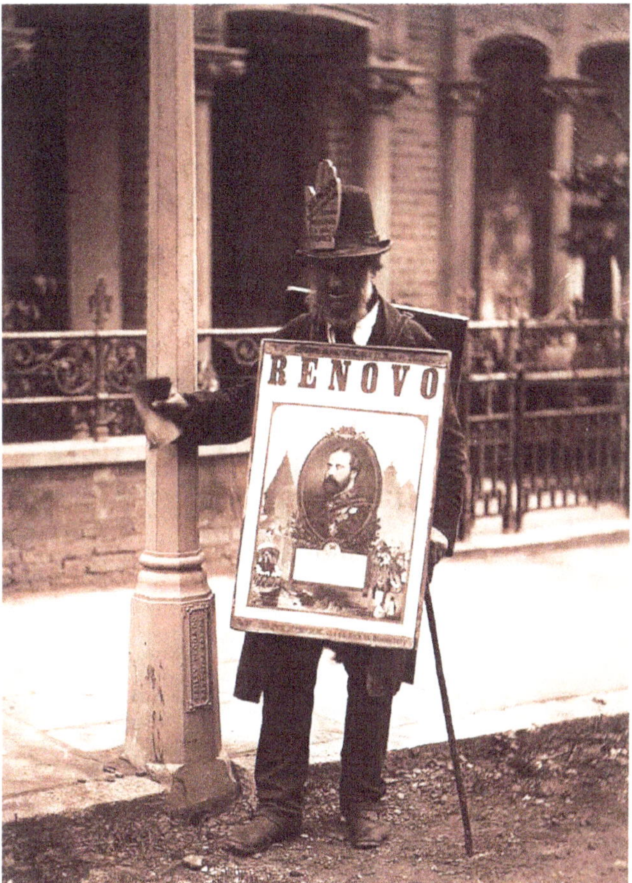

FIG 6.26: John Thomson, *The London Boardmen*, from Adolphe Smith and John Thomson, *Street Life in London* (London: Sampson Low, Marston, Searle and Rivington, 1877-78). Woodburytype.

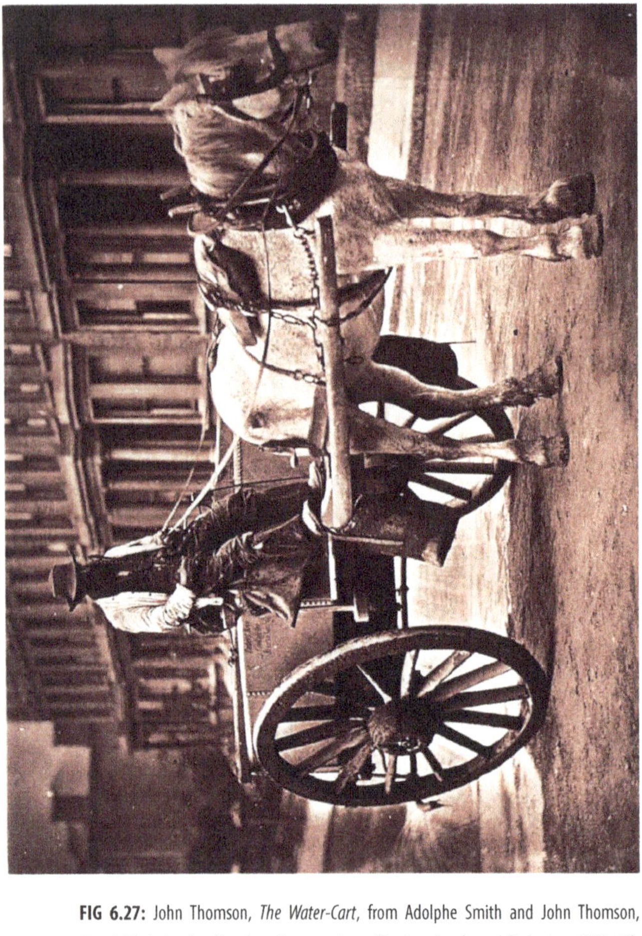

FIG 6.27: John Thomson, *The Water-Cart*, from Adolphe Smith and John Thomson, *Street Life in London* (London: Sampson Low, Marston, Searle and Rivington, 1877-78). Woodburytype.

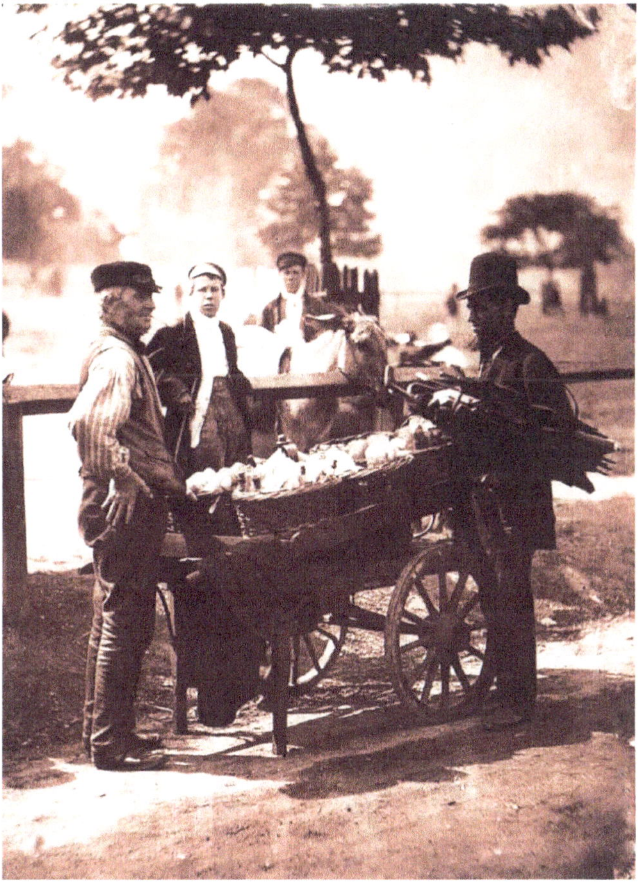

FIG 6.28: John Thomson, *Mush-Fakers and Ginger-Beer Makers*, from Adolphe Smith and John Thomson, *Street Life in London* (London: Sampson Low, Marston, Searle and Rivington, 1877-78). Woodburytype.

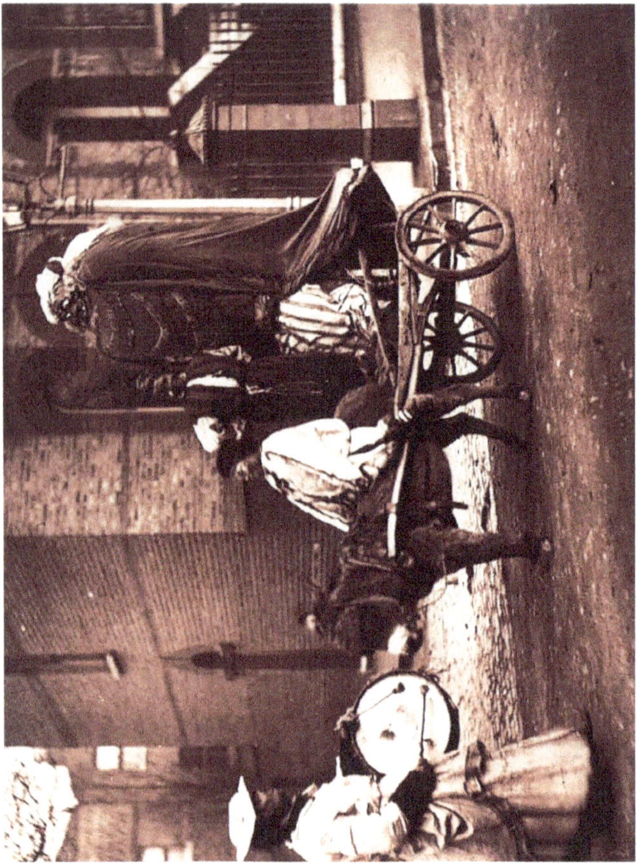

FIG 6.29: John Thomson, *November Effigies*, from Adolphe Smith and John Thomson, *Street Life in London* (London: Sampson Low, Marston, Searle and Rivington, 1877-78). Woodburytype.

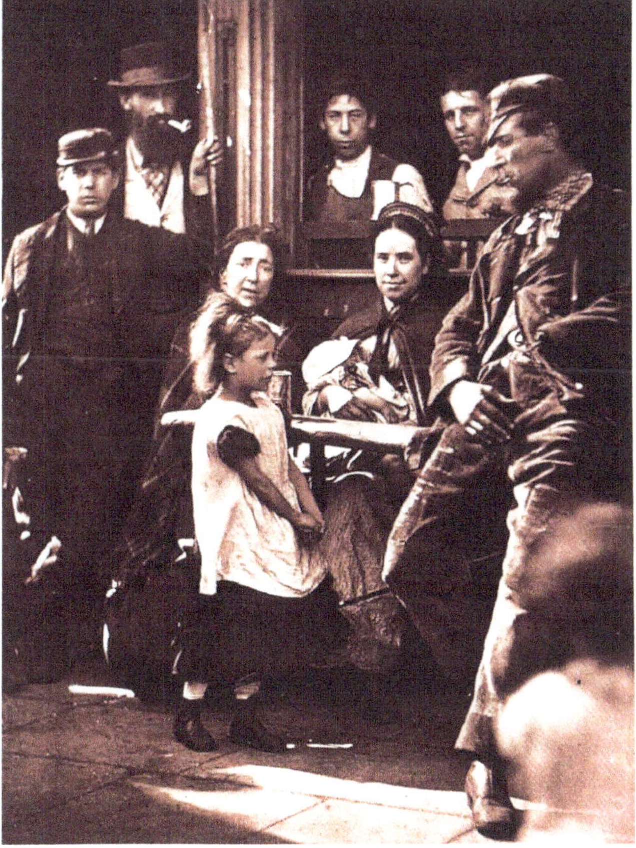

FIG 6.30: John Thomson, *Hookey Alf of Whitechapel*, from Adolphe Smith and John Thomson, *Street Life in London* (London: Sampson Low, Marston, Searle and Rivington, 1877-78). Woodburytype.

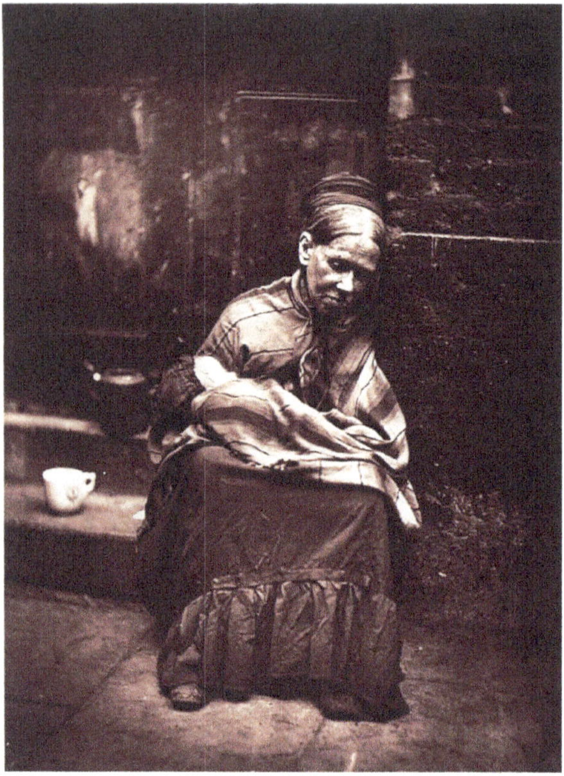

FIG 6.31: John Thomson, *The Crawlers,* from Adolphe Smith and John Thomson, *Street Life in London* (London: Sampson Low, Marston, Searle and Rivington, 1877-78). Woodburytype.

attempting to delineate between more- and less-helpful modes of philanthropic giving (Figures 6.29-6.31). Additionally, *November Effigies* (Figure 6.29) has clear seasonal appeal, as it discusses festivities related to the November 5 holiday, Guy Fawkes Day.

Little seems to bind the entries of the December 1877 installment. Unlike prior issues, this one and the next, from January 1878, had to be compiled well ahead of time, since their contents also appeared in the single-volume version of the publication that appeared in November 1877 as a Christmas book. The authors seem to have constituted this issue, in particular, out of leftover bits and pieces, images made and texts composed earlier. None of the December entries has seasonal appeal, an odd omission given the obvious holiday connections to be made, and all the photographs were made during much warmer weather.[66] *Italian Street Musicians* (Figure 6.32) discusses the training of child musicians; *The Street Locksmith* (Figure 6.33) profiles a prosperous worker; and *The Seller of Shell-Fish* (Figure 6.34) focuses on the titular figure and his trade.

The final installment in the series, from January 1878, also had to be compiled by mid-November for inclusion in the Christmas volume, and it too seems constituted of bits and pieces. Nonetheless it does

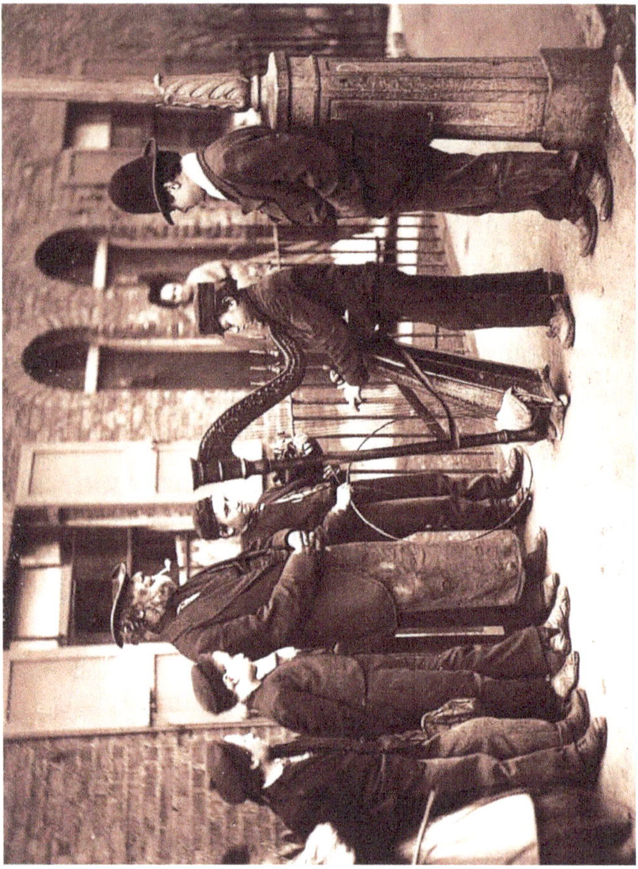

FIG 6.32: John Thomson, *Italian Street Musicians*, from Adolphe Smith and John Thomson, *Street Life in London* (London: Sampson Low, Marston, Searle and Rivington, 1877-78). Woodburytype.

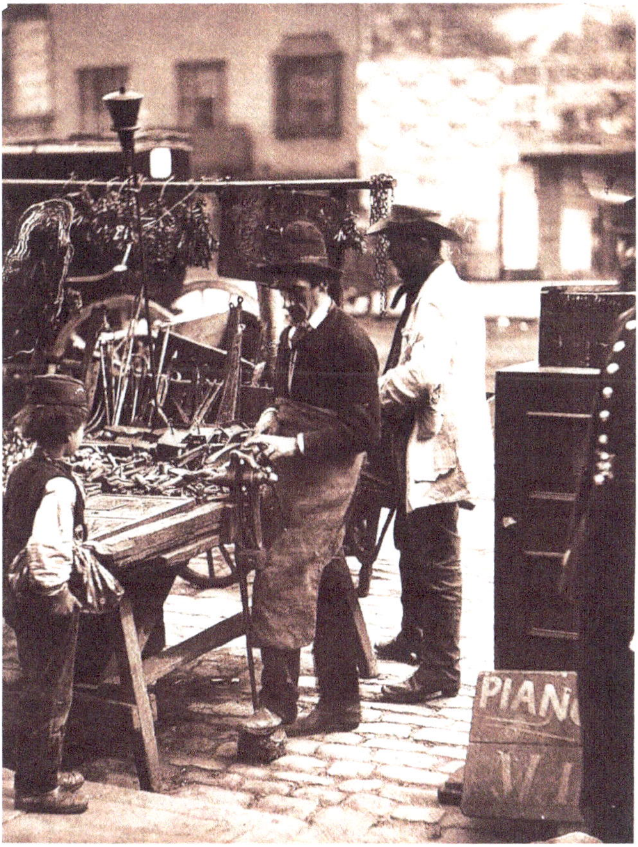

FIG 6.33: John Thomson, *The Street Locksmith*, from Adolphe Smith and John Thomson, *Street Life in London* (London: Sampson Low, Marston, Searle and Rivington, 1877-78). Woodburytype.

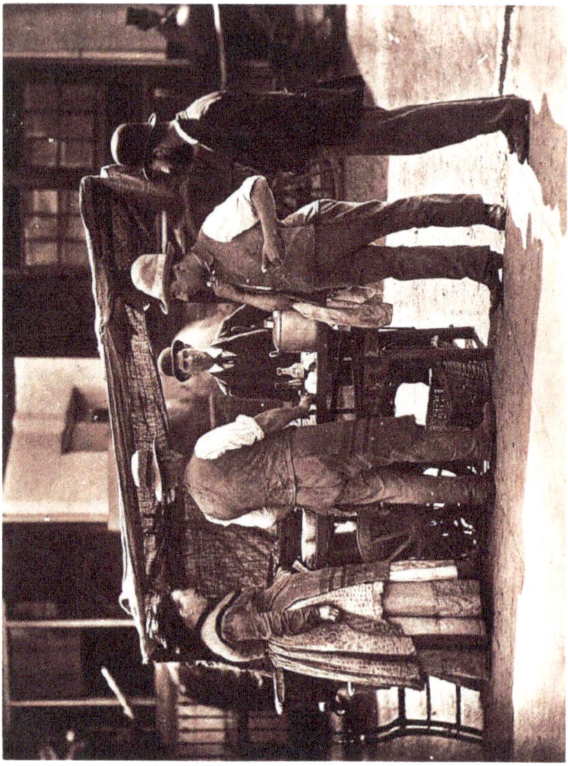

FIG 6.34: John Thomson, *The Seller of Shell-Fish*, from Adolphe Smith and John Thomson, *Street Life in London* (London: Sampson Low, Marston, Searle and Rivington, 1877-78). Woodburytype.

have a discernible theme, since in each of the entries a subject or profession is oppressed or repressed by official interference or prohibition. The *Flying Dustmen* (Figure 6.35) are illicit garbage men who come by after the regular, city-run trash services have passed, picking up trash from customers who have missed the city wagons – and perpetually on the run from the police and district inspectors. The seller of *Old Furniture* (Figure 6.36) suffered a greater indignity, his shop and the entire district housing it having already disappeared as part of a push for urban renewal motivated by well-to-do residents of a nearby street. And the *Independent Shoe-Black* (Figure 6.37) lives a peripatetic existence, "always on the move," Smith tells us, "carrying his box on his shoulders" and running from the police because he has no (expensive) license and no affiliation to the charitable "boot-black brigades."[67] The January 1878 issue, serving as the serial's parting address, thus returns in part to the reform-minded attitude exhibited by the earliest monthly issues, expressing sympathy at injustices wrought in the name of progress, modernization, and the maintenance of the social order.

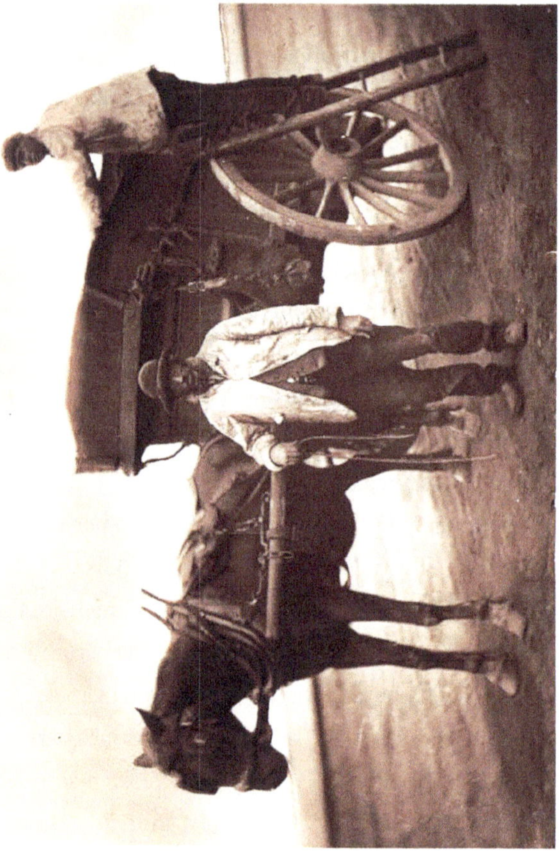

FIG 6.35: John Thomson, *Flying Dustmen*, from Adolphe Smith and John Thomson, *Street Life in London* (London: Sampson Low, Marston, Searle and Rivington, 1877-78). Woodburytype.

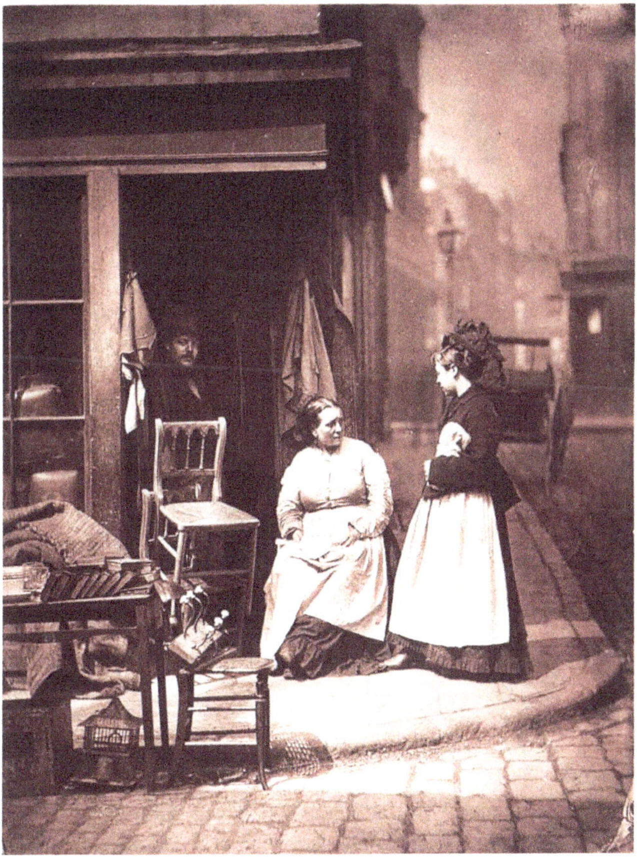

FIG 6.36: John Thomson, *Old Furniture*, from Adolphe Smith and John Thomson, *Street Life in London* (London: Sampson Low, Marston, Searle and Rivington, 1877-78). Woodburytype.

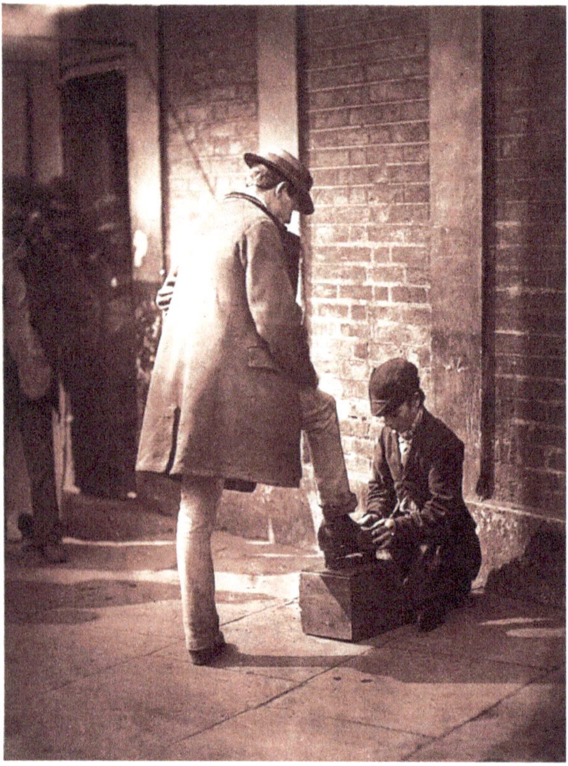

FIG 6.37: John Thomson, *The Independent Shoe-Black*, from Adolphe Smith and John Thomson, *Street Life in London* (London: Sampson Low, Marston, Searle and Rivington, 1877-78). Woodburytype.

NOTES

1 The Authors [Adolphe Smith and John Thomson], Preface, *Street Life in London* (London: Sampson Low, Marston, Searle and Rivington, 1877), n.p.

2 Anonymous, *The Sinks of London Laid Open* (London: J. Duncombe, 1848); Hector Gavin, *Sanitary Ramblings: Being Sketches and Illustrations of Bethnal Green, A Type of the Condition of the Metropolis and Other Large Towns* (London: John Churchill, 1848). See Chapter Four for more discussion of this literature.

3 Ialeen Gibson-Cowan, "Thomson's *Street Life* in Context," *Creative Camera* 251 (November 1986), 11.

4 Ibid.

5 In positioning the four adults, he took care to use their clothing to advantage. The two central adults, a standing man who leans against the wagon with his hands folded and feet crossed, and a woman seated on the ladder/stoop next to him, both wear clothing that appears dark in the monochrome image. The other two adults, a man seated on the traps at right and a woman, left, sitting on an unseen bench or stool, wear white shirts that serve as visual anchors for the composition.

6 The horses had probably been sold to spare their upkeep over the winter months. See Raphael Samuel, "Comers and Goers," in H.J. Dyos and Michael Wolff, eds., *The Victorian City*, Vol. I (London / Boston: Routledge and Kegan Paul, 1973), 130-31.

7 John Thomson, *London Nomades, Street Life in London*, 9.

8 Chapter Four offers a more thorough discussion of Mayhew's study.

9 Henry Mayhew, *London Labour and the London Poor: The Condition and*

Earnings of Those That Will Work, Cannot Work, and Will Not Work, Vol. I (London: Griffin, Bohn and Co., 1861), 3.

10 Ibid.

11 Ibid., 4.

12 Lesley Wylie, "Rare Models: Roger Casement, the Amazon, and the Ethnographic Picturesque," *Irish Studies Review* 18, no. 3 (August 2010), 316. See also Chapter Four where I discuss the literature of urban spectatorship, including the common tendency to compare one's superior knowledge of the inhabitants of other continents with inferior knowledge of other classes within one's own city.

13 Ibid.

14 Henry Mayhew, "Of Wandering Tribes in General," *London Labour and the London Poor*, Vol. I, 3.

15 John Thomson, *London Nomades, Street Life in London*, 9.

16 Ibid.

17 Ibid.

18 Ibid., 10.

19 Ibid.

20 Ibid.

21 Thomson concludes the account by noting that he was invited to play dominoes by one of Pradd's neighbors whom he had interviewed. He says that he declined, instead hastening "to note down as fast as possible the information received word for word in the original language in which it was delivered, believing that this unvarnished story would at least be more characteristic and true to life." The essay begins, then, with Thomson acting as narrator, and ends with him acting as faithful

transcriber of the actual words of the street sellers themselves. Quotes often appear in a kind of patois; consider this one from William Hampton: "'Edication, sir! Why what do I want with edication? Edication to them what has it makes them wusser. They knows tricks what don't b'long to the nat'ral gent. That's my 'pinion.'" Other informants "speak" in more neutral, less heavily-accented language. Overall, the entry conveys the effect of myriad voices coming together to prove that the world of the hawkers is indeed both "divided and subdivided," and "mingled into one confused whole."

22 "Literature: *Street Life in London*," *Lloyd's Weekly London Newspaper*, 11 March 1877, 5.

23 Ibid.

24 Adolphe Smith, *London Cabmen, Street Life in London*, 12.

25 Ibid.

26 Ibid.

27 Ibid.

28 Angela Vanhaelen, "*Street Life in London* and the Organization of Labour," *History of Photography* 26, no. 3 (Autumn 2002), 201.

29 Adolphe Smith, *London Cabmen, Street Life in London*, 14.

30 Ibid., 15.

31 Ibid.

32 This is not the great Cathedral but a smaller edifice, designed by Inigo Jones and also called the Actors' Church.

33 Among many other places, flower-women appear as romantic figures in Blanchard Jerrold and Gustave Doré's *London: A Pilgrimage*, in which both text and image wax poetic on their pretty pathos. See Gustave

Doré and Blanchard Jerrold, *London: A Pilgrimage* (London: Grant and Co., 1872; facsim. New York/London: B. Blom, 1968), esp. Jerrold's text, 117 and Doré's illus., 54 and 126.

34 Adolphe Smith, *Covent Garden Flower Women*, *Street Life in London*, 17.

35 Ibid., 18.

36 The final entry in *Street Life in London*, published in January 1878, profiles an "independent boot black" with an invalid father who works to augment his mother's pay. That child was probably this woman's son, since such "independent" boot-blacks, not affiliated with the "brigades" of licensed shoeshine boys, were a relatively rare breed and hard to find. See Adolphe Smith, *The Independent Shoe-Black*, *Street Life in London*, 139-42. There is thus a concrete connection between the first and last issues of *Street Life in London*, and between these profiles of seemingly-unaffiliated groups of people. See Chapter Five above for more discussion of this.

37 Adolphe Smith, *Covent Garden Flower Women*, *Street Life in London*, 18.

38 Ibid.

39 Lucy H. Hooper, "From Abroad: Our Paris Letters, March 17, 1875," *Appletons' Journal* 13, no. 317 (April 17, 1875), 505.

40 Adolphe Smith, *Covent Garden Flower Women*, *Street Life in London*, 18.

41 Blanchard Jerrold made exactly the same comparison in *London: A Pilgrimage*, also mentioning the Jockey Club flower-girl and also comparing her unfavorably to the more virtuous London flower-women. See Doré and Jerrold, *London: A Pilgrimage*, 117.

42 Notably, other contemporary reports contradict Smith's implication that Isabelle was sexually available to the Jockey Club members. Lucy

H. Hooper states that despite her vulnerable and publicly-exposed position, Isabelle's "reputation for virtue was unquestionable." See Hooper, "From Abroad: Our Paris Letters: March 17, 1875," 505.

43 Adolphe Smith, *Recruiting Sergeants at Westminster, Street Life in London*, 19-22.

44 Ibid., 22.

45 In this way, *Sufferers from the Floods* resembles many of Gustave Doré's engravings for *London: A Pilgrimage*, in which London's laboring classes seem to live and work in a kind of eternal twilight.

46 John Thomson, *Street Floods in Lambeth, Street Life in London*, 23.

47 Ibid., 25.

48 Ibid.

49 Ibid.

50 Ibid., 26.

51 Ibid., 23.

52 [Adolphe Smith and John Thomson], Preface, *Street Life in London*, n.p.

53 "Is it not the necessary garb of our suffering age, which wears the symbol of a perpetual mourning even upon its thin black shoulders? Note, too, that the dress-coat and the frock-coat not only possess their political beauty, which is an expression of universal equality, but also their poetic beauty, which is an expression of the public soul - an immense cortege of undertaker's mutes .... We are each of us celebrating some funeral." Charles Baudelaire, "The Salon of 1846 XVIII: On the Heroism of Modern Life," in *The Mirror of Art*, trans. and ed. Jonathan Mayne (Garden City, NY: Doubleday, 1956), 128.

54 Adolphe Smith, *Public Disinfectors, Street Life in London*, 31.

55 Ibid., 30.

56 Ibid.

57 Ibid., 28-30.

58 See Henry Mayhew, *London Labour and the London Poor*, Vol. I (London: Griffin, Bohn, 1861), esp. 213-306.

59 See Henry Mayhew, *London Labour and the London Poor*, Vol. II, 370-72.

60 Probably a location in Lambeth Borough, south of the Thames. See Chapter Five, above, for more discussion of locations depicted in *Street Life in London*.

61 See also Angela Vanhaelen, "*Street Life in London* and the Organization of Labour," 199-200.

62 Adolphe Smith, *Halfpenny Ices*, *Street Life in London*, 77-80.

63 [John Thomson], *Black Jack*, *Street Life in London*, 81.

64 "The best customers for the fish sold in the streets are… the Jews, for they not only buy the greatest quantity of fish, but give the highest price – a peculiarity not often attributed to the children of Israel… The Irish will not give half the money the Jews freely pay for fish, so that, perhaps, the French are the next best customers. They come in large numbers from Soho, and being such good cooks, can utilize fish in a number of dishes totally ignored by the English poor." Adolphe Smith, *Cheap Fish of St. Giles's*, *Street Life in London*, 87.

65 The September installment, unlike prior installments in the serial, incorporates not one but two unsigned texts. Earlier installments have routinely included two texts signed by Adolphe Smith, and a third bearing either Thomson's signature or none at all. Here, the unsigned essays probably resulted from collaboration between the two authors.

66 While the Italian street musicians may have been photographed at any time, Thomson probably visited and photographed the street locksmith – who works in the Whitechapel Road – at around the same time he made his iconic image of *Hookey Alf of Whitechapel*, mid-autumn of 1877. The shellfish dealer must have been photographed in early-to-mid-autumn, given the sunny weather and the apparent warmth of the day.

67 Adolphe Smith, *The Independent Boot-Black*, *Street Life in London*, 141.

CHAPTER SEVEN

STREET LIFE IN LONDON AS PHOTO-TEXT

THIS CHAPTER DEMONSTRATES how *Street Life in London* evolved over time, in response to a variety of external forces and pressures; and it examines *Street Life in London* as a photo-text, looking especially at entries in which the two means of representation – photography and writing – prove particularly harmonious or particularly dissonant. Changes to the publication over time were not neatly linear. As we have seen, the photographs did not appear in the order in which they were made, but rather in response to the internal thematic and seasonal logic of individual installments of the serial. The texts were usually written right before they appeared in print, but Smith and Thomson seem to have conceived some entries, particularly those related by thematic or other links, out of their final published order. And because the last two issues of the monthly serial were prepared in advance, in order to ready their contents for publication in the single-volume version of *Street Life in London* in mid-November 1877, they express these tendencies somewhat differently than do the several issues before them.

All that said, the project clearly did change over time, both in response to criticism and with an eye to improving poor sales. Thomson innovated less in the composition and construction of his images, presenting instead a vision of the streets more static and more eternal, less subject to the forces of time. Smith demanded fewer wide-ranging social reforms and engaged in less stringent social criticism, replacing these instead with increasing calls for personal philanthropy, and suggestions of how concerned readers might devote themselves to alleviating the conditions they encountered in the book. Overall, the project became more conventional, conforming more closely to the trends set by earlier works in the vast literature of urban spectatorship and street typology.

Between naturalism and typology: changes in Thomson's photographs

Because Thomson's images did not appear in the order in which he made them, the trajectory of his response to external pressures is not linear. Nonetheless, Thomson clearly did respond to criticism and probably also to requests from the serial's publishers, beginning to produce more traditionally typological imagery as a result. Street types sacrificed style for clarity, presenting street figures and the tools of their various trades as clearly as possible. In the first two issues of *Street Life in London* Thomson often broke from these standards, but his innovation did not continue unabated. In an effort to interest readers and appease critics, the publication began to temper its pictorial radicalism with doses of the known and comfortable. Thomson seems to have treated more conventionally those figures already familiar to readers from prior studies of street life, like Mayhew's. Conventional or familiar street figures get conventional treatment; unconventional or unusual street figures may be – but are not always – depicted in less stylistically-conventional ways.

By the fourth monthly issue, in May 1877, we find Thomson openly embracing typological convention in one entry, titled *The Temperance Sweep*. This entry focuses on a figure quite familiar from prior studies of urban poverty and street culture, a chimney sweep.[1] Sweeps bore considerable symbolic freight for middle class readers. They were untouchable figures, not only dirty but actually trading in filth; yet at the same time they were absolutely essential to the functioning of the hearth and thus of the home. Unlike members of other lowly professions, sweeps regularly gained admittance to well-heeled homes. Fundamentally familiar and fundamentally other, sweeps show up in many collections of street types.[2] Thomson's image (Figure 6.13) appears straightforward: the title character stands in the center of the frame, the tools of his trade prominently displayed, his face clearly visible, the wall behind him blank. The small boy behind him is probably another tool of the trade, an assistant and apprentice employed to scramble up narrow chimneys.

Close examination reveals that in order to force this image to conform to typological convention, Thomson had to crop it during printing. Most of the woodburytypes in the book have similar dimensions: roughly 4.25 to 4.75 inches at the longer dimension, 3.25 to 3.75 inches at the shorter. This print, however, is 3.625 inches high but only 2.25 inches wide, its odd dimensions indicating that this vertically-oriented image was in fact made from a horizontally-oriented negative, from which a full two inches were cropped.[3] The negatives are lost so it is impossible to know what has been cropped out, but the result of the change is an image that conforms to the standards of street typology. Again, Thomson did this primarily to satisfy readers' expectations with regard to the figures one would typically find in a collection of street types, including chimney sweeps. The other two entries in May, *Caney the Clown* and *Dealer in Fancy-Ware*, (Figures 6.11-6.12) profile less culturally-freighted figures, so Thomson relaxes away from the conventions of type in his images of them.

In June 1877, Thomson deployed a pose from the

portrait studio repertoire for *Tickets, the Card-Dealer* (Figure 6.15), creating a "portrait type" rather like the ones for which he became known in Asia. *Street Life in London's* only interior scene, the image depicts a man in the act of painting a shop-window advertising placard. But the picture is an outright fiction: the advertising poster he "paints" is already well-used and dirty, and indeed the accompanying text tells us that the man shown here is not a painter at all. Rather, he drums up business for a partner, not shown, who does the actual painting of the advertising placards. It seems strange that Thomson and Smith should put forth such a fiction. Why not depict the painter himself, rather than the solicitor? The content of Smith's essay offers an explanation, inasmuch as it focuses far more on this particular individual than on the type of work he performed. That is, the entry profiles not the job, but the man. Since the work of soliciting commissions proves difficult to depict, however, they resort to this construction, a pictorial lie that permits them to present textual facts. The subject is French, and Thomson has photographed him in such a manner as to clearly reveal his physiognomy for readers interested in attempting to discern the "foreignness" in his face.

But this image appears between two others, *The*

Dramatic Shoe-Black and *An Old Clothes' Shop, Seven Dials* (Figures 6.14, 6.16) in which something of the genuine activity and movement of the streets penetrates and disrupts the pictures' stillness. The former image depicts an unusual figure, an elderly shoe-black and sometime theatrical performer. He poses next to his stand and shoeshine-block and gestures dramatically, but a child customer stands with his back to the camera, partially blocking the view of the display stand.[4] In *An Old Clothes' Shop* the female shop owner and one of her customers appear before the shop, but at the lower left of the image, a shadow on the sidewalk reveals the crowd of gawkers standing just outside the frame.

The tension between Thomson's desire to innovate and his need to succumb to market pressures persists as the series progresses. The July 1877 image *A Convicts' Home* (Figure 6.17) is remarkably complex and must have been extraordinarily difficult to choreograph. It incorporates nine figures, including one, his head wrapped in a kind of turban, whom Smith identifies as "Ramo Sammy... the tam-tam man," a familiar street musician.[5] An earlier collection of street types would certainly have included someone like Sammy, a familiar figure and a representative of the type of the foreign street entertainer. However, he would have been represented *as* the tam-tam man, actually in the process of holding and beating his drum in the streets. Here we find him during his time off, going to a restaurant across the street from his home. Thomson and Smith thus defy the standards of typology here, acknowledging that the man has a home and a life beyond the streets. The entry represents a well-known "street type" but is not itself typological.

Another July 1877 image, *The Wall-Worker,* (Figure 6.18) shows three figures in a relatively static though not overtly typological composition; but with the third July image Thomson has attempted a kind of collective type. *Covent Garden Labourers* (Figure 6.19), although a multi-figure composition with a fair amount of environmental context, shows each of the four workers in either profile, full-face, or three-quarter profile, the four of them together thus providing one complete idea of the "typical" Covent Garden laborer. Despite Thomson's best efforts here, however, the streets refuse to conform completely to typological expectation: again, shadows at right reveal a crowd just outside the frame, gathered to witness the making of the photograph.

August 1877 perpetuates this tension between type and dynamism. *Halfpenny Ices* (Figure 6.20) shows its primary subject, an Italian seller of ices and ice creams, only from the back, a view hardly satisfying to devotees of street typology. It takes as its real subject the raucously eager crowd of children gathered around the ice-man's cart, and its vitality derives from the way the boys' personalities assert themselves. One boy, just opposite the Italian ice-man, stares down into the wooden cart, forlornly paralyzed by indecision. Two older boys at left struggle to hide their amusement at being photographed. These two in particular, on the threshold of manhood but not quite over it, activate the image, making it come fully alive not as a reified street scene but as a fleeting moment captured by the camera. Thomson presents in the image not a declarative statement but an open-ended question, a meditation on flux and change.

Cheap Fish of St. Giles's (Figure 6.22) another of the August entries, is charged with a similar energy. But *Black Jack*, the third image from August (Figure 6.21), has clearly been altered after the fact to accord with the standards of type. The figure in his donkey-cart seems lost in a placeless void, the background having been masked out. Thomson probably either painted on or pasted a piece of paper onto the undesirable portions of the negative to mask it, both techniques he used at other points in his career.[6]

However, in those instances the masking either corrected flaws in an area, such as a sky, that was already predominantly white; or it involved cropping of edges and corners to re-align a crooked image. Here, the extreme manipulation serves to erase London itself, causing the subject to exist in a kind of non-space. Such a drastic – and crudely-done – erasure speaks to a desire to make the image more conventionally typological, eliminating distractions and suppressing the vitality of the streets in order to improve focus on the singular central figure. Given Thomson's interest in aesthetics, such drastic and clumsy modification of the image surely rankled with him; thus this alteration was more likely made at the request of the publisher than of his own initiative.

The September 1877 issue presents the audience with three two-person compositions. Two of the images, *Cast-Iron Billy* and *Workers on the Silent Highway* (Figures 6.23, 6.24) foreground style over clarity. Indeed, the latter is among the most evocative images in the entire publication. In a city defined, even in 1877, by its almost completely man-made character, the Thames, with its tidal flooding and its quiet, inexorable flow, persisted as among the few natural features of the landscape. The river's quietude becomes the true subject of the photograph.

Although two workers stand on a barge's deck, they are positioned some twenty feet from the camera, the distance and the shadows on their faces making them difficult to read as types.

The third image from September, however, buys wholeheartedly into the street type genre. Again in this entry, Thomson resorts to convention when depicting a conventional street type, since street-sellers of fruits and vegetables appeared often in the literature of street exploration and typology.[7] Indeed, Thomson titles the picture *Strawberries, All Ripe! All Ripe!* (Figure 6.25), an explicit reference to the "street cries" print genre. He composes the street-sellers in accordance with the standards of the genre, arranging his tableau roughly parallel to the picture plane. The young man and woman are clearly posed, their bodies in profile but their heads turned to three-quarter profile, on either side of the cart. Even the donkey stands in profile, displaying its knobby legs and broken-down body.

Thomson clearly understood the standards of the form well. In the street cries genre, the cry in the title supposedly emits from a figure or figures in the image. As such, figures are frequently depicted with one hand raised to the mouth as though to amplify their cries. We see a similar device here: the boy at right raises his cupped hand to his face. But he seems not to understand what Thomson has asked him to do, placing his hand not before his mouth but next to his ear, as though massaging his jaw. The interaction with Thomson has clearly made him uncomfortable, and he eyes the camera warily, exuding hostility. The boy cooperates but does not acquiesce, and the image thus resounds with tension, belying the nostalgic reference in the title.

In October 1877 Thomson gave in almost entirely to market demands, presenting three straightforwardly typological images. *The London Boardmen* profiles a truly pathetic character, the sandwich-board wearer. Thomson's photograph (Figure 6.26) shows the poor man, filthy and grizzled, standing in the street next to a lamppost. Attached to his chest and back are advertising boards promoting a product called "Renovo," and he wears a wooden or cardboard silhouette of a hand with the same brand name attached to his hat. In his right hand, the man carries advertising flyers; in his left, a cane to steady himself. Gaze downcast and face caked with dirt, he presents a pitiable spectacle. The boards, while not completely legible, are clearly visible, as are the man's vacant facial expression, the silly hand attached to his hat, and his ragged clothing. The background is an anonymous street, appropriate for a street type. Apparently the publishers of *Street Life in London* also found this figure appealingly typical, for when the publication appeared as a Christmas book in late 1877, the boardman was one of the two figures embossed in gold on the cover and serving to advertise and (mis)represent the book as a collection of street types (see Figures 5.5, 5.6).

In *The Water-Cart* (Figure 6.27) Thomson endeavors to present the cart-driver, his horse, and the cart itself as clearly as possible in their accustomed environs, the London streets. He stands only as far from the subject as necessary to incorporate all three elements completely into his photograph. While he is still unable to render the face of the cart-driver clearly due to a shadow, the failure does not nullify the attempt. Thomson clearly intended to present the man as a "type," because in his accompanying text he uses the terms "type" and "typical" for both the man and the horse.[8] And the third October image, *Mush-Fakers and Ginger-Beer Makers* (Figure 6.28) is an outright construction, a performance for the camera. It brings together two men who otherwise would not be in the same place at the same time: although both could be found on or near Clapham Common, the ginger-beer maker worked primarily on sunny days and the "mush-faker" or umbrella repairman on rainy ones. Thomson poses the two workers in profile, facing one another – but formally, not conversationally – and displaying their goods clearly to the camera.

In the November issue, Thomson seems finally to have reconciled market demands with his desire to present the dynamism and the evocative potential of the city streets. Although one photograph, *November Effigies* (Figure 6.29) was made during a Guy Fawkes Day parade and seems hurried and ill-composed, as though Thomson had only a few moments to make it before the parade had to continue, the other two images in the monthly issue are justifiably among the best-known in *Street Life in London.* In these two images, *Hookey Alf of Whitechapel* and *The Crawlers*, the November issue reveals what the serial could have achieved, had it continued beyond its one-year run: an ideal synthesis of pictorial reification and ineffable vitality. The November issue thus reveals the potential promise of "true type."

Hookey Alf of Whitechapel (Figure 6.30), impresses the viewer with its lively, varied quality. It constitutes a kind of street microcosm, depicting representatives of both genders and compressing the hierarchy of the streets, from the well-off artisan to the dopey pot-boy to the destitute invalid, into one image. Though the subjects acknowledge the camera and pause for the duration of the exposure, the image does not feel posed or extensively manipulated by Thomson. The title character – Hookey Alf – stands at the extreme right of the image. He leans against something we cannot see, pipe clenched between his teeth, and looks not at the camera but down at the child approaching him. His left arm ends in a metal hook where his hand should be, and the child looks at the hook, fascinated and perhaps a bit fearful. Her light-colored hair, pulled back from her face by a band, stands out in a matted shock – a halo – at the back of her head. Thomson's presence elicits a telling variety of expression among the subjects: they appear confident, uncertain, quizzical, annoyed. These are not types but individuals, each imbued with distinct personality. Nothing at all in *Hookey Alf* appears with typological clarity, but the image overall conveys a sense of environmental or contextual accuracy that surpasses the artificiality of type.

The third November image, *The Crawlers*, (Figure 6.31) continues to resonate with present-day audiences as a powerful and affecting work of social criticism, generating palpable feelings of disgust and dismay at the plight of these pitiful figures:

a homeless woman so weak from hunger that she crawls from place to place, and the child in her charge. In contrast to *Hookey Alf*, the resonant quality here derives in part from the simplicity of the image, which is a straightforward street type. Thomson centered the figures and depicted little of the environment, just enough to reveal that this woman lives in a doorway. Beside her, on the steps that serve as her sole furniture, we see her meager possessions, a teapot and china cup. Thomson used the capabilities of photography to great advantage here, rendering visible even tiny details: the fine lines radiating out from around the woman's mouth; the wrinkled ruffle at the bottom of her dress, corresponding so neatly to that of the child's cap; even the worn decorative tracery just barely visible on the surface of the wall where the woman leans her head.

Much of the power of both this image and its accompanying text derives from the contrast between the woman's pathetic state and the dignity with which she remains able to conduct herself, a dignity Adolphe Smith emphasizes in the accompanying essay. Too weak to stand or even hold up her head, she props herself up against the wall and dozes but never really sleeps. But she dresses as neatly as possible under the circumstances. Looking down at the top of her head, we see her cap carefully placed and pinned; in front of it her hair is smooth and perfectly parted. Despite her weakened state she cares as well as possible for the child on her lap, burying its little body in her cape and clutching it to her to keep it warm.

To create the photograph Thomson stood far closer to the subject than usual, creating a sensation of intimacy and imparting to the viewer a sense of actually being the better-off passerby, looking down from a superior vantage point. Perhaps it was this photograph that prompted Susan Sontag to refer to *Street Life in London* as "a sustained look downward."[9] Sontag saw *Street Life in London* as one of the first endeavors in what would become photojournalism, a genre she regarded as glorified slum tourism, an extended exercise in exploitation. Such endeavors, she felt, did not help those they depicted; they did not alleviate suffering. Rather, they took advantage, aestheticizing the subjects' pain for voyeuristic audiences who could feel they had done something useful simply by looking at the pictures.

But Sontag had a fundamentally anachronistic attitude toward *Street Life in London*, placing on this book the entire weight of what came after it. Sontag regarded photography as almost universally exploitative, with photojournalism and documentary as its most insidious, because most seemingly-compassionate, forms. She formed her attitudes, however, during the twentieth century, when photographs of poverty, pain and suffering proliferated and the possibility that one might be satiated and numbed by such ubiquitous horrors had become very real. In 1877, by contrast, photographs in any genre other than portraiture were relatively rare. Few people would ever have seen such an image as *The Crawlers*. Hence while Thomson's photograph may be characterized, quite literally, as a "look downward" – he did, after all, photograph the woman from above – it also revealed to its viewers a vision of pain and suffering of which they might never otherwise have become aware. Thomson does not thwart the traditional conventions of typology here, but he brings them to life, revealing their potential. The camera's gaze here feels soft, sympathetic; the machine seems to regard this poor woman and her tiny charge with something like kindness.

The tension between typology and naturalism, between Thomson's desire to innovate and his need to satisfy the market demands, persists to the end of the serial. The January 1878 entry *Flying Dustmen* (Figure 6.35) profiles unlicensed trash collectors. Thomson depicts the two men alongside their horse and wagon, but in place of the city street in the background we find again, as in *Black Jack*, a placeless void resulting from the masking of the negative. If one's primary interest lies in discerning the looks and modes of the typical flying dustman, the image satisfies with its stiff, posed presentation of the men. Here, again, Thomson photographs a familiar figure in a familiar and traditional manner: trash-collectors, both licit and unlicensed, appeared in prior street explorations and indeed Mayhew profiled the business of refuse processing at great length.[10] However, one learns little from the image of the labor these men perform, and nothing of the neighborhoods in which they work. Though the book promises to present *Street Life in London*, here we find only the life, the city having been erased.

By contrast, the January 1878 photograph *Old Furniture* (Figure 6.36) reveals a great deal about London street life and about city spaces. Although the owner of this secondhand furniture shop is not literally a street laborer, his store does discharge many of its contents on to the sidewalks every morning, drinking them back in every night. The shop stands on a street corner and Thomson photographs from across the street, standing at an angle that permits him to see both the shop and the cross street beside it, curving away into the distance. This recession and depth of field are unusual in *Street Life in London*. This image, more than any other in the publication, gives a sense of the city as a three-dimensional space rather than just a backdrop.

The issue, and thus the publication as a whole, concludes with *The Independent Shoe-Black*. Thomson photographs a child laborer – a shoeshine boy – with a client (Figure 6.37). On the sidewalk the shoe-black sits cross-legged, looking downward at his shoe-shine stand and the foot of his customer atop it. We see enough of his face to discern his age as between about ten and fourteen, but beyond this we can tell little about him. The shoe-black's customer stands with his back to the camera, just a hint of his profile visible. As the boy shines his shoe, the customer looks down at the top of the boy's head. The image resists the typological standard in that it gives little information about the physiognomy of the shoe-black; but at the same time it conveys the nature of the work quite effectively. It encapsulates the brief, strange intimacy of the shoe-shining encounter, the physical proximity required for the job coexisting with the social distance, the difference in status and in stature between the shoe-black and his client.

Just visible at the left edge of the photograph, a group of men has gathered. Clearly what draws them is not the sight of a man having his shoes shined but rather the presence of Thomson and his camera. No doubt a crowd gathered behind Thomson to watch him make many of the photographs in *Street Life in London*. The shadows of such unruly gatherings appear in other images in the publication, but here at least four men appear actually in the photograph, jostling one another for space and eyeing Thomson warily.

Although Thomson made the image well prior to its publication as *Street Life in London's* final image in January 1878, it serves as an ideal summary to the book. Informative about the labor of shoe-shining while telling us little about the shoeshine boy himself, it neatly encapsulates the dance between typology and naturalism that characterizes so much of *Street Life in London*. With its unruly crowds, too, it demonstrates the movement of the streets. One senses the making of this photograph, and by extension all photographs for the book, as a kind of street performance, the spectators here unsuccessful at removing themselves from the stage.

From socialism to philanthropy: changes in the texts

Going back to the start of the publication and again working forward, we can trace similar changes in

Street Life in London's texts. This particular problem is complicated by the dual authorship, but both authors' essays do change, albeit in different ways. The changes in Thomson's writings come largely as changes in format. After his first two essays Thomson ceased signing his contributions because he regarded them as collaborations. Several of his "collaborators" are the street figures whom he quotes at length, their own words constituting the greater part of these entries. In other instances, he collaborated with Smith. As with much in *Street Life in London* the reason for this change is unclear. It probably resulted from a combination of factors: Thomson's limited time, his greater comfort with photographing over writing, his – or the publishers' – desire to put forth accounts of the streets that rang of authenticity and direct reporting to the same degree as the photographs they accompanied. The quoted accounts probably also increased the appeal of the publication to casual readers, who preferred a series of biographical sketches and first-person accounts to a more factual but also drier series of statistical reports on street conditions.

Smith's contributions change in a more complex way over the course of the serial's one-year run. Responding to the demands of critics and publishers, he began to deliver more reader-friendly fare.

Later essays incorporate fewer calls for changes to public policy or criticisms of overarching social structures, and more discussions of or suggestions for philanthropic endeavor. Although Smith advocated a relatively activist form of philanthropy, often encouraging readers to go into the streets and have direct encounters with needy individuals rather than to stand at a remove and throw money at the problem, the later essays nonetheless represent a diminution of the radicalism of his earlier texts, a backing-away from his socialist rhetoric.

It seems clear that he did not undertake these shifts entirely of his own volition, and so his later essays sometimes convey a degree of awkwardness and even a hint of frustration at the difficulty of the situation, a frustration expressed in some cases as a loss of patience with the subjects he profiles. He tends to express this impatience most frequently with female subjects, whom he was unable to take entirely seriously as laborers. Women, for Smith, engender pity and romantic associations, as in *Covent Garden Flower Women*; but they also earn a derision and scorn that he rarely directs at men.

Early entries like *Recruiting Sergeants at Westminster* reveal Smith's deep radicalism through their calls for reform. In that essay from March 1877 Smith criticized the class-based system of rank and promotion within the military, subtly condemning at the same time the entire construct of social class. He called for the military rank system to be completely overhauled and for promotion and rank to be granted based on merit alone. *London Cabmen*, from the serial's first issue in February 1877, sought to rehabilitate cabdrivers in the public eye, using statistics to demonstrate their trustworthiness, to diminish traditional perceptions of them as rough, unsavory characters, and to show how they were exploited by the large companies that often employed them. The latter entry, among others, also highlighted the emergence of trades unions as a positive development in the progress toward empowerment of the worker, an assertion that would have been regarded suspiciously by some members of the Victorian public.

As the serial progressed Smith began to tone down such overt calls for reform. More reader-friendly fare, like biographical sketches of the subjects, began to take precedence over dry facts and figures. His May 1877 essay *The Temperance Sweep*, for instance, accompanies one of the first straightforwardly typological photographs in *Street Life in London* (Figure 6. 13), and in the text Smith too retreats away from complexity. For many well-heeled Victorians, chimney-sweeps by their very nature connoted filth and degradation, but this essay focuses more on their diversions than on the nature of their work. Smith devotes considerable space to the sweeps' longstanding May-Day ceremonies and parades.[11]

The entry is not entirely lighthearted: it does address the widespread alcoholism among chimney-sweeps. Alcoholism was a significant problem in Victorian Britain, but unlike other problems Smith had previously addressed in *Street Life in London* it was relatively uncontroversial: most believed that responsibility resided with the individual alcoholic, not with society as a whole. Smith reduces the potential for controversy even more by treating it as he and Thomson often did with troublesome issues, holding it at a distance. They foreground as the entry's main character not a drunken and degraded sweep but a prosperous and upstanding one, a man who stopped drinking after a lifetime of it and began to flourish as a result. The subject, John Day, now not only practices temperance but preaches it to his fellow-sweeps.[12] Only through Day, i.e. only secondhand, do we hear of other, less upstanding sweeps.

This essay scants on facts and figures. One receives an impression of this individual but learns little of the sweeping profession as a whole. Context has been largely eliminated in the text, just as it was in the image. Thus in both, the entry conforms to the standards of typological representation at the expense of a sense of the complexity of London's social landscape or an idea of the industry of chimney sweeping *as* industry.

The emphasis on philanthropy over reform increases as the series progresses. In the June 1877 issue, for example, two of the three entries focus on a single individual and highlight how a specific, directed act of charity by a well-known figure assisted him. In *Tickets the Card-Dealer*, Smith profiles a peripatetic Frenchman reduced to destitution by the vicissitudes of international politics. After a stint abroad in America, the subject attempted to return to France but arrived in Europe just as the end of the Franco-Prussian War and the Commune created a dearth of employment in his home country. He found himself stranded, penniless, in England, but "a philanthropist whose name should be familiar to the reader," Mr. George Moore, assisted him and a business partner in launching a sign-painting venture.[13] The figure profiled in the second entry, *The Dramatic Shoe-Black*, became destitute through illness rather than through personal failings. His personal savior, who provided him the capital to outfit himself as a shoe-black, was none other than "the Ex-Premier, Mr. Gladstone," to whom the subject had written a letter.[14] Both Tickets and the shoe-black, as recipients of largesse from such respectable sources, become respectable poor themselves, thus raising the level of respectability of the serial overall. The impetus toward philanthropy becomes that much stronger in the publication; by setting such illustrious examples of philanthropic giving, *Street Life in London* encourages the reader to emulate the behavior.

By November 1877, Smith had given over much of his effort to delineating philanthropic opportunities, and to differentiating between good and bad uses of one's largesse. *November Effigies* details a bad, pseudo-charitable use of disposable income: donations to the makers of "guys" for Guy Fawkes Day parades. The "guys" were made by individuals and groups who then used them to solicit donations. Sometimes the makers were themselves poor, and donations to them genuinely helpful, but most people who made and paraded "guys" were better-off, using the floats to generate supplemental income. Most of the donations, too, came not from wealthy or middle-class donors but from the poor themselves. Smith regards such donations as wasteful, lining the pockets of the makers of the guys but generating no genuine social change.

The second November entry, *Hookey Alf, of Whitechapel*, begins by deploring another tradition on which the poor throw away their money, public drinking, but it also models philanthropic behaviors for interested readers. The title figure, Hookey Alf, continues to try to work and support his family despite two terrible workplace accidents, one of which left him with seizures and the other of which led to the amputation of his hand. After telling the man's story, Smith encourages readers to travel into the wilds of London themselves, to meet and get to know similar characters. "[It is] my belief," he states, "that time spent among the poor themselves is far more productive of good and permanent results, than liberal subscriptions given to institutions of which the donor knows no more than can be gleaned from the hurried perusal of an abbreviated prospectus."[15] Smith even plays on his audience's knowledge of and love for the work of Charles Dickens: "[I]n this manner Dickens acquired his marvelous stores of material and knowledge of the people... As I talked to 'Hookey' it seemed as if the shade of Captain Cuttle had penetrated the wilds of Whitechapel."[16] This reference to Dickens is rather gratuitous, since all Hookey Alf really has in common with Cuttle is the hook, but it again brings before the reader an illustrious example of compassion, encouraging emulation of such behavior.

The third November entry, *The Crawlers*, continues in compassionate mode, profiling two homeless women so hungry and destitute that they crawl from place to place rather than walk.[17] Like Hookey Alf, the women fell into unfortunate circumstances not through any fault or vice of their own but because of simple ill-luck; also like Hookey Alf, they deserve assistance but will not ask for it. In the essay, Smith himself models such assistance, noting how he bought a meal for one of them and stating outright how much money each would require to get back on her feet. At the end of the essay, he gives the reader a nudge and instills a sense of duty with his remark that these women's problems ought to be solved "with the help that will now be forthcoming" after their appearance in his book.[18]

As a socialist, Smith was preoccupied by questions about the obligations of one citizen to another. His preferred solution, however, was to alter oppressive policies, not simply to apply bandages to individual wounds. Here in the November issue he gives in to publishers' concerns and makes less ambitious suggestions. However, he does also reveal his own personal interests and proclivities, albeit subtly.

He uses the three November essays collectively to advocate increased personal contact between bourgeois and working-class individuals, a situation he no doubt believed would bring about greater change. Additionally, two of the essays here profile ways – unwise donating and excessive drinking – in which laborers are deluded into thinking they are free, fully-conscious social operators. What they really purchase with this money, Smith implies, are false hope and fleeting pleasure. Interest from bourgeois reformers – from more people like himself, that is – may bring about real change, empowering laborers to move beyond their enchained state and into true freedom.

Smith's worries about misguided philanthropy appear once more in the series, in the December 1877 entry *Italian Street Musicians*. Although his later entries tend to promote middle-class philanthropic activity over legislative reform, in this essay he concerns himself with delineating how such charitable energies may be misdirected. He begins by remarking that despite the general affluence and industriousness of Italians and the relative well-being of their children by comparison with many English children, something about Italian and Savoyard boys piques people's sympathy. By comparison with the "English mendicant," who is "coarse, ungainly, dirty, rude of speech, unartist-like in his appearance, out of tune when he sings, vulgar in all his deeds," and frequently drunk, Italians have about them an air of romance that permits them to benefit from beggarly status in England. Some even migrate to England specifically to become beggars, and many work in London as street musicians.[19] Charity organizations have become concerned, Smith writes, that the child street musicians are actually slaves, given up by ignorant Neapolitan parents who believe their children are being educated in the arts.[20]

Smith does not believe most of these rumors. While he implies that there probably is a traffic in children, he disagrees with the charitable groups that claim this situation has gone on for generations and constitutes one of the gravest threats to the poor living within England. How could such a trade have continued for generations – shouldn't the Neapolitan parents have realized the deception by now? Likewise, "I venture to doubt if they are worse off than in their own country, where they so often fall victims to a vice utterly unknown in England."[21] This unexplained vice – probably Smith's euphemistic reference to child prostitution – is worse, he argues, than the treatment they receive in England. Likewise, while the *padroni* who own them are no doubt cruel, they:

> *...have only followed the example set by innumerable manufacturers and other employers of labour both in England and abroad... I would welcome any measure that would protect the Italian children against the exactions of their padroni... but it is equally urgent to protect our native street arabs – to redeem from the starvation, drunkenness, degradation and immorality of their homes those poor English children, whose care-worn, haggard faces, peering from our back courts and alleys, testify that their lot is not to be compared with that of the bright, laughing, healthy foreign children, who, for some inscrutable reason, seem to have momentarily monopolized what little human sympathy can survive the business of charity organization.*[22]

In interviews with Italians unconnected with the music trade, he determined that most children are actually treated well, the one in the photograph included (Figure 6.32).[23] Smith's greatest concern is that the children are not being properly educated, an issue for which he suggests a legislative, not a charitable, solution.[24]

As throughout *Street Life in London*, Smith endeavors to educate the public. Here, however, he acts not to shed light on a dark, unexamined corner of street life, but to complain that rather too much light has already been shed. The imagination of the public has been captured by the idea of a white slave trade, particularly one involving children; and charitable organizations have mobilized to combat such a terrible evil. Smith worries aloud that this unnecessary battle will sap the already-limited charitable energies of the English public, leaving them too little compassion to care about problems faced by native-born English children. Rather than convince his audience that they ought to care about a particular social question, here he argues that they care a bit too much.[25] This anti-sensationalism and interest in the local ring true to sentiments he expressed throughout his career. The entry demonstrates his refusal to acquiesce completely to the market's desire for real-life melodrama.

Still, his frustration with the situation – *Street Life in London's* poor sales, the publishers' and critics' demands for more reader-friendly fare – did come through in some entries. He became more negative in his assessments of the poor over the course of the serial, growing increasingly likely to condemn them or to admit that endeavors to help them had failed. His September 1877 text for *Workers on the Silent Highway* hardly matches the compelling, evocative quality of Thomson's image (Figure 6.24). Focusing little on the experiences of individual watermen on the Thames, Smith instead concentrates on the confusion and competition that frequently arises among the many corporate entities with interest in the barge trade on the Thames. Smith writes that working men frequently "play the one off against the other" to their own benefit and their employers' expense.[26] Smith seems particularly frustrated by the barge industry's reputation as a haven for criminals. The disorder of the industry, Smith implies, leads to a greater social disorder, not only harboring criminality but fostering epidemics in which those who suffer most are the most innocent. "It is most revolting," Smith shudders, "to think that in the narrow and dark cabins of a barge, children are sometimes born."[27]

Oddly vitriolic, the entry presents a fairly unpleasant picture of life among the rivermen. The industry as a whole seems hopelessly mired in bureaucratic confusion, attached to bygone traditions and regulations that permit the employment of criminals and miscreants and the perpetuation of horrific living conditions for bargemen's families. While the photograph shows an evocative scene of two bargemen bathed in sunlight, the text belies this, decrying the unsanitary conditions of life just below deck where the sun never shines its disinfecting and purifying light.

October 1877's *The London Boardmen* seems similarly hopeless. "Few men," Smith writes, "...are better abused and more persistently jeered at than the unfortunate individuals who let themselves out for hire as walking advertisements."[28] Pelted with mud by urchins, kicked by passing omnibus drivers, whipped by coachmen, and thrown off the sidewalk by police, they have no friends in the street and find no rest, during their working hours, from constant ridicule and abuse. Typically employed by advertising firms, the men receive around eighteen pence per day, hardly a princely sum.[29] The work itself is mindless, but the constant abuse, the need to move all the time and the irregularity of the employment make the job difficult.

If Thomson's photograph (Figure 6.26) conforms to the standards for a street type, Smith denies that we can know anything of the typical boardman just by examining this one specimen:

> *Unlike many other street trades, this business is not followed by a special tribe. Costermongers, for instance, are almost a race apart, and differ both in their habits and even physically from the rest of the population, but boardmen are of all sizes, ages,*

> *shape, and complexion. Some are hopelessly vulgar and ignorant, others have received the education of gentlemen. They represent, to use a consecrated expression, all who have 'gone to the wall.'*[30]

Some, Smith continues, pursue the work as a stop-gap, while others serve as boardmen for years. Many resort to such work after a lifetime of crime or drunken dissolution.

Smith finds a few characters with whom he can sympathize here, but overall he tells a dark story. For every industrious, honorable boardman he meets, dozens more carry boards in order to fund their drinking habits. A Co-operative Boardmen's Society, admirably conceived, dissolved after half of the committee appointed to run it succumbed to drunkenness. Smith notes that "the only practical service that can be rendered" by a well-meaning philanthropist might be "the selection of individual and more worthy cases."[31] Even then, however, one's apparently careful choice might prove foolish, as one advertising contractor discovered when he endeavored to provide work for an especially promising boardman. "[W]hen sober," Smith writes of this man, "he was as industrious, as grateful, as it was possible to expect, but about once a week he yielded to his passion for drink, and finally became so unmanageable that he had to be dismissed."[32] The boardmen represent the dregs of society, their livelihood serving to maintain them only on a miserable plane of existence. By and large, Smith implies, they are unredeemable.

Women became particular targets for Smith's frustration, as in *The Old Clothes of St. Giles*, an entry focused in part on a female business owner. Smith begins by describing the old-clothing industry in general, then turns to discussion of secondhand shops like the one owned by this woman and shown in Thomson's accompanying image (Figure 6.16). "Few persons," Smith writes, "have a better insight into the hard side of life than the dealers in old clothes; for it is to them that are brought the refuse apparel which has been rejected by the pawnbrokers as unsuitable guarantee for even the smallest loan."[33] Given that pawnbrokers were known to accept such bizarre and nearly-worthless objects as men's razors, this statement bespeaks the pathos suffusing even an average day in a secondhand shop.[34]

Smith then notes that "the dealer whose portrait is before the reader cannot boast of a large business."[35] He implies that she is not a particularly good businesswoman: valuable books pass through her hands from time to time, but she undervalues them drastically. And yet, Smith writes:

> *...if the dealer was ignorant in matters relating to literature and fine arts, she was at least master in the art of keeping her home clean... As a rule, second-hand clothes shops are far from distinguished for their cleanliness, and are often the fruitful medium for the propagation of fever, smallpox, &c. In this case, however, the floor was well washed, the shop carefully dusted, the goods kept in order of merit, and ...a door at the back admitted a thorough current of air... Perhaps these rare qualities explain the fact that trade is slack with her. Cleanliness is essentially distasteful to, and is even considered 'stuck up,' by a large section of the population.*[36]

In this passage Smith transforms the woman from small-business owner to housekeeper. Although he has already explained that the old-clothes trade is currently in a slump, he attributes this particular woman's hardships to her personal qualities and circumstances: first bad luck and illness, then her failure to understand the value of her stock, and finally to the very cleanliness for which he praises her.[37]

Given Smith's lifelong commitment to women's rights, his reduction of this business owner to struggling domestic seems rather surprising. Confronted with a female worker, he demonstrates an inability to understand her *as* a worker, and to place her appropriately within the overarching narrative of this particular industry. When Smith conceived of street laborers as a body, he conceived them as male. The appearance of women – like this pawnshop owner, or the Covent Garden flower-sellers whom he describes as emanations of Nature herself – disrupted this conception and, consequently, all the solutions Smith imagined for the ills of the poor. We see here both his confusion when confronted by women workers, and his increasing frustration with the failure of this project, which manifests itself here as impatience with the poor overall.

Smith again directs frustration at women in his text for *Hookey Alf of Whitechapel* (Figure 6.30). The attitude is even more obvious here because the entry profiles a mixed group of men and women, and as he criticizes the women he is simultaneously solicitous toward the other, male figures in the entry. Smith writes that surrounding the tavern at any given time, one might see "a metropolitan mixture of good and evil in the countenances" of the customers:

> *Thus in the photograph before us we have the calm undisturbed face of the skilled artisan, who has*

> *spent a life of tranquil, useful labour... while under him sits a woman whose painful expression seems to indicate a troubled existence, and a past which even drink cannot obliterate. By her side, a brawny, healthy 'woman of the people,' is not to be disturbed from her enjoyment of a 'drop of beer' by domestic cares; and early acclimatizes her infant to the fumes of tobacco and alcohol. But in the fore-ground the camera has chronicled the most touching episode. A little girl... has penetrated boldly into the group, as if about to reclaim some relation in danger, and drag him away from evil companionship. There is no sight to be seen in the streets of London more pathetic than this oft-repeated story – the little child leading home a drunken parent... Inured to a life crowded with episodes of this description, the pot-boy stands in the back-ground with immoveable countenance, while at his side a well-to-do tradesman has an expression of sleek contentment, which renders him superior to the misery around.*[38]

He employs mostly pleasant descriptors for the male subjects here: "calm," "tranquil," "useful," "sleek," "superior." One of the female subjects, by contrast, wears a "painful" expression, and the other has abandoned her housework and performs her maternal duties in a deeply unsatisfactory manner. In this entry Smith displaces all his frustrations on to the women, reserving kinder feelings only for the men.

Smith's final entries demonstrate a kind of ambivalence about street labor and poverty. He comes to terms, it seems, with the complexity of the issues embodied in the endeavor to catalogue the streets, indeed with the impossibility of the undertaking. *Old Furniture*, from January 1878, profiles the trade in secondhand furnishings. More than that, however, it functions as an elegy for a working-class area of London that, between when it was photographed and when Smith wrote his text, was "improved" out of existence. The street, Church Lane, once housed a vibrant street market full of shops and stalls selling fruit, flowers, and vegetables. Nearby residents of upscale New Oxford Street, however, objected to the presence of the street market, "and the tax-payers of that important thoroughfare had to be conciliated," Smith sniffs.[39] In the entry Smith illuminates the trade in old furniture for his readers; but he acknowledges at the same time that the discussion, at least with regard to this particular shop, is moot.

Dealers in old furniture tend to obtain their stock from "brokers and bailiffs," and will buy nearly anything. Some repair items themselves, but others employ assistants.[40] These are "recruited from the street" and hail from no particular background, representing all walks of life and all forms of prior experience. Such work may, indeed, serve as a "stepping-stone," permitting street laborers to progress and become members of "the great artisan class."[41] Dealers also buy directly from the poor. In general, poor people sell easily-transported items first, and these usually to pawnbrokers. Furniture goes last, and its sale bodes poorly for the seller, indicating a downward slide from which few recover. "As a rule, second-hand furniture men take a hard and uncharitable view of mankind. They are accustomed to scenes of misery, and the drunkenness and vice that has led up to the seizure of the furniture that becomes their stock."[42]

Smith here provides a mixed view of the poor, commenting on both virtue and vice. The furniture-dealers provide a valuable service, but they develop their cynicism through contact with unsavory individuals and unpleasant circumstances. Smith highlights anxiety-provoking issues of class mobility here, too: furniture repairmen sometimes use the work as a stepping-stone to better trades and thus better lives, but the furniture itself is obtained from people moving in the opposite direction, downward on the social ladder. Smith also discusses urban improvement, and the relationship between improvement and social status: the well-heeled people of New Oxford Street look down upon the marketers of Church Street, and they exert their greater influence and clout to have the market and indeed the entire street removed. Smith is ambivalent about the character of the poor here, but certainly favors them over the middle-class taxpayers whose squeamish distaste for the street-market drove its closure.

The complexity and depth Smith offers in this text matches the unusual depth – literally, the depth of field – of Thomson's image (Figure 6.36). Image and text here work together to satisfy the promises Smith and Thomson laid out in their Preface. They do indeed use photography to portray a detail and variety usually not found in other modes of image-making; and they give in this entry a glimpse beyond the façade of "type" into the very real triumphs and tragedies in the lives of their working-class subjects.

The interplay of word and image: *Street Life in London* as photo-text

With this harmonious interaction between text and image, *Old Furniture* serves as an ideal departure-point for discussion of the final issue here, the nature of *Street Life in London* as a photo-text. Throughout the publication, image and text accompany one another, each conveying part of the overall message. But the relationship between the two hardly remains stable. Much of this instability, indeed the majority of it, originates in the book's dual authorship.

Often, it derives from the two authors' divergent perspectives toward the photographic imagery. As maker of the photographs, Thomson related to them and referred to them in his texts very differently than Smith did. In his first two entries Thomson refers quite frequently to his photographs, using them almost as props. He regards them not as reified "scenes" but as the products of his own effort, and he discusses them as such. In *London Nomades* (Figure 6.1) he writes of how he returned, months after photographing the subject, to deliver a copy of the image and conduct an interview. During the interview, he notes, the picture functioned as a prop and a prompt.[43] In *Street Floods in Lambeth*, from March 1877, Thomson refers to the photograph (Figure 6.5) even more frequently. He addresses the choices he made in creating the picture and he uses it as a tableau, identifying each figure and explaining how he or she was affected by the floods. He made the image in front of a rag shop and the wife of the shop's owner stands in its doorway, her livelihood threatened by water damage to the once-prosperous business. "The woman in the centre of the group with the child in her arms," Thomson continues, "is a skilled lace-maker" sickened by the flooding.[44] The man at the right served as rescuer of people and things during the flooding, and as clean-up crew after the water abated.

As Carol Armstrong has argued, such direct discussion of an image permits an audience to shift almost seamlessly from readership to viewership. The text illuminates and activates the photograph, and the photograph reinforces the authority of the text by demonstrating its veracity, showing that it really happened.[45]

Adolphe Smith, on the other hand, prejudices readership over viewership. The photograph is present as useful illustration, but for Smith, in general, the word is supreme. Indeed, he treats photography throughout the publication as a transparent representation of its referent, what Roland Barthes called "a message without a code."[46] To Smith, the photograph is a special kind of image, created by the action of light rather than the intervention of a human being. A photograph is not, as a print or painting would be, made by the hand of man and hence subject to its maker's assumptions and prejudices.

Most of the time, Smith makes little reference to the photographs that accompany his essays, and the references he does make are often vague. In *London Cabmen*, he summarizes at one point "the career, as related by himself, of the cab-driver who furnishes the subject of the accompanying illustration."[47] But there are actually two men in the image (Figure 6.2), both apparently cabmen. Smith does not bother to clarify which one he means. In *Covent Garden Flower Women*, he writes, "it is not my purpose to trace the history of the [Covent Garden] market. I have to deal rather with the group of women who may be seen daily standing by those ugly Tuscan pillars which Inigo Jones designed to ornament the church of St. Paul."[48] The accompanying photograph (Figure 6.3) shows precisely the scene he describes, the women standing before the pillars, but his reference to the image is oblique. He does not refer to the picture; rather, the picture and the text refer to the same real-life group of women.

He engages somewhat more with the photograph in *Recruiting Sergeants at Westminster* (Figure 6.4). He knows, and gives, the full name of each of the recruiters shown here, describing their positions in the image so the reader may follow along. Likewise in *Public Disinfectors* he writes:

> *...the accompanying photograph has been taken in the yard adjoining the Vestry Hall, close by Ebury Bridge, and the familiar countenance of Mr. Dickson, the Inspector of Nuisances for the Parish or Union of St. George's, Hanover Square, will be readily recognized by all who are well acquainted with this district. The group is gathered in front of the out-house where the disinfecting oven is situated.*[49]

But if he mentions and even briefly describes the latter image (Figure 6.6), he does not engage with it. He fails to address, perhaps even to recognize, its potential as a commentary on labor and class relations. The differences between the poses of the Inspector and the Disinfectors, for one, convey significant differences in their social status and in the nature of their work. Mr. Dickson stands as for a portrait, but the Disinfectors, unaccustomed to being photographed, slouch and stare. Likewise, the Inspector is unencumbered by the tools of any trade, since his labor is mental, while the Disinfectors are defined in part by their horse-like relationship to the handcart. But Smith, so attuned throughout his life to the vagaries and injustices of class difference, overlooks such dynamics here. Though they appear so starkly delineated, he is unable to read them in the image.

In some entries, like *Caney the Clown*, one wonders if he has bothered to look at the image at all. In the picture (Figure 6.11) the chair-caning clown sits outside the barred window of a middle-class home. A woman, probably a housemaid, stands in the window, almost as prominent a presence as the title figure. But Smith never mentions her. Her omission from the text actually makes her presence in the image that much more arresting, as it leads one to wonder who she is and why she is there.

In other entries, however, Smith depends on the photograph, alternately reporting on his firsthand knowledge and reading the image in front of him. Such is the case with *Cheap Fish of St. Giles's* (Figure 6.22). In the entry Smith spends considerable time discussing the photographic image directly, walking the audience through it figure by figure. While he clearly spoke with many of the people depicted – since he knows their names and some details of their lives – he must have encountered them as a group only within the image. As such, the image embodies the market community for Smith, and permits him to discuss its members' relationships, their obligations to and kindnesses toward one another.

The most remarkable example of this alternation between reading – or misreading – of the image and direct reportage comes in *Hookey Alf of Whitechapel* (Figure 6.30). Smith seems not to have interviewed anyone shown in the photograph apart from the title character. Smith calls the pipe-smoking man in the doorway an "artisan" and imagines him to deserve rest and relaxation at this tavern after a life of "useful labour," but gives no proof that he really knows the man's profession or work ethic. He also displaces his disapproval of alcohol consumption entirely onto the women in the image, claiming that the facial expression of the woman sitting at left indicates trauma in her past. She appears, however, more annoyed than distressed: peeved, perhaps, that Thomson has appeared with his camera to interrupt her leisure time. Smith finds the young woman next to her the very model of a bad mother, whereas in reality she looks well-groomed and her child properly cared for. Her only crime seems to have been going out in public, rather than staying at home.

Smith reserves his oddest observation for the little girl at the image's center. He imagines her to have come on an errand to fetch a drunk parent. But her attention is clearly arrested and her curiosity piqued by Hookey Alf's metallic prosthesis. Clutching one hand in the other and twisting her fingers in the way nervous children do, she opens her mouth slightly, perhaps to ask Hookey Alf what happened to his hand or if she can touch it. That she has asked or is asking a question seems likely, given Alf's reaction: rather than looking at Thomson he has turned his head to face this child, blurring his features in the process.

Smith has not relied entirely on the image for information. He clearly did interview the title character, if not the other figures in the photograph. Indeed, he explicitly encourages readers to do the same, to seek out street characters and talk with them as an effective form of philanthropy. But in a way – and not the way he intended – his own essay here becomes the best argument for the value of such direct contact. Smith sympathizes wholeheartedly with the title character, a man with whom he has spoken directly; but he reifies, and in some cases vilifies, the other figures in the photograph. His experience of them is much the same as the reader's: distant, secondhand, imagined. Contact, Smith argues in this entry, breeds sympathy. Certainly it did for Smith himself.

If we can learn much from entries in which text and image look past one another or work at cross-purposes, so too can we learn from entries in which they work together especially well. *Clapham Common Industries* offers one of the relatively few instances in *Street Life in London* in which the photographer's agenda and interests jibed with the journalist's. Uniquely in the publication, this entry includes two photographic images: *Photography on the Common* and *Waiting for a Hire* (Figures 6.9-6.10). As in the March 1877 issue, Thomson and Smith here expand the definition of "street labor," profiling subjects who worked in public but were not traditional street types: a photographer, and a man who rented donkeys for pleasure-riding.

In the first picture (Figure 6.9), Thomson photographs a photographer. A group of three stands nearby, waiting in the shade while the photographer prepares to make their picture. He appears to be inserting the ground glass focusing-screen into the back of his camera. The camera's lens points toward his mobile studio-cum-display cart, the lower part of which is hung with a cloth to serve as a backdrop for his portraits. We may assume that after the focusing-screen is in place, the photographer will arrange the family in front of this backdrop, grouping them around the little chair that stands next to his cart; and then he will focus the camera. Assuming this man uses the wet-collodion process, he will then prepare the negative and make the photograph. This difficult process demanded, among other things, that the subject be prepared and the camera focused before the negative could be readied, since it had to be wet to expose properly.

Thomson, of course, knew all the steps in this process intimately. As such, he chose carefully the best moment to make his image. Insertion of the focusing screen required the man to be standing behind his camera and thus identifiable as "photographer." However, only during this stage in the process would the man be clearly visible. While posing the family, he would neither stand near his camera nor remain still long enough for Thomson to create a legible image. During the process of focusing, he would be obscured, his head under a dark-cloth. While preparing the negative, he would be next to his cart, which probably also doubled as mobile darkroom; and he would be working as quickly as possible. During the making of the image, too, he would stand with his camera only as long as necessary to properly expose his negative. Thomson thus chose the wisest possible time to create his image, making a legible photograph of the subject and his labor but placing as little demand as possible on the man's time. While Thomson's photograph probably required everyone in the picture to stand still for a few seconds, it did not demand outright pantomime on anyone's part.

The other photograph, *Waiting for a Hire*

(Figure 6.10), shows two men and a donkey in the foreground, with a fenced enclosure behind. Thomson composes the picture statically, arranging both men and the donkey parallel to the picture plane. If the composition is uncomplicated, however, it is not straightforwardly typological. Rather, it appears casual, almost familiar. The subjects look relaxed, neither posing formally nor simply submitting to the camera's gaze. One man stands partially obscured by the donkey, his arm slung affectionately over the creature's saddle. The other, dressed in an oversized checked jacket, leans on a fence. The clear amusement on his face lends the photograph a degree of charm and contributes to its snapshot-like aura.

In the essay that accompanies these images, Adolphe Smith begins by discussing the benefits that come to workers like these on "holidays and idle days," including Sundays and "especially Good Fridays."[50] Clapham Common, a large area of parkland south of the Thames, sees considerable traffic on such days and thus attracts large numbers of vendors, photographers, and other "eager caterers to the public."[51] The photographer, Smith writes, is a fixture on the Common, coming regularly even in winter.[52]

Smith notes the importance of charm and a winning personality to such photographers, who rely for survival on their ability to reel in passers-by and make them comfortable while they "submit to the painful ordeal of having a portrait taken."[53] On holidays, a photographer might take in quite a lot of money, one skillful salesman having made thirty-six shillings, at a shilling per sitting, in a single hour; but in general an income of ten shillings per day was deemed satisfactory, with one-quarter of this going toward expenses. Some photographers – but not the one in the picture – leave Clapham Common in the off-season, traveling to other places like seaside resorts and racetracks where they photograph well-to-do and even royal patrons who give princely sums, £1 or more, per photograph. "It seems as if this fashion of patronizing photographers on the race-course is really but charity in disguise," Smith writes.

> *The ordinary glass pictures paid for so liberally are generally given over to the coachman, thrust into the rumble, and never see the light of day again. But the photographs taken on such places as Clapham Common, or at the corner of some quiet suburban street, meet with a more worthy fate. They are cherished in the homes of the poor... They serve to recall the past, to revive latent affection for the absent; they never do any harm and sometimes*

> *awaken the better and more tender instincts of our nature.*[54]

In this passage Smith touches on the complex functions of photography in relation to family and to class. To the photographs made by itinerants, purchased and immediately discarded by rich men, Smith contrasts the "worthy" images made by stalwart, steady, less-mobile characters like the man profiled here. Such photographs not only "never do any harm," but may actually serve as moral guides. The pleasures and passions of the laborer may appear smaller than those of the capitalist and the royal, but they are more appealing and more compelling than the empty gestures of the rich.

In a book distinguished by its use of photography, this image and text stand out for their self-referential qualities. This man and Thomson pursued the same profession, a proximity that introduces a degree of tension. What separated Thomson from this particular laborer? How was Thomson's practice of photography different from that of this portraitist? Angela Vanhaelen writes that Thomson and Smith seem to have been attentive to such issues, attempting to distance themselves from this subject:

> *[A]lthough this man may have had access to the same photographic technology as someone like John Thomson, the two activities cannot be equated. Inhabiting the feminine world of babies, mothers, and nursemaids, the street photographer obviously does not provide visual commentary on public issues of importance.*[55]

Thomson and Smith, on the other hand, explicitly do provide such commentary. Vanhaelen argues that because the portraitist does brisk business, his "labour… is thus linked with a desire for money and profit." This distinguishes him from Thomson, who practices photography with artistic discernment and in hopes of educating his audience.[56] Nonetheless, text and image convey a degree of anxiety about this separation; as Vanhaelen notes, a photographer's social status was hardly fixed, his success never guaranteed.[57] Smith says as much: "Many [photographers] have held higher positions, have been tradesmen, or owned studios in town; but, after misfortunes in business or reckless dissipations, were reduced to their present less expensive and more humble avocation."[58] Thomson was hardly unaware of this precariousness; his activities in and after his return from Asia, including *Street Life*, were themselves undertaken in the pursuit of an elusive financial security.[59]

In *The Making of English Photography: Allegories*, Steve Edwards examines the petit bourgeoisie's crucial contributions to the medium's development as profession, rather than polite avocation. Conflicts between the gentleman-amateur photographer and the profit-driven professional underpin much discourse in nineteenth-century photographic journals. Edwards sees such journals as largely aspirational, directed at petit-bourgeois hopes of respectability and anxieties over the uncertainty of studio photography as a profession. Upward social mobility could be arrested by a single unprofitable season, one's social standing diminished or destroyed by the vagaries of fortune. As an industry, the photographic medium was influenced far more by figures like the anonymous Clapham Common photographer and his petit-bourgeois brethren than by men like Thomson.

Edwards notes that in the literature of the period, a distinction was frequently made between art and work: "...art is seen as free and creative, while work is servile and repetitive."[60] While Thomson would not have classified himself as an artist, certainly he saw himself as doing something more artful, even in his portraiture, than this itinerant photographer. We see this photographer's dependence on "servile" repetition in the pedestrian cartes-de-visite and tintypes that cover the front of his cart; we see Thomson's freedom from such repetition in his rejection, here and in other *Street Life* images, of the strictures of typology.

The status of the photographer in the nineteenth century perpetually shifted: was he a businessman, an artist, or an artisan? Was he a laborer or a professional? Smith's statement that photographers' businesses might fail through "misfortunes... or reckless dissipations" is a crucial formulation. Whether by profligacy or through no fault of their own, photographers – like small-business owners in any other field – occupied precarious ground. "[T]his phantasm of labor," Edwards writes, "torments the petit-bourgeoisie, invading and corrupting their identity. The constant closure of studios invoked the ever-present threat that a photographer's own concern might fail and that he would slide down into the workers' world."[61] Thomson's image of his fellow-photographer could be seen to embody just such anxieties. In looking at this man, did Thomson see the specter of what he, without constant and feverish striving, might become?

By including the Clapham Common photographer in their book, Smith and Thomson classify him as a manual laborer, equating his work to that of the cabdriver, the advertising bill-paster, and the street doctor. Profiling him along with another laborer in this entry, they drive his status home: "By the side of the photographer, stands the donkey-boy."[62] Unlike the photographer, whose home away from the Common is never described, the so-called donkey-boy "lives in a slum hard by, and belongs to that peculiar and distinct race known under the generic term of costermongers."[63] Costermongers generally purchased donkeys as cart animals, but the owner of this donkey found it more profitable to rent out his animals for pleasure-riding than to put them in harnesses. Again, the affluent neighborhood serves this business well: ladies who live nearby rent the donkeys for entire days as entertainment for their children.[64]

As usual, Smith concludes by connecting the subject at hand to some overarching concern. Here he commends the Common and other public spaces as profitable business venues for street vendors, and for the fresh air they provide to people accustomed to working in places less well-ventilated and healthful. "A little oxygen," he writes, can be "the purest, most effective, and natural of tonics."[65] As a result, "all Londoners owe a deep debt of gratitude to those patriotic citizens who have combined and subscribed to defend the commons against the illegal and selfish encroachments of the neighboring landowners."[66] At once and with great economy, Smith addresses two critical social issues: first, the relationship of proper ventilation to public health; and second, the evils of enclosure, which by the mid-nineteenth century had claimed enormous swaths of public land in England.[67] A good socialist, Smith links the two issues, making privatization of land a crime against the public good and an anti-patriotic act. Thus the entry's subtle anxiety over the vagaries of capitalism and private endeavor becomes overt at the end, Smith making a decisive statement in favor of the power of the collective over the self-interest of the individual.

Text and image, type and naturalism, also come together in *The Crawlers*. Thomson's image (Figure 6.31) is a masterpiece of simplicity. Smith follows suit with evocative prose, paying homage to the dignity these women try so hard to retain. They sit at the absolute nadir of the order of beggars, reduced by starvation to a state of near-complete enervation. "Wrecks of humanity," they receive most of their sustenance from stale bread and used tea-leaves cast off by other beggars.[68] Though they have no energy to stay awake, they also never sleep, since they spend days on end sitting upright on the steps of the workhouse. Almost all elderly, they get drenched in the rain and pounded by the wind, and suffer from a variety of aches and pains as a result.

While some of the women have arrived at their fate through vice or improvidence, many simply ran afoul of fate, Smith writes. The woman in the photograph falls into the latter category, having lost her husband and then been driven out of her daughter's house by her disagreeable son-in-law. With her teenaged son, who refuses to do work he considers undignified – match-selling, for instance – the woman now lives on the street. She cannot work because she has no address to give and no connections to provide her with references. Her son pawned his clothes and now also cannot work because he goes about wearing only rags. Still, Smith writes, the woman has some ambition:

> *She would move heaven and earth to obtain a few shillings, and with these would proceed to the hop-fields, where she would earn enough to save about a pound... enough to start in life once more. Her son might get his clothes out of pawn, and then obtain work. She would, on her side, rent a little room so as to have an address, and then it would be possible for her to apply for work.*[69]

In relating this ambition, Smith emphasizes its modesty, its smallness: "a few shillings," "a little room." What she wants, really, is the minimum anyone could want.

The child shown with her in the photograph belongs to her friend, who works in a nearby coffeehouse. She minds the baby for most of the day, for which she receives as compensation only a cup of tea and some bread. She and the child spend the day together, huddling against one another for warmth. Smith notes that the child wheezes and coughs alarmingly, its sole environment being the street and its sole protection the thin cape of the crawler.

In the essay, Smith makes frequent reference to Thomson's photograph, using his text to amplify the image. The woman in the photograph acquires a story and a background, becoming a flesh-and-blood human being: a mother and a mother-in-law, a former laborer, and a widow. Because she minds another woman's child for so little compensation, she becomes compassionate, as well. To the silent image Smith also contributes sound, as the noise of the child's crying, coughing and wheezing animates the photograph.

Continuing, Smith relates the story of another crawler who was to have been photographed along with this woman. A generous donor, however, gave her an unexpected sixpence the prior evening, permitting her to obtain lodging for a night. "[S]he was so unaccustomed to the luxury of a bed," Smith remarks, "that she overslept herself and thus missed the appointment!"[70] This woman, a Scot, goes about clothed in a waterproof coat. "It is not known that she has any under-clothing," Smith continues, "only a muddy nondescript substance hanging loosely round the lower part of her legs... while the upper part of her feet are covered by soleless goloshes [*sic*]."[71] Having been admitted to the casual ward of the workhouse three nights in a month, she was sentenced to three days hard labor in the workhouse as punishment. Casual wards were intended to be options of last resort for vagrants, and designed only for single-night stays. They were deliberately harsher and more Spartan even than the residency wards in the workhouses, which were not in themselves happy places. Smith notes that this woman well understood that when she sought the third admittance in a month she would be sentenced to hard labor. It is a testament to the sheer misery of the streets, Smith writes, that she did it anyway.

She did not suffer such misery through faults of her own, being neither criminal nor drunk: "No amount of pressure on my part could persuade her to drink even a single glass of beer with the dinner which, of course, I found an early opportunity of giving her."[72] Rather, her misfortunes befell her through her husband's improvidence, and were compounded by his early death and her subsequent illness. Unable to work because of an eye condition, she could afford only common lodging while she recovered, and it was there that her clothes were stolen, leaving her nearly naked. Since no one would hire her in such a state, she went to live on the streets. Like her fellow-crawler depicted in the photograph, she possesses meager but realistic ambitions: first, to get some clothing; then to obtain work and a tiny, shared lodging; then to begin to save a little money.[73] Her refusal to beg limits her ability to achieve this ambition, but it demonstrates her strength of character and her desire to retain at least some dignity even in her near-naked state.

In both photograph and text, *The Crawlers* attests to the possibilities of what Thomson and Smith called the "true type." The image delivers both the detail and particularity viewers expected from a photograph, and the pathos they demanded of a street type. The text animates the image. It contributes sound to the picture's silence; it imparts a sense of place – the Short's Gardens workhouse near Seven Dials, an easily identifiable location – to the picture's gray placelessness. Smith even activates the woman's broken china teacup, placing in it the dishwater scent of weak tea. Here text and image come together to deliver, forcefully, on the publication's latent potential.

But in *Street Life in London* this cohesiveness and balance between text and image are exceptions. In entries like *Black Jack* and *The Flying Dustmen* where the backgrounds have been masked out, there is too much type, too little reality. In *London Cabmen* and *The Dramatic Shoe-Black*, among others, Victorian readers found themselves frustrated by the opposite problem, an excess of context and a dearth of legibility. *Recruiting Sergeants at Westminster* thrills the modern-day viewer with its dramatic lighting and asymmetrical composition, but it left Victorian readers cold.

Ultimately, the publication's very multiplicity caused its commercial failure. Two authors brought two agendas. Thomson aimed to innovate pictorially, to inject the stale street type genre with new life through art; Smith, to pique readers' pity and spur social change. The publisher brought a third agenda, commercial success. The subjects themselves brought their own histories, their own expressions, their own words. Even the streets asserted themselves, delivering forth crowds and errant children and wandering mongrel dogs. The resulting confusion overwhelmed readers and critics. Thomson and Smith endeavored, as we have seen, to render the publication more desirable to its audience, but their considerable efforts yielded no results. The publisher cancelled the series after just one volume, and the authors moved on to other projects. The lessons, if any, that the three parties learned from the volume went unreported and unremarked, and the impetus to what they called "true type" lay dormant into the twentieth century.

NOTES

1 See e.g. Henry Mayhew, *London Labour and the London Poor*, Vol. II, (London: Griffin, Bohn & Co., 1861), 338-382.

2 See Sean Shesgreen, *Images of the Outcast: The Urban Poor in the Cries of London* (New Brunswick, NJ: Rutgers University, 2002), 85.

3 Measurements taken from prints in the collection of George Eastman House, Rochester, New York. The missing material probably came from the right side of the image. In the photograph, while both of the figures clearly pose for the camera, they are looking not at the camera but off to the photographer's right toward the same unseen object or person, an object of interest which may have been visible in the original negative.

4 Another "customer" appears to be a shop-assistant of some kind, summoned into the sun from the gloom of his shop to pose for the image and appearing hatless, in his shirtsleeves, with a pair of carpet-slippers in place of proper shoes.

5 Adolphe Smith, "A Convicts' Home," *Street Life in London*, (London: Sampson Low, Marston, Searle and Rivington, 1877), 70.

6 Thomson's negatives from China and Cyprus reside in the collection of the Wellcome Institute, London. Thomson occasionally masked, painted on, or otherwise altered his negatives to improve them, to eliminate extraneous information, and other corrections. The Wellcome Collection, however, reveals no precedent for the masking-out of an entire background, as Thomson did with "Black Jack" and "Flying Dustmen."

7 See Henry Mayhew, esp. *London Labour and the London Poor*, Vol. I, 79-96.

8 "The accompanying illustration is a fair specimen of the modern water-cart and its accessories. . . . The horse is typical of the class of animal used for the work – large and powerful, so as to stand the strain of incessant journeyings two [sic] and fro, and of the weight of water in the tank. The man is a fair type of his class, being attired in a manner peculiar to watering-men." [John Thomson], "The Water-Cart," *Street Life in London*, 103.

9 Susan Sontag, "Melancholy Objects," *On Photography* (New York: Picador / Farrar, Strauss and Giroux, 1977), 57.

10 See Henry Mayhew, *London Labour and the London Poor*, Vol. II, esp. 159-338 and 383-465.

11 Adolphe Smith, "The Temperance Sweep," *Street Life in London*, 51.

12 Ibid., 54.

13 Adolphe Smith, "'Tickets,' the Card-Dealer," *Street Life in London*, 61. George Moore was a famed London philanthropist, profiled in a biography by Samuel Smiles in 1878. Samuel Smiles, *George Moore: Merchant and Philanthropist* (London: George Routledge and Sons, 1878). Among other acts, he often helped young men wanting "situations," as this subject and his business partner did.

14 Adolphe Smith, "'Tickets,' the Card-Dealer," *Street Life in London*, 59.

15 Adolphe Smith, "'Hookey Alf' of Whitechapel," *Street Life in London*, 116.

16 Ibid.

17 Only one of them appears in the accompanying image.

18 Adolphe Smith, "The 'Crawlers,'" *Street Life in London*, 120.

19 Adolphe Smith, "Italian Street Musicians," *Street Life in London*, 121.

20 Ibid., 121-23.

21 Ibid., 123.

22 Ibid.

23 Ibid., 124.

24 Ibid., 125.

25 It is worth noting that Smith tended throughout his career toward such reasonable anti-sensationalism. For instance, when, years later, he reported on the appalling conditions present in many Chicago slaughter- and packing-houses, he was careful to relate precisely what he saw. Hence while he found much worth deploring, he was also certain to report when he saw a particularly well-built or well-designed structure, or a clean and properly-managed facility. He found workers' housing, for instance, to be adequate in many cases, even presenting photographs in *The Lancet* to support his assertions.

26 Adolphe Smith, "Workers on the 'Silent Highway,'" *Street Life in London*, 92.

27 Ibid.

28 Adolphe Smith, "The London Boardmen," *Street Life in London*, 99.

29 18d., an entire day's salary for this man, was the price of a single monthly issue of *Street Life in London*. Obviously, the people purchasing *Street Life* were not the people shown in its pages.

30 Ibid., 100.

31 Ibid., 102.

32 Ibid.

33 Adolphe Smith, "The Old Clothes of St. Giles," *Street Life in London*, 64.

34 Ellen Ross, "'Fierce Questions and Taunts': Married Life in Working-Class London, 1870-1914," *Feminist Studies* 8, no. 3 (Fall 1982), 590,

citing James Greenwood, "Pawnbrokery in London," *Hours at Home* 7 (1868), 114.

35 Ibid., 65.

36 Ibid.

37 See Angela Vanhaelen, "*Street Life in London* and the Organization of Labour," *History of Photography* 26, no. 3 (Autumn 2002), 202.

38 Adolphe Smith, "'Hookey Alf' of Whitechapel," *Street Life in London*, 113.

39 Adolphe Smith, "Old Furniture," *Street Life in London*,136.

40 Ibid., 138.

41 Ibid.

42 Ibid.

43 John Thomson, "London Nomades," *Street Life in London*, 10.

44 Ibid., 27.

45 Carol Armstrong, *Scenes in a Library: Reading the Photograph in the Book, 1843-1875* (Cambridge, MA: MIT Press, 1998), see especially 330-32.

46 Roland Barthes, "The Photographic Message," *Image-Music-Text*, trans. Stephen Heath (New York: Hill and Wang, 1978), 17.

47 Adolphe Smith, "London Cabmen," *Street Life in London*, 12.

48 Adolphe Smith, "Covent Garden Flower Women," *Street Life in London*, 17.

49 Adolphe Smith, "Public Disinfectors," *Street Life in London*, 30.

50 Adolphe Smith, "Clapham Common Industries," *Street Life in London*, 39.

51 Ibid.

52 Ibid.

53 Ibid.

54 Ibid., 41.

55 Angela Vanhaelen, "*Street Life in London* and the Organization of Labour," 195.

56 Ibid.

57 Ibid.

58 Adolphe Smith, "Clapham Common Industries," *Street Life in London*, 41.

59 See Vanhaelen, "*Street Life in London* and the Organization of Labour," 195.

60 Steve Edwards, *The Making of English Photography: Allegories* (University Park, PA: Penn State Press, 2006), 15.

61 Ibid., 116.

62 Adolphe Smith, "Clapham Common Industries," *Street Life in London*, 41.

63 Ibid., 41-42.

64 Ibid.

65 Ibid.

66 Ibid.

67 See E.P. Thompson, "Custom Law and Common Right," in *Customs in Common: Studies in Traditional Popular Culture* (New York: The New Press, 1993), 97-184.

68 Adolphe Smith, "The 'Crawlers,'" *Street Life in London*, 116.

69 Ibid., 118.

70 Ibid., 119.

71 Ibid.

72 Ibid.

73 Ibid., 119-20.

CHAPTER EIGHT

CONCLUSION

THIS BOOK HAS illuminated the complex matrix from which *Street Life in London* emerged, and demonstrated the effects of that matrix on the publication itself. The inverse question of the publication's effects on its authors, its publisher, and its environs is also worth examining. John Thomson and Adolphe Smith probably benefited both tangibly and intangibly to at least a moderate extent from their work on the publication, each man presumably receiving modest payment and each gaining experience and exposure from the endeavor. Smith may have garnered something even more, an understanding of the possibilities of photography as a form of evidence: his series of *Lancet* articles exposing the poor sanitary and labor conditions in the Chicago meat-packing plants, published in early 1905, include his own photographs of both the interiors and surroundings of the plant to illustrate and reinforce his assertions.[1] Publisher Sampson Low and Co., for its part, suspended release of *Street Life in London* after its one-year run but did not abandon photographically-illustrated productions, continuing to produce other serials that included photography and remaining committed to the photo-book, especially for travel-related themes.[2]

The relationship of *Street Life in London* to subsequent productions in social exploration, and to the development of documentary photography in the twentieth century, is somewhat more complex. While *Street Life in London* did not play a causal role in the increase in both serious and touristic social exploration in the late nineteenth century, or in the later evolution of photojournalism, it does serve in some ways as a harbinger of both. Endeavors in urban spectatorship became more numerous, more participatory, and in some instances more voyeuristic as the nineteenth century came to a close. Charles Booth's *Life and Labour of the People in London* mapped and described conditions of poverty and labor throughout the city.[3] First appearing in 1889, by 1903 its third edition numbered seventeen volumes, far broader in scope than Mayhew's *London Labour and the London Poor* of the 1850s. During the same time period, other urban explorers ventured into the London slums in increasingly large numbers. Some came as tourists, others as resident missionaries. A number, following the example of James Greenwood in his 1866 pamphlet "One Night in a Workhouse," came in disguise. By the 1880s "slumming" had become both a popular pastime and, for the more philanthropically-minded, a means of educating oneself as to the conditions of poverty and the need for reform.[4]

In *Street Life in London*, Adolphe Smith had urged

readers to engage in just such activity, to visit the tenements and see the slums for themselves. "[P]ersonal investigation," he wrote, "is at once the truest and most useful form of charity."[5] Indeed, *Street Life in London* was designed in large part to emphasize the more approachable, non-threatening aspects of poverty, to make the poor seem deserving of sympathy. The publication's impetus to bring to light the "less observed" conditions of poverty in London anticipated the rise in participatory philanthropy over the following decades.[6] Similarly, the publication's groundbreaking combination of photography and text to show as well as tell the conditions of poverty presaged publications like Jacob Riis's *How the Other Half Lives* (1890). Just as photography itself was invented by several people almost simultaneously, so too did many people recognize at around the same time the potential of the photo-text to verify and testify to the less-desirable effects of the ongoing Industrial Revolution and the fundamental humanity of the afflicted.

Street Life in London also anticipated the shortcomings of such publications: the danger, all too frequently realized, that the photo-text may objectify its subject; the condescension inherent in evocations of the subject's need and desperation; the projection of the author's own prejudices onto the subject. Smith and Thomson aimed to expand the boundaries of street typology to include an increased measure of naturalism and a quality of casual realism, to demonstrate in some instances the lives of its subjects beyond the street. But without an alternative visual or verbal vocabulary they still often operated within typology's boundaries, sublimating many subjects' individuality to the demands of genre.

Their successors would find it impossible to do what they had attempted, to reconcile the demands of type and of truth. The street type would become increasingly a mode of the past.[7] Documentary photography, with its increasing naturalism and its aspirations to fidelity, accuracy, and for the most part sympathy, would arise to take typology's place as the primary means for the representation of poverty and working life. Despite its aspirations, however, documentary photography frequently has not proven to be any better at representing social problems, or at solving them, than what came before it. A candid image, it turns out, may be just as likely to objectify and condescend as one of Thomson's posed and sometimes manipulated "true types."

Prior scholarship has tended to regard *Street Life in London* as monolithic, in more than one sense:

as a single-volume publication, as the product of a unified artistic vision, as complete in itself. I have demonstrated that none of these assumptions holds true. Unfolding over time, the serial evolved and adapted. The authors' voices and their visions for the publication often competed, clashed, or worked at cross-purposes. They admitted the voices of their subjects to the degree that some entries became collaborations between authors and informants. They also, crucially, conducted work on the project with no clear end date in mind. Smith and Thomson did not regard the twelve monthly issues as a whole; they did not regard their production as a completed statement. What we encounter in *Street Life in London* is the start, but not the conclusion, of a conversation between text and image in the service of education, reportage, and social justice. Combining textual and visual analysis, I have offered a total view of *Street Life in London* as an ongoing process rather than a thing-in-itself, a dynamic rather than static entity. It responded to a wide variety of social pressures and forces and commented, often trenchantly, on the society that produced it. Ultimately *Street Life in London* should be recognized, as Henry Mayhew's *London Labour and the London Poor* and other works of social exploration have been, as a fascinating and valuable commentary on the complex and multifarious era from which it emerged.

NOTES

1 [Adolphe Smith], "Chicago: The Dark and Insanitary Premises Used for the Slaughtering of Cattle and Hogs – the Government Inspection," *Lancet* 165, no. 4246 (14 January 1905), 120-23; [Adolphe Smith], "Chicago: The Stockyards and Packing Town: Insanitary Condition of the World's Largest Meat Market (From our Special Sanitary Commissioner)," *Lancet* 165, no. 4245 (7 January 1905), 49-52; [Adolphe Smith], "Chicago: Tuberculosis among the Stockyard Workers – Sanitation in Packingtown – The Police and the Dumping of Refuse – Vital Statistics," *Lancet* 165, no. 4247 (21 Jan. 1905), 183-85; [Adolphe Smith], "Chicago: Unhealthy Work in the Stockyards – Shameless Indifference to the Insantiary Condition of the Buildings and the Cattle Pens – Pollution of the Subsoil – The Need for Legislative Interference," *Lancet* 165, no. 4248 (28 Jan. 1905), 258-60.

2 James J. Barnes and Patience P. Barnes, "Sampson Low and the Victorian Book Trade," *Journal of the Bibliographical Society of America* 105 (March 2011), 82.

3 Charles Booth, *Life and Labour of the People in London*, 17 vols. (London: MacMillan, 1902-03).

4 See Seth Koven, "Introduction: Slumming: Eros and Altruism in Victorian London," in *Slumming: Sexual and Social Politics in Victorian London* (Princeton: Princeton University Press, 2004), especially 1-14. Koven writes that slumming (the Victorians' own term) grew in popularity especially in the 1880s and 90s. See also Judith R. Walkowitz, "The Indian woman, the Flower Girl, and the Jew: Photojournalism in Edwardian London," *Victorian Studies* 42, no. 1 (Autumn 1998-99), 3-46;

and Tony Seaton, "Wanting to Live with Common People…? The Literary Evolution of Slumming," in Fabian Frenzel, Ko Koens, and Malte Steinbrink, eds., *Slum Tourism: Poverty, Power and Ethics* (London/New York: Routledge, 2012), 21-48.

5 Adolphe Smith, Hookey Alf of Whitechapel, *Street Life in London* (London: Sampson Low, Marston, Searle and Rivington, 1877), 116.

6 The Authors [Adolphe Smith and John Thomson], Preface, *Street Life in London*, n.p.

7 An openly nostalgic deployment of street typology may be found in Irving Penn's *Small Trades* project. Virginia A. Heckert and Anne Lacoste write that Penn based the project, undertaken in 1950-51, "on his admiration of Eugène Atget's photographs of workers and the larger, centuries-old tradition of representing the petits métiers, or 'small trades.'" In Irving Penn, et. al., *Small Trades* (Los Angeles: The J. Paul Getty Museum, 2009), 10.

BIBLIOGRAPHY

A. [PSEUD]. See Smith, Adolphe.

Advertisement of Events at London National Society for Women's Suffrage. *Examiner* (London) 3399, 22 March 1873: 316.

Advertisement of Sampson Low, Marston, Searle and Rivington's List of New Books. *Athenaeum* 2616 (15 Dec. 1877): 785.

Allen, Rick. *The Moving Pageant*. London/New York: Routledge, 1998.

Annan, Thomas. *Photographs of the Old Closes and Streets of Glasgow 1868/1877, with a Supplement of Fifteen Related Views*. With an introduction by Anita Ventura Mozley. New York: Dover, 1977.

Armstrong, Carol. *Scenes in a Library: Reading the Photograph in the Book, 1843-1875*. Cambridge, MA: MIT Press, 1998.

Barnes, James J. *Free Trade in Books: A Study of the London Book Trade Since 1800*. Oxford: Clarendon Press, 1964.

Barnes, James J., and Patience P. Barnes. "Sampson Low: Organizer of the Victorian Book Trade." *The Papers of the Bibliographical Society of America* 105 (March 2011): 69-89.

Barringer, Tim. "Will Your Honour Buy a Sweet Nosegay?" Review of *Images of the Outcast: The Urban Poor in the Cries of London*, by Sean Shesgreen.

Art History 27, no. 2 (April 2004): 331-35.
Barringer, Tim. *Men at Work: Art and Labour in Victorian Britain*. New Haven: Yale University Press, 2005.
Barthes, Roland. *Image-Music-Text*. Translated by Stephen Heath. New York: Hill and Wang, 1978.
Bartram, Michael. *The Pre-Raphaelite Camera: Aspects of Victorian Photography*. London: Widenfield and Nicholson, 1985.
Batchen, Geoffrey. *Burning With Desire: the Conception of Photography*. Cambridge, MA: MIT Press, 1997.
Baudelaire, Charles. *The Mirror of Art*. Translated and edited by Jonathan Mayne. Garden City, NY: Doubleday, 1956.
Bax, Ernest Belfort. *Reminiscences and Reflexions of a mid and late Victorian*. London: G. Allen and Unwin, 1918. http://www.marxists.org/archive/bax/1918/autobiog/ ch02.htm (accessed 11 July 2011).
Beach, Rev. William. *The Visit of His Royal Highness the Duke of Edinburgh to Hongkong*. With photographs by John Thomson. Hong Kong: Noronha and Sons, 1869.
Beale, Willert [Walter Maynard]. *The Light of Other Days Seen Through the Wrong End of an Opera Glass*. Vol. II. London: Richard Bentley and Son, 1890.
Blackburn, Sheila C. "'Princesses and Sweated-Wage Slaves Go Well Together': Images of British

Sweated Workers, 1843-1914." *International Labor and Working-Class History* 61 (Spring 2002): 24-44.

Boime, Albert. *Art and the French Commune*. Princeton, NJ: Princeton University Press, 1995.

Booth, Charles. *Life and Labour of the People in London*. 17 vols. London: MacMillan, 1902-03.

Bridges, Dr. J.H. "The Late Commune of Paris." *Bee-Hive*, 22 July 1871. Quoted in Harrison 1971, 470.

Briggs, Asa. *Victorian Things*. Chicago: University of Chicago Press, 1988.

"The Boyer Collection." *Image* (Rochester, NY) 2, no. 7 (October 1953): 1-8.

Buckland, Gail. *Reality Recorded: Early Documentary Photography*. Greenwich, CT: New York Graphic Society, 1974.

"Calls it a Jesuit Plot: Adolphe Smith Tells of Persecution of Dreyfus." *New York Daily Tribune*, 28 November 1904: 5.

Christ, Carol. *The Finer Optic: The Aesthetic of Particularity in Victorian Poetry*. New Haven and London: Yale University Press, 1975.

Christ, Carol T., and John O. Jordan, eds. *Victorian Literature and the Victorian Visual Imagination*. Berkeley/Los Angeles: University of California Press, 1995.

Clement, James. "Scottish Contributions to

Photography 1: The Exhibitions." *British Journal of Photography* 130, no. 17 (6 May 1983): 467-70.

Connell, Jim. "How I Wrote the 'Red Flag.'" *The Call,* 6 May 1920: 5.

Cooter, Roger. *The cultural meaning of popular science: phrenology and the organization of consent in nineteenth-century Britain.* Cambridge/New York: Cambridge University Press, 1984.

Cowling, Mary. *The Artist as Anthropologist: The Representation of Type and Character in Victorian Art.* Cambridge: Cambridge University Press, 1989.

Davidoff, Leonore. *Worlds Between: Historical Perspectives on Gender and Class.* New York: Routledge, 1995.

D'Avillier, Baron Charles. *Spain.* Translated by John Thomson. London: Sampson Low, Marston, Low, and Searle, 1876. Reprinted Bickers and Son, 1881.

de Rothschild, Alfred. *A Description of the Works of Art Forming the Collection of Alfred de Rothschild.* 2 vols. Compiled and with text by Charles Davis and photographs by John Thomson. London: Chiswick Press (privately printed), 1884.

Devonshire House Fancy Dress Ball, July 2nd 1897: A Collection of Portraits in Costume of Some of the Guests. Hammersmith: Privately Printed for the Committee, 1899.

Dickens, Charles. *Sketches by Boz and Other Early Papers 1833-39*. Edited and with an introduction by Michael Slater. Columbus: Ohio University Press, 1994.

Doré, Gustave, and Blanchard Jerrold. *London: A Pilgrimage*. London: Grant & Co., 1872. Reprinted New York/London: Benjamin Blom, 1968.

Doty, Robert. "*Street Life in London:* A Review of an Early Use of Photography in Social Documentation." *Image* (Rochester, NY) 6, no. 10 (December 1957): 240-45.

Dyos, H.J. "The Slums of Victorian London." *Victorian Studies* 11, no. 1 (September 1967): 5-40.

Dyos, H.J., and Michael Wolff, eds. *The Victorian City*. 2 vols. London/Boston: Routledge and Kegan Paul, 1973.

Eder, Josef Maria. *History of Photography*. 4th Ed., 1932. Translated by Edward Epstean, 1945. New York: Dover, 1978.

Edwards, Elizabeth. "Photographic 'Types': the Pursuit of Method." *Visual Anthropology* 3 (1992): 235-58.

Edwards, Elizabeth. *Raw Histories: Photographs, Anthropology, and Museums*. Oxford: Berg, 2001.

Edwards, Elizabeth., ed. *Anthropology and Photography 1860-1920*. London/New Haven: 1992.

Edwards, Steve. *The Making of English Photography: Allegories*. University Park, PA: Penn State Press, 2006.

"English Lecturers Touring France." *Bismarck Daily Tribune* (Bismarck, ND), 13 November 1915: 2.

"The Fabian Society and Socialist Notes." *Our Corner* 8 (July 1886): 59-64.

"The First Photojournalist: John Thomson." *Creative Camera* 43 (1968): 22-25.

Flukinger, Roy. *The Formative Decades: Photography in Great Britain, 1839-1920*. Austin: University of Texas Press, 1985.

Ford, Colin, ed. *An Early Victorian Album: The Photographic Masterpieces (1843-1847) of David Octavius Hill and Robert Adamson*. New York: Knopf, 1976.

Fox, Celina. *Londoners*. London: Thames and Hudson, 1987.

Frenzel, Fabian, Ko Koens, and Malte Steinbrink, eds. *Slum Tourism: Poverty, Power and Ethics*. London/New York: Routledge, 2012.

Gavin, Hector. *Sanitary Ramblings: Being Sketches and Illustrations of Bethnal Green, A Type of the Condition of the Metropolis and Other Large Towns*. London: John Churchill, 1848.

Gernsheim, Helmut. *Creative Photography: Aesthetic*

Trends 1839-1960. New York: Bonanza Books, 1962.

Gernsheim, Helmut. *Incunabula of British Photographic Literature, 1839-1875*. London/Berkeley: Scolar Press, 1984.

Gernsheim, Helmut, and Alison Gernsheim. *The History of Photography from the Earliest Use of the Camera Obscura in the Eleventh Century Up to 1914*. London: Geoffrey Cumberledge/Oxford University, 1955.

Gernsheim, Helmut, and Janet Lehr. "Correspondence: John Thomson." *History of Photography* 4, no. 4 (October 1980): 343.

Gibson-Cowan, Ialeen. "Thomson's Street Life in Context." *Creative Camera* 251 (November 1985): 10-15.

Gibson-Cowan, Ialeen. "John Thomson on Cyprus." *The Photographic Collector* 5, no. 3 (1986): 309-19.

Goldberg, Vicki. "The Art of Reality: John Thomson's far-reaching view of the Far East." *American Photographer* 17 (Nov. 1986): 28-30.

Grandville, J.J. *The Public and Private Life of Animals*. Translated and edited by J. Thomson. London: Sampson Low, Marston, Low, and Searle, 1877.

Grant, James. *The Great Metropolis*. 2 vols. London/New York: Saunders and Otley, 1837.

Green-Lewis, Jennifer. *Framing the Victorians:*

Photography and the Culture of Realism. Ithaca: Cornell University Press, 1996.

Green-Lewis, Jennifer. "Landscape, Loss and Sexuality: Three Recent Books on Victorian Photography." *Victorian Studies* 39, no. 3 (Spring 1996): 391-404.

Green-Lewis, Jennifer. "At Home in the Nineteenth Century: Photography, nostalgia, and the will to authenticity." *Nineteenth-Century Contexts* 22, no. 1 (2000): 51-75.

Green-Lewis, Jennifer. "Not Fading Away: Photography in the Age of Oblivion." *Nineteenth-Century Contexts* 22, no. 4 (2001): 559-85.

Greenwood, James. *A Night in a Workhouse.* London: F. Bowering, 1868.

Greenwood, James. *The Seven Curses of London.* London: Stanley Rivers and Co., 1869; reprinted with an Introduction by Jeffrey Richards, Oxford: Basil Blackwell, 1981.

Greenwood, James. *In Strange Company.* London: Henry S. King, 1873.

Greenwood, James. *The Wilds of London.* London: Chatto and Windus, 1874; repr. New York/London: Garland, 1985.

Greenwood, James. *Low-Life Deeps.* London: Chatto and Windus, 1876.

Hamilton, Peter, and Roger Hargreaves. *The Beautiful and the Damned: The Creation of Identity in Nineteenth Century Photography*. London: Lund Humphries/ National Portrait Gallery, 2001.

Harker, Margaret. "Scottish Contributions to Photography 2: The Symposium." *British Journal of Photography* 130, no. 18 (13 May 1983): 492-93, 502.

Harker, Margaret. "Scottish Contributions to Photography 3: The Symposium Continued." *British Journal of Photography* 130, no. 19 (20 May 1983): 526-27, 530, 537.

Harrison, Royden. "Marx, Engels, and the British Response to the Commune." *The Massachusetts Review* 12, no. 3 (Summer 1971): 463-77.

Headingley, Adolphe S. See Smith, Adolphe.

Herbert, Christopher. "Rat worship and taboo in Mayhew's London." *Representations* 23 (Summer 1988): 1-24.

Highmore, Ben. "Street life in London: Towards a rhythmanalysis of London in the late nineteenth century." *New Formations* 47 (Summer 2002): 171-93.

Hooper, Lucy H. "From Abroad: Our Paris Letters, March 17, 1875." *Appletons' Journal* 13, no. 317 (April 17, 1875): 505.

Houghton, Walter E. et. al. *The Wellesley Index to Victorian Periodicals 1824-1900*. 4 vols. Toronto:

University of Toronto Press/London: Routledge and Kegan Paul, 1987.

Humpherys, Anne. "Mayhew, Augustus Septimus (1826–1875)." *Oxford Dictionary of National Biography Online*, Oxford University Press, 2004. http://www.oxforddnb.com/ view/article/18432 (accessed 20 July 2012).

Hyndman, H.M. *The Record of an Adventurous Life*. New York: Macmillan, 1911.

Jerrold, Alice. See Smith, Alice Jerrold; Smith, Mrs. Adolphe.

Jones, Gareth Stedman. *Outcast London: A study in the Relationship between Classes in Victorian Society*. Oxford: Clarendon Press, 1971.

K., J.S. "Obituary: John Thomson." *Geographical Journal* 58, no. 6 (1921): 470.

Knight, Charles, ed. *London*. 6 vols. London: Charles Knight & Co., 1841.

Koven, Seth. *Slumming: Sexual and Social Politics in Victorian London*. Princeton: Princeton University Press, 2004.

"The Last Thirty Years." *The Lancet* 202 no. 5223 (6 October 1923): 750.

Lehr, Janet. "John Thomson (1837-1921)." *History of Photography* 4, no. 1 (January 1980): 67-71.

MacCormac, William. "Recollections of Work in an

Ambulance." Pts. 1-9. *The British Medical Journal*, 5 Nov. 1870: 483; 12 Nov. 1870: 525-26; 19 Nov. 1970: 548-49; 26 Nov. 1870: 575-76; 3 Dec. 1870: 601-02; 17 Dec. 1870: 652-53; 14 Jan. 1871: 33-34; 4 Feb. 1871: 113-14; 11 March 1871: 249-50.

Mason, James. *The History of the Year 1876*. London: Ward, Lock and Tyler, 1877.

Mavor, Carol. *Pleasures Taken: Performances of Sexuality and Loss in Victorian Photographs*. Durham, NC: Duke University Press, 1995.

Mayhew, Henry. *London Labour and the London Poor: A Cyclopaedia of the condition and earnings of those that will work, those that cannot work, and those that will not work*. 4 vols. London: Griffin, Bohn and Company, 1861-62. Reprinted New York: Dover Publications, 1968.

McGowen, Randall. "Getting to Know the Criminal Class in Nineteenth-Century England." *Nineteenth-Century Contexts* 14, no. 1 (1990): 33-54.

"Medical News." *Lancet* 181 no. 4687 (28 June 1913): 1840.

Milner, John. *Art, War and Revolution in France 1870-71: Myth, Reportage and Reality*. New Haven/London: Yale University, 2000.

Mouhot, Henri. *Travels in the Central Part of Indo-China (Siam) Cambodia and Laos During the Years 1858,*

1859, and 1860. 2 vols. London: John Murray, 1864.

"Mr. John Thomson, F.R.G.S." *The Photographic Journal*, 20 Nov. 1878: 20-22.

Newhall, Beaumont. *Photography 1839-1937*. New York: The Museum of Modern Art, 1937.

Newhall, Beaumont. *Photography: A Short Critical History*. New York: The Museum of Modern Art, 1938.

Newhall, Beaumont. *The History of Photography from 1839 to the Present Day*. New York: The Museum of Modern Art, 1949.

Newhall, Beaumont. *The History of Photography from 1839 to the Present Day*. 4th ed. New York: Museum of Modern Art/Rochester, NY: George Eastman House, 1964.

Newsome, David. *The Victorian World Picture: Perceptions and Introspections in an Age of Change*. London: John Murray, 1997.

Obituary of Adolphe Smith. *Times* (London) no. 44118, 13 Nov. 1925: 14, col. E.

Obituary of Adolphe Smith. *Lancet* 206, no. 5333 (14 Nov. 1925): 1033.

Obituary of Mrs. Adolphe Smith. "Deaths." *Musical World* 60, no. 12 (25 Mar. 1882), 183.

Obituary of Mrs. Adolphe Smith. "Literary Gossip." *Athenaeum* (London) no. 2841 (8 April 1882), 446.

Obituary of Mrs. Adolphe Smith. *Union and Advertiser* (Rochester, NY) 57, no. 102, 1 May 1882, 1.

Obituary of Mrs. Adolphe Smith. *Daily Courier* (Syracuse, NY), 8 May 1882, n.p.

"Obituary: Sir William MacCormac, Bart., K.C.B., K.C.V.O." *British Medical Journal* 2, no. 2137 (14 Dec. 1901): 1771-75.

Oliver, Barret. *A History of the Woodburytype: The First Successful Photomechanical Printing Process and Walter Bentley Woodbury*. Nevada City, CA: Carl Mautz Publishing, 2006.

Ovenden, Richard. *John Thomson (1837-1921) Photographer.* Edinburgh: National Library of Scotland/Stationery Office, 1997.

Ovenden, Richard. "Thomson, John (1837-1921)." *Oxford Dictionary of National Biography Online.* www.oxforddnb.com.ezproxy2.library.arizona.edu (accessed 4 January 2010).

"The Paris Universal Exhibition of 1889," *Lancet* 134, no. 3453 (2 Nov. 1889): 924.

Parker, Elliott S. "John Thomson, 1837-1921: RGS Instructor in Photography." *Geographical Journal* (London) 144, no. 3 (November 1978): 463-71.

Penn, Irving, Virginia A. Heckert, and Anne Lacoste. *Small Trades.* Los Angeles: The J. Paul Getty Museum, 2009.

Poovey, Mary. *Making a Social Body: British Cultural Formation, 1830-1864*. Chicago: University of Chicago Press, 1995.

Prasch, Thomas. "Fixed Positions: Working-Class Subjects and Photographic Hegemony in Victorian Britain." Ph.D. diss., Indiana University, Bloomington, 1994.

"Rare Photograph Book Slips Past the Experts." *British Journal of Photography* 139 (July 11, 1991): 4.

Reed, John R. *Victorian Conventions*. Athens, OH: Ohio University Press, 1975.

Review of *Illustrations of China and Its People*, by John Thomson. "Our Editorial Table." *British Journal of Photography*, 28 November 1873: 569-70.

Review of *Monaco and Monte Carlo*, by Adolphe Smith. *Bookman* 43, no. 255 (December 1912): 64.

Review of *Monaco and Monte Carlo*, by Adolphe Smith. *Academy and Literature* 2124 (18 January 1913): 80.

Review of *Monaco and Monte Carlo*, by Adolphe Smith. *Lancet* 181, no. 4671 (8 March 1913): 693-94.

Review of *Street Life in London*, by Adolphe Smith and John Thomson. "Photography in and out of the Studio: More Photographic Publications." *Photographic News*, 26 January 1877: 37.

Review of *Street Life in London*, by Adolphe Smith and John Thomson. "Annotations." *Lancet* 109, no. 2789

(10 February 1877): 213.

Review of *Street Life in London*, by Adolphe Smith and John Thomson. "Our Editorial Table: *Street Life in London.*" *British Journal of Photography* (16 February 1877): 80.

Review of *Street Life in London*, by Adolphe Smith and John Thomson. "Our Editorial Table." *British Journal of Photography* 24, no. 878 (2 March 1877): 104.

Review of *Street Life in London*, by Adolphe Smith and John Thomson. "Literature." *Lloyd's Weekly London Newspaper*, 11 March 1877: 5.

Review of *Street Life in London*, by Adolphe Smith and John Thomson. "Critical Notices: *Street Life in London.*" *Photographic News* (8 June 1877): 271.

Review of *Street Life in London*, by Adolphe Smith and John Thomson. "Politics, Sociology, Voyages, and Travels." *Westminster Review* (July 1877): 116.

Review of *Street Life in London*, by Adolphe Smith and John Thomson. *British Journal of Photography* 24, no. 896 (6 July 1877): 324.

Review of *Street Life in London*, by Adolphe Smith and John Thomson. "Our Editorial Table." *British Journal of Photography* (10 August 1877): 382.

Review of *Street Life in London*, by Adolphe Smith and John Thomson. "Our Editorial Table." *British Journal*

of Photography 24, no. 910 (12 October 1877): 489.
Review of *Street Life in London*, by Adolphe Smith and John Thomson. "Christmas Books." *Saturday Review* 44, no. 1153 (1 December 1877): 694.
Review of *Street Life in London*, by Adolphe Smith and John Thomson. "Christmas Books," *Times* (London) no. 29115, 3 December 1877: 3.
Review of *Street Life in London*, by Adolphe Smith and John Thomson. "Our Editorial Table." *British Journal of Photography* 24, no. 919 (14 December 1877): 595.
Review of *Street Life in London*, by Adolphe Smith and John Thomson. "Gift-Books." *Athenaeum* 2616 (15 December 1877): 778.
Review of *Street Life in London*, by Adolphe Smith and John Thomson. "Politics, Sociology, Voyages, and Travels." *Westminster Review* (January 1878): 254.
Review of *Street Life in London*, by Adolphe Smith and John Thomson. "Politics, Sociology, Voyages, and Travels." *Westminster Review* (April 1878): 515.
Richards, Thomas. *The Commodity Culture of Victorian England: Advertising and Spectacle, 1851-1914*. Stanford, CA: Stanford University Press, 1990.
Room, Adrian. *Dictionary of Pseudonyms*. 5th ed. Jefferson, NC/London: McFarland, 2010.
Rosen, Jeff. "Posed as Rogues: The Crisis of

Photographic Realism in John Thomson's *Street Life in London*." *Image* (Rochester, NY) 36, nos. 3-4 (Fall/Winter 1993): 8-39.

Ross, Ellen. "'Fierce Questions and Taunts': Married Life in Working-Class London, 1870-1914." *Feminist Studies* 8, no. 3 (Fall 1982): 575-602.

Royle, Edward. "Bradlaugh, Charles (1833-1891)." *Oxford Dictionary of National Biography*. Oxford: Oxford University Press, 2004; online edn, Jan 2011. http://www. oxforddnb.com/view/article/3183 (accessed 19 July 2012).

Ryan, James R. *Picturing Empire: Photography and the Visualization of the British Empire*. Chicago: The University of Chicago Press, 1997.

Rylance, Rick. *Victorian Psychology and British Culture 1850-1880*. Oxford/New York: Oxford University Press, 2000.

Samuel, Raphael. *Theatres of Memory I: Past and Present in Contemporary Culture*. London: Verso, 1994.

Scharf, Aaron. *Pioneers of Photography*. New York: Harry N. Abrams, 1976.

Seiberling, Grace, and Carolyn Bloore. *Amateurs, Photography, and the Mid-Victorian Imagination*. Chicago/London: University of Chicago Press, 1986.

Sekula, Allan. "The Body and the Archive." *October* 39

(Winter 1986): 3-64.

Shafer, David A. *The Paris Commune: French Politics, Culture and Society at the Crossroads of the Revolutionary Tradition and Revolutionary Socialism.* New York: Palgrave, 2005.

Shesgreen, Sean. *Images of the Outcast: The Urban Poor in the Cries of London.* New Brunswick, NJ: Rutgers University Press, 2002.

The Sinks of London Laid Open. London: J. Duncombe, 1848.

Slater, Michael. "Jerrold, Douglas William (1803–1857)." *Oxford Dictionary of National Biography.* Oxford: Oxford University Press, 2004. http://www. oxforddnb.com/view/article/14789 (accessed 28 July 2011).

Slater, Michael. "Jerrold, (William) Blanchard (1826–1884)." *Oxford Dictionary of National Biography.* Oxford: Oxford University Press, 2004. http://www.oxforddnb.com/ view/article/14790 (accessed 27 July 2011).

Smiles, Samuel. *George Moore: Merchant and Philanthropist.* London: George Routledge and Sons, 1878.

Smith, Adolphe [A., pseud.]. "Prud'hommes in Difficulty." *Examiner* (London) 3391, 25 January 1873: 85-86.

Smith, Adolphe. "Bohemia Beautified." *Food Journal* (London) 4, no. 58 (1 March 1873): 67-70.

Smith, Adolphe [A., pseud.]. "Spanish Socialism." *Examiner* (London) no. 3397, 8 March 1873: 245-46.

Smith, Adolphe [A., pseud.]. "The Co-operative Movement in France." *Examiner* (London) no. 3404, 26 April 1873: 430-31.

Smith, Adolphe [A., pseud.]. "The Industrial Crisis in Belgium." *Examiner* (London) no. 3407, 17 May 1873: 498-500.

Smith, Adolphe [A., pseud.]. "Federalism and Solidarity." *Examiner* (London) no. 3413, 28 June 1873: 658-59.

Smith, Adolphe. "Amadeo." *The Dark Blue* 5, no. 1 (March 1873): 1-8.

Smith, Adolphe. "Co-operation Under the Septennate." *Examiner* (London) no. 3455, 18 April 1874: 397-98.

Smith, Adolphe [unsigned]. "Report of the Lancet Special Commission on the Contamination of Uniforms Provided by the Army Clothing Depot." *Lancet* 111, no. 2841 (9 February 1878): 217-19.

Smith, Adolphe [Adolphe S. Headingley, pseud.]. *The Biography of Charles Bradlaugh.* London: Remington, 1880.

Smith, Adolphe. *The Garden of Hyères: A Description*

of the most Southern Point of the French Riviera. London: Fleet Print Works/J. Evans and Co., 1881.

Smith, Adolphe. *Pneumatic Drainage: A Description of the "Berlier System"*. London: E & F. Spon, 1883.

Smith, Adolphe [Adolphe S. Headingley, pseud.]. *The Biography of Charles Bradlaugh.* 2nd ed. with an appendix by W. Mawer. London: Freethought, 1883.

Smith, Adolphe. "The Science of Health: The Fourth International Congress of Hygiene (From our Special Correspondent)." *Phrenological Journal* 76, no. 1 (January 1883): 40-45.

Smith, Adolphe. "Report of the International Trades Union Congress, Held at PARIS from August 23rd to 28th, 1886." London: Foulger & Co.1886.

Smith, Adolphe [unsigned]. "The Sixth International Congress of Hygiene (From our Special Correspondent)." *Lancet* 130, no. 3344 (1 October 1887): 683-85.

Smith, Adolphe. "A Critical Essay on the International Trade Union Congress, held in London, November, 1888, by Adolphe Smith (Interpreter to the Congress)." London: Published by the Author, 19 Barclay Road, Walham Green, SW, 1889.

Smith, Adolphe. Testimony before the House of Lords Select Committee on the Sweating System, 22

March 1889. *House of Commons Papers: Reports from Committees: Vol. 5: Sweating System: Third Report from the Select Committee of the House of Lords on the Sweating System, With the Minutes of Evidence and Appendix*. London: Henry Hansard & Son, 1889: 397-407.

Smith, Adolphe [unsigned]. "The Paris Universal Exhibition." *Lancet* 133, no. 3435 (29 June 1889): 1324-25.

Smith, Adolphe [unsigned]. "The Paris Universal Exhibition." *Lancet* 134, no. 3437 (13 July 1889): 89-91.

Smith, Adolphe [unsigned]. "The Paris Universal Exhibition (From our Special Correspondent)." *Lancet* 134, no. 3449 (5 Oct, 1889): 713-15.

Smith, Adolphe [unsigned]. "The Paris Universal Exhibition." *Lancet* 134, no. 3451 (19 Oct. 1889): 813-17.

Smith, Adolphe [unsigned]. "The International Congress of Hygiene and Demography." *Lancet* 134, no. 3547 (22 Aug. 1891): 441-58.

Smith, Adolphe [unsigned]. "Federation of the Medical Unions of France." *Lancet* 138, no. 3561 (28 November 1891): 1250-51.

Smith, Adolphe [unsigned]. "The Cholera in France." *Lancet* 140, no. 3605 (1 Oct. 1892): 792-96.

Smith, Adolphe. "Are We Prepared to Resist a Cholera Epidemic?" *New Review* 9, no. 53 (October 1893): 353-61.

Smith, Adolphe [unsigned]. "The Eighth International Congress of Hygiene and Demography: The Excursion to Constantinople." *Lancet* 144, no. 3711 (13 October 1894): 884-86.

Smith, Adolphe [unsigned]. "The Battle of the Clubs." Multi-year series, c. 1895-1908. See e.g. "The Battle of the Clubs at Brussels." *Lancet* 146, no. 3756 (24 August 1895): 476-77; "The Battle of the Clubs." *Lancet* 154, no. 3961 (29 July 1899): 304-06; "The Battle of the Clubs: A Five Years' Struggle at Shipley." *Lancet* 170, no. 4400 (28 Dec. 1907): 1876-77; "The Battle of the Clubs." *Lancet* 171, no. 4417 (25 April 1908): 1240-42.

Smith, Adolphe [unsigned]. "The First International Congress on Medical Ethics or Deontology, Held at Paris, July, 1900." *Lancet* 156, no. 4013 (28 July 1900): 275-79.

Smith, Adolphe [unsigned]. "The First International Congress of the Medical Press, Held at Paris, July, 1900." *Lancet* 156, no. 4015 (11 August 1900): 454-56.

Smith, Adolphe [unsigned]. "The Eleventh International Congress of Hygiene and Demography." *Lancet* 162, no. 4178 (26 Sept. 1903): 913-17.

Smith, Adolphe [unsigned]. "The World's Fair at St. Louis." *Lancet* 164, no. 4239 (26 Nov. 1904): 1527-29.

Smith, Adolphe [unsigned]. "The World's Fair at St. Louis (From our Special Sanitary Commissioner)." *Lancet* 164, no. 4241 (10 December 1904): 1681-83.

Smith, Adolphe [unsigned]. "Sanitation at St. Louis, Missouri (From our Special Sanitary Commissioner)." *Lancet* 164, no. 4242 (17 December 1904): 1753-54.

Smith, Adolphe [unsigned]. "Chicago: The Stockyards and Packing Town: Insanitary Condition of the World's Largest Meat Market (From our Special Sanitary Commissioner)." *Lancet* 165, no. 4245 (7 January 1905): 49-52.

Smith, Adolphe [unsigned]. "Chicago: The Dark and Insanitary Premises Used for the Slaughtering of Cattle and Hogs – the Government Inspection." *Lancet* 165, no. 4246 (14 January 1905): 120-23.

Smith, Adolphe [unsigned]. "Chicago: Tuberculosis among the Stockyard Workers – Sanitation in Packingtown – The Police and the Dumping of Refuse – Vital Statistics." *Lancet* 165, no. 4247 (21 Jan. 1905): 183-85.

Smith, Adolphe [unsigned]. "Chicago: Unhealthy Work in the Stockyards – Shameless Indifference to the Insantiary Condition of the Buildings and the Cattle Pens – Pollution of the Subsoil – The Need for Legislative Interference." *Lancet* 165, no. 4248 (28 Jan. 1905): 258-60.

Smith, Adolphe [unsigned]. "The International Association of the Medical Press Committee Meeting at Berne." *Lancet* 165, no. 4262 (6 May 1905): 1230-32.

Smith, Adolphe. "Political Refugees." In *London in the Nineteenth Century*, by Walter Besant. London: A. & C. Black, 1909: 399-406.

Smith, Adolphe [unsigned]. "The Third International Congress of the Medical Press." *Lancet* 174, no. 4495 (23 Oct. 1909): 1242-46.

Smith, Adolphe. "A Spiritist Revival." *Contemporary Review* 98 (July-December 1910), 315.

Smith, Adolphe [unsigned]. "Monaco's Model Hospital." *Lancet* 177, no. 4575 (6 May 1911): 1229-31.

Smith, Adolphe [unsigned]. "The Drainage Problem at Monaco." *Lancet* 177, no. 4577 (20 May 1911): 1384-85.

Smith, Adolphe. *Monaco and Monte Carlo*. London: Grant Richards Ltd./Philadelphia: J.B. Lippincott, 1912.

Smith, Adolphe [unsigned]. "The International Congress on Tuberculosis at Rome." *Lancet* 179, no. 4628 (11 May 1912): 1301-05.

Smith, Adolphe. "The Present Menace of Cholera." *Fortnightly Review* 92, no. 548 (August 1912): 348-49.

Smith, Adolphe. "The Old and the New International, A Reminder of Facts." Letter to the Editor. *Times* (London) no. 41568, 28 August 1917: 5 col. E

Smith, Adolphe. "The International: German Domination and the Trade Unions." Letter to the Editor. *Times* (London) no. 41885, 3 Sept. 1918: 4 col. E.

Smith, Adolphe. "Direct Action: Labour and Foreign Affairs: Propaganda of Kaiserism." Letter to the Editor. *Times* (London) no. 42140, 1 July 1919: 8 col. A.

Smith, Adolphe. "The Pan-German Internationale: I – Marx and his Successors." *Times* (London) no. 42164, 29 July 1919: 14 col. C.

Smith, Adolphe. "The Pan-German Internationale: II – Trade Unionists Abroad." *Times* (London) no. 42165, 30 July 1919: 14 col. C.

Smith, Adolphe. "The Pan-German Internationale; III – the Capture of the Machine." *Times* (London) no. 42166, 31 July 1919: 10 col. F.

Smith, Adolphe [unsigned]. "Science as Made in Germany." *Lancet* 194, no. 5006 (9 August 1919): 258.

Smith, Adolphe, and John Thomson. *Street Life in London*. London: Sampson Low, Marston, Searle and Rivington, 1877-78. Reprinted with Publisher's Note. New York: Benjamin Blom, 1969.

Smith, Adolphe, and John Thomson. *Street Incidents: A Series of Twenty-One Permanent Photographs with Descriptive Letter-Press.* London: Sampson Low, Marston, Searle & Rivington, 1881.

Smith, Alice Jerrold [Alice Jerrold, Mrs. Adolphe Smith]. *A Cruise in the Acorn.* London: Marcus Ward and Co., 1875.

Smith, Alice Jerrold. [Mrs. Adolphe Smith]. *Love Without Wings.* 3 vols. London: Tinsley Brothers, 1877.

Smith, Alice Jerrold. [Mrs. Adolphe Smith]. *A Woman of Mind.* 3 vols. London: Sampson Low, Marston, Searle and Rivington, 1879.

Smith, Lindsay. *Victorian Photography, Painting, and Poetry: The Enigma of Visibility in Ruskin, Morris, and the Pre-Raphaelites.* Cambridge, England: Cambridge University Press, 1995.

Smith, Lindsay. "The Shoe-Black to the Crossing Sweeper: Victorian Street Arabs and Photography." *Textual Practice* 10 (1996): 29-55.

Smith, Mrs. Adolphe. See Smith, Alice Jerrold; Jerrold, Alice.

Sobieszek, Robert A. *Masterpieces of Photography from the George Eastman House Collections.* New York:

Abbeville Press, 1985.

Sontag, Susan. *On Photography*. New York: Picador/ Farrar, Strauss and Giroux, 1977.

Stafford, David. *From Anarchism to Reformism: A Study of the Political Activities of Paul Brousse within the First International and the French socialist movement 1870-90*. Toronto: University of Toronto Press, 1971.

Stallybrass, Peter, and Allon White. *The Politics and Poetics of Transgression*. London: Methuen, 1986.

Stocking, George. *Victorian Anthropology*. New York: Oxford, 1987.

Stott, William. *Documentary Expression and Thirties America*. New York: Oxford University Press, 1973.

"Street Photography." *British Journal of Photography* 25, no. 942 (24 May 1878): 241-42.

Tagg, John. *The Burden of Representation: Essays on Photographies and Histories*. Amherst: University of Massachusetts Press, 1988.

Tagg, John. *The Disciplinary Frame: Photographic Truths and the Capture of Meaning*. Minneapolis/London: University of Minnesota Press, 2009.

"Tales of the Paris Commune." *New Castle News* (New Castle, PA), 17 Mar. 1905: 2.

"Tales of the Paris Commune: Delegate to the Peace Congress Lectures on his Experience in the Siege." *Sun* (New York), 28 November 1904: 10.

Taylor, Jenny Bourne, and Sally Shuttleworth. *Embodied Selves: An Anthology of Psychological Texts, 1830-1890*. Oxford: Clarendon Press, 1998.

Thompson, E.P. *Customs in Common*. Harmondsworth: Penguin, 1993.

Thomson, John. "Practical Photography in Tropical Regions." Pts. 1-6. *British Journal of Photography*, 10 August 1866, 380; 17 August 1866, 393; 24 August 1866, 404; 14 September 1866, 436-37; 5 October 1866, 472-73; 12 October 1866, 487.

Thomson, John. *The Antiquities of Cambodia: a series of photographs taken on the spot, with letterpress description*. Edinburgh: Edmonston and Douglas, 1867.

Thomson, John. "Enlargements from Small Negatives." Pts. 1-2. *British Journal of Photography*, 4 January 1867: 3; 11 January 1867: 13-14.

Thomson, John [misprinted as G. Thomson]. "Notes on Cambodia and its Races." *Transactions of the Ethnological Society of London* 6 (1868): 246-52.

Thomson, John. *Foochow and the River Min*. London: Autotype Company, 1873.

Thomson, John. "Notes of a Journey in Southern Formosa." *Journal of the Royal Geographical Society* 43 (1873): 97-107.

Thomson, John. "Notice of a Journey in Southern

Formosa." *Proceedings of the Royal Geographical Society* 18, no. 3 (1873): 144-48.

Thomson, John. "The Antiquities of Cambodia." *Journal of the North China Branch of the Royal Asiatic Society*, New Series 7 (1873): 197-204.

Thomson, John. *Illustrations of China and Its People, a series of two hundred photographs with letterpress description of the places and people represented*. 4 vols. London: Sampson Low, Marston Low, and Searle, 1873-74.

Thomson, John. *The Straits of Malacca, Indo-China, and China, or Ten Years' Travels, Adventures and Residence Abroad*. London: Sampson Low, Marston, Low, and Searle, 1875. Reprinted in 2 volumes as *The Straits of Malacca, Siam and Indo-China: Travels and Adventures of a Nineteenth-century Photographer*, with an introduction by Judith Balmer. Singapore: Oxford University Press, 1993; and *Thomson's China: Travels and Adventures of a Nineteenth-century Photographer*, with an introduction by Judith Balmer. Hong Kong: Oxford University Press, 1993.

Thomson, John. "Proverbial Photographic Philosophy." *The British Journal Photographic Almanac and Photographer's Daily Companion*, 1875: 128.

Thomson, John. *Through Cyprus with the Camera in*

the Autumn of 1878. 2 vols. London: Sampson Low, Marston, Searle and Rivington, 1879. Reprinted as one volume with an essay by Ialeen Gibson-Cowan. London: Trigraph, 1985.

Thomson, John. "A Journey Through Cyprus in the Autumn of 1878." *Proceedings of the Royal Geographical Society and Monthly Record of Geography*. New Series 1, no. 2 (February 1879): 97-105.

Thomson, John. "Blackberrying." *The British Journal of Photography*, 13 April 1883: n.p. and 214.

Thomson, John. "Exploration with the Camera." *British Journal of Photography* 32 (12 June 1885): 372-73.

Thomson, John. "Photography and Exploration." *Proceedings of the Royal Geographical Society and Monthly Record of Geography* New Series 13, no.11 (November 1891): 669-75.

Thomson, John. *Through China with a Camera*. Westminster: A. Constable and Co., 1898. 2nd ed. New York/London: Harper and Co., 1899. Reprinted San Francisco: Chinese Materials Center, 1974.

Thomson, John. "Geographical Photography." *Scottish Geographical Magazine* 23 (1907): 14-19.

Thomson, John, et. al. *China Through the Lens of John Thomson 1868-1872*. Bangkok: River Books, 2010.

Tissandier, Gaston. *A History and Handbook of Photography*. Translated and edited by John Thomson from *Les Merveilles de la photographie*. London: Sampson Low, Marston, Low, and Searle, 1876. Reprinted Edinburgh/Boston: MuseumsEtc., 2013.

Tissandier, Gaston. *A History and Handbook of Photography*. 2nd Rev. ed. Translated and edited by John Thomson. London: Sampson Low, Marston, Low and Searle, 1878.

Tombs, Robert. *The Paris Commune 1871*. London/New York: Longman, 1999.

Trachtenberg, Alan. *Reading American Photographs: Images as History, Mathew Brady to Walker Evans*. New York: Hill and Wang, 1989.

Tuer, Andrew. *Old London Street Cries and the Cries of Today*. London: Field and Tuer/The Leadenhall Press; New York: Scribner's, 1885.

Urban, Sylvanus [pseud.?]. "Table Talk." *Gentleman's Magazine* 16 (February 1876): 252-56.

Vanhaelen, Angela. "*Street Life in London* and the Organization of Labour." *History of Photography* 26, no. 3 (Autumn 2002): 191-204.

Wade, Louise Carroll. "The Problem with Classroom Use of Upton Sinclair's *The Jungle*." *American Studies* 32, no. 2 (Fall 1991): 79-101.

Walkowitz, Judith R. "The Indian woman, the Flower Girl, and the Jew: Photojournalism in Edwardian London." *Victorian Studies* 42, no. 1 (Autumn 1998-99): 3-46.

"The War." *Lancet* 185, no. 4776 (13 March 1915): 575.

"The War: A Lecture on the War." *Lancet* 185, no. 4777 (20 March 1915): 629.

Ward, John. "Beard, Richard (1801–1885)." *Oxford Dictionary of National Biography Online*. Oxford: Oxford University Press, Oct 2006. http://www.oxforddnb.com/ view/article/66897 (accessed 20 July 2012).

Warner, John. "John Thompson [*sic*]: Compassionate Photographer." *Arts of Asia* 6 (1976): 42-53.

White, Stephen. *John Thomson: A Window to the Orient* (published in the UK as *John Thomson: Life and Photographs*). New York/London: Thames and Hudson, 1985.

"Wills and Bequests [Adolphe Smith]." *Times* (London) no. 44144, 14 Dec. 1925: 17 col. E.

Wilson, Colette E. *Paris and the Commune, 1871-78: The Politics of Forgetting*. Manchester/New York: Manchester University Press, 2007.

Winter, James. *London's Teeming Streets 1830-1914*. London/New York: Routledge, 1993.

Wolfreys, Julian. *Writing London*. Vol. I, *The Trace*

of the Urban Text from Blake to Dickens. London: MacMillan/New York: St. Martin's Press, 1998.

Wylie, Lesley. "Rare Models: Roger Casement, the Amazon, and the Ethnographic Picturesque." *Irish Studies Review* 18, no. 3 (August 2010): 315-30.

Yeo, Eileen, and E.P. Thompson. *The Unknown Mayhew*. New York: Pantheon, 1971.

ACKNOWLEDGEMENTS

I WOULD HAVE been unable to complete this book without the help of a number of individuals and institutions. Stephen White showed me extraordinary generosity, sharing his knowledge of the life and work of John Thomson and granting full access to his research materials. Archivists Amy Rule and Leslie Squyres and the staff of the Center for Creative Photography taught me a tremendous amount about photographs as physical objects. The staff of the Wellcome Institute and Library, particularly William Schupbach, were kind and patient in answering my questions about John Thomson. I would also like to thank James J. Barnes; the staff of the British Library; Graham Hogg of the National Library of Scotland; Catherine Stanton and Sarah Williams of the Museum of London; Hilary Thomas; and Darren Treadwell of the Labour History Study Centre, Manchester, UK.

This book originated as a dissertation at the University of Arizona. Tremendous thanks go to the community of mentors who encouraged and supported me through the project. Sarah Moore provided insightful criticism, advice, and much-needed encouragement. Keith McElroy taught me a great deal about photography and offered consistent and thoughtful guidance and support throughout my years of study at Arizona. Kate Palmer Albers, Paul

Ivey, William Jenkins, Douglas Nickel, Britt Salvesen and Alan Trachtenberg also contributed invaluable wisdom. At Arizona I was also lucky to find a group of colleagues whose enthusiasm for photography mirrored and encouraged my own: Erin O'Toole, Katie Samson, Daphne Srinivasan, Mary Statzer, and James Swensen. Thanks also to the many others who offered guidance and friendship, including Katy Alexander, Tricia Amato, Megan Bartel, Kara Burns, Larry Busbea, Christina Lindeman, Nancy Lindsay, Therese Martin, Julie-Anne Plax, and Leslie Walfish.

My colleagues at Iowa State University have been unfailingly kind and encouraging. Thanks to Greta Anderson, Grant Arndt, April Eisman, and Cullen Padgett-Walsh for their insightful advice and criticism; and to Roger Baer, John Cunnally, Marwan Ghandour, Nancy Girard, Emily Godbey, Heather Hess, Ingrid Lilligren, Andrea Quam, Luis Rico-Gutierrez, and Kimberly Zarecor.

Finally I would like to thank my family: my parents, Peter and Sally Morgan, for their constant and loving support; my husband, Aaron Gassmann, for his patience and encouragement; and my daughter Vivian, for being delightful always.

ABOUT THE AUTHOR

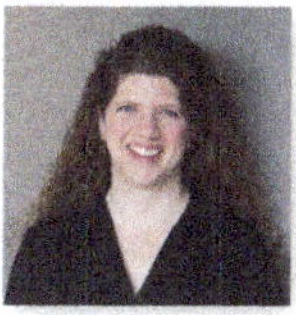

EMILY MORGAN is a Senior Lecturer in Art History at Iowa State University. She received her MA and PhD in Art History from the University of Arizona, with a concentration on the history of photography. Emily's research interests include photography and social exploration, photographic imagery of conflict and war, and photographic modernism, among other topics.

ALSO FROM MUSEUMSETC

Street Life in London

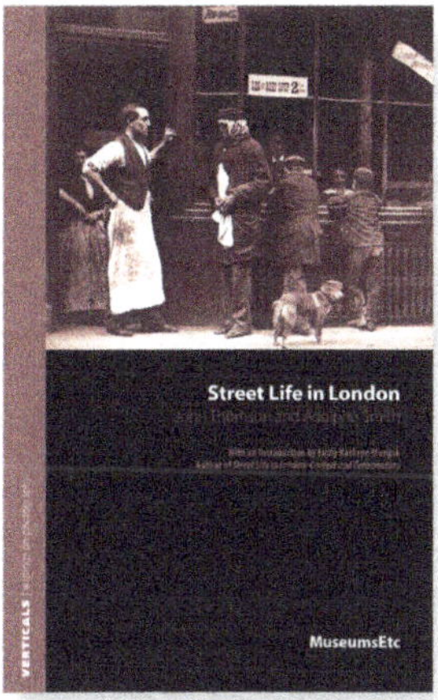

John Thomson and Adolphe Smith

203 x 127mm
ISBN: 978-1-910144-25-1 [paperback]
ISBN: 978-1-910144-26-8 [hardback]

Order online from
www.museumsetc.com

This is a new edition of Thomson and Smith's pioneering *Street Life in London,* first published in 1877-78, with an Introduction by Emily Kathryn Morgan, author of *Street Life in London: Context and Commentary,* and produced in colour on premium 105gsm paper, with modern design and typesetting.

The new format allows today's readers to view Thomson's deep purplish-brown Woodburytype photographs – among the most perfect photographic reproductions ever made – and to study Adolphe Smith's complete text with fresh eyes. In *Street Life in London* we see the start, but not the conclusion, of a conversation between text and image in the service of education, reportage and social justice.

"In terms of the concept of the photographs, and the volume's aims and ambitions as a book, *Street Life in London* is one of the most significant and far-reaching photobooks in the medium's history."
The Photobook: A History Volume 1,
Martin Parr and Gerry Badger.

A History and Handbook of Photography

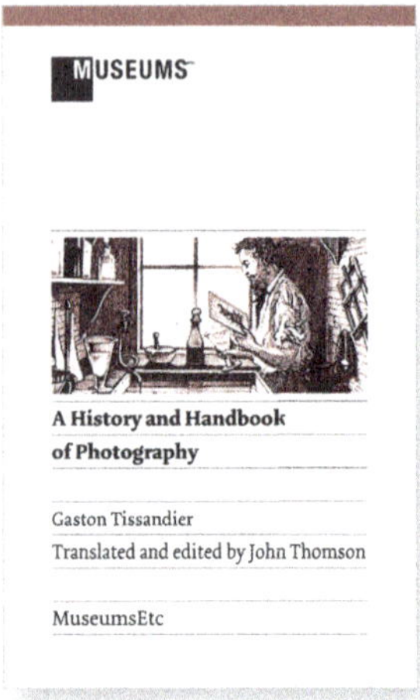

Gaston Tissandier
Edited and translated
by John Thomson

276pp | 203 x 127mm
ISBN: 978-1-907697-82-1 [paperback]
ISBN: 978-1-907697-83-8 [hardback]

Order online from
www.museumsetc.com

Scottish photographer John Thomson (1837-1921) is renowned for his pioneering book *Street Life in London*, widely regarded as a classic of social documentary and as laying the foundations for today's photojournalism.

In a career which also included a series of outstanding photographic portfolios - shot in challenging conditions - documenting life, landscape and architecture in the Far East, followed by a successful studio portraiture business in London, Thomson also took time to translate and edit this edition of Gaston Tissandier's book.

First published in 1876, it was a standard reference work of the period, and blends a concise and highly readable history of the invention and development of photography with a uniquely readable account of late-19th century photographic practice - a time when the making of a new image could be measured in hours rather than seconds.

This newly-designed and typeset, richly illustrated edition provides - for the first time - a highly readable and accessible selection from the original.

The Photographic Studios of Europe

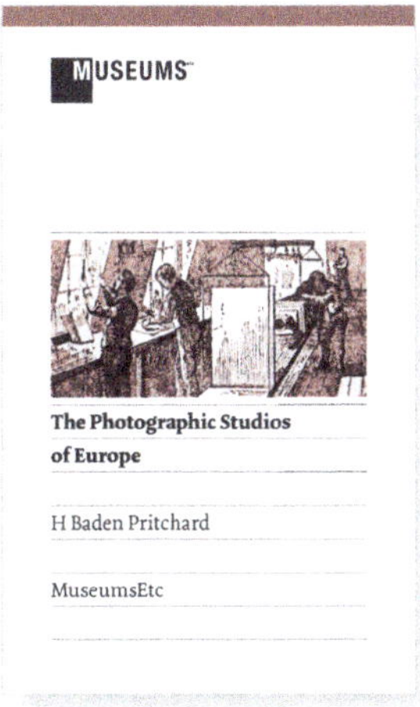

H Baden Pritchard

294pp | 203 x 127mm
ISBN: 978-1-907697-79-1 [paperback]
ISBN: 978-1-907697-80-7 [hardback]

Order online from
www.museumsetc.com

First published in 1882, this the only detailed account available of working practices and conditions in the studios of the leading photographers of the Victorian period.

Revealing, surprising, perceptive and authoritative, this first-hand report is based on seeing scores of photographers and their workshops in action.

The result is fascinating and valuable both as a social historical record and as a classic of photographic literature.

This newly-designed and typeset edition provides - for the first time - a highly readable and accessible selection from the original Victorian edition.

Adopting a "colloquial style" author H Baden Pritchard leads us on a "house-to-house visitation among the principal studios of Europe... determined to write down great things and small alike... and so produce a record of practice."

Recording in detail the physical environment of each workplace, the range of photographic work undertaken, the employees, clientele, pricing policies and unique techniques of each studio, this book provides unparalleled insights into the burgeoning business of photography in the Victorian period.

Books on Museum Practice

10 Must Reads: Inclusion – Empowering New Audiences
10 Must Reads: Interpretation
10 Must Reads: Learning, Engaging, Enriching
10 Must Reads: Strategies – Making Change Happen
Academic Museums: Exhibitions and Education
Academic Museums: Beyond Exhibitions and Education
Alive To Change: Successful Museum Retailing
Contemporary Collecting: Theory and Practice
Collecting the Contemporary: A Handbook for Social History Museums
Conversations with Visitors: Social Media and Museums
Creating Bonds: Successful Museum Marketing
Creativity and Technology: Social Media, Mobiles and Museums
Engaging the Visitor: Designing Exhibits That Work
Inspiring Action: Museums and Social Change
Interpretive Master Planning: Philosophy, Theory and Practice
Interpretive Master Planning: Strategies for the New Millennium
Interpretive Planning Handbook
Museum Retailing: A Handbook of Strategies for Success
Museums and the Disposals Debate
Museums and the Material World: Collecting the Arabian Peninsula
Museums At Play: Games, Interaction and Learning
Narratives of Community: Museums and Ethnicity
New Thinking: Rules for the (R)evolution of Museums
Reimagining Museums: Practice in the Arabian Peninsula
Restaurants, Catering and Facility Rentals: Maximizing Earned Income
Rethinking Learning: Museums and Young People
Science Exhibitions: Communication and Evaluation
Science Exhibitions: Curation and Design
Social Design in Museums: The Psychology of Visitor Studies (2 volumes)
Sustainable Museums: Strategies for the 21st Century
The Exemplary Museum: Art and Academia
The Innovative Museum: It's Up To You...
The New Museum Community: Audiences, Challenges, Benefits
The Power of the Object: Museums and World War II
Wonderful Things: Learning with Museum Objects

VERTICALS | writings on photography

A History and Handbook of Photography
Gaston Tissandier (trans. John Thomson)

Naturalistic Photography
P H Emerson

Photography and the Artist's Book
Theresa Wilkie, Jonathan Carson & Rosie Miller (editors)

Poetry in Photography
P H Emerson

Street Life in London
John Thomson & Adolphe Smith

Street Life in London: Context and Commentary
Emily Kathryn Morgan

The Photograph and the Album
Jonathan Carson, Rosie Miller & Theresa Wilkie (editors)

The Photograph and the Collection
Graeme Farnell (editor)

The Photographic Studios of Europe
H Baden Pritchard

The Reflexive Photographer
Rosie Miller, Theresa Wilkie & Jonathan Carson (editors)

COLOPHON

This edition published in 2014 by MuseumsEtc Ltd
UK: Hudson House, 8 Albany Street, Edinburgh EH1 3QB
USA: 675 Massachusetts Avenue, Suite 11, Cambridge, MA 02139

www.museumsetc.com

MuseumsEtc books may be purchased at special quantity discounts for business, academic, or sales promotional use. For information, please email specialsales@museumsetc.com or write to Special Sales Department, MuseumsEtc Ltd, Hudson House, 8 Albany Street, Edinburgh EH1 3QB.

A CIP catalogue record for this book is available on request from the British Library.

ISBN: 978-1-910144-01-5

The paper used in printing this book comes from responsibly managed forests and meets the requirements of the Forest Stewardship Council™ (FSC®) and the Sustainable Forestry Initiative® (SFI®). It is acid free and lignin free and meets all ANSI standards for archival quality paper.

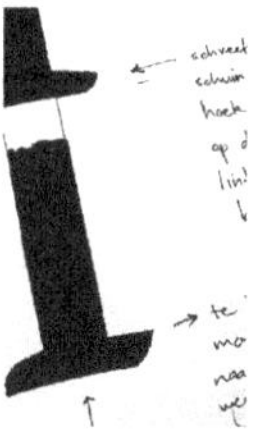

Dolly Pro, the typeface in which the main text of this book is set, is designed by Underware, a specialist type design studio founded in 1999 and based in The Hague, Helsinki and Amsterdam. The font is "a book typeface with flourishes", designed for the comfortable reading of long texts. The asymmetrically rounded serifs give the type a friendly but contemporary look - and it uses old-style numerals, which we love.

Myriad Pro was designed by Robert Slimbach and Carol Twombly for Adobe Systems and is the sans serif typeface best known as Apple's corporate font.

VERTICALS | writings on photography

For almost 200 years, the work – and the writings – of pioneering photographers have transformed the way we see the world, and each other. Their ideas have inspired heated debate and dissent. And their images have helped form those we see all around us now. *Writings on Photography* brings you the thinking of these radicals and visionaries in their own words, and authoritative commentary on them.